The First Great Race

Alaska's 1973 Iditarod

Dan Seavey

Foreword by Terry O. Adkins, D.V.M, M.P.H.

Publication Consultants Since 1978

PO Box 221974 Anchorage, Alaska 99522-1974
books@publicationconsultants.com—www.publicationconsultants.com

ISBN 978-1-59433-389-7
Library of Congress Catalog Card Number: 2013-942964

—First Edition—

All photos appearing in this book are from the Dan Seavey collection unless otherwise credited.

Manufactured in the United States of America.

Dedication

The First Great Race is dedicated to Shirley, my partner in life and matriarch of the Alaska clan of Seaveys.

And to the memory of Scott Hagen (1956-2011), a beloved family friend whose love for people was equaled only by his love for dogs and books.

(Photo: Jonathan Sewall)

The First Great Race

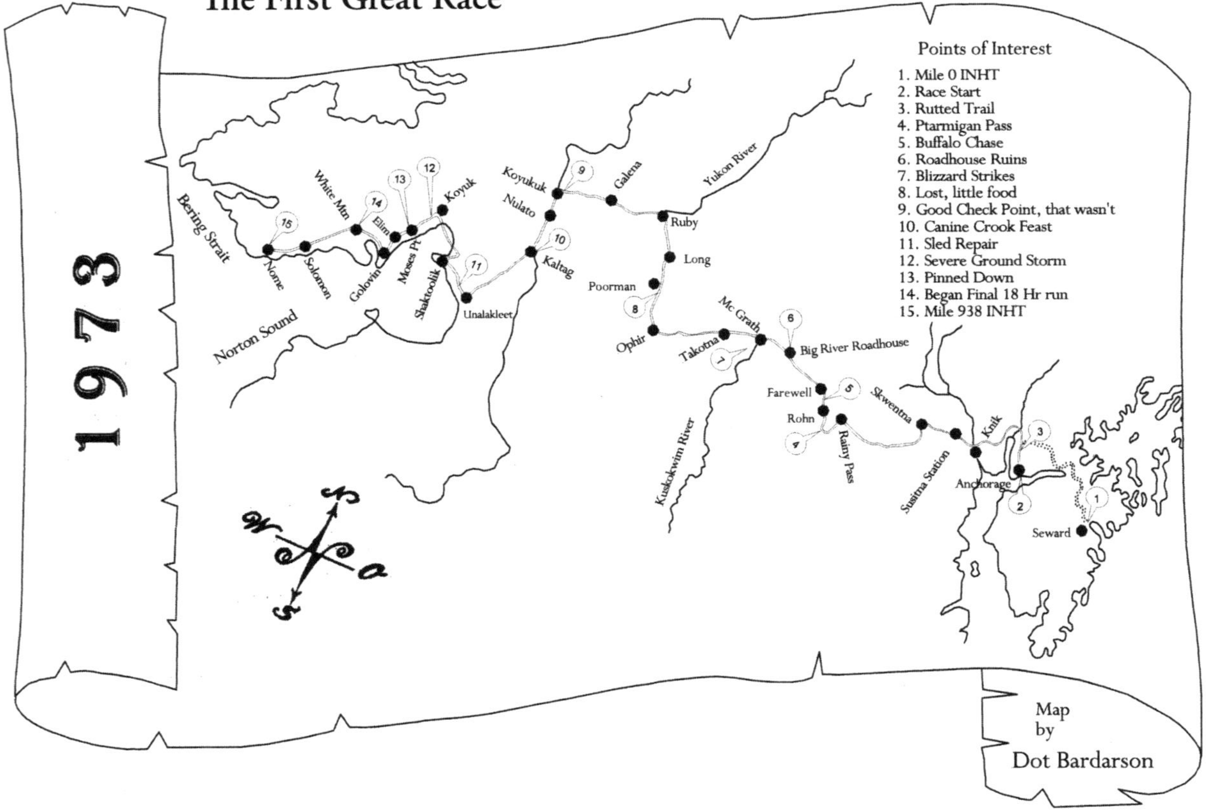

Acknowledgements

Many family members, friends, neighbors, and acquaintances have contributed immeasurably to this book. Some have kept the faith for nearly forty years that indeed a book would come to fruition. It is my ardent hope that I have not disappointed you, that your wait has been rewarded.

I humbly acknowledge my indebtedness to each of the following. Family members: Shirley Seavey, Mitch and Janine Seavey, Conway Seavey, Tyrell Seavey, Danny Seavey, and Louis Audette.

Old Friends: Louis Raymond, Bob and Shirley Hill, Don and Ruth Mai, Bill and Judy Larson, Lee Poleske, Dot Bardarson, Doug Capra, and Jonathan Sewall.

First Great Race Friends and Associates: Gleo Huyck, Dick Mackey, Terry Adkins, D.V.M., John Norman, Pam Randles, Howard and Julie Farley, Leo Rasmussen, George Sabo, Don Rosevear, Dody Nesbit, Joanne Potts, and Greg Bill.

Thank you Audrey Jackson, Annie Hood, and Hannah Moderow for yeoman service rendered.

Special acknowledgement is due: Ron Aldrich, George Attla, Bill Arpino, Ken Chase, John Coffin, Howard Farley, Owen Ivan, Robert Ivan, Victor Katongan, John Komak, Dick Mackey, Tom Mercer, Terry Miller, Bruce Mitchell, Herbert Nayokpuk, Isaac Okleasik, Ron Oviak, Rod Perry, John Schultz, Bud Smyth, Bobby Vent, and Dick Wilmarth. Each an Iditarod Race pioneer and founder.

Genghis, Casper, Crazy, Flame, Snippy, Eska, Kiana, Koyuk, Shiak, Kuchik, Bandit, and Sonny, canine pioneers whose perseverance during the First Great Race helped assure meaning and purpose for unborn generations of their kind.

Foreword

I met Dan Seavey in 1973 when he raced and assisted in planning the first Iditarod. I was stationed at Elmendorf AFB as the base veterinarian in the early 70s. From this extraordinarily-fated assignment led my journey to Iditarod and the pioneers that have made the Iditarod, 'The Last Great Race.' In actuality, I was the only sucker Joe Redington Sr. could talk into going along as a veterinarian to appease the Humane Society and reference medical care for the dogs, and at times, anyone or thing else that may need care. I was gone from my office for 35 days flying up and down the trail. During this time I saw a world-class event being born and was allured to the life of mushing.

Although I was deemed the expert, watching Herbie Nayokpuk and Isaac Okleasik providing dog care at Rohn River with moose quarters in their sleds to feed because the donated, up-scale, commercial dog food was causing diarrhea in their dogs was new to me. And watching Dan Seavey apply 'Neats Foot Oil' and pine tar for foot protection was educational (nothing in the curricula at Auburn.) Koppertox® was the only foot product I had in my bag and it was for foot-rot in cattle. After applying this product, there were a lot of green tracks left by dogs loping down the trail.

The early Iditarod dogs were tough and hearty and so were the people who ran these teams. The first races took many days/weeks. During these early Iditarod runs, there were no headlights, no booties except the rare hand-sewn seal-skin bootie, no reflective trail markers (spruce bows if anything), no quick-change runners, and no pre-race drop-bags assigned to each checkpoint. The mushers that ran were experts in survivalist arctic living and elite dog-men; many times these individuals were the trail-breakers as Iditarod was a trail and not a highway at that time. I remember air dropping dog food to the mushers at Poorman; they were snowshoeing in front of their teams. Mushers camped and rested at night. The dogs were more trap-line dogs than anything. Today's Iditarod dogs are trained better and selected for more speed. Please note however, a good dog is a good dog--in 1974, I was given a dog from Herbie that I tried to buy in 1973. One of that dog's pups, April, ran 10 Iditarods for me; April's son, Oly, ran 11 Iditarods. Some of their descendants went over the trail for my son in 2010.

We, the mushing community, are blessed with a degree of comradery like no other sport. Granted while you are racing, you are trying to beat the other contestants but you also feel a kinship to those you are racing. Camping with Herbie, Isaac, Joe Sr., Dan, Frank Teasley, Rick Swenson and many other mushers is the very fondest of memories for me. The Iditarod is a smaller fraternity than those who have climbed Everest.

The Iditarod is a way of life for many people; I feel it still calls to me each year. I said once to complete that race makes one feel as if they could spit in a tiger's eye. It is more than an addiction. The oneness of you and your team coupled with the beauty, the harshness, and the satisfaction of going over the trail proves to me there is a God.

From the warmth of my house and the luxury of GPS tracking, I proudly watched Dan (and yearned to be on the trail AHEAD of him) run the 40th anniversary of the race this past year--along with his son and grandson. This pioneer that I watched so long ago from a bush plane and learned of artic living across a campfire has inspired many. I appreciate Dan's immense contribution to the race, his commitment to the sport and dog-care progression, and the passing of a tradition.

Enjoy the ride from the pages of this book. Dan pays tribute to the joy and sacrifice it takes to follow a dream and try new things despite the obstacles. After this many years, I had forgotten some of the details that launched this exploration into a world-class, annual event. Dan's on-the-trail account captivated my thoughts and stirred fantastic memories of how extreme it really was.

Terry O. Adkins, D.V.M, M.P.H

Every year this race has run since 1973
To put in place another face in halls of victory
The spirit of Alaska, dogs will do the job
They run the race relentless pace
They call IDITAROD

They run Alaska's rough terrain, more than a thousand miles
Men and women brave and true, will enter Nome in style
The roughest race that's known to man, would run the wrath of God
We make the case Alaska's race
They call IDITAROD

From song: "Alaska's Race Iditarod"
By Louis Albert Raymond

Table of Contents

Part Two: To The Finish

Part One

1

When We Grow Up

The author, an adventure bent boy
in backwoods Minnesota, 1949.

"There! Ahead and a bit to my right. Could it be? Yes, it had to be, for there, on the landward side of the frozen Bering Sea, loomed Cape Nome." Even the almost total darkness of that Arctic night could not hide such a massive headland. "Whoa!" My tired team, of eleven huskies, that had been in harness since early morning – sixteen hours by then – gladly obliged. That distant glow in the night sky had to be Nome. Nome, Alaska, end of a punishing twelve-hundred-mile sled dog trail, now just twelve miles distant. I had been traveling by dog team over twenty days in the first-ever Iditarod Trail Sled Dog Race. What a beautiful sight!

Oh, the thoughts that whirled through my fatigued and confused mind. Thought flashes, I suppose. Like watching a slideshow projected on a wall: A fierce blizzard, caribou, vandalized sled, native villages, lost and near starvation, a trailside turkey dinner, buffalo chase, knee-deep water, minus forty degrees F. campouts, Anchorage race start, my family, our Seward homestead, Good Friday Earthquake, move to Alaska and how it all had its beginnings in a little country school, so far away in time and distance.

The spell was brief. Reality took over. I had twelve miles to go. The finish line was just two hours away and I was a front-runner in the First Great Race. No time to tarry. Those lights beckoned. "Ok, guys. One last time. Let's go."

"When we grow up, let's go to Alaska." I uttered those, or similar words, some sixty-five years ago.

The "we" were my friend Helmer Olson and me. Helmer, a few others, and I at fifth- and sixth-grade level were finishing up a geography lesson on the far-off Territory of Alaska. Helmer and I made up the snappiest map team in the entire one-room Hamlet Lake Township School.

When it came to geography, we were the original 1949 Whiz Kids. We knew, if only given a chance, we could beat all the map teams in Crow Wing County, all of northern Minnesota—all the whole darn state, for that matter. Our beloved teacher, and she truly was, Mrs. Irene Koloski, consistently gave Helmer and me flattering grades in geography, balanced with not-so-flattering grades in deportment.

We had Alaska down pat. Juneau, Fairbanks, Anchorage, and Seward—we could find them and spell them. We knew what a panhandle and an island chain were. We could point out on a well-used, roll-down map the homes of the Athabascan, Thlingit, Shimsian, Aleut, and Eskimo peoples, though the correct pronunciations of most all the Eskimo villages escaped us. But what got us most fired up over Alaska were the captivating stories Mrs. Koloski dramatically told and read to us. Stories of crafty trappers, fearless big game hunters, and rich gold prospectors. Stories of fishermen and dog team mail carriers. Wonderful tales of adventure and of riches in gold and furs. In Alaska, we learned, there was free homestead land just for the taking. All one had to do was find a nice place on a stream full of fish with enough trees to build a cabin, drive four stakes in the ground, and it would be his.

Helmer and I spent hours on the details of our move to Alaska. We would save money we earned the next three summers. After they let us out of school at the end of the eighth grade, we would strike out for the North Country. Probably hitchhike or maybe hop a freight train west from Minnesota to Seattle, Washington. There, just like Yukon Mike in one of the adventure books we had shared, we planned to sneak aboard a freight ship bound for Alaska. Maybe hide in one of those big wooden barrels like Jim did that time in *Treasure Island.* There shouldn't be any problem knowing when we had arrived in Alaska because there would be lots of fishing boats around, just like in our geography book.

Now the hard part. In order to get to the gold fields and where the trapping was best, we had to pack all of our supplies on our backs all the way to the Brooks Range of mountains. We figured if we set our minds to it, we could make it in two or three days. Much, we reasoned, would depend on how many rafts we would have to build. Or how much trouble the polar bears gave us. Since I was the bigger of the two, I would pack the Yukon stove and Helmer the Yukon tent. Both of these items were necessary in case we did not get our cabin with its fireplace built before our first winter. We had to arrive in Alaska prepared. It might be a long way to a trading post and the only way we could get there would be on snowshoes, at least until we trained our first dog team.

If our plan for going to Alaska was a bit sketchy, we knew pretty well what we would do once there. The beauty of our plan, indeed the key to our success in Alaska, hinged on the proper selection of our homestead. By carefully picking a wild, remote, well-timbered site along a fish stream, our success was assured. It was very simple really: the land would provide. From our woods we planned to build our snug little cabin. From our stream would come fish halibut for us and salmon for our dog team. We would dry the fish on racks, just as the Eskimos did in the pictures. But the touchstone of our Alaska fortune would be the gold, lots of gold. Sluiced right out of our own stream. That would be our summer job. In winter, using both snowshoes and a dog team, we would run our traplines. Since Helmer lived to the north of me in Minnesota, over on Stony Brook

Road, it only made sense that his trapline would run north of our cabin. He obviously understood the North Country better than I, having lived there longer than I had. It followed then that my trapline would extend south, the direction of my experience, thus into the realm of my expertise.

Before the snow melted in the spring, we would travel to the nearest trading post, probably Nome, and trade our furs for sugar and tea. If we had extra money, we would send it to our folks so that they could feel a little better about our running away from home. We reasoned it would require a large dog team to transport our large cache of furs to the trading post. Our expected catch was a couple of hundred wolves, five or six hundred mink, about as many fox, and maybe fifty saber-tooth tigers each. Or was it saber-toothed lynx?

We had no plans to spend much of our accumulated hoard of gold. Just like Klondike Mike, we would take it with us when we went back to Minnesota, looking for wives, when we got old enough for such things.

It was a long way in both space and time from that Hamlet Lake one-room country school in Minnesota, 1949, to Seward, Alaska, 1963, where folks were adjusting to their newly won statehood. However, I got there as directly and as quickly as I could. Childhood dreams for me did eventually come true.

My country school days ended in the spring of 1949 due to the consolidation of schools to central education hubs. With the final good-bye to a most wonderful teacher and our family-like student body, an important era in my life came to a close. For me, those two years (1947-49) spent in that little white schoolhouse were the most memorable, most rewarding educational experiences of my whole life, bar none, including the earning of a master's degree on the college level. I would be hard pressed to list why those particular years have come to mean so much to me. Perhaps it's because I remember them and that's enough. Or is it because it was the time an adventure-bent boy stood before a ragged roll-up map and conceived the notion that when he grew up, he would go to Alaska?

Time passes. But doesn't it? Our country school family was transported to a big, consolidated junior high school at Riverton, Minnesota. Then to a bigger high school at Crosby-Ironton. Then off to college. And what of Helmer, the kid who plotted all those thrilling Alaska adventures and riches with me? By high school, we had lost contact. I do hope he found his life's Eldorado, even if not in the Far North.

In July of 2008, my wife Shirley and I celebrated our golden wedding anniversary at our home in Seward, Alaska. Fifty years of "wedded blitz," as we kid one another. Fifty-two years of acquaintance, actually, when two years of courtship are figured in.

That courtship started when I fell "head over heels" for that beautiful, blond Swedish farm girl from Milaca, Minnesota. It was the summer of 1956. Her name was Shirley Anderson. There was no turning back. We were married on July 12, 1958, in the Lutheran Church of that little farm town. First came love, then came marriage, then came both of us with the baby carriage. In that precise order. Apart from the usual vows, the only prenup understanding Shirley and I had was that we would go to Alaska as soon as possible, just for a couple of years, to see what it's like.

"I fell head over heels for that beautiful, blonde, Swedish farm girl..." Shirley, 1957.

My poor wife. Had she known just what she was getting into, our story might have been quite different and no doubt considerably shorter. She literally worked my way through college. I began my two-year associate degree at Brainerd Junior College, Minnesota, in September of 1958. Shirley worked, gave birth to Mitchell Blake, who was destined for a future Iditarod championships. She worked some more with the added duties of a baby to care for and tons of college papers to type for me. Then she got pregnant again, and gave birth to our daughter, Tracie Beth, in 1960. By that time, we had moved to St. Cloud, Minnesota, where I was attending the Teacher's College. Again, Shirley bore the burden of my college degree—and another son, Darian Blayne. By no coincidence was the college housing development where we lived in duplex Quonsets called "fertile flats." Rent? Twenty-five dollars per month.

Next stop, Red Wing, Minnesota, and my first teaching job. In January of 1962, we arrived amid a good old-fashioned Minnesota blizzard. We traveled with a smallish U-Haul trailer containing all of our earthly possessions, including a seventeen-inch black and white TV, hooked to our new Rambler station wagon. Shirley reminds me that after unloading our goods and chattels, I made a beeline back to St. Cloud, one hundred seventy-six snowy, slippery miles distant, in order to avoid paying another day's trailer rent. With gasoline priced at twenty-nine cents per gallon (that's cents, not dollars), it made the trip cost effective. After all, we had splurged by agreeing to pay seventy-five dollars per month rent on a beautiful, little two-bedroom house. A beautiful house in the beautiful town of Red Wing, home of popular Red Wing Boots and famous Red Wing Pottery, situated on the west bank of the mighty Mississippi River.

I taught social studies at the high school level within the Red Wing Reformatory for boys, commonly referred to as the "Training School." I was hired by the Minnesota Department of Corrections. My job was very interesting and enjoyable, exciting really. Counseling students was a big part of the job. I soon came to consider one-on-one rapport with students to be of greater importance than assigned academic duties.

Our twenty months at Red Wing winged by quickly. We splurged yet again on housing and moved into an eighty-five-dollar-per-month house. Busy with our three babies, Shirley employed her magical transformation powers to convert our new rental into a home. Training

School duties kept me amply occupied. In addition to regular classroom work and counseling, I volunteered to coach introductory wrestling to a large crop of eager boys.

That February 1963, I began sending job applications to Alaska schools. Thirteen in all. I got addresses from materials sent by the Alaska Department of Education at Juneau. Since I didn't have much teaching experience to flaunt, I banked on the fact that, in general, Alaska had a high turnover rate for teachers. Applications sent to thirteen high schools resulted in eleven flat-out rejections and two maybes by mid-April. One prospect was on the island of Kodiak, and the other was from Seward, on the Kenai Peninsula. We were not dead in the water, but things weren't looking all that rosy, either.

"Das vater unser, vater unser der du bist in himmel…" Fritz Reuter, a fellow teacher at the Training School, was braving another German language lesson for me, using the Lord's Prayer as a vehicle. We were seated on a bench under one of scores of mostly budded elms that accented our beautiful riverside campus. My "das vaters" being mixed with mouthfuls of sandwich from my brown bag lunch. It was an idyllic early April day—birds, squirrels, the whole bit. Fritz was the industrial arts instructor, a master craftsman of the old German order. He expected master crafts from his students, and he got them. By setting high expectations and demanding absolute perfection, he cultivated needed pride and self-esteem in his students. It was a given that when "Fritz's boys" entered a project in statewide industrial arts fairs, they would bring home blue ribbons.

We had finished our lunches and I was still in the process of demonstrating to Fritz my non-proficiency in the German language, when a boy assigned to the office approached and handed me a message: "Call home as soon as possible."

"Now what?" I wondered as I dialed our home number. "Hope one of the kids didn't swallow a chicken bone. Maybe the oven won't come on—again."

Shirley was genuinely excited. Before she had the receiver to her ear, she was shouting, "A telegram has come. You have a job offer in Alaska!"

"Where in Alaska?"

"Seward!" she exclaimed.

That evening, I sent a return telegram of acceptance. From that moment on, our Alaska die was cast.

The spring and summer of 1963 were busy times for the young Seavey family. Since the academic school ran year round at the Training School, I had my normal teaching load right through the day of my resignation. Shirley began to pack for the long road trip ahead. We had to be in Alaska before the end of August. There seemed to be a million things to do before we cranked up our red and black Rambler station wagon to head in that direction.

There were questions, lots of questions to ask and answers to be found. Just where was this Seward anyway? Could we drive there? How far was it? How long would it take to get there? What was the community like? Would we have enough money to get there? I suppose every family who makes a move, even across its home state, has the same questions and suffer some of the same anxieties. We, however, had one additional problem. Shirley's mother, as well as mine, not-too-silently disapproved of their grandchildren being "dragged off to the edge of the earth." The slogan "Alaska, the Last Frontier," didn't lend much comfort to those wonderful but overly worried grandmothers.

A few excerpts from letters written to me by Seward Public Schools superintendent, George Fabricius, the man who escalated my Alaska dream to reality, follow:

April 8, 1963

Dear Mr. Seavey:

I just sent off a wire offering you the social studies position in Seward High School and will now go into details of the matter... salary would be $6,500.00...teaching of World History, American Government, Economics and possibly U.S. History...enrollment would run from 15 to 25 per class... Please wire collect your acceptance or refusal of the position.

April 15, 1963

Dear Mr. Seavey:

I am pleased that you have chosen to cast your lot in Alaska and especially with Seward... The contract enclosed states a salary of

$6,500.00, but there was a new salary bill just recently and I would believe that this will be raised no less than $300.00… You may be interested in knowing that high school wrestling is coming into recognition here in this part of Alaska… I am certain you will have many questions, so just send them along and I will do my best to answer them.

June 19, 1963
Dear Mr. Seavey:

I will try to answer your questions as far as possible… Seward teachers have a Group Blue Cross Plan… There is a National Guard unit in Seward… We have a local publication called the *Petticoat Gazette*. Not a regular newspaper as you might consider one… Seward has a local teacher association (S.D.T.A.), which is affiliated with A.E.A. (Alaska Ed. Assoc.) an d the NEA…There is a public library… I have made a personal change of plans since last contacting you. I requested and was granted a release from the last two years of my contract in Seward… I will be in Seward until about July 8th if you should have other questions.

Yours very truly,
Geo. J. Fabricius, Supt.
Seward Public Schools

One of the many regrettable things in my life is that I never got to meet face-to-face that patient, helpful man, George Fabricius.

During the months of May, June, and July, most of my questions were answered. I continued teaching and even managed to mow the lawn. I built a cargo box for atop the Rambler, purchased a twenty-five-dollar utility trailer, and added a 7MM magnum Remington bolt-action rifle to my growing arsenal. Shirley and I undertook an Alaska geography study, which rivaled that of my country school days. We purchased the latest (1963) *Milepost*, the bible for travelers of the Alcan, also known as the Alaska Highway.

That led to more important chores. The Alcan, it turned out was an all dirt road, stretching from about one hundred miles north of Dawson Creek, British Columbia, to the Alaska border. It was reportedly some twelve hundred miles of mud and dust. The headlights, grille, windshield, and gas tank of the station wagon needed protectors. We purchased four spare tires—two for the Rambler, two for the trailer. We also acquired cans for spare gas and water, and a new set of mechanic's tools.

August 2 was my last teaching day at the Training School. A couple of days were spent on last-minute details like cleaning the rental house and turning in the keys. We then made a final round of good-byes to friends and nearby relatives. The prolific Seavey clan was taxing at a time like this. It was a clear, hot summer day when we said our good-byes to Shirley's folks at their Milaca farm, and a few hours later, to mine near Duluth. Our poor mothers. Can you imagine with what horror they received the devastating news some seven months later that "Seward is burning to the ground" in the aftermath of the Great Alaska Earthquake?

August 5, 1963: Good-bye Minnesota. We were off to a new life in a new country, some thirty-five hundred miles away. Fourteen days later, road weary but very happy and excited over the prospect of our new home, the old Rambler, dirt encrusted, rolled to a stop in downtown Seward. It had been an arduous but wonderfully exciting journey.

Goodbye, Minnesota. August, 1963.

Psychologists tell us that the human mind has a tendency to forget the unpleasant. I believe it. That first trip over the Alaska Highway, as it finally became known, proved it. Pushed to the most remote recesses of my mind were the realities of the trek: Bumps, potholes, washboard, mud, dust, and more dust. Flying rocks, smashed headlights, broken windshield, flat tires with no spare left, and a hundred miles to the next gas station. Rainy, soggy nights of camping. Hot afternoons, windows up in a car with no air conditioning in a futile attempt to keep dust out. Dust and more dust. We inhaled it. We ate it. All of those experiences now distant memories.

Alaska Highway, 1120 miles of dirt, mud, dust, and more dust.

What remains after nearly fifty years is indeed the pleasant: Slow, long, leisurely days of travel, stopping frequently to exercise the kids. At the time, Darian was two, Tracie was three, and Mitch was four. Taking time to throw the ball, fix lunch, splash in the water—be it puddles or lakes.

The prairie foreverness of North Dakota and the Canadian Provinces fascinated us Minnesota "stump jumpers." We imagined ourselves to be the wild and free Sioux, traversing the great emptiness on horseback. Our station wagon—now a covered wagon—rolling westward toward the setting sun. We prepared our evening meals over an open campfire. Then came the mountain magnificence of British Columbia. Grandeur, the like unseen before by us "flatlanders." As the overburdened six-cylinder Rambler struggled up steep sections of road, the kids recited, "I think I can, I think I can," a line from one of their favorite books—*The Little Engine That Could.* Jaw-dropping scenery in every direction. Our little Brownie Hawkeye snapshot camera was working overtime, shuttering onto 120-size film God's handiwork to go.

Can I ever forget crossing the fabled Yukon River the first time or the absolute elation upon seeing the Yukon Territory sign? A myriad of thoughts overwhelmed me: Dawson City, Klondike Gold Rush, *Call of the Wild*, and Hamlet Lake country school. All so old and familiar, now given a new and exciting life. At the time, the thought never occurred that I would someday drive dog teams on that storied Yukon waterway.

"Welcome to Alaska," the sign read. At last, the Promised Land. The land of my fifteen-year dreams. Shirley clicked the shutter with the Hawkeye aimed toward the kids and me standing beneath that sign. We made it. Here was a sign personalized and erected, it seemed, just for us.

"At last...the land of my 15 year dreams."

Our thirteenth night on the road was spent in the Bird Creek Campground, a few miles south of Anchorage. Lofty Chugach Mountains towered north, south, and east. At our doorstep lay the Alaska Railroad, and just beyond, tidal crazy Turnagain Arm. We speculated how the *Milepost* came up with that name, Turnagain Arm.

It had been a long day traveling from Deadman Lake just inside the Alaska border, to Bird Creek. It was late. We were tired. It was raining—hard. Not so, come morning. The rain had stopped. In its place, a brilliant blue, cloudless sky. Overnight, Turnagain Arm had replaced its dismal mud evening jacket with one of calm, high-tide water. On that ripple-free water surface was a re-creation of our surrounding world. Perfect, undistorted mountains, glaciers, snowfields, forested slopes, blue, blue sky, all these reflected in the water, duplicated. Beautiful beyond description. To the east, a big old sun was beginning its daily climb along craggy mountain crests, turning night into day as in eons past. This day was different from the countless millions of the past. Old Sol probably didn't even notice, but he had brought this day into being just for this young Seavey family. Everything conspired that last hundred miles down the Kenai Peninsula to grab us, to hold us, to claim us, to indelibly imprint upon our minds that this is home. This is where you belong. You may, in the future, roam far, but you will always return.

Nowadays, there are signs posted along the Seward Highway, proclaiming it to be a National Scenic Byway. If the modern Joe Tourist thrills to each turn in that stretch of God's green acres, just a fraction of what we did our first time, he will be more than amply repaid for his time and expenditure. He had indeed saved the best for last. Besides, that gorgeous Alaska day was August 19, my birthday. No finer present, ever.

Breaking camp for the last time with nearly thirty-five hundred miles behind us, we headed south, driving for the first of what now would be thousands of times, the Seward Highway to the seaport town of Seward. For us, the drive was magical, a kaleidoscope of awe-inspiring beauty. We really did "turn again" to get around Turnagain Arm. We drove by Portage with its little Union 76 gas station. Up into Turnagain Pass with more "I think I cans" from the kids. Snow was practically down to the road at the summit. Silver Tip Creek highway maintenance station, Hope Road cutoff, just beyond the twisty Canyon Creek Bridge. Two usual mountain highway features were missing: guardrails, because no one had troubled themselves to put them up, and billboards, because we were traveling in the Chugach National Forest, where trees had boldly marched right up to the highway's narrow shoulders. We made a stop to get the Hawkeye out at the road's crown jewel, Summit Lake. There was a log-constructed lodge with gas pumps. On the mountain to the west, Gilpatrick, the *Milepost* continued to instruct, was a flock of Dall sheep, "mountain goats" to the uninformed newcomers.

Back on the road. The sun was by then high in the brilliant sky. Not a cloud to be seen in any direction, the Kenai Mountains, mostly snow capped, here and there displayed a blue tinge of ancient glacier. Down from Summit Lake to the village of Moose Pass. A two-gas-pump place and a motel. The kids were put on alert to be watching for moose now that we were at Moose Pass. Less than thirty miles to go.

Next came the picturesque Trail Lakes, and soon a sign that proclaimed "Crown Point," apparently a railroad siding. Then off to our right, the west, appeared yet another jewel of the drive, twenty-five-mile-long Kenai Lake. As with the Yukon River, first seen just a few days previous, I had no inkling that Kenai Lake would become so important in my preparation for the first Iditarod Trail Sled Dog Race.

Finally, up and over Mile Twelve Hill, a short-enough climb as not to warrant even one "I think I can." From the south side of Mile Twelve Hill, it was downhill all the way to Seward at sea level, remaining inside the Chugach Forest, almost to the edge of town.

Mile 7, Grouse Lake; Mile 6, Bear Lake Road; Mile 4, Metcalf's Cash Grocery; Mile 3, The Pit Bar; Mile 2, Nash Road; Mile 1, The Country Store; and…there it was…Seward, Alaska. It's setting indescribably beautiful. Resurrection Bay, the Pacific Ocean, its entrance guarded by islands way to the south, completely ringed by some of the most spectacular mountains on earth, all dipping their feet in the briny water of the bay. The town site itself, some seven blocks wide and one mile long, was situated between the mountains and the deep, blue sea at the head of the most picturesque of fjords.

With craning necks, we crossed the saltwater lagoon into town, following the paved Seward Highway to its logical conclusion at Mile 0, at the south end of town. Here we hooked a left and glided a block east onto the dusty, unpaved main street, where the trusty old Rambler came to a stop.

2

A Puppy for the Kids

A puppy "for the kids." Chignik II,
a little magnet with a big force.

Shirley and I have often joked that the reason we aren't millionaires is that we arrived in Alaska with too much money—all of twenty-three dollars and a used-up Texaco credit card. In contrast, former Alaska governor and United States Secretary of the Interior, Walter Hickel, landed in Seward, as the story goes, with thirty-nine cents in his pocket. He went on to build his fortune. We went into dog mushing.

Fact is, my last paycheck from the Training School did not greet us at General Delivery, Seward, as hoped. It was to be September 1 before we could move into the rental we decided on, with the help of fellow teacher, Monty Richardson, head of Seward Public Schools' "Sunshine

Club." No problem here. We simply stayed in camp-out mode, residing at First Lake, a nice park-like setting, for several days. Eating, or should I say, the lack of eating, did become a problem, however.

"Dad, do we have to eat this stuff again?"

"Why not? Beans are good for you."

Postmaster Clarence Larson to the rescue: "Go talk to the Stanton boys. They will probably give you credit."

Brothers Bob and Bart Stanton were longtime proprietors of the long time in business, Seward Trading Company. I explained our plight to Bob, a tall, businesslike man sporting a baseball cap. The result was our first shot of Seward hospitality. "Mr. Seavey, help yourself to what you need for as long as you need it. Pay when you can." It was just about that simple. The presence of a wife and three raggedy kids might have accentuated my need.

A few days later, while huddling over a soggy breakfast on a soggy picnic table after a very soggy, rainy night at First Lake, we got company. Introducing himself as Red Griffith, this rawboned, red-haired, middle-aged man turned out to be the manager of the Marathon Apartments on 4th Avenue.

One apartment was vacant at that time.

"You sure are welcome to camp out there until your house can be occupied. Won't cost you a dime, and it's dry."

We gladly took him up on his kind offer. More Seward hospitality.

By September 1, we had relocated to our 3rd Avenue rental, just across the street from the Lutheran Church, later Resurrect Art. The little stucco house was snuggled up to a much larger stucco house, owned at that time by Walter and Elsie Blue. It was Walter whom I replaced in the Social Studies Department at Seward High. Elsie ably served as administrator for Seward General Hospital. Situated in the upper part of town, our first and only Seward rental had a commanding view of Resurrection Bay and its guardian islands south, toward the open North Pacific Ocean.

In rapid fashion, we became settled Sewardites. We were off the streets and out of the parks before the fall monsoons set in. With our first Sunday attendance at Seward Lutheran Church (what else could we be, coming from Minnesota?) we joined a wonderful, supportive "church family." Fact was, the whole darn place was steeped in "frontier spirit." Seward's guiding principle was that a newcomer was accepted at face value until he or she proved to be something less. Until then, the hand of welcome is always extended. Early Seward, all of Alaska for that matter, never seemed to question one's motives for being there, but puppy like, wriggled with the joy of seeing you. Everyone we met during our first few weeks in Seward seemed members of an orchestration designed to capture this new Cheechako family, making sure we never escaped. That openhanded helpfulness of Seward's Stanton boys, and so many others like them, has served as a lifelong lesson for me.

Happy new Alaskans. L-R: Darian, Mitch, Tracie.
As quickly as possible – off came the Alaska Highway dirt –
on went our Alaska plates.

School was the same. It took no time to get into the swing of things. A couple of teacher meetings prior to school's start afforded the opportunity for me to become acquainted with the teaching staff, administration and other school personnel, including school board members.

The idea I had gotten that Alaska in general had a huge teacher turnover rate proved true. To Seward, in the fall of 1963, came fifteen fresh, new teachers of a total staff of thirty-four, both high school and elementary taken into account. In addition to mandatory weekly "teacher meetings," various occasions conspired to weld us together as a teaching staff and further our bonding with the Seward community. From the PTA (Parent Teacher Association), each teacher received a well-polished apple and a plywood paddle with the words "Board of Education" prominently inscribed.

Then there was the "Meet the Teachers" luncheon held at Del Zentmire's Harbor Dinner Club, an affair whereby, for a free lunch, new teachers were placed on public display, sponsored by the Seward Chamber of Commerce. Highly recommended by the administration was the Seward District Teachers Association. "Oh bother!" I thought, "another meeting!" I must admit, however, my attendance at this organization's very first gathering completely turned me around. The main business conducted was lively professional discussions centered on captivating topics such as hunting and fishing.

Teachers held crab feeds, wild game feeds, and just plain everyday feeds. There were poker games and beer parties, both of which Shirley managed to steer me clear of with "more important things to do." On top of all the teacher activities, we had a whole host of community-sponsored activities from book clubs—no TV for Seward yet—to ski parties up on Mile Twelve Hill. That dreaded mid-winter malady, cabin fever, had to run pretty fast to catch up with your average Sewardite.

Certainly, by mid-October of my first of twenty Alaska school years, I was settled in. Family was out of a tent and into a house. I integrated with school staff, and students. Classes organized and, as far as I could tell, going well. I had planted the seed for a wrestling team. I liked the new superintendent, Lawrence Brent, up from Mill City, Oregon, as well as the new principal, Larry Bourger, a recent Cold War refugee from Hungary. Also, before my first Alaska winter descended, I had our teaching staff pretty well sorted out and grouped into two categories: "like" and "can probably live without."

When I first met Tom Johnson, I had no inkling that I had taken a giant step toward fulfilling one of my youthful dreams. Tom preceded me at Seward High by one year, coming from Rockford, Illinois, to teach English in the autumn of 1962. Prior to that, he had landed a summer job with the Alaska Department of Fish and Game as a salmon stream guard on Kodiak Island. That job, Tom told me, entailed reporting boats fishing upstream from the limits markers and keeping from being eaten by grizzlies that routinely chose to ignore the signs. Tom was a robust man with close-cropped brown hair after the "butch" fashion of the day. He was above average in size, trim and youthful. Johnson was in Alaska for one purpose—adventure. Well, maybe two purposes. A few years down the road he would ask one of the most beautiful girls in his first senior English class to marry him. She did.

Tom and I hit it off at our first teacher's meeting. A natural storyteller with skills honed by study of English and drama, he treated all who would listen to garnished tales of his adventures and misadventures. Mostly misadventures: Up a tree for the night with a patient grizzly waiting on him below, renegade fishermen out to get him for reporting their illegal activities to Fish and Game over on Kodiak, waking up in the middle of the night to discover he had pitched his tent in the way of the incoming tide on Cook Inlet's Chickaloon Flats, while on a duck hunt. He, with others, attempted to traverse the Harding Ice Field between Seward and Homer, only to get pinned down on the Seward side by gale-force winds and five feet per day snowfall. After many frightening days, they made an escape back to Seward only by the grace of God. You get the picture. Tom's favorite poet was "The Bard of the North," Robert Service. His authors of choice were Jack London and Herman Melville. Like me, he grew up on, indeed reveled in, the adventures of radio's Sergeant Preston of the Royal Canadian Mounted Police. He knew of the marvelous exploits of the sergeant's lead dog, Yukon King. In fact, he was, at the time I met him, in the planning stages of his next Northland adventure—dog mushing.

Fellow teacher John Hall and Tom were roomies, bachelors in a little rental just two houses north of the new Seavey residence. They had adopted a stray male husky, or so John thought, about a year previous. Several weeks into the new school term, it had several pups! Genghis, Tom's male Siberian, was the hoped-for father.

"The cutest little things you ever saw," according to Tom. "I am thinking of going into dog mushing myself. I just read a book about this archdeacon of the Yukon, an Episcopalian who, back in the old days, traveled all over the place by dog team, like ten thousand miles in one year. What a business trip, huh? Hudson Stuck was his name. Yup! I am thinking about becoming a musher. Maybe getting up a competitive team in a couple years. Maybe entering the Fur Rendezvous Race in Anchorage. Show George Attla and that outsider, Doc Lombard, a thing or two about racing dogs."

The point to all this is Johnson and I spoke the same language, sang the same tune, and thought the same thoughts regarding things Alaska. Over intervening years together, we would share many wonderful adventures and misadventures as well. Thus, my lifelong love affair with sled dogs actually began that 1963 autumn day when I trekked north two houses and got easily talked into taking one of John and Tom's husky pups home "for the kids." That first cuddly pup to the dormant dog musher must be like that first few drops of drink to the latent drunk. For me, that darling little guy was the beginning of a lifelong sled dog binge.

Hoonah, Chena, Koyuk, Adak, Hyda, Kiana, Eska, Ruby, Karluk, and Kiska. Shirley, our two older kids, Mitch and Tracie, and I discovered a treasure trove of dog names printed all over our Alaska map. We tried at least a hundred of them on this seemingly disinterested little fur ball. Kenai, Kodiak, Kobuk. Yes, at least a hundred "how 'bouts." Even the mighty Yukon was advanced as a possibility, but rejected since Sergeant Preston long ago had dibs on it. One would have thought we were in the throes of naming the nation's newest aircraft carrier. After a lengthy period of self imposed agony, we settled on—sound the trumpets—Chignik, a village and ocean bay located on the east side of the Alaska Peninsula. "Chignik," it had a nice sound and, for some reason, don't ask me why, it fit.

For about the first ten years of my mushing experience, most of my dogs were "map dogs," the Kianas and Kenais. So here is a litter comprised of Skwentnas and Yentnas, pups resulting from a Kobuk-Koyuk cross, confusing even with good genealogy records. Fortunately, I eventually stumbled onto a much better way of accounting for my dog lot denizens—the theme system. Nowadays, each litter is named based on a theme. These six in the corner of the lot are fishes—Salmon, Sable, Cod, Bass, Pike, and Flounder. Or, as with a litter in my present "retirement team," based on weather phenomena: Dusty, Misty, Gale, Breeze, Storm, and Thunder. Theme possibilities are even more numerous than place names on an Alaska map.

Our family's love affair with Chignik was, sadly, short lived. Two weeks at the most. Neighbor Bob Morgan's mixed breed female strayed into our yard one school day afternoon and munched the little rascal. Shirley had put him out for a bit as part of her carpet spot reduction campaign. The kids were there too, although not for the same reason as the pup. Tragic as the resulting scene was, it was a valuable life's lesson. Long-faced countenances of the parents and loud lamentations of the children, notwithstanding, came the realization that animal ownership is not all peaches and cream. There is a downside. Daughter Tracie, who grew up the animal lover of all times, put it this way: "Animals live just long enough to break your heart."

I reminded Bob of Seward's leash law, collected $25.00 from him and put feelers out for another carpet spotter. This unfortunate incident did set me to wondering about dog behavior. How is it that this mother dog, the assassin, had raised two families of her own, was people friendly, a good mother to her own kids, can in two chomps annihilate another dog's son? Confusion time. After many, many litters in the dog lot setting, pups numbering in the hundreds, I still have no answer to that question. Without exception, whenever the Chignik scene has been reenacted in my dog lot, the villain is always female. Males never. Sinook comes to mind in that regard. He was one of my big original males. A seventy-five pounder, yellow/whitish in color. A litter of five puppies in our dog lot took a shine to him. They slept with him and as they got bigger, forced Sinook to vacate his own home, preferring to sleep atop his house in order to accommodate the invaders. I literally had to ward off the little mooches, giving Sinook an opportunity to eat his own food from his own dish, his natural inclination being to defer to his house guests. He would lie for hours on end without as much as a retaliatory snap, allowing himself to be mauled by this miniature wolf pack. Go figure.

L-R: Tracie (with Chignik II), Darian, Mitch, on first Alaska snow. December, 1963.

We needed to find another puppy "for the kids," right? Returning from a Sunday afternoon drive to Moose Pass, not very long after the Chignik incident, we encountered the most incredible sight. It was four-year-old Mitch who first spotted it. "Look!" he squealed. "There goes a dog riding a motorcycle."

Sure enough, pulling out of John Hardcastle's Country Store onto the Seward Highway, was a high-school age boy astride a very small red Honda cycle. From the rear, the driver was completely obscured from view by a towering canine, perched confidently atop a platform over the rear wheel. Stopping, starting, turning, this dog was at complete ease, appearing to own not only the Honda but its driver as well. The chauffeured—the chauffeur.

The driver, I found out, was not only one of my students, but had signed my preliminary roster for Seward High's first wrestling team. Dick Rogers would prove to be a top-notch student and athlete, a true credit to our school. Besides, his motorcyclist, Kobuk, a Mackenzie/Siberian cross, was to be a father in a few weeks. The expectant mother? A very pretty Siberian husky whose name was Chena, and who also belonged to young Mr. Rogers. "Mr. Seavey, would you like one of the pups?"

"You bet."

If ever there was a chance for a reincarnation of radio's Yukon King, this was it. Kobuk and Chena were the most awesome, beautiful creatures I had ever laid eyes on. Friendly, people-oriented, and extremely trainable. Their offspring was bound to make a wonderful family pet.

"Dad, have the puppies been born yet?"

"No. Be patient."

Patience paid off. The first week in February 1964, Chena had weaned her litter of five. There were two boys and three girls. Another learning experience was at hand for me. Never take three small children to help pick out a puppy. After what seemed like an eight-hour United Nations debate, and amid loud acclaim and violent protests, we left the Rogers' residence one puppy richer and ten dollars poorer. Unanimity was achieved on one proposal, however: the new puppy would be named Chignik II in honor of his dearly departed namesake.

3

Earthquake!—Digging In

An aerial view of our adopted hometown, Seward, Alaska, morning following the Good Friday Earthquake of March 27, 1964. (Photo: U.S. Army. Resurrection Bay Historical Society.)

We had been in Seward seven months when on Good Friday, March 27, 1964, at 5:36 p.m., the Great Alaska Earthquake occurred. Shirley was at home with the kids preparing dinner. She was scheduled to sing in the Community Choir that evening which was to perform the annual Good Friday concert. I had walked the half block north to return snowshoes I had borrowed from Tom Johnson. That afternoon, Maynard (Pete) Wilburn, a fellow teacher and I had snowshoed up the South Fork of the Snow River, located fourteen miles north of town, east of the Seward Highway.

On his table, Tom had a small glass jar filled with fifty-cent pieces, which he nonchalantly promised me I could have if I could guess their value. I rose to the challenge with an equally nonchalant estimate of fifty dollars. Tom's facial expression said it all: I had guessed correctly. That's when we heard the first rumbles, felt the first vibrations and looked questioningly at one another. "What's going on?" I questioned in rhetorical fashion.

Then, as with one voice we both shouted "EARTHQUAKE!"

And earthquake it was. Over two minutes of the worst shaking ever recorded in North America. Electric poles whipped like flexing fishing poles. Vehicles did a strange dance. The earth rolled and cracked as if a giant underground snake was making its way north. Tom and I held fast to whatever was handy, staggering like a couple of drunks to stay upright. Buildings teetered, their chimneys crumbled and slid to the ground in a heap of billowing dust. On the railroad dock, three blocks south, a mammoth gantry crane appeared to walk to the edge and topple into thirty fathoms of water. Things were far from settling down when I lit out for home, running wide open. It did not dawn on me until years later that Tom still owed me fifty dollars.

Our family's earthquake experience is quite well documented in John Nance's excellent book, *On Shaky Ground*, a thesis on America's earthquake unpreparedness. On the heels of the quake came several tsunamis which, combined with uncontrollable fire, erased a large portion of our town from the map. Before dark, the night of the earthquake, male teachers had been deputized and assigned patrol duty in the downtown area as a precaution against looting. Come morning, happily, we had not a single incident to report. School closed a month and a half early. Students were sent home and grade books turned in. I was assigned emergency housing manager by Civil Defense officials and took up my post at the Army Recreation Camp on the north edge of town. Within two weeks, school reopened. Too many hysterical people were leaving the sinking ship. Officials reasoned that by opening the school, people would be given a reason to stay. Students and teachers did not exactly sit and stare at one another that remaining month. Likewise, not a whole lot of knowledge was imparted, either. Regardless, this strategy worked. Reconstruction was well under way by the time school adjourned a second time. Things were looking up.

As one may imagine, all kinds of stories resulted from the quake experience. Some frightening and tragic. Some humorous and strange. Most strange, unexplainable tales centered around animal behavior, like canaries refusing to sing the entire day of the quake. A horse that stood statue still in its paddock, gazing out to sea from mid-morning right up to the 5:36 p.m. event. One resident reported her calico tomcat, which generally prowled the neighborhood both day and night, "a real bum" in her words, decided to stay at home on quake day. He selected a never before used spot behind the couch to spend the day sleeping.

More firsthand, however, is the quake story told by young Dick Rogers. Dick reported that on that fateful Good Friday morning, his two homebody dogs had disappeared. Both Chena and Kobuk. Chena left behind her two remaining pups, sisters to our Chignik. After school, riding his Honda, Dick had scoured the town for the two waifs. No luck. He returned to his family home, located on the north-south street closest to Resurrection Bay. There he and family members took the same earthquake thrashing as the rest of us. Minutes later the Rogers had looked on, horrified as the first tsunami, filled with flaming debris, swept within feet of their home. A full twenty-four hours later the two wayward dogs came home. No explanation offered.

Midnight and midday, on perhaps a half dozen occasions following the quake, a police sound car, speakers cranked up to max, patrolled Seward streets advising residents to head for higher ground. In our case, higher ground meant up Jefferson Street two blocks to the hospital. These rude awakenings and loud intrusions were reactionary precautions prompted by violent "aftershocks" as massive portions of sunken earth snuggled into more comfortable resting positions following the original upheaval. Into the back of our Rambler went kids and puppy, all unimpressed by the gravity of the situation. Shirley and I by then, having observed the colossal devastation of our town, needed no urging. The fear was that those aftershocks would cause more destructive tidal waves. It was our good fortune that they did not.

To say the 1964 Alaska Earthquake played a hand in shaping our family's future is really an understatement. It had, in fact, a profound effect. First, there was the quake experience itself. We shared it equally with all survivors. We grieved those we lost. We were beneficiaries of that free, openhearted, openhanded spirit that is Alaska. That is Seward. We, in turn, tried to emulate that spirit. Comparing notes with Shirley, probably ten years later, we discovered that neither of us, not even once, entertained a thought of abandoning ship, of getting out of Seward during that chaotic time immediately after the calamity. I do remember thinking that to leave a place when it needed you the most would be the act of a traitor. In short, the quake became a bonding event. The Seaveys were in Seward for the long haul.

Another significant result of the quake was that an inordinate amount of property came up for sale in the Seward area. Cheap. So many folks wanted out. A buyers market resulted. As somebody quipped, "A half million dollars would have bought you the whole darn place." Not having the requisite half million, we settled on a five-acre purchase for fifty-five hundred dollars on the installment plan $500.00 down and $75.00 per month plus 6% per annum.

Our Alaska Shangri-La was located three miles north of Seward, plus over one mile west of the Seward Highway, up Resurrection River Valley along Box Canyon Creek, a tributary. Access to the homestead was over a mile-long former logging trail, which in itself, is telling. In addition to our unspoken bonding with Seward, other factors prompted purchase of this remote parcel: I had been offered a teaching job for the next school term and by then, I had been bitten by the dog mushing bug. I needed a suitable place to keep a "few" sled dogs.

So what did we get for our $5,500.00 plus 6% per annum? Well, for starters, five acres of gravel and stone crowned with stately Sitka spruce plus a scattering of moss-covered stumps, monuments to an earlier logging operation. There were two small streams gushing down a high foothill which formed its north boundary. And a house start. Place emphasis on the word start. It had a foundation, framing covered with weather sheathing, rolled-paper roofing, window openings covered with sheet plastic, basement floor covering of a natural material, namely, gravel. But look at all that space for a dog lot!

A better picture of our newly acquired "Blue Heaven" can probably be painted through liberal use of the "no" word: no improved road, electricity, telephone, running water, indoor plumbing, central heat, window glass, mail service, or school bus. The move meant some tough living for a few years—for Shirley, in particular. She had three kids to keep safe from moose and bear, real and pretend. Now let's add trips to the laundromat, the telephone, grocery store, post office, and elementary school. There were wood stoves to persuade, water to carry, kerosene and gas lights to tend. All of this and much more. A real Alaska pioneer woman, that one. Matters were not helped by my unavoidable absences for school, wrestling practice and weeklong road trips. There was another reason for what seemed unavoidable disappearances on my part—dog mushing. That Shirley never bought one-way air tickets back to Mama for the kids and herself is proof positive of my sales ability for the idea that things would improve, and Shirley's abiding faith that indeed they would—someday. Then too, it may have been that we didn't have enough money for the tickets.

Daughter Tracie (4 ½ yrs.), just one of her many "favorite" dogs. Homestead, June, 1965.

Son Darian (3 ½ yrs.), with juvenile Chignik II. Homestead, June, 1965.

Future Iditarod champ's first ride on dog sled.
Mitch, 5 ½ yrs. January, 1965.

Jumping ahead a few decades, following the 2009 Iditarod Sled Dog Race, Shirley and I drove from Seward to Sterling for an ingathering of the extended Seavey clan, held at the home of Mitch and his wife Janine. It had become, over the years, almost a family tradition. What this special assemblage really amounted to was a rehash of the current race without the inconvenience of being on the trail. It was an opportunity for the many Seavey participants to compare race notes, with an eye always on improvement for "next year." Innumerable "I probably should haves," "what ifs," "maybes" and such were routine. For us elder Seaveys, this particular gathering was even more interesting than those of the past. For that race, the thirty-seventh Iditarod, there were enough Seaveys involved to make up a respectable-sized dog team. Mitch had tallied sixteen races; his son, twenty-two-year-old Dallas, had completed his third and Jen Seavey, Dallas's pretty young wife, a rookie. Oh! The fourth one was yours truly.

My part was minor compared to those of our racers. So minor, in fact, I had starting position 0. Here's the deal. My retirement dog team was dubbed the Iditarod Trail Centennial Team, and I, "Centennial Seavey," by the Iditarod Historic Trail Alliance, of which I am a member. Our job was to publicize and celebrate the trail's one-hundredth birthday. Amid a great deal of media noise, we were first out of the chute at the Anchorage ceremonial start. I mushed with an old-fashioned freight sled, old-fashioned garb, and special advertisement coats on the dogs proclaiming: Iditarod National Historic Trail Centennial. The fifth Seavey was Conway, Mitch's youngest son, twelve years old at the time. He ran the whip sled, which is simply a second sled, trailing the main sled. Conway and I showed off for the benefit of the historic trail, all eleven of those grueling ceremonial miles. As may be guessed, we didn't get much in the way of high billing when the real race was recounted that day.

After much pre-meal race talk, and after much race talk during the two-fisted meal Janine had served, those who retained interest in the topic took up stations in the spacious living room for more–surprise, race talk. Danny, our first grandson, and I made a wild dash for a favored spot on a plush couch. He won. In the process of losing, I knocked an object off a coffee table. It landed with a lot of fanfare on a hardwood floor, but unbroken. Picking it up, I asked Mitch what it was, in rhetorical fashion. Before he answered, I saw it to be a tiny, maybe six-inch-tall cup-type trophy, mounted on an equally small wooden base.

"That's my favorite trophy," Mitch stated in a manner that left no doubt. "It is the only one allowed in the living room."

There was no doubt about that either. With the passage of some twenty years of professional sled dog racing, the guy had assembled a most impressive array of laurels. Big first place trophies and plaques from every major Alaska event. A dozen beer-stein-sized cups recording finishes in the Iditarod: top twenty, top ten, top five. He had, by that time, earned the granddaddy of all trophies—the 2004 Iditarod Championship trophy—made of solid bronze. It was done in the likeness of Joe Redington Sr., now proclaimed the "Father of the Iditarod." That trophy requires two strong men or one good Alaskan woman to move. It is heavy enough to sink a battleship, well, almost. Even that edifice to sled dog racing perfection was not to be seen.

I picked up for the second time what was apparently one of Mitch's truly prized possessions. I inspected it in more detail. Small, chipped, stained, nicked, aged, all descriptive. And there below the little silver cup, a small inscription plate that read: "Aurora Dog Mushers, Jan. 15, 1972, Jr. Preliminary 3-dog, First Place." Instantly, before the last word was read, a wave of emotion swept over me. Memories past, realities of the present and still future hopes. Our children, our grandchildren, our great-grandchildren, all mixed together. Throw in remembrances of many a fine dog team and their leaders, trail experiences, family fun with dogs and a very volatile emotional situation had been created.

Now, it wouldn't do for the patriarch of all those present to be witnessed bawling like a baby over a $2.50 piece of tinsel. But it was close. In the next instant I realized why that Tom Thumb of trophies meant so much to Mitch. It took him back in memory. Back to the exciting, exhilarating days of boyhood. Days dawning one upon the other, each creating the world anew. Worlds to explore, to conquer, to record in one's life stream which flows from fountains of memories to guideposts of the future.

Mitch poses with Tom Johnson and his all-time favorite trophy earned in an Aurora Dog Mushers Club kids' race. January, 1972.

Seavey Homestead as first viewed, April, 1964.
"No improved road, electricity, telephone, running water, indoor plumbing, central heat..."

During our drive home to Seward that evening, Shirley and I discussed the profound effect that little beat up trophy had on me. She asked me if I could have any trophy from boyhood years, what it would be. After several miles of thought, I answered, "That old ragged Alaska map from the Hamlet Lake one-room school, back in Minnesota." Yes, if I had that map today it would hang in a place of honor on our most prominent living room wall. I confess, I am not the sharpest pencil in the box, but I did begin to see the light. That map would have been my trophy of boyhood dreams come true, of a wonderful, satisfying life in Alaska. For Mitch the same, that little dog mushing trophy is a symbol of his boyhood dreams come true. Only Mitch's little one-room schoolhouse had been the Seavey Place near Seward. Mitch, his sister Tracie, and his brother Darian all enrolled that first day of May so long ago, when we moved to the homestead, right after the Great Alaska Earthquake.

4

Looks Like a Husky

An early milestone. Seven dogs going in one direction. Genghis in lead.

Another of my lifelong regrets is that I did not keep a daily journal over the years. Fortunately, I have kept what amounts to several file folders of mementos, photos, clippings, shorthand written narratives, and the like. Quite a collection, really. Another bit of good fortune and display of foresight is my Dog Diary. From the first dog Chignik on, this record has been kept mainly in an attempt to keep straight who's who in the present dog lot. Not as simple as you may think. The book, in fact, makes reference to several the likes of this: "Karluk, six pups, two male, four female, father unknown, born October 7, 1965."

Here and there throughout this stubby little record book is found information other than that depicted by genealogy charts and notes on results of canine bedroom activity. Happy, indeed, am I that I have both "the files" and Dog Diary to assist in dissipating the mists of my foggy memory.

An early entry:

> January, 1964. My first sled ride and actual experience with sled dogs was on a weekend during winter, 1963-64 at Mile 18 campground road. With two of us (myself and four-year-old Mitch) on a sled, were clocked (by Tom Johnson) at eighteen miles per hour. What a thrill. Speed, power, beauty.

Our homestead proved fertile ground for my growing interest in sled dogs, as evidenced by their increasing numbers. Further events conspired to draw me into dog mushing early in our Alaska experience. One such was Tom Johnson's move out north of town, to a rented place on Salmon Creek Road, for no other reason than to have a place to "keep dogs." He began his collection almost as soon as he threw his sleeping bag on his new bed. That was September 1964. He and I would soon become inseparable partners in the crime of dog mushing.

Another factor in my growing addiction involved the Jesse Lee Home, a Methodist orphanage which moved from Unalaska to Seward in 1925. The 1964 earthquake brought to a close its long and intimate relationship with Seward. Instead of replacing its well-shaken and destroyed buildings, the decision was made to move "the home" to Anchorage. This decision left in limbo a score of Jesse Lee students, who were in attendance at Seward High. The home gave these students an option: Go to Anchorage with the younger students, or find a place to stay in Seward. As a result, Shirley and I became foster parents to two young men: Larry Tyone of Athabascan descent and Frank Trigg, whose ethnic background was Eskimo. Frankie came with Sam, a well-mixed sled dog who Frankie had been training with other equally well-mixed dogs residing at the home. Sam took his place in my growing dog lot to be hitched with occupants of Tom's growing dog lot.

As strange as it may sound, like young lovers, moonlight has an inexplicably alluring effect on aspiring dog mushers. A good share of this activity, out of necessity, was done by light of the moon. For starters, there are only about six hours of daylight at 60°N latitude in the dead of winter. We went to school in the dark and returned in the dark. Plus, most weekends were taken up with wrestling trips or home meets. Not complaining. There was something magical, mystical, even spiritual about driving dogs by moonlight. To this very day, I thrill at the prospect.

I should mention that at the time Tom and I took up the gentle art, there was not a single dog team to be found in the Seward area. Except for a few minor league sprint teams around Kenai and Soldotna, the entire Kenai Peninsula was devoid of dog teams for any purpose. This condition would remain until after the first Iditarod race of 1973. One of the initial objectives established for the Iditarod Sled Dog Race in the first place was to prevent the complete demise of the Alaska sled dog. The first race was pivotal. Soon, dog teams began to crop up, not only around home, but ultimately around the world. By the first Iditarod, I had put in ten seasons on the runners and certainly had made my share of mistakes. Notwithstanding, I managed to cover several thousand miles behind a dog team during that period.

My love affair with sled dogs began in typical fashion, for recreation. Fun for the family was the reason I started our dog collection. First, the original, short-lived Chignik. Next, our earthquake baby, Chignik II, who is remembered for being hurried to higher ground (don't forget the kids) following Alaska's Good Friday Earthquake. Then, came that first sled ride at Mile Eighteen campground, accounted for earlier. That was a first for both myself and four-year-old Mitch. With hook firmly set, dog acquisitions, just for the fun of it, followed. Space won't allow, nor, I suspect, will reader patience, a complete acquaintance with all genealogies of all the hundreds of dogs recorded over the years. Interesting to me is the fact that dogs best remembered are those first acquired.

From Dog Diary: (recorded January 1968)

Chignik—Born February 1964, MacKenzie/Siberian, 50 lbs. male, ran in wheel. From Dick Rogers.

Genghis—Born February 1962 (?) Seppala Siberian, 55 lbs. lead dog, male, from Earl Norris through Tom Johnson.

Guba—Male, 65 lbs. born (?) mixed breed, team dog, from Tom Johnson.

Baranof—Background unknown. Got from Dave Utecht (fellow teacher) and later Tom Johnson— a stray in town. Appears Siberian. According to teeth, young. Est. birth-1962. Wheel dog, male.

Sam—Frank Trigg brought him from Jesse Lee Home. Red in color. Very mixed breed, 50 lbs. Born about February 1964. Team dog, male.

Sinook—Born October 1965, Samoyed/Siberian cross, 60 lbs. lead or point (swing) from Homer area. A freebee.

Chignik II, our first, a family pet in every sense of the word. Ghengis, my first leader, was so instrumental in my completion of the first Iditarod. He had a big heart for wilderness travel, a big heart for forgiveness of every one of my beginner's ignorant blunders. Guba, a steady solid uncomplaining, let's-get-the-job-done kind of guy. Baranof was the most kid-friendly, patient, and kindest dog of the bunch. Sam was honest when not distracted, and in memory, he and Frankie, the young man, were inseparable. Sinook, large puppyish to the end, a family pet. He did more than his share in harness as well as under pack during family summertime hikes in the mountains. My daughter Tracie once so aptly remarked, "They all in due time leave us with only fond memories."

So it went between the years 1963 to 1968. Dogs and more dogs, with a stable dog lot population of perhaps not more than thirty critters. Tom remained that indefatigable dreamer, a co-babe-in-the-woods, or was it a briar patch? As our rising recognition as Seward's up and coming (and only) mushers increased, so did our vulnerability. Every Tom, Dick, and Harry who had an unwanted dog contacted us. "No, we are sorry, but a smooth-haired dachshund is too low to the ground to make a sled dog. Besides, it will freeze to death. No, sorry, we are sure a St. Bernard is too large. No, we cannot use it even if it does come with a barrel that attaches conveniently around its neck." Same answer for various and sundry others; hounds, spaniels, police dogs, you name them.

Seward's Justice of the Peace, Genevieve Schaefermeyer, was about to issue an order to have a rogue, trouble-causing stray put down. Would we like to try him out first? Well-marked, large, husky male. I named him Shiak, broke him of some bad habits like attempting to devour teammates, and drove him to Nome in my first and second Iditarod teams. A rare success story, I must admit.

"But this one even looks like a husky, mask and everything. Big, strong, gets up to forty miles, maybe fifty miles, per hour chasing cars."

"Looks like a husky, huh? Well, bring him out. We will give him a try."

Persistence and a maturing resolve paid off over the long haul of those formative years. Tom and I became more selective, more critical of freebies while giving closer scrutiny to dog lot hanky-panky. The payoff was more honest, forward-oriented dogs per litter. In many instances, five for six or even six for six. The overall result became more gratifying as those years rolled by. Our teams grew better, going down the trail faster, farther, with fewer problems. It became increasingly apparent that our dog collection and breeding were on the right track. In place of a bunch of mangy, frustrated mutts being driven along by an equally frustrated (and mangy?) musher, there developed an organized team of genetically-driven, happy animals. With evolutionary improvement of dog quality and concurrent acquisition of musher skills came a growing sense of accomplishment and well-earned enjoyment of those marvelous animals.

By talking with the few old-timer-type individuals available to us and reading such literature as could be procured, Tom and I, quite early, developed our mind's eye ideal sled dog.

From Files: 1965 (Desirable Sled Dog Traits)

> 1. Above all others, must be genetically forward-oriented. Self-driven, trail aggressive. 2. Medium size, males 50 -75 lbs; females 50-60 lbs. Good body conformation. Well furred. 3. Good feet. 4. Siberian husky appearance. 5. People-oriented (friendly). 6. Trail endurance, capable of a long day's work.

What an eye-opening, interesting experience it was for me to recently rediscover and analyze these traits penciled on scratch paper over forty-five years ago. It should be borne in mind that at that time, there were no endurance sled dog events. No long-distance races. The last All Alaska Sweepstakes of Nome had been run long before our time. True, it would become known as the granddaddy of long-distance racing—all four hundred and eight miles—but only with the advent of the Iditarod. Alaska and other parts of the country did have active sprint-racing circuits, however. As the name implies, sprint mushers go like mad behind twenty-plus very forward-oriented dogs for a relatively short distance, up to thirty miles. Alaska hosted three main event sprint races in the 1960s and 70s. Held at Kenai-Soldotna, Anchorage, and Fairbanks, these races attracted such renowned mushers as Alaskan George Attla and New Hampshire's Roland Lombard, and huge crowds of enthusiastic spectators, including Seavey and company. Long-distance endurance racing, however, had died with the last Sweepstakes Race in 1917. In 1965, by the time Tom Johnson, my dreamer friend and I were in the throes of becoming something resembling dog mushers, the Sweepstakes had faded into oblivion.

Thinking back, it is apparent that those ideal dog traits were more mine than Tom's, because he entertained hopes of picking off sprint championships at Soldotna-Kenai, in Fairbanks, and finally at the Anchorage Fur Rendezvous. Except for forward orientation and possibly good feet, our shrewd list of desirable sled dog traits didn't mean a whole lot in selection of a typical sprint dog.

On the other hand, my direction was toward what I came to call a "utility team," a middle of the road team. Not too big. Not too small. Not screaming speed demons, but fast enough to ascertain as I moved down the trail that indeed that tree up yonder really was getting bigger because I was moving toward it, not because it was growing fast. I envisioned, at first, a team for family fun. Maybe winter dog team expeditions, winter campouts with an affordable, manageable number of dogs. Endurance racing was dead, all but forgotten. Sprint racing held only spectator appeal for me.

By 1968, I had developed a pretty clear idea of the kind of dog I wanted, and the kind of dog team I desired. In that regard, giant steps had been made beyond, "Oh, isn't he cute? Let's make a sled dog out of him," to a more realistic approach to dog acquisition based on a pretty darn reliable list of criteria. The diminutive Alaska Purchase Centennial Race (1967) over a short segment of the old Iditarod Trail was in the past. That event, though I had read about it in the news, didn't register with me as being very significant. I may have been a "kind of, sort of" musher, but a racer I was not. There was plenty yet to learn just to get a mediocre dog team down the trail.

5

...Harness Upside Down

A young Tom Johnson with his dog "team."

It should come as no surprise that I brought absolutely nothing to the table in the way of sled dog knowledge or mushing experience. According to my ever-optimistic friend, Tom, that was not a problem.

"Sled dogs just know instinctively what to do," he declared. "We outfit them with a harness, hook them to the sled, and away we go." In Tom's view, the most difficult part of the whole operation was to determine which of the pack would be the lead dog. That took time. First, we needed to pick the biggest, strongest male dog and then turn our team loose with him in a big pen. Tom said, "There most likely will be a lot of fighting, blood, and all until the big guy completely exerts his dominance, just like in *Call of the Wild.* After that, all we need to do is tell the leader what we expect, and he sees to it."

"Yeah, sure, Tom, I think you put that harness on upside down."

What to do? Where to turn? How about sage advice from old-timers? The only old-timer we found willing to even talk with us about dog mushing lived in Moose Pass, twenty-nine miles north of Seward. On one of our earliest trips to new trails, with one of our earliest rag-tag dog teams, Tom and I visited Ed Estes at the Estes Brothers Store. Ed, at that time perhaps in his late sixties, was of small slender stature, raw boned, as the saying goes. Pleasant, with laughing eyes of steel gray. Hair grey-white. A roguish, playful demeanor. He was a true pioneer of the area. We were attracted to him because he had carried mail between Moose Pass and Hope-Sunrise by dog team back in the "old days."

What a disappointment that visit turned out to be for a couple wannabe mushers with that born-again zeal. Yes, he had done the mail route with dogs in the 1930s. Then, as ever, the mail must go through. For Ed, this fact—or slogan or whatever—brought nothing but bad, bad memories. He told of times, after heavy, wet snowfalls, when he would break trail on snowshoes. He'd leave the dogs, and snowshoe ahead a mile or so, backtrack, drive the team forward, and do it all over and over again for miles. Backbreaking work. Spirit-breaking toil. There were times, he recalled, when he sat down in the trail and sobbed out of frustration and weariness.

Ed related that a small dog in his team of twelve weighed in at 100 pounds. Most were larger. The rule-of-thumb load was 100 pounds on the sled per dog in harness. His favorite sled was a fourteen-footer. At times, one or more auxiliary sleds were attached tandem style, as required. Big dogs meant big dogfights to Ed. Bone-crushing, flesh-shredding free-for-alls—one-hundred-twenty-five pound brawlers, ten or twelve having it out in the most dreadful manner. That was when the lead-filled handle of the whip found service. Any other means were both ineffective and extremely dangerous. The burly perpetrators would be rendered unconscious by means of that weighty end and, according to our playful informant, "After their lights came back on, we would proceed down the trail."

Not much glamour here for my idealist friend, who asked Sourdough Estes about his best memory of dog mushing. Tom, no doubt, expected something along the lines of crisp, frosty, moonlight dashes with Ed's favorite girlfriend. We got something quite different. Ed's favorite memory, it turned out, was the day he learned someone had underbid him for the mail contract. He went out back, shot every single dog, and buried them all.

"By the way, you guys are school teachers, right? Supposed to be smart, right? Then tell me, why in hell do you want to spend your time cleaning up after a bunch of fish burners? Aren't there any women left in Seward to chase?" So much for sage advice from revered elders. I still remember those playful, laughing eyes, filled with merriment as we exchanged our good-byes.

Fortunate we were for the printed page. I read with growing fascination of the power, endurance, utility, the captivating roles played by the draft dog in exploration of both north and south ends of the earth. I studied, enthralled with the triumph and tragedy. How often it seemed a dog's chief value was not in his ability to pull but rather his presence in the expedition's stew pot. Richard E. Byrd, Roald Amundsen, Robert E. Peary, Frederick A. Cook, and Hudson Stuck had interesting stories, but alas, they were not informative about the nitty-gritty of dog mushing.

Lee and Mel Fishback came to the rescue. The husband-and-wife team had published a very practical how-to manual called *Novice Sled Dog Training*, published by Raymond Thompson Company of Lynwood, Washington. Their little booklet was invaluable, covering in a concise, instructive manner all one needs to know for those initial steps into dog mushing. My matured ideas on sled dog equipment and training, including my favorite activity, leader training, are only refinements of those offered me by the Fishbacks over forty-five years ago. I acknowledge my indebtedness. Other Fishback publications I found helpful were *Sled Dog Conformation* and another on use of dogs under pack. Sage advice? Yes! From our elders? I think so. Even Tom Johnson seemed to profit. His annoying idealism faded into acceptance and practice of the realistic approach to sled dog training, detailed for us by those common sense writers, Lee and Mel Fishback.

As priceless as information gleaned from books or even as time went by, talking with knowledgeable, helpful sled dog people, nothing was more instructive than one's own experiences. Could it have it been otherwise? Try something, make mistakes, learn, profit, and store the lesson away in a small but growing bank of sled dog wisdom.

There were so many problems to solve, so many puzzling occurrences. How many times in a period of fifty years have I hooked up a dog team and driven it over a stretch of trail? Hundreds? Thousands? I never kept score. One thing was certain no two runs were ever alike. Warm today, sticky trail, slow going. "What a bum stretch of trail. Better stop and bootie up. Darn, that bonehead chewed another neckline. Wonder why Gale is pulling off to the side like that. Easy now, moose holes in the trail ahead. Breeze, get up there. You need to learn to do your business on the run. No! No! Lead dog, I said gee! Oops, sorry, that is gee, isn't it?" So it went. A five-mile run, a hundred-mile run. This year or forty of them ago. None alike. All teachers to some degree.

Speaking of teachers, during the winter of 1996-97, I trained up a team to enter the 25th Anniversary Iditarod Race. A few were my own, but most team members were dogs from Mitch's racing kennel. For me, it was not so much a race as it was a sentimental journey to relive past experiences from the First Great Race of 1973. Tyrell, Mitch's number two son, came with the loaner dogs as handler. Back during those formative years, before the first Iditarod, the thought never entered my mind that, one day, I would take mushing lessons from a grandson.

Tyrell, as with all four of Mitch and Janine's sons, was home schooled. Home schooled not only in academics, but in life itself. A big part of life for a dog mushing family is, what else? Dog mushing. Grandsons Danny, Tyrell, Dallas, and Conway all cut their teeth on the subject. Graduation, indeed the rite of passage, seemed to be running the Iditarod. Tyrell, my twelve-year-old loaner/handler, was obviously pleased to spend the winter on the training trails with his grandpa. I was thrilled he wanted to help.

On a very cold February night, Tyrell and I went into a cold "siwash" camp while on a two-day training run. Our dog chores done and ourselves fed, Ty crawled into his sleeping bag spread out in his sled bag. Zipped up and from the depths of two layers came a very at ease, at peace with the world, "Good night, Boppa." And that was it.

I had cut some spruce boughs and placed them atop the snow. Down went my old trusty red REI foam pad, dating back to that first race.

Then I, too snuggled into a minus twenty-eight degree F down-filled, relatively new bag and looked up at the star-filled heavens. How many times on a crisp, clear, winter's night such as this had I laid in a slowly warming sleeping bag after a hard day on the trail and soaked up the magnificence above me? "Yes, good night, Ty Guy. See you in a few hours."

As I started to doze off, it came to me as almost a dream that I had been there before, said the same thing to a young person there on the Mystery Creek Trail, within yards of that same spot. Defeated at my last feeble stab at staying awake, I slipped into unconsciousness with the assurance that indeed, I had been there before, almost to the day, twenty-four years before, with Tyrell's dad, my thirteen-year-old son Mitch, who was likewise getting me ready for a race.

That kid, handler, trainer, teacher was, in reality, my chief critic for several months running.

From Files: Winter 1996-97 (Tyrell's Selected Suggestions.)

1. You can give me more than eight dogs to drive. I can handle them.
2. Forecast is for colder weather. Next run better take some extra fat. (For dog rations.)
3. King isn't much of a leader; he needs to go back in wheel to learn what work is about.
4. My dad uses Algyval on the feet. It's the best.
5. Don't you think we should run the hills more?
6. I will make you up a cable towline. Throw that old poly stuff away.
7. There are much better headlights out now. (Than mine, of course.)
8. Donate it (my personal gear) to the Salvation Army. Buy a Northern Outfitters cold weather system.
9. There's a lot better sleeping bag than your down filled one.
10. Bops (that's me), where did you get that sled? The antique store?

The above is only a sampling. I do sincerely thank Ty for the wonderful trail time we spent together and all his patient efforts to bring me into the modern age. In this, I must confess, he was only moderately successful. Still, my education as a musher has progressed considerably from Tom's and my Dark Age fumblings to the age of high-tech sleds, lithium-battery-powered headlamps, and GPS tracking of Iditarod racers.

Nowadays, I can put off painting the gable ends of our house for years, stall cutting the grass for days, not get too concerned when the last rick of firewood appears, and, at times, shamelessly sleep in past 9:00 a.m. That was not so back then in my earlier mushing days. I truly marvel at the active, energetic life we led—the "we" being Shirley, my longsuffering and patient wife, and, as they matured, our three children. We all learned early on in our Alaska lives what work was, and what it took to make things go successfully as a family.

There was much going on: An active church life, involvement in community affairs following the earthquake, full-time school attendance for the kids with accompanying activities, my teaching job, plus the initiation of the wrestling program at Seward High. Shirley literally and figuratively kept the home fires burning. She kept the cold, squirrels, porcupines, and bears away. There was much to do: house to make habitable, mile-and-a-half road (trail) to maintain and snow to plow, well to dig, septic to put in, firewood to cut, vehicles to maintain, garden spot to grub out, game and fish to harvest. On and on it went.

Through all the work, we made time for relaxation and family fun. We spent Sunday afternoons with a growing group of church and community friends, tea, conversation, laughter. There were school activities, wrestling meets, programs, plays, and proms. We found time for hunting and fishing trips, and summer and winter picnics with family and friends. We made infrequent summer trips "outside" to visit back-home friends and to demonstrate to our mothers that their grandkids survived another Alaska stint. There would be animals: cats, a skunk, rabbits, guinea pigs, squirrels, birds, chickens, and, eventually, horses. And a house dog, hound-type named Scruffy, a souvenir of my sabbatical leave and a master's degree at Northwest University in Natchitoches, Louisiana. But mostly, there have been sled dogs, fifty years worth of mushing and still counting.

6

You Guys Lose a Dog Team?

Sledding out the groceries. Early Fuller Lakes moose hunt.
Pictured: Mitch, ahkio with meat, Sinook foreground.

My first dog sled wasn't a dog sled at all. It was a military surplus "ahkio" purchased at Ralph Andrews' Army Store in Seward. It was made of white fiberglass. It had several hardwood, thin narrow strips attached to its bottom to provide grip on snowy mountain slopes. It also sported double ends with upturned sides and a canvas cover under which a battle casualty could be secured for transport by a military ski team. I cut away the canvas cover, leaving the many convenient lashing rings affixed to the perimeter of the seven-foot, toboggan-type conveyance. Because of its distinctive shape, it became a "banana sled" in the Seavey lingo. Under hard use, this sled, and later ones, invariably fatigued and broke into two almost equal halves, rendering "half bananas." Since an ahkio had fasteners on both ends from which to be drawn, half bananas were ready to go. They made handy kid-size sleds for pulling dog food buckets or kid-size loads of firewood. Though a bit rough on one's posterior, they provided an exhilarating ride down a bumpy, obstacle-filled trail behind three to five hard-charging dogs.

Ahkios were a good investment. They were tough, abundant at the time, and cheap. I purchased my first one in the fall of 1964, when we moved out into the woods. Its bottom was nearly worn through and fatigue lines appeared before the first serious November snows fell. Four immense Sitka spruce trees were toppled by wind several years prior. With my newly acquired Homelite chain saw, I limbed and bucked these giants into "rounds" of sufficient length to fit our ever-greedy wood-burning stove. Three dogs, as I recall, my entire team at the time, were hitched to the banana sled. Shirley and our three small children took a post on the tree end of the operation and I on that of the wood pile near the house, about one-half block in distance. After a whole lot of trial and error, we had those mutts pulling over bare ground, three or four, often three feet in diameter "rounds" from woods to home. Shirley and her child labor force would roll rounds onto the ahkio, point the dogs toward home, and send them on their way. I received the three panting dogs at the woodpile, unloaded, turned them around, and sent them trotting back for another load. This routine was a carryover used by my brother Joe Seavey and me, as kids, skidding trees from the woods of our Minnesota "stump farm" with a trusted draft horse team. By that means, our first winter's firewood was put by. There was family involvement. We were learning something of the capabilities of draft dogs that always seemed enthusiastic for any pulling tasks. Best of all, we had initiated a pattern of family connection with those most remarkable animals.

Team on firewood duty, 1970.
Notice the ever-so- handy ahkio (sled).

Homestead potatoes. Daughter Tracie displays just the largest from one hill. Heaviest was 5 pounds, 4 ounces, 1966.

A variety of uses was soon found for banana sleds, usually on snow, unlike our first wood-gathering efforts over bare ground. We had no water well for several years after moving to the homestead. However, there were two small springs flowing (until freeze-up) close to the house. I rigged up a flow to the house from the closest spring that sort of worked during above-freezing parts of the year. The nearest winter source was just under one mile away at Clear Creek. Our dogs hauled five-gallon "military surplus cans" with large, gasketed openings, up to thirty gallons per trip on an ahkio. We often turned a bothersome chore into family fun by making as many moonlight runs as possible.

Also, in a few instances, the kids and I made "fish runs." Three kids, a large wooden box, and I crammed on the banana sled. Five crazy-to-run dogs made quick work of getting to a nearby shallow stream with a late autumn run of humpback salmon. Catching, with our hands, enough slippery prey to fill the box, getting sufficiently wet and cold in the process, we made an equally rapid trip home. Hot chocolate for the crew. Coffee for me. Fish for the dog food cook pot. Fun to boot.

Many a hundred weight of moose meat were conveyed by ahkio and dog team. We figured on two moose plus other assorted wild game and fish to keep our family fed for a year. I didn't find time to hunt small game and it was only an occasional caribou or black bear bagged. Moose meat was our mainstay. Other than a local, whose misfortune it was to stumble into our yard during moose season and end up in the freezer, most of our moose meat came from the Fuller Lakes Basin of the Kenai Peninsula, just north of the Sterling Highway near Cooper Landing.

During those early years, that game unit boasted two moose seasons, one in late August and another around Thanksgiving time. Usually, a fellow teacher and I hunted the late fall season. With luck, there was adequate snow cover to give us an excuse to use dogs in sledding out meat, thus avoiding a good deal of toil as human pack animals.

During the 1960s, we took an even dozen of these giant ungulates from the Fuller Basin over a steep, rough trail about two miles in length. A routine was soon developed. We hiked in and hunted one weekend, usually while on Thanksgiving vacation from school, and hung the meat out of reach of at least the non-feathered scavengers. On the following weekend, three or four dogs were brought in to transfer meat from tree to truck. This entailed hitching that rather modest-sized dog team to an ahkio and driving it up a mountainside to the cache site. At the cache site, the first order of business, usually, was to wrest our winter's meat supply from feathered scavengers such as crows, ravens, magpies, and an occasional bald eagle. Next, we lashed moose quarters securely to the sled with a light, strong nylon line. That job was accomplished quickly and easily thanks to the presence of all those lashing rings built into the ahkio. Keep in mind that an average butchered moose weighs six hundred pounds or more. I found it better to make two trips for one moose than attempt to haul the whole thing at once, even though it could be made to fit on the banana sled. With half a moose plus a few odds and ends, I was able to ride atop the load on flat and slightly downhill stretches of trail. On serious downhill portions, which were all in the last mile, I attached myself to a long "snub line" dangling off the rear, upturned end of the sled. I would hold back as long as possible in what can be loosely termed as an upright position. There was only one way to go from there—down. With heels dug in and a prayer on my lips that my weightiest part might avoid frozen clods, embedded sticks, roots, and rocks, we made for the truck "hell-bent for leather." Happy was I that I had but a few, manageable dogs and only half a moose to hold back from overtaking and running over those eager workers.

There are in memory's storage a couple of noteworthy unusual happenings that go with our Fuller Lakes hunting experience. The first, was quite a heart-stopper.

In the late 1960s, my kid brother, nineteen-year-old Dale Seavey, left our kith and kin in Minnesota to spend a few months with my family in Alaska. He landed a fish-processing job with Icicle Seafoods in Seward, which was good, profitable summer work. Come autumn, our thoughts naturally turned to hunting. Dale wanted to bag a moose while in Alaska. He wanted the experience. I wanted the meat. The day after our Thanksgiving repast, we loaded our hunting and camping gear into my new, yellow Dodge pickup and drove to the Fuller Lakes trailhead near mile 60 of the Sterling Highway. We packed in on foot, and just before dark, about 3:30 p.m. that time of year, Dale downed a very nice, if not a record, bull. After congratulations, we field dressed him by flashlight. The next morning, Sunday, we completed the job, leaving some six hundred pounds of moose cached high up in a sturdy spruce. Our plan was to fetch it come the following Saturday by dog team.

On the appointed day, Dale and I arrived at the trailhead, in the early grayness between night and day. This time, however, we were accompanied by fellow teacher and budding dog musher, Bob Hill. Packing his trusty Marlin rifle, Bob had hopes of duplicating our earlier success. Dale and Bob would proceed up the trail in hunting mode. I was to follow an hour later with the banana sled and dog team in transport mode. All went as planned. I gave the dauntless stalkers a good hour, hooked up four dogs, and was able to ride most of the way up over a hard-packed trail. Up near the lakes, there was a skiff of new snow, maybe an inch and one-half, enough to plainly reveal Bob and Dale's footprints. I followed them along the east side of Lower Fuller, a lake perhaps the size of three football fields, bordered with alders, willows, and thin stands of spruce. They abruptly left the trail, heading west, and crossed the lake toward our cache, located on a ridge that ran north and south between lakes. In no time at all, dogs, with noses glued to the men's tracks, covered the width of the lake. I scanned the far shore, trying to determine where the best landing place might be. Not too brushy. We were maybe fifty yards from shore. I glanced over the dogs to see how they were doing. Yup. Everyone pulling. We were still on the hunters' tracks. But then I saw the open water. "Whoa! Whoa!" A dark, ominous spot, about the size of a pickup truck, and leading right to it—here's the heart-stopper—two sets of human tracks, ending abruptly at the near edge. Not a sign of struggle. Nothing floating. "How in the world could they walk into open water like that? This just cannot have happened. I am seeing this wrong." My heart, by then, was pounding a hundred miles per hour. Thoughts rushed through my confused mind. Thoughts of things to do. Action to take. All only contributing to inaction. A frozen immobility. Then, as I began to come to grips with the situation, studying the scene further, a great sense of elation and relief came over me. There, on the side opposite me, were two sets of footprints heading for shore, undisturbed, unhurried, straight as an arrow. "Thank God!"

Here again, I was thankful I had a small, easy-to-handle dog team. Genghis, the Earl Norris Siberian, was at lead. He was getting better with each season's use, but could be hard headed at times. I was all too acquainted with horror stories of the trail, of dog teams sticking fast to a track, which led to inevitable disaster. With only my two dug-in heels for brakes, those dogs could have effortlessly delivered the whole shebang to an icy bath, if not grave. With much apprehension, but with a calm voice, I gave the "haw" command, knowing full well that had the team elected to stick to the tracks stretching out before them, we would, without a doubt, end up in the drink. Big sigh of relief. I was able to talk the team into a wide, safe arc away from the danger zone, gaining the shore without mishap.

Discussing the situation a bit later with the unsuccessful hunters, we concluded that they had unknowingly traversed an extremely thin area of ice covering a small, slow-moving incoming stream. Their combined weight was sufficient to sink the ice down some without breaking through. Since they never looked back, they were completely unaware of the actual danger they were in. By the time I came along with the team, the sunken ice had mostly melted, due more to current action than temperature. "All's well that ends well," someone once said. That slogan was surely true on that trip.

Fuller Lakes moose hunt. November, 1968.
Brother Dale (left) and me. Dogs front to rear:
Genghis, Baranof, Sinook, and Chignik.

I recall another day like that. Back when we used polypropylene-braided weave rope to make up our lines, which connected the dogs to the sled. Though very strong for its weight, its chief drawback was that sled dogs loved to chew on it. One of the main lessons taught in doggy elementary school was to never chew on any line. However, every musher soon learned that dogs never completely learn not to chew. This fact, generally, was realized after hours of searching for the front half of a team, chewed free in less time than it takes to say "Jack Robinson" by an overly rambunctious team dog. The point being, I sure wish I had known about Tyrell's cable towline long before he made my first one in 1996.

It was on another hunt, this time with Les Loraff, an elementary teacher and church friend. The weekend before, we had gotten lucky and, before Sunday noon, had two moose butchered and cached on the mountain slope off the south end of the smallest Fuller Lake. Les, four dogs, I, and my faithful ahkio had gotten a rather late start up the trail. Apparently, a strong wind had gone through the area during the week and felled a good-sized poplar tree across our path, maybe a quarter mile from the parking lot and midway up the first ascent. No problem. I drove the team around this annoyance with no further thought.

It was nearly dark, about 3:30 p.m., by the time we had our load for the day secured atop the banana sled. It was a big load, nearly a whole moose. We had two guys now with a snub line each to hold the team back and to prevent the load from running over the dogs on treacherous downhill trail sections. No easy job with a load well over six hundred pounds, but we made good time despite a heavy load and fading light. Les and I jogged along, clutching our respective snub lines with death-like grips. We stopped often to give the dogs a rest. Always thinking of their welfare, you know. (Gasp, gasp.)

Coming to the final descent, we simply became human drags, sitting down, digging in our heels while exerting a double death grip on our lines. The four dogs with a single goal—to get to the truck as fast as possible—were doing just that, when without an inkling, the whole show came to a sudden stop. Well, most of the show, that is. The dogs kept going.

In the dark, I had not spotted the windfall we drove around on the upward trek. The dogs elected to use their habitual trail, forget the detour, the closest route home was under the fallen tree. They fit. Our stack of moose meat did not. To our dismay, the poly towline broke and the sled-less team quickly disappeared down the trail, into the dark night.

Not to worry. The dogs would run down to the truck, some quarter-mile distant. They probably would pile into the pickup since the tail-gate was left down and I commonly ran a small team into the covered pickup box, sled and all, to be sorted out when I unloaded at home. Even the ahkio, with its monstrous load, presented no real problem. We extricated it, wedged as it was under the fallen tree, and pulled it around the detour. With Les steering by a line attached to the front, and I, being the brakeman from behind, we covered the downhill run to the truck without further incident. Only one problem. We were there, but our dogs were not.

Even the placid-natured Les got excited about that. We hurriedly unloaded the contents of the banana sled, tying moose quarters and sled to a rack astride the pickup topper. Now the question was: which way should we go looking for the runaways? Toward Soldotna or toward Seward? An absence of dog tracks on packed snow or clear asphalt offered no clue. One thing was for certain: We had a dog team loose, in the black of night, on a major Alaska highway. No small worry.

We had just fired up our vehicle and were waiting to get a safe gap to pull out into traffic to head toward Seward, a logical direction for home-loving animals, when a familiar dark-green pickup pulled in front of us, coming from the direction of Seward.

"You guys lose a dog team?" It was Roscoe Livingston on his way to Kenai. Roscoe, a Seward Junior High physical education teacher and coach, had some rather interesting news. He had seen a dog team heading toward Seward, pulling a Volkswagen Bug. Dangest thing he had ever seen. Pulling it along the shoulder, heading for Seward. Thanking Coach Livingston for such welcome information, we zoomed off in the direction of home.

Les speculated that our "Good Samaritan" might be a certain fellow from Seward who drove a Bug. I, it turned out, correctly pondered the notion that a dog-musher type had come along, caught the team, attached it to his vehicle and driven it to Gwin's, a popular restaurant/lodge about five miles toward Seward. So it proved. A sprint musher from the Soldotna area, whose name I am sorry to say is lost to my Dog Diary, files, and memory, came upon them nicely traveling at a fast trot along the right shoulder of the road. No tangles, no fights. They had been on the road for about one mile when he happened upon them. With help from his VW Bug, he delivered them to Gwin's where we found them attached to a porch post. Again, a situation that could have resulted in a major calamity, ended well. I have had a bunch of those over the years.

Tom left Seward for a teaching job at Palmer High, commencing with the 1967 school year. Knowing that at least initially, he would be living in town, he sold his sled dog holdings to me. Included was that wonderful Seppala-type Siberian male named Genghis, whom he had acquired from well-known musher and breeder, Earl Norris. The Norris kennel was, at that time, located where the British Petroleum building was later built in Anchorage. I also acquired Guba, a young male who Tom purchased from Wasilla musher Charlie Bassett. Baronof was the third dog from Tom, a town stray of unknown parentage. And finally, I acquired "Old Oak," a sled Tom had purchased from Sewardite Ralph Hatch.

Old Oak was my first stand-up sled with a handlebar and brake. Far from the classic beauty of Tom's eye, it could more truthfully be described as rugged and ugly. So much so that recently, I had the thought that maybe Ralph Hatch, who had forgotten how he acquired it, did, in fact, build the thing, but was too ashamed to admit it. Everything about it was heavy. Thick, wide oak runners, extra hefty stanchions, beefy oak basket slats, and a substantial handlebar and brush bow. The side rails were of such dimension as to have likely been members borrowed from the bull pen down at the rodeo grounds. Add about ten pounds of steel shoe to each runner and you have redefined the meaning of a heavy-duty sled.

That sled, nevertheless, served me faithfully during my formative years as a musher. Old Oak and a special birch sled made by early Wasilla sled smith, Keith Poppert, were the only two real dog-powered vehicles I had until the first Iditarod in 1973. I "wiped out" on many occasions. I broke brush bows, handlebars, side rails, runners, and basket slats. Wore out steel shoes, grinding over sand and rocks. One time, I traveled over ten miles using a shed moose antler for a runner after destroying the whole right side of Old Oak on the Resurrection Pass Trail. By the time it met its final demise in the mid-1980s, only two stanchions were the original sled. Other parts had been replaced at least once. Sadly, Old Oak came to an inglorious end, backed completely over by a dog truck driven by an inattentive person who will remain unnamed. By the time of that unfortunate incident, I had nearly ten years' experience building my own sleds.

7

Fix the Brakes or Else!

First "dog truck." Add 8 dogs, 2 sleds, 3 persons, and a mountain of gear and we were good to go.

As with sleds, my mode of dog transport underwent somewhat of an evolution. The fact is, the Seward area in the 1960s lacked dog trails for training any serious distances. It still does, for that matter. Recently, Seward has justifiably been recognized as the southern terminus of the Iditarod National Historic Trail. As such, we have made significant progress in the re-establishment of a physical tread on the Kenai Peninsula. Back then, I needed a truck to get to trail heads beyond which stretched adequate miles of usable trail for long-distance training.

My first "dog truck" wasn't even a truck, just as my first sled wasn't a real dog sled.

From Files: Sales Agreement
November 3, 1964
Seward, Alaska

Sold to Daniel B. Seavey one (description of property) 1943 Willy's Jeep #W20 37 2019 as is and to which I have good title for the consideration of three hundred fifty dollars ($350.00) to be paid as follows: One hundred dollars ($100.00) at time of delivery of the above property and the balance paid at the rate of fifty dollars ($50.00) per month, with the first such payment due December 5, 1964. No interest will be charged. Payment due on or before the fifth day of each month. It is understood that should any violation of this agreement occur, the above-described property may be repossessed by me after thirty (30) days from the date of such violation and without notice to the buyer.

Signed: Larry L. Hawn, Seller 11/3/64
Signed: Daniel B. Seavey, Buyer 11/3/64

This twenty-year-old World War II relic continued with its reputation for dependable service, albeit not completely unblemished during its tenure with the Seaveys. Its main feature, in addition to its four-wheel drive ruggedness, was a homemade plywood cab that used to be painted some "sale bin" shade of green. Two other postwar modifications had been added: a hand-operated windshield wiper (single blade) and a heater that had laid down its labors perhaps a decade before. In fairness to seller Larry Hawn, he gave me an up-front warning about the vehicle's brakes. Something to the effect that they were nearing the end of their enlistments and hadn't been the best soldiers lately.

Shirley later found this to be true when, at a most inconvenient time, they decided to go on leave. To prevent crashing into Metcalf's Cash Grocery, she quickly jammed it into reverse and came to an abrupt halt, just inches from the store. That unnerving experience prompted her to lay down the law: "Fix the brakes or else!" Being unsure of the "or else," I fixed them.

Frivolity aside, what can one expect for $350.00, purchased on credit with no interest?

It is difficult to even imagine now, but up to eight large dogs in harness were crammed toward the back of that old warrior. On top, one or two full-sized dog sleds and associated paraphernalia. Now stuff in Tom, perhaps a kid or two or three (Shirley drew the line here). Oh yes, and myself, with dogs oozing over the works and we are good to go. Except, that is, if you had forgotten to gas up the vehicle before loading. In which case, most would have to be unloaded in order to get to the fill spout, which somehow had found its way to a permanent inside location, just forward of the left rear wheel. Speaking of gas, whenever an errant amount of that substance from whatever digestive source was detected via olfaction, the dogs were invariably blamed by us human occupants. Dogs are so forgiving in matters of that sort.

Kids and sled dogs, a natural.
L-R: Darian 7 yrs., Tracie 8 yrs., 1968.

"Oogruk" one of an assortment of collected canines on my way to becoming a novice musher. A nice dog but not "racey" enough even for my team.

For nearly four years, our old, frumpy, unglamorous military surplus Jeep served us. Not always well. Not always willingly, but it served us, nonetheless. It plowed through heavy, deep snow. It sloshed through knee-deep floodwaters, and hauled dogs, people, and firewood. Certainly, I got my three hundred and fifty bucks' worth.

All good things come to an end. A short time after Irv Metcalf's store jumped out in front of our poor old Jeep while Shirley was driving, I put in an order for a brand new, full-sized, three-quarter ton four-wheel- drive Dodge pickup. Maybe it wasn't as fancy as the one Mitch would win in 2004 as the Iditarod champion, but it did have automatic non-hand-operated windshield wipers and a gas tank that quite handily filled from the outside. The price was right also, compared to the 2004 models, $4,286.90 delivered to Seward.

My friend Bob Hill lent a hand to render my new canary yellow Dodge something resembling a dog truck. Bob Hill, like myself, was a refugee of the iron mining camps of northern Minnesota. He, too, had landed a teaching position at Seward High School, becoming our total Industrial Arts Department. Coincidentally, his wife's name was Shirley, and by moving to our community, they also contributed three small children to our kid population. Over the years, our families have become tried-and-proven friends. Not content to support me in my habit by constructing dog boxes, dog houses, and dog sleds, Bob eventually fell victim to the siren call of mushing. Bob's laughter at his own antics, and a contagious habit of finding humor in just about everything that happened, produced a whole new, comical dimension to my mushing experiences.

Family friend Bob Hill and I reminiscence our experiences together, which most often had to do with dog mushing.

The first dog box Bob constructed for me wasn't really a dog box at all. It was your basic plywood truck shell. With an understanding principal and use of the school shop after hours, we whipped it out. By this, I mean Bob allowed me to run the "dumb end" of the tape measure for him and to daub his handiwork with paint, once completed. The box itself was bolted securely to the truck bed. Likewise, I bolted a tethering chain all around the inside of the bed. For one skilled in stuffing a little jeep cab with large numbers of people and dogs, this newly won space became a newfound challenge. By careful planning and a non-combative dog population, I, on a regular basis, double decked eighteen of them. The upper deck being a sturdy sheet of plywood affixed to the upper surface of the truck bed. Sled and most mushing paraphernalia were roped securely atop the shell. In that box/

shell, I carried dogs for training all over the road system of Alaska and transported my first Iditarod team to the "Big City" of Anchorage for the start of the first Iditarod Race in 1973.

I suppose every endeavor elicits its peculiar stories, be it car racing, farming, or chess. It is certainly true of dog mushing. In particular, beginners' dog mushing. The moral to most dog-driving stories is that one can learn from one's mistakes. In an effort to demonstrate my growing mushing prowess, I now turn to some early noteworthy episodes of that process.

8

Damn the Traps!

Sinook, a trap victim. Litters of pups took over
his house and ate his food with impunity.

In addition to the Hills, we developed a long friendship with Bill and Judy Larson, who were also from Minnesota. Bill, too, was an educator who taught junior high science. Through our association both at school and church, we quickly became friends and so remain to this day. Another commonality was wrestling. Bill wrestled for Mankato Teacher's College, while I was a member of a rival but underdog squad at St. Cloud Teacher's College.

It wasn't long before I cashed in on Bill's ("Swede Larson" to friends) knowledge of electricity and enlisted his services in wiring our house. This was done in anticipation of a line being strung from Doc Gentles', our closest neighbor, over a half mile away. Bill, a trim, one-hundred-thirty-five-pounder, also came in handy as a wrestling referee for our home meets. An avid trapper and hunter of all game, Larson wasn't overly interested in sled dogs, certainly not to a degree where he entertained ideas of becoming a musher.

The Larsons lived in Alaska for two event-filled years, before returning to Minnesota to take a science teaching position at Bemidji. While in Seward, however, Bill made the most of it. I helped him. We pursued moose, caribou, goat, bear, ducks, geese, and ptarmigan. We sport fished both summer and winter, and we trapped. Now, besides catching muskrats in abundance and a rare weasel or mink back in Minnesota, I was not much of a trapper. Bill, on the other hand, was an insatiable one.

In the winter of 1965-66, Bill set up a trapline along a new dog trail I was building up Resurrection River Valley. As the musher, my job was to handle a five-dog team pulling an ahkio loaded with trapping gear. Bill's targets were the canines: fox, coyote, and wolf, for which he had made a dozen or so sets, placed well away from the trail on the upland mountainside. A couple of wolverine traps—big, deadly-looking ones—were also set after Bill ran across a set of its distinctive tracks. All these trap sets were baited with fish, deceased chickens or skinned-out carcasses of prior catches. On the first Saturday after our trapline had been established, we had "run" it clear to the end, with creatures great and small remaining free. Bill decided, in gathering darkness, to relocate the wolverine set, farthest from home, inland a bit more. Since this entailed cutting away several good-sized lower limbs from a large spruce, I anchored the dog team securely and, with axe in hand and snowshoes on foot, went to lend my able assistance a short half block away. The whole process didn't take ten minutes. Back at the sled, however, my seventy-pound, yellow-white lead dog Sinook had become impatient with us. He was gone. Even poorly lighted evidence revealed that the rascal had nipped his single trace clean as a whistle and hightailed it in the direction of his food dish.

Sinook's mischievous act of sabotage, as such, wasn't a big deal. The four remaining dogs knew their way home and had plenty of zip to get there. I was not too worried. Sinook would be there waiting for us. Of course, it was as dark as it could get on a clear, moonless, winter night by the time we covered those six or so miles of homeward trail. One little problem, though. No Sinook. Where in the world did that scoundrel go? Then, as if on cue, we both blurted out, "I bet he's in a trap!"

Our old wind-up clock had struck 11:00 p.m. when Bill and I entered the house at the end of our second trapline excursion for the day. With Sinook gone, we had harnessed a couple more dogs, one of which claimed to be a leader and headed back up Resurrection Valley, this time bearing a flashlight each. I tried to keep my imagination under control: Yes, it was getting colder, but he hasn't been trapped very long. No, I reasoned, he's not in one of those big, bone-crusher traps, probably a small number two. Anyway, who's to say he is in a trap at all? What if a wolverine or wolf comes along? He would be practically defenseless. Oh, so what? Stupid animal shouldn't have chewed himself loose in the first place. Seems the wind is building. Doesn't that mean that a trapped foot without circulation will freeze more quickly? Mind games played with one's self.

We had started to check each trap site as we came to it on the second outward run. Fortunately for both trapper and trapped, we found the captive held fast in a number three jump trap at the second site. It was fortunate, too, that the trap's hold was not around the ankle, where most certainly, bones would have been crushed, but midway on the right front foot, which was protected somewhat by thick, tough pads. Sinook appeared strangely calm under the circumstances and as happy to see us as we were to have found him.

All happiness ended the moment Bill attempted to release the victim. Only heavy leather mittens prevented injury from the dog's lightning-fast bites, directed more at the pain, the trap, than the hand. We probably spent the better part of a half hour in thwarted attempts, all ending in human failure and prolonged animal suffering, not to mention dimming flashlights. Then, as if divinely inspired, Bill shot up from a kneeling position, gleefully shouting, "I've got it! A trapper friend of mine back in the Old Country (Minnesota) used to catch foxes for zoos and I remember what he told me, how he removed them alive from traps." With that proclamation, he proceeded to remove his parka, then with one swift motion—those Mankato wrestlers always did have good moves—he had safely employed it to restrain and engulf the dog. With a nod from my genius trapper friend, coupled with all the strength my two hands could muster, I compressed the trap's double springs, finally releasing Sinook's much-swollen foot.

In a surprisingly short time, Sinook was back on all four, acting as if being trapped was part of his job description. By the time Bill had retrieved his trap, and I had turned the dog team around, Sinook was his old self, except one foot was a little bigger than the rest. We ran him home in the team with only a neckline attached, excusing him from working the night shift. Three days later, I ran Sinook thirty miles in a pretty fired-up team. He seemed no worse for wear.

Jumping ahead a few years with the topic of traps, my team fell victim to yet another while we were training for the first Iditarod.

Aside from an occasional dog mushing foray "up north," most of my training for the first Iditarod was done closer to home on the trails of the Kenai Peninsula. One was the Resurrection Pass Trail, which runs between Cooper Landing and Hope. The other, Mystery Creek Trail, located in the Kenai National Moose Range, of the time, was accessible at Mile 66 of the Sterling Highway. If run to its end, going east, the round trip was about seventy-five miles. It was on the Mystery Creek Trail that another frightening trap incident took place. At the outset, it should be realized that in 1969, when I first "discovered" that trail, the current snowmachine craze was hardly a murmur. Fact is, during the three training seasons leading to the 1973 Iditarod, I saw only one lone snowmachine. It belonged to "Trapper Joe" of Soldotna. His was the only snowmachine track and mine, the sole sled runner track. Trapper Joe's line extended nearly the entire distance of the Mystery Creek Trail, east and west, around eighty miles. Lynx and wolf were his main targets. Thus, large number three and four traps were spread over an extensive area.

Sometime prior to my Mystery Creek debut, a musher acquaintance related a true horror story involving dogs and traps. He was driving his team over a little-used trail when he found himself the star in a musher's most tragic nightmare. A large wolf trap had been set in the middle of the trail, baited, covered with a few light tree leaves and a sprinkling of snow. Everyone likes a well packed trail since it makes for easy travel. His team was moving along at a good clip on a good trail when his leader sprang the trap, which instantly crushed its lower right front leg, and, of course, stopped him instantly. Before the driver could possibly realize what was going on, his remaining team bunched up on the poor unfortunate dog. Its high-pitched, pained squeal unexplainably served as a signal for the whole mob to attack not only the down and wounded, but one another as well. It wasn't over quickly and the brutal fray did not have a happy ending. Not for the three brawlers who didn't survive it. From that harrowing experience, a pair of bolt cutters became standard equipment to be faithfully carried on his sled. A bolt cutter can be used to snip the steel jaws of a trap almost as easily as a scissor cuts paper. Thinking it was a good idea, I bought an inexpensive version, threw it in my sled bag, and all but forgot it.

Then, sure enough, the second training season on Mystery Creek, the winter of 1971-72, that rusting bolt cutter came in mighty handy. The previous winter, I utilized Trapper Joe's snowmachine trail with nary a thought of traps. I saw not a trap or trapper in person all season, but I had heard that I was on a trapline trail. Rumor became reality quite abruptly on a December day, 1971.

From Dog Diary:

> Dec. 18—Bad day today, Snippy caught in wolf trap twenty miles out on gas line (Mystery Creek Trail). Damn the traps. The outcome could have been worse, no doubt.

That day, I had Genghis, the Earl Norris Seppala-style Siberian in lead, a similar athletic male at left swing, and Snippy, an aggressive, hard-driving female, in right swing. The Dog Diary is silent on the total team size, due to shortsightedness of its author, but I suspect I had twelve or thirteen dogs, which would have been normal. It was still very cold at midday when I came upon Trapper Joe's snowmachine trail eleven miles out from the parking lot off the Sterling Highway. Fairly well packed, it followed the gas line route, which runs west to east, from the Swanson River oil field to a point about eight miles west of Hope, where the pipe is laid under Turnagain Arm on its way north to Anchorage area military establishments.

We had been running on this "bonus trail" (snowshoes not necessary) for about an hour. The team was midway up a small hill, moving smartly, when suddenly, Genghis slowed to nearly a stop and veered to his left. Just as he had begun to regain his forward momentum, there came a rather muted, but instantly recognized, snap of a steel spring trap. This was followed by the super high-pitched squeal of a dog in the throes of excruciating pain. Snippy had planted her left rear foot squarely in the waiting jaws of a number four wolf trap.

Instantly, I hit the brake, though not too effectively, as the team lunged forward in an effort to put an end to the squealing and to end her intense pain. Next, I stomped the snow hook deep into the compacted, frozen trail surface. Thankfully, it held. As quickly as I could, I made my way to the front of the team, unsnapping traces as I went, hoping those crazed animals wouldn't be able to pop the snow hook, pulling by just their necklines. I remember an overwhelming feeling of despair and helplessness as I viewed the scene.

The only way to release the short, stubby springs of a heavy jump trap is to place it on a solid surface and use both feet and all one's weight to depress the two springs located on opposite ends of the trap. That couldn't possibly happen. Not on snow. Even on rock-hard ground or ice. Without a Bill Larson to constrain the dog in a heavy parka, one only invites being chewed to pieces by a pain-ridden, unhinged dog. More than one musher, finding himself in this dreadful situation, has resorted to destruction of the trapped victim. A humane solution, for sure, but one not relished. Every single dog continued its high-pitched, frenzied attempt to get at the down and wounded prey.

"If only I could cut those trap jaws and release the poor, writhing creature. Cut! Yes, the bolt cutters!" Back to the sled I stumbled, yelling like a wild man for the dogs to "stay!" I dug through the contents of my sled bag while standing on the snow hook as added protection from its giving in to the team's efforts at dislodging it. At last, I brought forth to the light of day my savior tool. I rushed forward to the victim; I clipped both ends of one jaw more quickly than it took to tell about it. Poor

Snippy immediately ceased her complaint about her rough handling. Just as quickly, my whole team settled down, as if it weren't a big deal in the first place. Again, as with Sinook, the trapline dog who became the trapped, nothing was broken in Snippy's foot.

Not wanting to risk another possible incident, I loaded Snippy, who, by then, had a hugely swollen foot, and turned the team toward home. Not two miles in that direction, I met a man driving a yellow snowmachine, pulling a sled filled with traps and related gear. We stopped to chat. A few questions later, I realized I was in the presence of Trapper Joe himself. To this day, I am quite proud of myself at the restraint used to mask the volcano of anger that welled up within me. Anger toward traps, trappers, and the world in general as I related to Trapper Joe the jeopardy in which his unthinking trapping method had placed me and my team. He promised, since he knew dogs would be on the trail, no more traps would be set in their way. To his credit, year upon year, he kept his promise.

Lessons learned:

1. Be more religious in teaching dogs not to chew lines.
2. Do not leave a dog team unattended.
3. Loose dogs and traps don't mix.
4. It is all but impossible for a lone musher, unaided, to remove a dog from a trap without paying a huge price in one's own blood.
5. Attention to sled gear is vital: Not only what you carry, but its location in the load. Those cutters saved the day. But so could have an axe, a gun, a knife, snowshoes, matches, or one of a dozen other items on another day.
6. A good snow hook is absolutely essential. My snow hook may not have been the best on the shelf, but it was a good one. Had it not held in that emergency, I, no doubt, would have been facing a much greater tragedy, one possibly taking me out of the first Iditarod.

9

Close Calls—Avalanche and Wolverine

On another trail into the unknown –
at times, unknown dangers as well.

Again, it should be emphasized that during my musher embryonic stage, I had zero aspirations for dog racing. My interest in that aspect was pretty much confined to Anchorage trips during the Fur Rendezvous to cheer Alaskan George Attla on to another victory over that pretender from the "Outside," Roland Lombard. The result of this non-race mind-set enabled me to explore many places via dog team rather than simply training on groomed racing trails. Since long-distance wilderness racing was yet to be reinvented, I was content, indeed thrilled, with each of the dozens of short dog team treks made. For me, at that time, a long trip would have been a fifty-miler and resulted in preparations that rivaled those made by polar expeditions.

From Dog Diary: Jan 20 (1969)

Ran South Fork. First time. Close call with avalanche and trapped wolverine. Froze right earlobe, minus ten degrees, clear, mild wind from north.

My January 1969 mush up the South Fork of the Snow River certainly wasn't an expedition. Even its claim as a trek comes into question; foray might be a better term. As I recall, it was already well past noon when I left the Seward Highway parking lot, just north of Mile Twelve Hill. Although I anticipated a full moon, I expected to return before dark. In single lead was Genghis, who, by then, was my most experienced and trusted leader. Behind him was a small team of not more than seven dogs, as I remember. A well-defined snowmachine trail led up the South Fork in a southeasterly direction. On a good trail, with an exuberant dog team, I moved out in fine style. About a quarter mile out, off to my right, I heard a rattling noise, like that made by a trap chain. Since I was bundled up against a minus ten degree F temperature, the sound was muffled, something in the distance. Local trapper, Doug McRae, whose son was a student at Seward High, had parked his pickup in the same turnout as I had parked. Simple explanation: Doug was over in that thin stand of timber yonder, setting a trap. That was about the total thought process as I turned my attention toward remaining upright and in one piece as the trail began to weave through a patch of sturdy Sitka spruce.

On I went without any serious interruptions, covering the first seven miles in about an hour. There was only one open-water crossing, which I managed to bypass thanks to a willing leader and a team accustomed to "swimming" in deep, loose snow.

Another half hour and we crossed the base of an obviously active avalanche chute, knifing into the South Fork Valley from a nameless mountain to the north. Although mostly snow covered, littering the chute's east side were scores of broken and twisted hemlock trees, some a foot and more in diameter. Perhaps victims of a slide, which may have rumbled into the valley early the past spring, leveling all before it. Glancing upward, maybe two thousand feet, I noticed a fairly small, snow-filled bowl sentinelled by jagged cliffs. Many of these were supporting what appeared to be extra-heavy, wind-shaped snow loads. The tallest and most heavily laden of these cliffs reminded me of the Pillsbury Doughboy. It was pointed where a head would be and covered by a fat, puffy, overhanging flock of snow, and rendered a beautiful pink-orange by a lazy winter sun off to the south. A north wind created a localized blizzard on its top, adding drama to this spectacular scene. These were quick, fleeting observations made in less than the minute it took to negotiate the slide area, made by small, recent avalanche deposits. As with the trap chain noise earlier, I dismissed this zone of devastation as just another interesting feature of this newly traveled valley.

Progressing upriver, the valley began to narrow to a point where we were running mostly on the diminutive South Fork itself. Then, possibly a half hour upriver from the avalanche chute, we came face-to-face with what appeared to be impassable, vertical bluffs. The river, such as it was at this point, flowed under layers of ice and snow from between two of these rocky and wooded obstructions. My ever-faithful snowmachine track had made a sweeping turnabout and headed home.

Later that same winter and spring, I would make several more exploratory trips well past this point, and beyond to a point where I could look down into King's Bay of Prince William Sound. It took a whole bunch of work, a lot of it on snowshoes, but words cannot do justice to the benefits derived. The awe-inspiring winter beauty of the Nellie Juan Lake region beyond those forbidding bluffs simply leaves me stuttering for descriptive words.

Nowadays, pickups pull their large trailers, chucked full of high-powered snowmachines, into the parking area from which I left that winter's day in 1969. Commercial operations, mostly. Their clients, perhaps first-time operators, can get a view of King's Bay and be back to the Pit Bar or Yukon Bar, talking about it in less than four hours. And talk they do. Boast of the power and speed of machines. Boast of their prowess as operators of those snow rockets. Complain of snow conditions, river overflow, weather, and innumerable other offences perpetrated on only them by a vengeful Mother Nature. Even their snow steeds are not immune to complaints: They get stuck. Their throttles get sticky. Hand warmers go out. Gas lines freeze. They refuse to start and suffer a never-ending list of maladies laid at the doorsteps of Skidoo and Arctic Cat.

Even so, generalizations aside, there must be an occasional fast tracker who, high atop the world at a place like Nellie Juan Lake, turns off his engine and, in reverent silence, sits facing east, absorbing into every pore of his being the majesty with which God puts to bed another of His days. Pinkish-orange, snow-laden mountains all around. A slow, breath-taking transition to ink-sketch dusk. But before he is surrounded by real darkness of night, there, behind that nearest mountain to the east, the upper edge of a huge full moon appears. Soon, all inkiness disappears, replaced by the brilliance that only a full, new moon on pure-white snow can bestow. And now the moon is up. So big, so close, it seems one could step onto it from Earth. Now a sensation our fast-tracker will never forget. The snow-covered bowl and surrounding snow-smoothed mountains are transformed it seems, into large, cumulus-type clouds, and as the moon continues to rise, there is produced a most stunning effect. The whole of our friend's immediate universe seems to him to be floating through space. Floating slowly, to be sure, but with increasing speed, as a growing number of stars make their appearance. Too soon, Mother Nature's induced spell comes to an end, as all good things do. The moon grows smaller as it moves off toward the south to attend other chores. Starting his engine, the snowmachiner, feeling the chill, but in a reflective mood, turns and drives slowly homeward.

My personal mountaintop experience would have to wait for another two months or more from the time I first laid eyes on those "guardian bluffs." Eventually, I was by snowshoe and dog team, able to view King's Bay and camp on thirty or more feet of snow blanketing Nellie Juan Lake basin. Bob Hill, my shop teacher friend, being well into dog mushing by then, accompanied me on a couple of these trips. Only once, however, were the stars aligned, so to speak, to produce the moving experience described above. I was alone, but for my dog team. I obviously was greatly affected. My canine camping partners, having worked hard all day, however, were unimpressed. They curled up and slept through the whole show.

Running out of daylight and not knowing if the way was passable beyond the guardian bluffs, as I came to call them, I turned the team around on the same convenient snowmachine track followed on the outward-bound leg. One of my team dogs had stepped over its neckline, so I set the hook and went forward to straighten things out. It was then I heard from down the valley toward home a sound like a distant train, rumbling along the track. It lasted but a short time and was gone. Made sense. A train, since the Alaska Railroad parallels the Seward Highway. In fact, from where my dog truck was parked, I could throw a rock and hit the tracks. Well, some guys could.

What a terrible shock I was in for. Moving smartly down the trail toward home and rounding a sharp bend, we came up hard against a wall of snow and tangled debris, and to a sudden stop. All the dogs, as if on cue, shot a glance back at me, as if to ask, "What do we do now?" There could be no doubt. What I had heard a few minutes earlier was definitely not a train.

It seemed the whole mountainside had slid down into the valley and attempted to climb up the opposite side. A quick perusal of the avalanche chute now off to my right revealed that its original width had at least tripled, and a new swath of trees was mowed down on its right (east) side. Snow-laden cliffs high above weren't so snow laden any longer. Mostly bare, vertical cliffs now dominated that lofty scene. Doughboy had been "de-pantsed," standing stark in his nakedness. Even the rapidly setting sun, which an hour ago had added such brilliance to his snowy mantel, now deserted him to the first gloomy shadows of darkness.

No way could we negotiate a route directly forward. The top of the slide was up there maybe twenty feet. Straight up. I hawed Genghis over to a ramped-up spot, then gee'd him up the incline onto the top. What a picture. A wintertime scene of a World War I no-man's land. A forest of broken, splintered, scattered trees, and brush, some one hundred and fifty yards in breadth. With a minimum of crashing and banging, I worked Genghis and the team through the tangle, making a fairly gradual easy exit on the downriver side.

Not until I was well on my way toward the Seward Highway did I get to thinking of the gravity of what I had just experienced. Scary thoughts. Had I left the truck a half hour later or turned around to go home somewhere before the guardian bluffs, my timing could have been perfect for a up-close and personal encounter with a world-class avalanche. Not a comforting thought. No, a mind's eye picture of team and driver, broadsided and buried by such a brutal, overpowering force wasn't very pretty.

Thus were my thoughts as we closed in on the pickup even as darkness closed in on us. Hearing highway sounds, the dogs had, without encouragement, stepped up our pace to a slow lope. Then, catching me completely off guard, deep in avalanche thoughts, the team bolted from the trail to the left. In less than two team lengths, they came to an abrupt halt, leader and swing (point) dogs buried among the lower boughs of a medium-sized spruce. As rapidly as possible, I nabbed a small tree on the crook of my snow hook, halting the disappearance of any more dogs under the tree.

My thoughts, directed at Genghis, were not nice thoughts, as I ungracefully stumbled forward to drag that son-of-a-so-and-so out from under the tree and back on the trail. What in the blankety-blank got into him? Just as I reached down, intending to wrench the three wayward dogs out from under the tree, I heard the all-too-familiar rattle of a trap chain. No doubt the same one I heard on the outward run. Parting thick tree boughs, I beheld a most remarkable sight. There, held firm by its left rear leg, was a trapped, very unhappy, very large wolverine. The largest member of the weasel family, it has a reputation for being nasty. Even a giant grizzly will go out of his way to avoid a wolverine's wrath. This particular one gave no quarter to my three intruders. It was nose to nose with Genghis, hissing its fury, baring its teeth and charging as far as the trap chain would allow. There was a foot-deep trench all around the tree's base, where it had dislodged a thick carpet of frozen moss.

Strange canine behavior ensued. None, neither team nor wheel dogs, and certainly not those under the tree, inhaling wolverine venom, seemed at all eager to have at this formidable defender. Absolutely no "let me at him, I'll shred him into little pieces and spit them out" business. Where Genghis and my swing dogs were concerned, it was like "What in tarnation have we gotten ourselves into? This little side trip really wasn't a good idea. We should be going now!" I had no difficulty extracting Genghis and company from under that tree or coaxing the whole outfit into a speedy retreat to our waiting truck.

Lessons Learned:

1. Practice Trail Awareness: It is one thing to build one's dog-driving skills, but just as important is to learn the skill of reading the

environment through which one travels. I should never have, and as far as I know, have not since, risked crossing that avalanche zone with such dangerous conditions as described above. The brutal truth was that just a few minutes' difference in timing and in all likelihood, I would not be here telling about it. That God watches over fools was true that day. Pitching in as backup are mortals like Jill Fredston and Doug Fesler at the Alaska Mountain Safety Center, whose efforts to bring about awareness of avalanche danger has not been futile where I am concerned.

More than avalanche danger is involved here. A great deal more: Trail conditions affecting dog's feet, Thickness of ice, Wind speed and direction, Temperature, obstructions, and other trail users, such as moose, snowmachiners, and trappers. On and on it goes. Had I been more aware that day of below-zero temperatures, I could have saved having my right ear turn black due to frostbite. "Live and learn," it is hoped.

2. Sled Dog Behavior: At its best, it is unpredictable. Stay alert. It is perhaps universally true that a sled dog, and thus, collectively, a dog team, loves to chase moose down the trail - predictable behavior. A dog team will go after that loose dog ahead. - predictable behavior. There will be a riotous uproar of approval when one approaches the dog lot with the food bucket in hand - predictable behavior. An animal in distress needs to be slain. Even a trapped, screeching teammate - predictable behavior? Not where the trapped wolverine was concerned that day. We shot right past it on the way out. Desire to be on the trail overrode curiosity perhaps. Not so on the homeward leg. Same dogs. Same trail. Same desire, this time to get to their truck. Same animal, in the same trap, under the same tree. In the blinking of an eye, we ended up nose to nose with one of the most ferocious critters on the globe, a hissing, spitting, defiant, dangerous animal. He expected no quarter, nor did he offer one. No squealing in pain. No invitation to end it all for him. It took only an instant for the dogs to size up the situation and they wanted out of there. Figure that one out.

10

The Great Snow Hook War

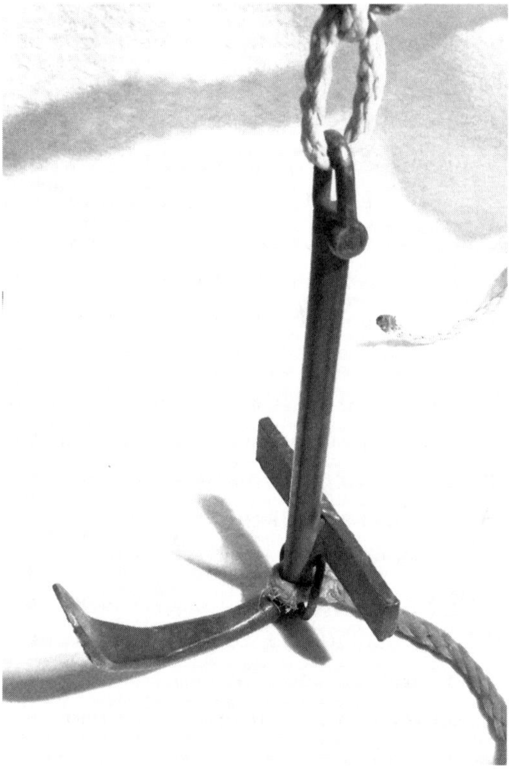

"Battle lines were formed to define the ideal snowhook, and for two winters the war raged on." (Photo: Resurrection Bay Historical Society.)

Here is as good a place as any to mention the "Great Snow Hook War." To dispel any visions of snow-hooked, impaled, bleeding victims, at the outset, let it be known it wasn't that sort of war. Tom Johnson started it. Soon after his move from Seward to Palmer, during the summer of 1966, he began rubbing elbows with musher types of the

Matanuska Valley. Folks the likes of Gleo Huyck, Charlie Bassett, Jerry Crum, Joel Kotke, Dave Olson, Bill Cotter, Keith Poppert, Dick Mackey, the Redingtons (Joe Sr., wife Vi, Joey, Raymie, and Tim), and others. Most belonged to the Aurora Dog Mushers Club, an organization destined to effect great changes in the world of the northern sled dog.

Of course, as one would expect, there was a good deal of talk among that crowd of dogs, mushing, and equipment. Through the medium of talking, my friend Tom took an authoritative role on all subjects relating to dog mushing. Whenever we met, he brought with him, for my enlightenment and gratification, copious amounts of mushing information, generally in the form of pure, indisputable fact. Admittedly, for a novice such as myself, our hours-long, one-sided discussions were interesting and, to a degree, instructive. On one issue, however, I stood my ground. I knew a good snow hook when I met one, which, obviously, Tom and the Matanuska Gang did not. Antagonists were identified as Tom and myself. Battle lines were formed to defend the ideal snow hook, and for two winters, the war raged on.

So as not to belabor our carryings-on, let it be said that between the fanatic combatants' many designs were advanced and championed as the ultimate snow hook. My original (first) snow hook was fashioned for me by Chuck Lechner, a second-generation Seward machinist. It was copied from my recollection of that used by George Attla in the Anchorage Fur Rendezvous Race. It was made of one-inch square steel bar. Chuck heated and hammered out a rounded point on one end, bent it into a nice hook, then cut to length the result and welded an eye for rope attachment. Finally, a six-inch crossbar of lighter material was welded to the upper side of the hook, midway to its overall length. This was the hook that held my team while I extracted Snippy from that Mystery Creek Trail trap. Price? Five dollars.

Tom countered with the latest from the Valley. He started with a trailer leaf spring. Thin, flat, and about three inches wide, no crossbar. Weight? Too heavy. To lighten the thing, I suggested he remove it from the trailer. Tom countered that my snow hook was so heavy, it would take a freight sled and twenty strong dogs just to move it—downhill.

Hooks and counter hooks. Round stock, flat stock, square stock. Angle claw, double claw. No crossbar. One crossbar. Two crossbars. Steel.

Aluminum. Tom was satisfied with a double-barreled tire iron hook, whereas I was going with a double-flattened claw hook, created by machinist Lechner from five-eighths-inch round steel stock. The Great Snow Hook War ended in stalemate. It also ended without production of a truly all-round effective, trustworthy snow hook. No! That's not totally true. Both Tom Johnson's and my snow hook worked very well with hard-packed snow, but, to our chagrin, mostly did not work on ice. Some of my most exciting, if not enjoyable, mushing moments have been being dragged clutching onto an overturned sled, toward open water over glare ice. This maneuver was most often accompanied by a prodigious quantity of verbal abuse directed toward a dog team that had forgotten the desired response to the command "whoa." No laughing matter. There comes to mind two teams and drivers pulled into open, ice-free spots on rivers and lost in separate tragedies. A reasonable assumption is that had those mushers had a hook capable of stopping their teams on smooth, windblown ice, their stories would have had happier endings. Had I such a hook for both the first Iditarod Race and the second, I would have been spared several frightening, potentially fatal incidents. As with so much mushing equipment, the modern musher can justifiably lord it over us primitives when it comes to the snow hook. My grandson Tyrell, in his campaign to modernize me for the 1997 Iditarod, introduced me to a truly remarkable combination snow and ice hook. Over the intervening years, I have developed an absolute, unshakable trust in the device. Should I be given a choice of a million-dollar paid life insurance policy for the next Iditarod or use of a Critterwoods hook tied to my snub line, I'd take the hook every time.

There are other hooks nowadays of similar design. The one with which I am most familiar, however, bears the Critterwoods brand name. Manufactured in Corinth, Maine, this stainless steel beauty is an ice-snow combination hook. It has double, very sharp, ice-chipping claws between which a perforated snow-scoop type plate is affixed. With its prominent lift handle and splayed-out hooks, it is designed to self-right when bounced over frozen tundra behind a loose, runaway team. A musher's hope, and under most circumstances, prayer, is that the sucker will grab onto something team-stopping before he or she runs out of jogging breath. This hook works equally well on snow or zero-friction ice. A fault-finding person will point out that it is extremely difficult to retrieve from hard-packed snow when set fast. This same person will gleefully point out the cost, one hundred thirty-five dollars when I last checked. A bit more than Chuck Lechner's five-dollar 1968 model, for sure. But then, I bet our fault finder would agree that even at a hundred thirty-five dollars, when faced with certain disaster ahead, it beats a life insurance policy at twice the price.

By the way, my first experiences with the super hook were not super. Moving along at a fast trot, I knelt on the runners and, as an experiment, slammed this new hook into a patch of glare ice. In less than one foot of travel, it set with a finality that left me on my back atop the sled bag, staring upward at a cloudy sky. No question about that. It works on ice. The next day, while running among a stand of giant coastal spruce, where little snow had reached the trail, this same hook bounced loose, immediately righted itself, just as the advertisement stated, and grabbed an exposed tree root. Everyone except me stopped instantly. I continued the journey crashing through handlebar and rear stanchions before coming to rest, this time, face down atop my sled bag, gazing at the ground framed by the brush bow. Yes, Sir! No question, it works on tree roots also.

What was to be had from all this snow hook business?

Lessons Learned:

1. Acquire by whatever means the very best equipment (dogs as well) possible. Be willing and able to make changes as dictated by necessity. Avoid all compromise where your safety, and that of your animals, is at stake. This goes for every bit of equipment. Snow hooks serve to illustrate the point.
2. Once acquired, use equipment properly. The only reason I was stopped in such an undignified manner by that tree root was that I failed to secure the hook in a safe way. Under a different set of conditions, the towline could have snapped, releasing my team to who knows what perils. Or I could have impaled myself on a jagged, broken sled stanchion. Maybe worse. Given that both claws of that particular hook are razor sharp gives rise to a variety of gory likelihoods.

11

Of Fish Heads, Bears, and Porcupines

Homesteader kids have to put up with a lot to be in a photo.
L-R: Tracie, Mitch, Darian, 1964.

Year round, year upon year, musher son Mitch shows up at the doorstep of Icicle Seafoods/Seward Fisheries. Attached to his pickup is a very large, covered trailer. Present manager, Charles McEldowney, sees to it that two totes weighing upward to a ton each are loaded into his trailer. Off he drives with a load of extremely valuable dog food, to be stored in walk-in freezers located at our Seward home place or Mitch's Sterling dog lot. Thirty to forty thousand pounds per year, whole salmon, salmon heads, halibut, black cod, you name it, all finds its way to our dogs' dishes. This is all nicely containerized and held in cold storage, awaiting Mitch's arrival. With ample reason, Mitch brags on Seward Fisheries as his most-valued sponsor. When he does, he perpetuates a boast originating with yours truly in 1965.

Shortly after moving to the homestead and accumulating a fair number of sled dogs, I began to bum dog food from the Fisheries. A facility operated by Seward Halibut Co-op had been completely destroyed by the 1964 earthquake and tidal waves. Icicle Seafoods/ Seward Fisheries became the new kid on the new dock, relocated at the head of Resurrection Bay. Linné Bardarson, a rather refined Viking, served as Seward Fisheries' first manager. It was he who would drop whatever he was doing and, with a genuine friendly, helpful spirit, provide me with tubs and totes of free dog food.

One weekday evening, in early October 1965, I hooked my two-wheeled trailer to the Rambler station wagon and bounced over a washboard, potholed surface of a recently rebuilt section of quake-damaged Seward Highway. I crossed three equally rough temporary bridges spanning Resurrection River on the way to Seward Fisheries. A hurried but cheerful Linné himself fork-lifted a tote of red salmon heads, prime dog food, to a spot where Mitch, Tracie, and I could pitch them into our waiting trailer box. It was all but dark when we struck out for home without benefit of taillights on the trailer. Dogs do love to chew electric wires. Come to think of it, they relished gas lines, brake lines, towlines, necklines, harnesses, rocks, tin cans, dropped gloves, occasionally a neighbor dog, and dog houses as well. We took a fairly good bump up onto the south end of the first bridge, thought no more of it while jiggling our way home. In complete darkness, I parked the fish wagon, calling it a day.

Seagulls screaming. Lots of them. That's what aroused me from peaceful slumber before Big Ben started his 6:45 a.m. wake-up serenade. Being a school day, Mitch, then a first-grader, and I left for school around 7:30 a.m. "Darn seagulls, I am going to have to cover that trailer or there won't be a head left by tonight," I remember thinking as I dashed to the rescue. Big surprise! I couldn't believe my eyes. There were remaining of the original thousands, two—that's one, two—fish heads in the trailer. Period! My first thought was: "That must be an industrious gang of gulls to have made off with a whole trailer load of heads, and before breakfast at that." Then I noticed a number of those rapacious loudmouths working a long, thin line of heads stretching beyond the first curve of our driveway. Almost at the same instant, it registered. Both sideboards of the trailer had given way and my tailgate was gone.

I had a hunch that the long, thin line of fish heads would end in town! It did. Both fish and seagulls ended at the southern end of the first bridge from town. A line of fish heads and joyous gulls three miles long. Not surprisingly, where the line ended, there also lay my tailgate. Mitch exhausted his youthful counting ability at one hundred. One hundred gulls the first half mile with two and a half miles to go. One can only speculate on what country-to-town commuters thought that morning as they dodged fish and feathers on their way to work. Gulls by the hundreds were competing for as many salmon heads. What a sight! One of those times when one kicks himself for leaving his camera at home.

"Dad, that's our tailgate. Stop and I will pick it up for you."

"Ahhh. That's OK, Mitch. We'd better keep going or we will be late for school." I learned from local sources that in less than one hour, the fish head chow line had vanished. All but vanished, that is. That evening, when I began repairs to my much-shaken trailer, there in plain view of the world, and seagulls of the world, was one, and only one, red salmon head.

A year later, in autumn of 1966, I learned that seagulls weren't the only wild-fish-loving creatures about. We had just polished off Shirley's moose pot roast dinner, replete with stewed-in-the-juice potatoes, carrots, parsnips, and rutabagas. Delicious is a rather limp-wristed word to describe such a meal. Doubly so when one throws in a loaf of freshly baked, still hot out-of-the-oven French bread, a Shirley Seavey specialty made perfect by the use of rendered bear fat. Her bread-baking mastery was made all the more remarkable by the fact that it was being pulled off in the oven of a temperamental, crotchety, old, oil-fired cook stove. Had the cook stove been a living creature, without a doubt, it would have been a wooly mammoth. Finally came the fresh berry pie, again, as only Shirley knows how to create one. Fresh (frozen) wild blueberries in a crust made perfect by years of practice. A topping of real whipped cream gave new meaning to the word delicious.

The "we" participants in this repast were, of course, the Seavey family. There were also foster kids: Frank Trigg and Larry Tyone. And another, Archie Wemark, a former Jesse Lee Home resident who was then a junior at Seward High and a longtime buddy of Frankie's.

Shortly after dinner that fall evening, Archie was saying his good-byes and thanking me profusely for "letting" him build dog houses all day when, without prelude, our dog lot went into a horrendous uproar. From past experiences, I knew only a loose dog or a foreign invader such as a moose could elicit such a crazed and universal response. Frankie, being the eldest of the young, was dispatched to "catch that loose dog." He was trailed by an inquisitive six-year-old Mitch.

"Bear! Bear!" Frankie yelled. Our front door burst open to reveal a wide-eyed, fast-breathing Frankie, with his dark-rimmed glasses askew. Two steps behind came Mitch, shouting the same information.

"There's a bear in our dog lot!"

Leaving the house, our mile-long "driveway" passed through the dog lot, which sprawled along both sides about one-half block away. Head down, or perhaps scanning a different direction for the suspected loose dog, Frankie came nearly nose to nose with a large—as in really large—black bear. It "whuffed," and darted into a patch of nearby devil's club bushes. My guess is that Frankie and Mitch didn't "whuff," but for sure, they darted toward the house.

No sooner had the youthful informants settled down enough to convey the story when, once again, the dogs went crazy with high-pitched excitement. It was, without mistake, an intruder alarm. We all lined up anxiously, peering out our kitchen windows to witness an extraordinary scene. Over in "South Dogville," the left side of the driveway, we had positioned an abbreviated fifty-five-gallon barrel. It had been cut down to about two-thirds of a barrel, and filled with halibut heads. These became my preferred supplemental dog food. Lots of fat and protein. Dogs loved the stuff. Located between two dogs that could just about touch it, the barrel was situated for feeding convenience. Again, the barrel had been filled with halibut heads. Had been! Methodically, one at a time, Mr. Bear grasped fish heads in his mouth and disappeared into those devil's club bushes and, after a short interval, returned to repeat the process. Interesting to watch, but what made this whole affair so incredible was that each time this black-hearted robber returned for more loot, he was greeted by two gone-crazy fish guards, not more than two feet away from him. Seventy pounds of canine ferocity came at him from two directions. Still, in a most unperturbed manner, he went about the heist. Not even the chiming in of another twenty-five super-charged antagonists deterred him. Tipping over the barrel to reach the final head, he faded into the underbrush for the last time.

Out go the older boys and myself. I had my trusty Remington Model 700 7mm magnum ready, just in case. Since the sun was well on its way toward setting, there was an unspoken understanding among us. We were not in hunting mode. It was by now an established routine. Whoever shot a bear was obligated to salvage both hide and meat. The latter went directly into the dog food cook pot, the use of which, we all perceived as being akin to a medieval torture rack. No one, Frankie, Larry, Archie, nor I, wanted to do the night shift. As it turned out, we didn't have to. Mr. Bruin was gone. There, mostly buried with a mixture of moss and dirt, was the bulk of our barrel contents. One could only imagine the dog ruckus that would have ensued with each return of that blackie for his daily meal until all were consumed. We refilled the barrel and manhandled it to the center of a big patch of dogs. That did the trick. Not long after Archie had taken the trail homeward, there was another big, but final, uproar from the dog lot. The unseen intruder must have returned, sized up the impracticality of the situation, and decided the few remaining humpies down in Clear Creek were a much better dining option.

Aside from the rare loose dog, which had slipped its collar, the usual dog lot commotion was incited by denizens of the wild: moose, bears, and, believe it or not, porcupines. Stray dogs were of no consequence at this time, as our closest neighbor, Doctor Gentles, was over a half mile away, with a mostly tied-up dog team. Of the three wild ones, porcupines, by far, gave me the most grief. That is, porcupines and more porcupines.

During our first two or three years on the homestead, we were, to put it mildly, plagued with porcupines. They were everywhere. Worst of all, the "where" was, of course, the dog lot. They loved the succulent willows bordering the dog lot. They loved the urine-saturated dog houses and relished creosoted power poles, in particular, the one in the center of our dog lot. There are those who assert that your average husky sled dog isn't extremely bright. Nowhere is this assertion given more credibility than when it comes to dog-porcupine interrelationships. A porky, believing himself to be invincible, wanders into a dog lot for a little salty dog house snack. A dog, in turn, views this trespasser as nothing more than an incredibly slothful, dull-witted dog toy, something to chew upon until dead. Now, if a given dog acted on that misguided view but once, and profited accordingly, he might be reasonably classified as educable. However, when that same dog chomps three separate porcupines on three separate occasions, that champion chomper might be reasonably classified as, well, not too bright.

So it was that for the first two autumns in the country, Frankie and I pulled quills from dogs, sometimes two or three times per week. The plague became so bad that on school days, we were getting up an hour early, checking the dogs and, too often, pulling scores of well-implanted barbed quills from a not-too-happy dog. One time we had two victims on the same morning. All before going to school. At times, due to some early morning school commitment, this less-than-enjoyable task was left to Frankie with assistance from Shirley.

"Quill duty" entailed first wedging the poor victim's mouth wide open by placing a short section of broom handle crosswise in its mouth, and tying it over the head with a light cord. The device was worked far back on the jaws so as to hold the mouth as wide open as possible. Next, the assistant rolled the animal tightly in a heavy blanket and proceeded to immobilize it. Long, sharp-nosed pliers went to work. Like small arrowheads, porky quills have no reverse gear. They only go ahead, so as a quill is pulled it is forced out against the grain, so to speak. The bigger, thicker quill shafts can be snipped with scissors, which results in a diminished shaft diameter, which seemed to ease their extraction somewhat. We attempted to get all quills pulled the first go around. Rarely were we successful however, as there would likely be many quills broken or chewed off. This necessitated at least one more session to pull those remaining as they worked their way through tongue, lips, or lower jaw. No fun for either man or beast. Eventually, I managed to acquire a good injectable sedative, and the orally administered Thorazine, albeit by somewhat dubious legal means. This made the recurring job much easier for the dog and much safer for those on quill duty, since the calmed patient ceased fighting and attempting to bite the hand releasing it from a hundred fiery darts. It should be understood that no veterinarian resided in Seward at that time. That service being 130 miles away in Anchorage, I learned to doctor dogs.

With a *Merck's Manual* in one hand and an old, late 1800s vet's how-to-do-it book in the other, I did what had to be done. I removed dew claws, sewed together ripped ears and other parts, extracted teeth, treated beat-up feet, and vaccinated and administered antibiotics, to list the most common.

A final note on porcupines. They seemed to be on a high-reproduction cycle during our first years on the homestead. This was evidenced not only by the couple of dozen or more that we dealt with, but by the large numbers observed flattened by vehicles on the Seward Highway during that time. I offered the kids (Mitch, Tracie, and Darian) a bounty of one dollar each, provided the porcupine was bagged within one-half mile of our dog lot. This bold and generous gesture on my part admittedly played a very minor role in the eventual decrease in porcupine numbers. As I recall, I paid out but a single-dollar bounty. The porkies that paid the ultimate price, either by the hand of man or mouth of dog, ended up in the dog food cook pot.

12

Babes in the Woods

A commonality, me and these pups,
we had much to learn about mushing.

From Dog Diary: (February 13, 2004)
Frenzy's pups arrived. Three males, three females. Sired by Nascar, Genghis line, twenty generations removed.

With the birth of those six pups, I had embarked on a new phase of my mushing experiences. They became the core of what I now refer to as my "retirement team." Seems an appropriate handle. I am, in fact, retired from teaching, commercial fishing, and operating a couple of small businesses. Of equal importance is the fact that this truly great bunch has been trained to accommodate the real and imagined frailties of one not as young as he used to be. I suppose it wasn't coincidental that the male I selected for intense leader training looks and possesses mannerisms similar to my first canine love, Genghis Kahn.

Recall that this "Seppala Siberian" had been the property of my lofty-minded friend, Tom Johnson. Tom bought him from Earl Norris's Anchorage kennel during the summer of 1963. Born in February of 1962, Genghis was a mere six months of age when he took up residence in Seward. The Seppala title comes from the alleged ability to trace his bloodlines back to dogs owned, bred, and raced by the great Leonhard Seppala during Nome's sled dog heyday. No commonplace, prosaic name would do for Tom's personal Yukon King. No Yukon or Kenai or Kobuk. Nothing short of a world conqueror would fill the bill. To Tom, "Genghis Kahn" sounded just right. Considering some of the Mongol hordes he was expected to lead during the start-up phase of my mushing career, Genghis wasn't all that inappropriately named, it turned out. I came into possession of this gray-and-white masked dog with an independent air, when Tom left his Seward High School English teaching job for a similar one at Palmer, the summer of 1966. Genghis was three and one-half years of age at the time.

Cashing in on the dog's natural instinct to aggressively move down a trail and pull at the same time, Tom had done a good job of developing Genghis into what is referred to as a "trail leader," a term used to denote the basic generic, garden-variety leader. A good trail leader needs to know many important things. Everything, in fact, but taking turn commands. Included is the all important job of keeping the mainline tight, thus preventing the team from becoming bunched up and inevitably tangled. Another is to start on command, that command generally being "hike," "OK," "let's go," or the like. Real mushers do not use the exclamation "mush!" to start a team. The only exception to this rule, it seems, is now historic. Joe Redington, Sr. did. No one in my acquaintance disputed Joe's claim to being a real musher, so we made the allowance. Once a leader had its team moving, it had to learn to adjust its speed according to the dictates of its driver. This skill can be taught by consistent use of a certain whistle to "hike up" a team and judicious use of the brake accompanied by an "easy" command to slow the outfit. Of course, an intelligent, well-trained leader also knows the absolute meaning of stop, usually at the command "whoa!" That command is most important on those not-too-infrequent occasions when sled and driver end up off the trail or unexplainably on the trail-less side of a tree. "Whoa!" not only tells a leader to stop instantly, but to remain in one spot until directed otherwise. Ideally, the same stop and stay put order applies to the entire team, provided there is but sparse representation from the Mongol hoard in its makeup.

Genghis quickly became my "main man." Due to his innate intelligence and desire to please, his development into a crackerjack "gee-haw" leader was rapid, if not always smooth. With the Fishbacks as my instructors via their booklet, *Novice Sled Dog Training*, and a whole lot of trial and even more error, Genghis, inside a couple seasons, became, if not a world conqueror, a very confident, trustworthy command leader. He overcame all my blunders, both great and small. He taught me patience and humility. By licking the hand that had struck him, so to speak, this beautiful creature of God demonstrated the meaning of true forgiveness. By refusing to give up when the going was at its worst, he extracted from me more true grit than I knew was mine. We traveled together for years and over thousands of miles of trail, including the trail of the first Iditarod Race. He gained a spot in my heart reserved for only the most cherished objects or beings. And when it fell to me to end our long and faithful partnership, due to a paralytic stroke at fifteen and one-half years of age, I did something unknown to me since childhood. I sat atop his then empty house and wept. Silly, I suppose. Still, after passage of some thirty-five years, scores of leaders and hundreds of team dogs, it is Genghis who appears to me when my fondest memories come to call.

Training Genghis and other early leaders was not all "peaches and cream." From run to run, I rode an emotional roller coaster. Initially, most runs were not good. It seemed everything that could go wrong did. Leaders often turned toward home on their own. At times, the whole team refused to start, as if on an organized strike. Leaders went blind and deaf at the same time, seemingly unable to hear that screaming, half-crazed person twenty feet to the rear, or able to see the trail off to the right. "GEE, you knucklehead! GEE!"

Soon, out of necessity, I started to put two and two together. The eye-opener for me came through close, day-to-day observation of natural sled dog behavior and the realization that such behavior could be directed to efficiently and pleasurably get a dog team over the trail. Once I learned to work with all the team members, rather than against them, the downside runs became less frequent, replaced gradually by pure pleasure dog team experiences.

Gold claim cabin on Quartz Creek near Cooper Landing served as a mushing camp for years. Photo c1967.

Tom's first winter at Palmer in "the Valley" was dog-less. This state of privation would soon end, however, with his 1967 move to a suitable dog-keeping location near Wasilla, off the Knik-Goose Bay Road (Joe Redington, Sr. Memorial Trial), at the corner of Hollywood and Vine Streets. Johnson's team-less status over the 1965-66 season did in no way prevent us from planning a dog team expedition over our school break for the Christmas holiday. We decided to partner up and drive my team of nine pretty raw rookies. Genghis, who already had been doing remarkably well traversing trailless and trackless stretches of local turf, would be in lead. Our first real dog team expedition was to Upper Russian Lake, accessible by trail from the Sterling Highway, near Cooper Landing.

Since we were many years away from telephone service at the homestead, many planning letters passed between our respective post offices. Lists mostly: Dogs, dog food, dog gear, people food, people gear. Unfortunately, these worked and reworked lists would prove noteworthy more for necessary items omitted than for the many superfluous ones included.

Tom traveled to Seward to spend Christmas with our family, starting a tradition that would continue for many years. Two days after celebrating our third wonderful Alaska Christmas, Tom and I, with nine dogs and what seemed to be a ton of equipment, headed over to Cooper Landing. Not in the old, tired Jeep, but Tom's new Ford pickup.

It began to snow as we wheeled into the unplowed parking lot at the head of the Russian Lakes Trail, coming to a stop in axle-deep snow. Our growing suspicions were confirmed. Not only was the cramped parking lot not maintained, the trail itself was obviously unused by even so much as a rabbit. We hurried the process of hooking up and sled packing as much as possible. Just past the winter solstice, the shortest day of the northern year, we were eager to squeeze as many miles out of the brief winter daylight as we could, daylight made shorter by the snow-producing cloud cover. Even so, it was well past noon when our dual musher team of Seavey/Johnson pulled the hook and hiked the team up, heading for Upper Russian Lake, some dozen miles into the mountains. Genghis was in lead.

We didn't get far. Not only hadn't a rabbit used the trail recently, nobody had. Our hope had been that perhaps skiers had traversed the route. There was zero hope for a snowmachine track, as that was about the number of "iron dogs" in the country at that early date. Dogs were forced to wallow in the snow without bottom for footing. Tom and I waded along behind, sweat beginning to flow profusely. After a pathetic half mile, it became apparent, even to my eternally optimistic buddy, this wasn't going to work. Time to regroup.

As I recall, we flipped a coin to decide who would hike back to the truck and fetch the pair of snowshoes inadvertently left behind. I lost. However, huffing and puffing my way down to the truck and back worked out satisfactorily as by agreement I took a break while Tom took the first "shift" at the snowshoes. Well, it seemed like a good deal at first. Each shift was to be one hour in length. About one-half hour after the snowshoer left, the musher was to start the team along the freshly made track, catching up about at the end of the snowshoer's shift. You have heard of "best laid plans"—right?

Tom took off. The dogs immediately did likewise, dragging me along clutching to the handlebar, snowplow fashion. This very undignified method continued until enough of the rascals tired of the sport and stopped after two or three blocks, conveniently near a sapling, which I managed to snag with my snow hook. This was a precarious arrangement at best, since none but Genghis had even a dim concept of the meaning of "whoa!" much less "stay!"

That they were quite eager to follow the now long-vanished Tom was evidenced by one neckline after another being severed by exuberant chewers, screaming in chorus to be on the road. All the while slamming into their harnesses. Through it all, thirty minutes by the watch, Genghis, though whining in eager anticipation, much to my delight, never once violated the "stay" command. I trudged forward and replaced necklines as I waited. I was startled to discover the section of plastic rope towline just forward of the first set of team dogs was chewed nearly in half. Not good. Like, really not good. Should a towline be parted, all the force ahead of the break is transferred through the necklines of the dogs to the rear of the break. The necks of those dogs then become the connection to team members to the rear of them and to the loaded sled. Potential for severe injury was obvious. I made necessary field repairs to the towline, thankful to have warded off almost certain disaster.

Nowadays, with use of plastic-coated steel cable for towline, a great worry has been all but eliminated. Even while I strained to repair that critical piece of mushing paraphernalia, my thoughts were diverted to the problem of making a towline break safer for the set of dogs where such a rent occurs. Our next trip out, I had loosened all the collars so as to allow them to slip off the dog before the forward force became too severe. Also, each animal was equipped with a very light duty brass snap on its collar, reasoning that it would pull apart or otherwise break before injurious stretching of the neck could happen. The latter trick in particular has paid off many times while running a tight trail through timber and an individualist decides to go on his private side of a tree. In every incident, the collar snap has flown apart with no appreciable harm done to dog or tree. It should be added that light duty (one-quarter inch) plastic accordion braid-style rope for necklines became standard. Again, the expectation was that it would give way before a dog's neck did. So, the short, flimsy neckline, which is affixed to the main towline, is attached to an easily slipped collar by means of a breakaway snap. Triple protection.

After going to the rescue of one of my scarce harnesses, which was in the process of being shredded by an impatient youngster, I regained my entangled snow hook from its tenuous grip on the poor little sapling. Off we went in hot pursuit of our intrepid trailblazer. The hot part of our pursuit was short lived. Immediately, it became apparent that a single snowshoe track was not a great improvement over none at all. A dog running in the snowshoe track had relatively easy going, while his partner did not. Therein lay my new problem. Dogs hitched side by side began to wage a pitched battle (shoving contest) for the preferred footing offered by Tom's narrow track. Our progress was slow, laborious, and not at all pleasant for the driver or the driven. What seemed much longer than the anticipated half-hour run, we came upon Tom, catching his breath beside the trail. We discussed our options for trail improvement. Not long before, Ed Estes, the old Moose Pass dog team mailman, had related to us how, of necessity, he would leave his team, snowshoe a distance ahead and return, drive the team forward, and repeat the process until he reached either better going or his destination. In doing this, he created a double snowshoe trail wide enough for even his monstrous-size dogs to pull side by side. Another solution, we reasoned, would be to rearrange the dogs in single tandem fashion so as to avoid canine competition for our present single-snowshoe track. Tom championed this latter remedy, highlighting his pro argument with a verbally painted picture of a painting he once saw, he thought in a Chicago fine arts museum. From what I gathered, it was a rendition in oil by some famous artist of a French-Canadian trapper on the march through a formidable stretch of wooded Canada. He was on long "trailer" style snowshoes, while in his slender track, followed five rather ruffian-looking dogs, hitched in single tandem, pulling with gusto a flat-bottomed, very narrow toboggan, stacked high with the bounty of the silent places, bundles of animal pelts.

Tom suggested that since I was a history teacher, certainly I was privy to the common knowledge that French-Canadian fur hunters had hundreds of years' experience traveling with dogs over some of the most barren wastes on earth. Why reinvent the wheel? All we needed to do was to adopt the "Canadian hitch." Who was I to doubt the wisdom of those august foreigners? Besides, we were running out of daylight with no indication that the snowfall would end anytime soon. Certainly, the prospect of covering the same ground twice on snowshoes, Ed Estes style, held little appeal.

Tom set to work rearranging the team in single tandem. I, donning the snowshoes, took my turn at trail breaking. Except for a few long, steep climbs, the going wasn't extremely difficult. As I recall, each shoe sank perhaps one foot into the upper, softer layers of snow. Still, I moved along quite well, stopping occasionally for a short breather. Finally, after my one-hour shift had come to an end, I stopped beneath a stunted hemlock. My hopes for a recuperative interlude were dashed, however, by the arrival of Tom with the team almost on my heels. Through a bit of experimentation he had found, with the dogs all following the single snowshoe track, things went better if he just rode the sled runners and let the dogs do the work. When attempting to assist the team by pedaling or pushing, he often sank into the snow up to his knees, requiring extra effort on the part of the dogs to haul him out.

By the end of my second go at the handlebar, the cloud cover was breaking up, allowing a new half moon to take an occasional peek at us. Tom had halted his march a few minutes early and was waiting for me on the porch of a Forest Service public use cabin on the far edge of Lower Russian Lake. It was all but dark by then, about 3:30 p.m. Did we want to cash in on the comforts of a cabin or push on after our fashion for another nine miles and a "siwash camp"? Encouraged by an evaporating cloud blanket, moonlight, though not full, and a promise of better travel occasioned by dropping temperature, we made the decision to strike out for the upper lake.

Following another hour of snowshoe duty, I found the eagerness level of the team, like the clouds, pretty much dissipated. There were two exceptions, however: Genghis, my leader, and a fairly large, beautifully marked grey-and-white female swing dog, Chena. Where the other seven lay, quite content with no obvious display of anguish over the imposed half-hour delay, Genghis and Chena remained standing, whimpering, traces tightened. Chena was a mere eighteen months of age at the time. I had purchased her as a weanling from Chistochina musher, Dick Gilliand.

Both Chena's parents were aggressive, forward-oriented team dogs whose greatest joy in life seemed to be that of going down the trail. Sure enough, Genghis and Chena remained strong and itched to go until we came to our final stop in a heavy stand of spruce on the near border of Upper Russian Lake. Home sweet home for the night. It had taken nearly eight hours to cover twelve miles. Not a staggering distance, nor an epic journey, but a satisfying beginners' trek just the same.

Except for having to be performed on snowshoes and under the light of a half moon, camp chores were not arduous. We chopped down a small, six inches in diameter, green spruce tree, and limbed and cut it into about three-foot lengths. We piled these side by side to form a platform on which to build a fire. Had we skipped that step, we soon would have been standing on our heads (down on our knees) to reach a reluctant fire that had melted its way to firm footing. Next, we built the fire itself from abundant and convenient dead tree limbs. We cut green tree boughs and placed them springy side up, on which we rolled out our foam pads, followed by down-filled sleeping bags. Had it snowed, a light, breathable canvas dust cover would have been spread over the bags. Tea water was made by setting snow to melt in our "tea can," a two-pound coffee can with a hay-wire bail. A can of beans and other frozen groceries were placed in strategic proximity to the fire so as to assure the least-possible amount of burned fare.

Next,came the dog chores. Tom began to stomp out a path between two trees, to which a relatively light tethering chain was to be strung, as close to the ground as possible. About every six feet along that main chain, a short, eight-inch piece of chain was affixed, to which the dogs were attached by use of their collar snaps. Early in my career, I learned to unharness dogs for an overnight stay, thus preventing dogs from turning valuable and necessary equipment into shreds during the night. Feeding was a simple matter. We would have, in all likelihood, thrown each a frozen fish or frozen chunks of prepared (cooked) food or, in a pinch, dry kibble mixed with snow. I have no record of what was fed to them that night.

For that matter, the tether chain routine didn't get pulled off, either. Not that time. While Tom labored to provide space for the tethering chain, I rummaged through our sled, attempting to locate it. Then came the inevitable sinking feeling. Not there! We had failed to pack that most vital piece of equipment. It was apparently a matter of one guy assuming the other had tossed it in the sled load.

How to handle this situation? One solution could have been to cut a stout stick for each of the nine dogs, about three feet in length and an inch plus in diameter, one end of which is attached to an anchor point with a strong cord while to the dog end is affixed, to, well, a dog, by the same means. We rejected this method, not really thrilled at the prospect of spending all night doing it. In the end, we scrounged spare necklines, tug lines, and, hesitantly, our one spare harness—all were pressed into service as ties for the various dogs, which were secured hither and yon to trees, bushes, and even to the sled. We were soon to discover that the sled was not the best place to tie dogs. Had it been extremely cold, and for sure, had it been cold without an insulating snow cover, we would have cut spruce boughs for dog bedding. This practice later proved to be a good one during the first Iditarod race and even more so for the second race, in 1974, when we experienced many overnight temperatures of well below minus fifty degrees F. Keep in mind, those were from the time periods I call B.C. and B.S. Before coats and before straw along the race trail. But back then, we selected an animal with an eye for hair quality: dense undercoat, abundant guard hair, and no bare bellies. These are the true Arctic travelers, capable of withstanding the most brutal conditions by simply lying down with bushy tail curled about the face and head. Let it snow. Let it blow. A snow-buried dog is a warm dog.

"Genghis and Chena. Genghis and Chena." This thought floated through my mind with decreasing regularity as my bag warmed and I slowly drifted into a deep, exhaustion-induced sleep. "Genghis and Chena, I need to cross them. Should get some good puppies…"

"Hey, Seavey! Get up! We have a problem!" Tom was already up with a freshly kindled fire crackling away.

Poking my head out of my bag, two things became instantly obvious. It was cold out there, and we had a beautiful clear day going for us. Sitting upright in order to get my boots on, the problem Tom referred to began to sink in. A glance in the direction of our sled told it all. Scattered to the four winds was just about the entire contents of our sled pack. People food, dog food (what little there was left, that is), spare gear, clothes, everything in a sickening state of disarray.

Closer inspection, however, placed our strewn gear into the minor aggravation category, for the babiche (rawhide) ties holding two sled uprights (stanchions) on its right side had been chewed nearly to disappearance. Likewise, both villainous perpetrators of those dastardly deeds had freed themselves using identical tools employed to render our sled useless. Interrupting their explorations of the immediate section of the trail they helped make the night before, they came bounding toward us. Without a speck of shame, guilt, or the tiniest bit of remorse, they wiggled their "good mornings" and nuzzled their sincere joy in seeing us up and around. Dogs! Those particular ones were named Genghis and Chena. If only we had remembered to bring our tethering chain.

Over morning tea, we discussed our predicament. No food, people or dog. No problem, it's only a few hours back to the truck. On the plus side, though, dogs ran loose during the night, but no fights ensued, which are not uncommon events under that circumstance. The real stickler was finding material to refasten those two sled stanchions. The oak sled would be useless until we found a solution. Sipping tea and lamenting our lack of means to repair the damage, I reached rather absentmindedly for the tea can boiling away on a dying fire. As quickly as I picked it up, even more quickly did I drop it. The bale was flesh-burning hot. As I un-sizzled my hand with cooling snow, the lights came on. The tea can bale wire would work. Several feet of light wire had been used in fashioning the can's handle.

Tom set to work disassembling the tea can and reassembling our sled. Since he had no proper tools, expedience ruled the operation. He used an ax to cut lengths of wire and short, strong sticks to twist wire ties tight and secure. While Tom was busy at that job, I broke camp, packed, and lashed the load. Next, I harnessed and hooked up the nine. Genghis, again, was in the lead. All were supercharged to be on the trail toward home. Sporting one musher per runner and the promise of a firm, mostly downhill trail, we began the return run mid-morning.

From Dog Diary: December 28 (1965)

Tom and I back from two-day trip to Upper Russian Lake. Broke trail up to lake. Dogs single file about eight hours. Camped. Little over two hours back on yesterday's trail. Genghis and Chena best. Cross those two. Genghis a very aggressive, straightforward dog in lead. Forgot stake out chain.

Lessons Learned:

1. Even the best dog team needs a trail with a firm base. Allow time for a newly packed trail to set up before use, when possible. On our outward leg to the Russian Lakes, very little set up time was allowed and, consequently, the dogs floundered some eight hours to reach our destination, where it took only a couple of hours returning on trail firmed up overnight in below-zero temperatures.
2. Develop two mushing gear lists. One "standard" list. Another "spare" list. My standard list came to include those items that, by experience, I learned I should never leave home without. Examples: Tethering chain (as Tom and I found out), ax, gun, snowshoes, sled repair kit, spare footwear, survival kit (includes fast means to start fire), rough lock chains, bolt cutter, tea can. The "spare" list was comprised of items that may be thought of as expendables—towline sections, necklines, harnesses, snaps, and collars.
3. It is of utmost importance to constantly monitor each dog's performance, for a couple of reasons: First, to determine if a given animal is going to make a satisfactory sled dog in every sense of the word. Second, to detect, as early as possible, any physical problems a given dog may develop. An aside to this is the fact that some dogs work more comfortably in certain positions within the team, a situation that necessitates a good deal of positional experimentation. When all is said and done, by the end of the mushing day, my most aggressive, in tune, rarin'-to-go team members ended up in lead and swing positions or in wheel, an extra demanding position as well.

13

Swede Larson Rides Again

Bill and Judy Larson pose proudly with their all time favorite sled dog, Genghis. 1965 (Photo: Bill Larson)

On a rare sunny July day in 2009, I phoned our old Alaskan friends, Bill and Judy Larson. They were then retired and residing on a beautiful, piney property west of Bemidji, Minnesota, home of the fabled Paul Bunyan and his famous blue ox, Babe. After leaving Seward, this wonderfully openhearted couple settled into a North Woods life in the "Land of Ten Thousand Lakes." Bill is long retired from a teaching career in Bemidji Public Schools. The couple still run at full-throttle involvement in outdoor activities as well as those of church and community. Many years have flitted by since Bill

("Swede") Larson and I wrestled to extricate poor old Sinook from that trap up Resurrection Valley. "A lot of water under the bridge," as the saying goes. Over that long succession of years, we have kept in touch. The Larson home became ours for occasions, bringing us to northern Minnesota. I headquartered there while attending summer school at Bemidji State University for a couple of summers. The Larson place once became our sled dog training hub. In January of 1999, the Seavey horde invaded in force. Grandsons Danny, Tyrell, Dallas, and I staked out twenty-two boisterous sled dogs in Larson's front yard. We represented what proved to be son Mitch's victory vanguard for the mid-distance Grand Portage Race premier.

The Seavey family had the good fortune of providing some reciprocal hospitality when, during the summer of 1988, Bill and Judy retraced their former route to Alaska. Many a reminiscence of our earlier Alaska days were placed on parade over their leisurely sojourn with us. Bill and I even managed to effect a new misadventure to be added to an already impressive list of the same. As with the Sinook ordeal, this more modern one played out up Resurrection River Valley. Bill and I decided to "shoot-the-rapids," as in the old days, down Resurrection River, some eight miles to salt water. The result might be described as a minor disaster. Not a quarter mile from our launch site, we rolled, losing a borrowed canoe, paddles, and, not the least, our pride as great whitewater men. We hauled out at different spots, separated by a mile of angry, silty river, and another story was born.

That was the reason for my 2009 call to Larsons. A story, I explained to their wonderment, that I was in the throes of an attempted book. Would they be kind enough to collaborate on a story for the same?

"No! Not the one about our moose hunt to Fuller Lake."

"The Sinook story?"

"No!"

"You mean the goat hunt where we were stuck on the mountain for three days?"

"No!"

"How about our latest canoe mishap?"

"No. I most decidedly do not want that to go public. Here is the deal. I want to convey my experience with dogs as a lead up to the first

Iditarod. I have somewhat introduced Genghis and was reminded of your storied experience with the rascal back about the time we were removing Sinook from the trap."

There followed a long, drawn-out pause. An extended period of silence, really. "Okay, okay! Tell you what I will do. Just in case my book never materializes, so all your work is for something, I will throw in a copy of Mitch's much-acclaimed book, *Lead, Follow or Get Out of the Way.*

That was the clincher. What follows is an unedited account of a 1966 occurrence involving three of the best friends this musher ever had—Bill, Judy, and Genghis.

Dog Days in Seward, Alaska
By Bill "Swede" Larson

"Ah, the romance of dog sledding the snowy river canyons of the Kenai Peninsula." That was the foremost thought in our minds as I harnessed the seven sled dogs to a WWII fiberglass "banana boat" sled in preparation for taking my wife, Judy, on her first dog sled ride.

The owners of the sled dogs were our good friends, Dan and Shirley Seavey of Seward, Alaska. They were among the first people we met when we moved from Minnesota to Seward in 1964. Dan and I both taught in the Seward Public School System.

Together Dan and I had run the sled dogs up the Resurrection River canyon toward Exit Glacier many times. I was running my winter trapline and Dan was teaching the dogs proper behavior and respect for commands. I seemed to have a good rapport with all of the dogs, except for Genghis, the lead dog. For some reason, he didn't seem to like me very much. In time, the feeling became mutual. As he ran, he would occasionally glance back over his shoulder at me with a "who are you?" look.

Now the day had arrived for me to take the dogs on a run up the canyon—without Dan. Dan had borrowed my green Dodge van to take his high school wrestlers to the state tournament in Fairbanks, 500 miles away. He had requested that I run the dogs while he was gone. I eagerly accepted.

By this time I had been running the dogs with Dan for two years, so I was brimming with confidence on this, my first solo run. With the sled securely chained to a big spruce, we harnessed the dogs and Judy got into the sled. The dogs were ready and raring to go, straining in their harnesses to move out. Somehow, in spite of all that nervous energy, I was able to unsnap the taut chain and hang on. The impact was shoulder-shocking as the dogs surged forward, pulling me behind the sled on my slick-bottomed mukluks and then dragging me as I fell. I shouted at Genghis, "Stop!" He turned around and just looked at me with those wolflike eyes and charged on! I pulled myself hand over hand on the chain until I heaved myself onto the sled behind my very nervous wife.

Soon we came to the place where we should turn off the road to the right to follow our designated route to the trapline, which would take us up the canyon. This was it! I mustered up all the authority I could and bellowed "Gee!" Now, any sled dog knows that gee means to turn right. But lead dog Genghis had other ideas. He turned his head as he ran and looked at me with a defiant gleam in his eyes. He knew very well what gee meant, but he also knew I wasn't Dan. He continued to race down the road, leading the whole pack of dogs and pulling the Larsons with them.

At the junction where the gravel road we were on met the highway was a bar known as The Pit. When Dan ran the dogs, they always stopped at this spot to turn around to race back home again. When Dan was giving the commands, they always stopped. But given my experience of a few minutes earlier, I wasn't sure if they would heed *my* command to stop. I couldn't let the dogs continue to run onto the highway with the possibility of them becoming casualties.

So the decision was made to position myself on the front of the sled, hurdle my body forward, and grab the two wheel dogs around their necks, wrestling them to the ground with the idea that the other five dogs wouldn't be able to pull us all. The jump was perfect and both wheel dogs went down with me. But the remaining dogs didn't slow down—they were pulling this whole mass and the end of the road was coming into view! "It's all over now!" I thought. I yelled to Judy to jump off and I'd do the same. However, I found myself entangled in the dog's harnesses! My foot was wrapped in the sled cords and my arm was wrapped in the harnesses. This heap of tangled flesh and fur dashed into The Pit parking lot—and stopped short. Thank goodness for the dogs' training and routine!

At that moment, an elegant, fur-clad lady stepped out of a big black Cadillac. Coming over and looking down at us, she said, "Dog sledding, how nice." It's a good thing she couldn't read my mind right then. I simply smiled in acknowledgement from my horizontal position on the parking lot ground.

Then things took a turn for the better. The dogs turned around easily and they set their noses back toward the Seavey home. By this time, a small crowd had gathered to watch and wish us well. With Judy and me aboard the sled and the dogs once again harnessed and pointed in the right direction, we flew out of that Pit stop. (I must admit I was feeling a little guilty for having briefly entertained the thought of allowing Genghis to run onto the highway and possibly into the path of a big truck!)

We rattled over a small bridge and rounded a bend in the road. And there, to our dismay, stood a little black cocker spaniel. Where did he come from? When he saw us coming, he began barking and running. I know from experience that a moose would distract the dogs from their designated path, but what would happen with a little barking dog? It didn't take us long to find out. Genghis, leading the whole team, took off, hot on the trail of that cocker spaniel, which ran right through his "doggie door" in the Gillespies' screened-in porch. I didn't even have time to think before all seven dogs and the front of the sled crashed into the screened porch, leaving a gaping hole.

The ruckus brought the Gillespies pouring out of their house. When they saw what had happened, after a brief period of shocked silence, they began laughing. And then they good-naturedly helped us untangle the dogs and re-harness them up. We waved good-bye and were on our way once again, racing toward home.

Finally, we were on the homeward stretch, about a half mile to go. We rounded the last corner and ..."Oh no!" A lady was walking her Dalmatian dog on the road. The Dalmatian hit the ditch with the seven sled dogs piled on top of him. The lady screamed (and maybe we did, too).

I entered the fray, hollering and grabbing dogs by their harnesses, trying to get them off that Dalmatian. None of the dogs were listening to me. Somehow, in that snarling, biting bunch of furry bodies, I spotted the white and black fur of the Dalmatian dog on the road. Pulling him out of that mess was a challenge, but I managed to fling him onto the road. The stunned lady grabbed her poor dog in her arms and walked away as fast as she could. I hoped the dog was okay, but I was too preoccupied with trying to calm and untangle the sled dogs to find out. Finally, we got them back in order.

Exhausted, Judy and I flopped onto the sled and I angrily yelled at the dogs, "Do whatever you want!" And they did. As they shot forward, the momentum tipped me backward, with my head landing on Judy's lap. From this comfortable position, I gazed at the peaceful sky above. This proved to be the most relaxing part of the whole excursion. Perhaps we discovered a new element in dog sledding.

Suddenly, the dogs stopped. We were in the Seaveys' yard! Unbelievably, we had made it home intact. The next twenty minutes were some of the happiest moments of the day—taking the dogs out of their harnesses and chaining them near their dog huts.

Ah, the romance of dog sledding in Seward, Alaska

14

In Quest of Hope

Shirley drives an abbreviated team, the remainder running free in the direction of Hope, 1966. Note parted towline.

Genghis played a star role in yet another episode at my introductory "Mushing School of Hard Knocks."

From Files: (*The Seward Phoenix Log*, December 16, 1966)

"Musher Tackles Snow-Go Trail"

Local musher, Dan Seavey, will prove that the snowmobile has nothing over the dog team, Alaska's earliest form of transportation, if plans for his Christmas vacation trip over the Forest Service trail from Cooper Landing to Hope and back work out as expected.

Departing Seward on this seventy-four mile round trip on December 28, Seavey, high school teacher and wrestling coach, has scheduled overnight stops at Caribou Creek and Juneau Lake cabins…

Mushing with Dan will be his wife, Shirley. She's planning to enjoy the nice long ride and Dan is looking forward to an assistant musher when the going gets tough.

"You get lots of physical activity with dogs." said Dan. "Snowmobiles are fine for people over 90, but we can't become soft just because of the snowmachine."

This local interest piece was given third-page prominence, just above the School Hot Lunch Menu: "Mon. Dec. 19—Mexican goulash, peas and carrots, rolls and butter, fruit, milk." But hey! It helps to know someone. In that case, Joanne Hoogland, the paper's editor, who also happened to be an English teacher of long standing at Seward High. Further, Shirley and I had just recently become godparents to one of her children, daughter Carol.

My Dog Diary reveals that Shirley and I were on the Forest Service trail, running north out of Cooper Landing along Bean Creek by midday, December 29, with nine dogs, Genghis in lead. We had on board our sled a super abundance of all things, both people and dog, plus a trifling hundred pounds in the form of Shirley. Our sled was heavy. With six to eight inches of recent snow, it was a heavy pull. Fortunate for all concerned, beneath this new layer of snow was a firm base made by snowmachines. I remember thinking that perhaps those new contraptions weren't all that bad, that they made pretty darn good dog trails.

It is a thirty-nine-mile traverse from the Bean Creek southern terminus to the north trailhead in the vicinity of Hope. There are many crooks, switchbacks, and hills en route and the lofty two-thousand-six-hundred-foot Resurrection Pass. Beautiful wooded miles they are. The only treeless landscape found, as to be expected, is in that appropriately named Devil's Pass. Generally, that trail, which I eventually came to know so well, meanders northward up the Juneau Creek drainage to its headwaters in Resurrection Pass, continuing down Resurrection Creek to Hope.

From Files: (*The Seward Phoenix Log*, Jan. 12, 1967)

"Mushers to Try For Hope Again"

Even though he didn't make it through on the Forest Service Trail from Cooper Landing to Hope on his first try by dog team during Christmas vacation, Dan Seavey reports he is still game to try again. Leaving on schedule on Dec. 29, he and his wife Shirley got as far as the Swan Lake cabin where they were unable to locate the trail across the twenty-seven-hundred foot pass north of Swan Lake. Heavy snow and lack of marking along the trail (as there are no trees or bushes there) made it impossible to get across the Pass.

They stayed the night at Swan Lake and returned to Seward the next day.

This weekend Seavey plans to snowshoe out a trail along Juneau Creek. As soon as he gets the trail in, he, his wife, and dogs will be off again.

That follow-up article in our local paper recorded for all time our failed first assault on Resurrection Pass, but it is devoid of the more interesting "facts of the case."

Shirley, packed and ready to hit the trail "in quest of Hope."
December, 1966.

December 29, the date of our departure, was a warm, twenty degrees F, gray day. Mid-morning found Shirley and me settled in, our nine-dog team making slow but steady progress on the climb along Bean Creek, a tributary of Juneau Creek. Six to eight inches of snow covered a solidly packed base. Occasionally, we halted to tie the snowshoes down more securely or untangle one of our odd assortment of canine draft animals. Each pause invariably prompted a mighty clamor from impatient dogs to be getting on up the trail. The racket was accompanied by nine dogs, all lunging forward to their own drumbeat, as if in the grip of some demon. I would pull the hook and off we would shoot as if we were a sprint team at the end of the countdown: "five, four, three, two, one—and they're off!" A short burst of speed ensued, then a return to a more dogged pace.

We had just made one of those equipment adjustment halts when our good fortune turned instantly bad. I did whatever necessary to get us back on the road; Shirley retook her risky position atop our load. I retrieved the hook from around a small spruce and shouted out a rather unnecessary "hike!" In an instant, the whole outfit catapulted from zero to twenty, and with the elapse of another moment, back to zero. We had plowed into a substantial stump beside the trail on the inside of a right-hand twist. I ended thrust fast against the handlebar; Shirley, almost in front of the immobilized sled. Both, to our relief, uninjured.

The implication here is that we all stopped very suddenly. Not so. Some of us did. Namely, Shirley, myself, and the two sets of dogs closest to the sled. The front five dogs however, with my super trained, lovable, faithful, personal Yukon King, Genghis, in lead, were gone and out of sight before we had regained our shaken composure. Exclamations, both mild and obscene, had no effect in halting the runaways.

Now, to see one's dog team vanish down a trail is closely akin to the sensation created upon viewing one's automobile rounding a corner on the end of a tow truck cable. Sinking and a whole lot more. What-ifs, mostly. "What if those crazy dogs run all the way to Hope? What if they get themselves in a trap? What if they get tangled and into a big, bloody brawl?" Then a more practical question: "Can the remaining four dogs move us up the trail on a sustained march of unknown length, to wherever our unencumbered vagabonds may lead them?"

Upon inspection, the cause of our sudden change in fortune became vividly apparent. The towline, which is added to or subtracted from by use of individual two-dog sections, had parted. This released two sections with attached dogs and the leader, who was secured to the front section by means of a single, three-foot-long line. But what was the cause of the mishap? Immediately, I suspected the most common—a dog had chewed them free. Before the advent of modern cable towlines, this indeed was a good hunch. But absence of chewed, frayed ends laid that suspicion to rest. "How about the line just plain breaking due to impact caused by the sled's abrupt stop? No, there were the nicely heat molded ends. Nothing telltale here." Slowly, by the old process of elimination, the real cause emerged. I had met the villain. It was me. For whatever the reason, I had failed to securely tie, in a nonslip fashion, one end of that particular towline section. How could I have been so negligent, so careless in handling such an important detail? If I could have figured a way to kick myself, I certainly would have. Good thing the thought to ask Shirley to do so didn't come to mind just then.

Things turned out much better than we could have reasonably expected. Our four remaining dogs, by both of us riding the runners and giving assistance as needed, handled the pulling job.

Every curve rounded, every hill crested, brought new anguish. We had covered about two miles of physical trail and ten miles of mental torment when, at last, we came upon the objects of our great anxiety. There they sat. All fine, cool, and calm. Not tangled. No fighting. No blood. All glancing over their shoulders with a look of puzzled dismay as to the inordinate amount of time it had taken us to cover a mere couple of miles.

Stopping the abbreviated team somewhat short of the runaways, I hoped the latter would not take to the trail ahead of us once again. I began to walk the short distance separating us. Big mistake. Here they came, now a big snarl of wagging tails, towline, harnesses, and slobbery tongues. Nor did they slow their progress toward their waiting comrades even as I went flying, both feet taken out from under me by a tightened, fast-traveling towline on its way to the team reunion. There I sat, crestfallen, and watched in dismay as the newly united team went through an intricate process of becoming an even larger, more complete snarl. Thankfully, no fights ensued.

Shirley's willing and able assistance notwithstanding, it had to have been well over a half hour before that mob was reorganized into something the likes of which resembled a dog team. Rest assured those towline sections were well knotted when, once again, we took to the trail. Another lesson indelibly imprinted.

As our pathway ascended to higher elevations, snow depth increased noticeably. Seemingly unaffected, Genghis and his swing dog assistants set a good, rhythmic pace, thanks to the continued firm trail base beneath. Another hour's travel brought us to the south edge of Juneau Lake. Our goal for the first day's run was Caribou Creek Forest Service cabin. Accordingly, we halted only briefly to inspect the snugly built Romig log cabin, serenely positioned on the margin of that beautiful, mountain-hemmed lake.

We pressed on northward along the lake's east shore, passing midway a second Forest Service accommodation, the Juneau Lake cabin. Due to drifted snow, the trail grew heavier as we approached the lake's north border, ending in no trail at all. No obvious path lay before us, leaving nothing to do but mount my trusty snowshoes. By then, the team had the edge worn off, becoming tolerably manageable for Shirley to drive, aided by an effective claw brake, which compensated for the little weight exerted upon it by its operator. For me, the next three and one-half miles along Juneau Creek, which ran through open, nearly treeless country, were an attempt to prevent being overtaken and rundown by the tame wolf pack, which ran nearly always on my snowshoe tails. For Shirley, the challenge was twofold: Don't run me down and keep the sled upright and in one piece. At times, we were on the creek itself or its sloughs, or bending around the numerous deadfalls and hummocks. We expended a full two hours of precious daylight covering that challenging stretch.

Jagged Kenai Mountains to the west had thrown their cloud-softened, end-of-the-day shadows across the full width of Swan Lake by the time Genghis drew our team to a halt beside its east shore cabin. We were, after all, only one week into winter with a niggardly six hours of usable daylight, less on a cloudy, low overcast day, such as we had been given. After discussing the situation, we made the decision to forge on. Convinced we would not make it over Resurrection Pass and on down to Caribou Creek cabin that day, we steeled ourselves for a cold camp should we not even achieve the midway cabin located in treeless Devil's Pass, at 2,200 feet elevation. The Devil's Pass trail came in from the Seward Highway to the east and connected with the Resurrection Pass Trail. At that point, the Forest Service positioned the Devil's Pass cabin some four miles above, (north) of the cabin at Swan Lake.

We started up in the same manner used to traverse the distance between Juneau and Swan Lakes—Shirley on the sled, myself ahead on snowshoes. No snowmachines had traveled this segment recently, perhaps ever. Consequently, there was no "bottom" or solid snow base on which to travel. Slowly, laboriously, we ascended the first half mile above the lake. Not once did the team refuse yet another go at it. Genghis, in particular, seemed to suffer an attack of separation anxiety whenever I put too much distance between the halted team and myself. The trail over that half mile was well defined by a wide slash through stunted willows and alders. Where the brush eventually quit, so did we, for beyond not a trace of trail presented itself. There was not a bush, cairn, ribbon, or tripod, indeed, nothing but a dimming scene of white. This being my maiden trek into that neck of the woods, I had not a clue as to the trail's course ahead. Over the following five or six years, I would travel this route scores of times and would come to know it intimately. For the there, and then, however, it made no sense for us to flounder about on an uncertain course in failing light.

With feelings more of relief than regret, Shirley and I managed an about-face of our outfit, though not without difficulty. After straightening the inevitable tangles, we beat a rapid downhill retreat to the beckoning Swan Lake cabin.

Dog chores that night were a simple affair. Unlike the earlier Johnson-Seavey Russian Lakes Expedition, members of this outing had remembered the tethering chain. In short order, it was strung, and the dogs unharnessed, secured, and fed. The latter being a matter of pitching a three- to four-pound halibut head to each eager eater. Amid much ripping and chomping, each ration disappeared, and in a short time, all were bedded down, snuggled in for the night. As at Russian Lake, there would be no all-night romp with the girls for Genghis. Darkness had come to dominate the scene by the time we made for the cabin, a darkness accentuated by an occasional snowflake.

Come morning and daylight, about 9:30 a.m., we greeted another gray day. The odd snowflake of the previous evening had evolved into a light snowfall with negligible accumulation overnight. I guessed the temperature to be in the upper teens. All promised a swift, relatively easy run down to Cooper Landing over yesterday's hard-won trail. And so it proved.

Resurrection Pass Trail, which seemed so daunting on our Christmas vacation excursion, would by the 1970-71 mushing season become almost routine. Almost. For sure, snowshoes had to be strapped on in more than one instance. But the most unforgettable trip of that season had me pinned down for nearly three full days in the Devil's Pass cabin by an extraordinarily heavy snowfall driven by a hurricane force wind. By a wind so fierce it literally threatened to rip that A-frame cabin from its very foundation. The term "cold camp" was redefined that time. Being above timberline, the Devil's Pass cabin was, and still is, equipped with an oil-burning stove. Now, don't be thinking I lacked the foresight to pack fuel oil up there. I had abundant fuel for my intended one-night stay. That said, it proved useless to me. Forced off the vanishing trail by that rapidly worsening gale, I secured my team on the lee side of the cabin, entered, and proceeded to light the stove. No luck. That same kind of luck prevailed all but the last few hours of my three-day imprisonment, during which time, my dogs went on half rations. With extreme, constant wind velocity and off-the-chart gusts, there was simply too much chimney down draft produced for my puny match flame to overcome. Cold camp indeed. Luxury was to be had in my goose-down-filled sleeping bag and a thick, insulated pad. How thankful I was that I had brought both and that the heavy steel cable, anchoring the cabin to Earth, held.

I had still another misadventure, if there is such a word, along the Resurrection Pass Trail.

From Dog Diary: (no date, but during 1968-69 season.)

Ran Res. Trail yesterday. Too little snow. Broke right runner on Old Oak (sled name) ahead of back two stanchions. Used moose horn (antler) I had found on trail as runner. Pretty good lash job. Made it from Swan Lake to Cooper Landing trailhead.

Lesson Learned:

It is true. First impressions, like first lessons, are the most indelible, best learned of all. Be they those of early childhood or the basics of some new skill, like mushing. Shirley's and my Christmas vacation mush, resulting in Genghis and half our team vanishing before our disbelieving eyes, taught me a lifelong lesson where a dog team is concerned: Pay close, close attention to gear detail. Or, put another way, small negligence (and/or ignorance) can lead to big problems. In that particular instance, I was well acquainted with a safe, nonslip weave for towline loops. Upon inspection, all other loops had been done correctly. Be it due to a distraction, mental drift, or some other reason, I had messed up big time. Grave injury, even death for dogs, driver, or both could have been a far different result than our fortunate outcome. This is serious equipment and must be regarded as such at all times After all, God may just get tired of His close watch over fools. Ever since that first attempt on Resurrection Pass, I have vowed never to let a gear oversight put me at fault again.

Expanding the gear failure theme a bit, it is sad but noteworthy that dog mushing is a fertile activity for such incidents, resulting in mishaps ranging from minor irritations to major tragedies. Whole books could be written on the subject. A sampling based on actual accounts follows:

1. A well-known Wasilla, Alaska, sled builder and musher failed to clear his snub line (the one to which a snow hook is attached) of granny knots. His team lurched forward, pulled the hook, and in the confusion, he grabbed the snub line and tripped, still holding it. A rogue square knot tightened around his thumb, which continued its journey down the trail minus its owner.
2. My friend and fellow musher, Bob Hill, was nearly knocked senseless when he applied the claw brake on his stanchion sled. The claw grabbed a large rock, which was solidly frozen to the ground, causing the hinged end of the brake board to break off, digging into the trail. After the sled traveled over the entire assembly, the claw end, still attached to the sled by bungee cords, sprang up, administering a severe blow to the back side of Bob's head, felling him to his knees.
3. Once, hauling back on a rickety handlebar in an attempt to get a team turned onto a trail leading away from home, I caused more injury to my pride than to my rear, on which I came to rest. The ancient handlebar broke completely off just above its rear supports. The dogs ran home the seven miles. I walked.
4. Teen-aged sons, Mitch and Darian, driving separate teams, both were dragged into open, armpit-deep water near the Moose Pass railroad trestle. Notwithstanding, good fortune smiled on those two youths. In both cases, leaders and swing dogs were able to gain purchase on the far shore of the slow-moving stream and hauled the soggy works to safety. At minus twenty-seven degrees F, they arrived at the Moose Pass Inn, a half-mile distant, in a nearly frozen state. There, a kind and generous proprietress, Erma, "Ma Wesley," thawed them out, dried their clothes, and fed them royally. One shudders at thoughts of all that could have happened. What if the current had carried teams and drivers downstream and under thick, solid ice? What if it had taken place on a remote trail, away from almost immediate warmth and aid? Etcetera, etcetera!

   Better still, what if the whole drama had never played out? Both sleds were sporting very poor claw-type brakes, no stopping on ice with those. Worst of all, the Chuck Lechner style snow hooks in vogue at that time were good on packed snow, but had zero purchase on ice. The boys' near catastrophe, resulted not so much from failed equipment as from the inadequacy of that being used. A modern snow-ice hook is capable of halting a large team in its tracks on the most icy of surfaces.

5. Another mushing buddy, Gene Jorgenson, living at Mile 42 of the Seward Highway, in the Summit Lake area, at the time, trucked his team to the Mystery Creek trailhead, Mile 65, on the Sterling Highway. Gene had all eleven or so team members hitched, all carrying on like crazed maniacs over the joyous prospect of being on the trail. Tied off to the truck's rear bumper with clearly a too small, too weak snub line, his team bolted, parting the line, leaving Gene amazed, frantic, and walking. And more walking. He bunny booted over eleven miles, a five-hour hurried march. Arriving at the trail's junction with the Gas Line, he turned east to follow the usual dog route. After another half-hour hike, he met Iditarod musher, Tim Osmar, with a large team on a west-bound training run. Osmar, who had been traveling west for a full three hours, had not encountered Gene's runaways. Gene hitched a ride on Tim's sled for nearly an hour, at last locating an extremely balled up, but un-bloodied, dog squad tangled in the brushy bottom of the East Fork to the Moose River. All this work and anxiety for want of a proper snub line.
6. An equipment malfunctions can be invisible, silent, and deadly—this time again involving mushing partner Bob Hill. On a brilliant, sunny, early May morning, Hill and I hooked our teams up for an overnight mush over our favorite Mystery Creek trail. Our plan was to travel east toward Hope following the Gas Line, some forty miles, camp, and return the next day, a pleasant excursion with dogs before the snow season came to an end. I "pulled the hook" first; Bob planned to leave fifteen minutes or, thereabouts, after. On previous runs, Hill, having a faster team, would soon overtake me, but on that day, he did not. Becoming increasingly concerned with his "no show," I finally stopped, set the hook, and waited—and waited some more. Finally, after maybe three quarters of an hour, he came into

sight. Dogs scarcely crawling, Bob alternating between walking and pedaling. When Bob gave the "whoa" command, his whole outfit dropped to its belly as if one animal. Every one of his nine or ten well-conditioned dogs was all totally exhausted by the time it had covered the first mile of trail and got worse as it progressed to where I waited, approximately three miles' total travel.

"Sickness in the kennel?"

"No!"

"Food. Had the team's diet been drastically changed recently?"

"No!"

"What experience had this whole team had lately that could conceivably have caused its breakdown?"

Bingo! In a flash, it dawned on me. Their ride over there from Seward in the box of Bob's truck. Carbon monoxide poisoning. And so it proved to be. A malfunctioning dog truck exhaust system had put that team far too close to death row.

Stories of this nature are sadly common within the mushing community. Just about everyone who had driven dogs to any appreciable degree has a litany of such happenings. Many have ended in ways much more dire than those sighted above. If it is true that experience is, after all, the best teacher, I, from my infant beginnings with sled dogs, have stayed awake in her class. As a result, I am confident in stating that I learned a fair amount about equipment as it relates to safe and efficient handling of sled dogs. Many times, I was taught through experiences of fellow mushers. But the lessons best learned are those that have come to me in a private, personal way over a nearly fifty-year-long trail of experiences. Shirley's and my 1966 aborted dog team assault on Resurrection Pass and its memorable equipment malfunction episode being but one of many such entries in my Dog Diary. Yet another lesson well learned the hard way.

15

Genghis in Ivy Halls

Genghis, my trusted leader, a key figure
in Seward High School's Seavey-Bell Wager, 1968.

Name of your instructor's lead dog.
(a.) *Spot* **(b.)** *Yukon* **(c.)** *Genghis* **(d.)** *none of these*

By correctly answering the above question on one of my World History final exams, a certain Seward High sophomore managed to stay in the passing column by one skimpy point. Lucky kid. He thus avoided having to listen to me rave on for another year about Genghis Kahn—not the great thirteenth-century world conqueror, but his namesake, my budding Seppala Siberian leader.

Genghis, in fact, did go to Seward High, though his attendance was rather poor. It all depended on the creation of snow bridges, naturally drifted, firm snow, over open river channels. This allowed me to run small teams from home south across Resurrection River into town and on to the high school. Dogs were then tethered behind the school during the school day and run home at its conclusion. I broke several dogs to lead over several school years following that routine. It was Genghis, however, who outshined them all and without exception became my favorite. My students, I suspect, heard far more than they ever wanted about that animal. I applaud their indulgence. Faculty members were seemingly less well disposed to my—well—bragging.

Weir Bell was one of many "characters" on our high school staff who helped make my twenty-year tenure there such a joy, fun really. A Purple Heart recipient, veteran of the Pacific Campaign of World War II, Weir, it seemed, had an argument, bet, or confrontation brewing with someone nearly all the time. For the amiable, pleasant-natured guy, it all was a big game, played with a devilish, kiddish smile on his fifty-year-plus countenance.

The Johnson-Bell Debate of 1965 serves to illustrate. Somehow, my mushing comrade, Tom Johnson, and Weir got crossways on the winning pitcher of a certain World Series, and we denizens of the teachers' lounge were drawn into the squabble, if only as long-suffering bystanders. For days, the battle raged. First, a several day verbal barrage perpetrated on each by each. Reinforcements from staff were mustered, Johnsonites and Bellites, according to a questionable understanding of each partisan. Foreign mercenaries appeared in the form of old newspaper clippings and yellowed almanacs. Then at a crucial moment, when it appeared a capitulation by Johnsonite forces was imminent, Tom strategically produced and deployed his most secret and destructive weapon, a rather ancient *Encyclopedia Americana.* To the assembled war conference, Tom triumphantly presented "irrefutable evidence" in favor of his champion, bringing at last to a close but one more faculty room controversy. Well, almost. Amid clamorous Johnsonite cheers and equally boisterous Bellite jeers, Weir quit the field, disputing the validity of *Americana* to the end. "After all, people write encyclopedias, don't they? We all know people make mistakes, right? We are not, after all, infallible, right?" Truth was, though battle scarred, and,often as not, humiliated in the face of his antagonists, Weir, in his own mind, never lost a battle.

It was this merry combatant who, hearing, no doubt, more than he ever wanted about this budding miracle leader of mine, thought it was time to prove the pudding. "Five bucks say you cannot run a five-dog team with your marvelous Genghis in lead down the length of the high school—inside."

He was on. Eager for some new excitement, various faculty members made hefty side bets. The Seavey-Bell Wager of 1968 was to be settled the following evening, after school had been dismissed. It was fortunate for me that I left home early, driving a seven-dog team on wager day morning. I encountered no problems crossing the first two channel snow bridges on Resurrection River. The third and closest to town, however, had gone out overnight. Since it had spanned a deep flow of water between three to four feet high vertical snow banks, there was nothing to do but turn and run for home. Into the old Jeep went seven dogs, pretty much unrestrained. On top of the Jeep, I tied my sled, to which was secured rigging, harnesses, tethering chain, and midday dog snacks. From the Jeep, there arose, to state it in a delicate manner, an oppressive doggie stench. It permeated my clothing, both interior and exterior, and was punctuated by an assortment of dog slobbers and kisses administered en route to town. I arrived at school quite odiferous, and, I fear, I remained so for most of the day. My poor fellow academes.

Bet time arrived. While I was hooking up the seven out back, Weir arranged for a doormen at either of the school's ground floor doors, which opened to the east. Before entering the building, I detoured toward home, letting the dogs go wide open down First Street, along the west edge of the saltwater lagoon. After about a half mile, we reversed directions. All this to take the edge off the dogs, giving me better control once inside, where, of course, using a sharp claw brake on beautiful marble floors would probably have negated any positive feelings school administrators might have had for me. I used the heels of my boots as my only braking device.

We approached the north doorway straight on. Up two steps from street level, I stopped a dozen feet from the now open door, set the hook, and proceeded to unhook traces of the two rear sets, leaving just Genghis and the two swings in full pulling mode. Back to the sled, I pulled the hook and gave the "hike" command. We proceeded up two more exterior steps to the ground floor level of the building and into the commons area of the school. Frankly, except for a bit of uncertainty over strange footing, those dogs acted as if they belonged there—or that they had been there in the past. Indeed, all the males proceeded to mark their territories in the customary manner. A sharp "haw" command would line us out for the run south, down the length of a smooth-sailing lower floor hallway. Straight ahead, however, (west) was the landing to the upper floor. In a flash of inspiration, I decided to take the high road. Without incident, we negotiated the two flights of steps and a midway landing necessary to reach the second floor. We then trotted smartly down the length of the upper floor—a duplicate in looks and length of the lower.

Coming to the south end of the upper floor, I gave the "haw" command, which turned us down two flights of stairs to the lower floor. This was followed by a "gee" turn, which lined us up for the homestretch run down the lower hallway. I gave Genghis his final "gee" signal, and we expertly exited the building through the same door that saw our entry. Genghis and I clicked wonderfully throughout.

The whole affair went off smoothly, disregarding the fair amount of paint we scraped from the mid-landing wall on our bouncy way down. Most amazing, though, a big surprise for me, was the almost immediate adaptability of those dogs to such strange surroundings. None ever had anything to do with the inside of a building before, except maybe as very small pups being cuddled by kids inside our house.

A few weeks prior to the Seavey-Bell Wager, I had run that same team lengthwise over a snowbound, abandoned car alongside a road. We approached from the front, and Genghis and the swing dogs had to claw their way up onto the car's hood and then again up onto its snow-covered top, followed by a high leap off the back. Team dogs and wheelers followed, trusting their leaders. I followed the works on the sled, not at all certain of my own wisdom as I bounced my way over the derelict. It was an unorthodox performance requested of a dog team, but out of doors and on somewhat familiar footing. I wasn't at all sure the team would run so well through the school, but they did.

After anchoring the outfit to our front yard flag pole, I went up to the teachers' lounge to collect my five bucks. It took some doing. Weir reasoned that I had not lived up to the terms of our bet. I was supposed to have traversed the bottom floor; only, nothing was mentioned about doing the upper floor as well. Besides, the wager called for the use of five dogs, not seven. In the end, following much lively and prolonged banter, I was paid my due. Weir's parting shot being to the effect that I really had lost by default but the whole affair was worth a five-dollar bill in entertainment. It is noteworthy that our principal was away that day, attending an administrators' meeting in Kenai.

From Dog Diary: (no date recorded, likely during March 1968)

> Won a five-dollar bet with science teacher, Weir Bell, that I could drive a five-dog team down the hall of our high school building. Genghis in lead.

Had there been more and better trails available to me, I might not have conceived the idea of driving dogs to school at all. However, sometime during my second mushing season, 1965-66, it began to dawn on me that not only were there not many trails in the Seward area, the ones present were poor at their best. Winter went like this: rain – freeze, snow – freeze, freeze – thaw, thaw – freeze. A one-liner describing Seward winter weather can well be: Water on ice. Generally, when snow did fall, it came deep, wet, and heavy. On one memorable occasion, it began to snow at about 1:30 p.m., heavy and wet golf-ball-sized flakes. It was 5:30 p.m. by the time I could get away from school, collect Shirley from her insurance office job, and round up our kids. In that four-hour period, over three feet of snow had accumulated on our self-maintained road. Our poor old Jeep. It pushed snow well above its headlights. Even so, the only way to make progress between Doc Gentle's and home was by repeatedly ramming forward, backing up for a new start, gaining maybe fifty feet per attempt. It took over a half mile of this operation in order to get home that evening.

No snowmachines were on the scene in those early years to break trail after a snow event of that nature. Snowshoe, dog team, and a fair amount of sweat on the part of the musher were all necessary. To that list should be added axe and saw. Normal snowfall in the Seward area would bend across a trail, sometimes block after block—alder, willow, and poplar saplings effectively rendering movement along it virtually impossible. All had to go. The means? Musher, axe, saw, snowshoes, perspiration, and precious winter daylight. Given the poor condition of existing short trails and a complete lack of a single trail that, even with a good imagination, might have been termed long, I resorted to what now seems an extremely rash expediency. We, Tom Johnson and I, routinely ran dog teams on city streets, public secondary roads, Seward Highway, and the Alaska Railroad.

As noted above, I took advantage of windblown snow bridges over Resurrection River to run a small team to school in the morning, and back home at night. In the dead of winter, this meant running in darkness in both directions. Crossing the river, my course traversed the city dump, through Forest Acres Subdivision, among the "Hickel Homes" of the Clearview Subdivision, over Dairy Hill, past Second Lake and First Lake into the backyard of the high school, located on Second Street, at the very foot of Mount Marathon. My team was tethered among the spruce during the day, where they patiently waited for me to appear for the evening run home.

State-maintained Nash Road, during my formative years, served as a dog trail as frequently as did Seward's city streets. In those years, Nash Road ended near the northeast corner of Resurrection Bay, close to the present Afognak Logging Company. There was no Seward Marine Industrial Park or Spring Creek Correctional facility beyond as there is today. Round trip, the trail, was about ten miles with very little vehicle traffic, as there were probably no more than a half dozen residences along the way.

Another trail was Bear Lake Road. Coming out onto the Seward Highway on our homestead trail, it was a gee (right turn) south one mile toward Nash Road or a haw (left turn) north three miles to Bear Lake Road. Both enter the highway from the east. Bear Lake Road did and still does terminate on the southern shore of a most beautiful Bear

Lake. Again, this was sparsely populated at the time. There were two homes only near the highway and on the lake's edge, the Kenai Lumber Company mill, owned and operated by the Tressler brothers, Erv and Ray. Round trip from home was ten miles unless the lake to the north shore was included, which made it a fourteen-mile trip.

Tom and I frequently ran the Seward Highway (on the shoulder) from home to Moose Pass and return. Mostly, though, it was from home to mile fourteen and back on nice, moonlit nights. Most often, it was late night—early morning—when only a rare vehicle would be on "our trail." Those who were, however, made no secret of their opinion that we were idiots of the first class for being on the road at night with a dog team without a light of any kind. "Hey! Was that your team I nearly hit last night coming down Mile Twelve Hill?" We heard that sort of remark quite often from townspeople. We gained twenty-four miles round trip by that admittedly foolhardy means.

Once again, the Alaska Railroad saw dog team traffic. From the beginning, in 1903, the railroad provided a dog team route both on idle tracks and unfinished grades. In 1908, Walter Goodwin's Alaska Road Commission survey party drove its teams to the end of the line at mile fifty-four. From there, the party continued north, laying out a trail whose destination was Nome and would become known as the Iditarod Trail. Tom and I, of course, had neither permission nor train schedule. Although the matter of permission—or more precisely, the lack of permission—to be on the tracks never gave us much concern, ignorance of the train schedule did. While a fear of meeting or being overtaken by a train was always in the back of our minds, it certainly migrated to the forefront during our travel through tunnels located on the southern slope of Mile Twelve Hill. Crossing trestles (bridges) was a most difficult undertaking. Railroad bridgemen, it seemed, didn't have a dog's natural gait in mind when determining their tie and trestle timber spacing. Also, open air between trestle ties was disconcerting to a dog, its team position notwithstanding. However, after a few crossings, the dogs got things figured out, just as they had learned to run the road shoulders.

Son Mitch was more forthright with Alaska Railroad folks when, in 1995, he and musher friend, David Lindquist, ran teams from downtown Seward to Anchorage. They became the first mushers in probably eighty years to cover that stretch by dog team. Mitch went on from Anchorage to Nome as an Iditarod Race participant, thus completing his "Home to Nome" trek. For the rail part, he sought and received one-time permission to run teams on the railroad-right-of-way from Seward to Anchorage. Unlike his trespasser dad, he was provided with a train schedule. As a footnote, I enjoyed handling for those fellows during their three-day drive up the tracks. We were all treated royally by both the Trail Lake Lodge in Moose Pass and Alyeska Prince Hotel "roadhouses" during our overnight stops en route.

A final local trail is noteworthy. Over my first three mushing seasons, I extended Bill Larson's Resurrection Valley trapline trail from home upriver to the foot of Exit Glacier, some eight miles. I had used the trail for many years before there was a Kenai Fjords National Park or a road to it. It certainly beat running on the public streets and roads. Present-day Exit Glacier Road (Herman Leirer Road) follows generally that pioneer trail.

Lessons Learned:

1. The sled dog is highly adaptable. Once taught to run on the shoulder of a road or up on a plowed berm or to pussy-foot across a railroad trestle, little further reinforcement is necessary. Soon, I came to feel quite safe driving a dog in seemingly unsafe environments.
2. Be seen as much as possible. Carry a flashlight while running at night. Use it to signal approaching vehicles. By the 1969-70 season, I had ceased running on the highway, roads, and railroad. However, fast-moving snowmachines had begun to make their presence felt in greater numbers, so being seen at night became ever more important safety-wise. It would be some years after the first two Iditarods that I finally began to use a headlight routinely and reflective tape on harnesses, sled, and parka. Both are standard safety equipment nowadays.

16

Gold Trail to San Francisco of the North

An estimated 65 tons of gold was freighted by dog team over the Iditarod Trail to Seward. Figure that at today's gold prices. (Photo: Resurrection Bay Historical Society.)

Confession time. I came about the first Iditarod Race not through eyes of a fierce sports competitor or even those of a sled dog racer, but rather, those of a bookish student of Alaska history. Going a step further, it is an unvarnished truth that this was the case, not only for the first, but all five of my Iditarods. My second Iditarod, in 1974, was the only possible exception. Prior to that first great event, I had undergone a ten-year apprenticeship in the art of dog mushing, not sled dog racing. A natural spin-off of traveling by dog team over remaining segments of Alaska's historic trails was a desire to know something about them. Why a particular trail was placed geographically, topographically as it was? What use did it see in the past? Why was it important to people and the communities it connected? Who had passed over it? What human dramas were played out along its course? What were the circumstances leading to its disuse and decay?

Vicariously, I traveled many thousands of miles with the likes of Hudson Stuck and James Wickersham by way of their superb dog team travelogues. It must be admitted, however, that often, the how-to part of these wondrous travels, were ignored as being too prosaic. Things most travelers of that day would have been bored to read, somewhat akin to the modern sportswriter instructing Tiger Woods on golf stroke technique.

A fifty-year infatuation with Alaska's history probably would have started without being assigned to teach the subject to high school seniors. But that's what happened my second year at Seward High. Mr. Larry Bourger, who had been principal my first year, moved into the superintendent's slot for the 1964-65 school year. It was he, a stout, balding, intense Hungarian refugee of the Cold War, who handed out the new contracts along with new teaching assignments. In my case was included a semester of Alaska history to seniors. Mr. Bourger was a refugee in every sense of the word. He had escaped under, through, or around the then very real Iron Curtain, leaving behind loved ones for which he carried an unrelenting burden of worry.

Early in my acquaintance with the nearly forgotten Iditarod Trail, I became intrigued with Seward's all-important role in its development. Knowledge of Seward's prominence and a growing appreciation for it came in a piecemeal fashion. By talking with the real "old-timers," rummaging among old newspapers and gleaning snatches from an odd magazine article, I became even more enthralled. I was a frequent visitor of local museums along the old route. With an eye out for things Iditarod, I became active in our newly organized (1965) Resurrection Bay Historical Society and the founding of its museum. To have served on its board of directors for the past forty-two years has given me much pleasure. Our historic society sponsored my race efforts in the first Iditarod, and subsequent ones as well, a gesture for which I have taken unabashed pride.

It became an intriguing source of wonderment as I came to realize the significance of my new home to the growth and development of the great Territory of Alaska. And why not? Seward early became both a key center of disembarkation to the vast interior and of embarkations to the world "outside" Alaska. Docks were in. Railroad tracks extended toward the gold fields. By winter of 1912, the Seward-Iditarod Trail was complete from Knik to Iditarod and beyond to Nome, with much-needed improvements being undertaken south toward Seward. Winter transportation belonged to Seward over the trails leading to the western Kenai Peninsula, Tyonek, and north to the Iditarod and Nome districts. Heavy two-way traffic ensued. Come summer, focus shifted to water transport up the Knik and Turnagain Arms of Cook Inlet, Susitna drainage, and nearly the entire Yukon drainage, including the Innoko and Iditarod Rivers. Ocean-going ships set their course directly to Nome, taking advantage of a short shipping season. Even here, Seward played a central role, becoming a depot for mail, goods, and persons to be redistributed northward and out westward along the Alaska Peninsula and Aleutian Chain.

After a few months of Mr. Bourger's forced Alaska studies, I found myself devoting disproportionate amounts of time to studying the North Country gold rushes and requisite dog team travel. In particular, I wanted to learn how Seward fit into the overall picture. First to occur was the 1896 Cook Inlet Stampede, then the granddaddy of stampedes, the 1898 Klondike with satellite rushes to Nome in1900, Fairbanks in 1902, and Iditarod in 1909. To me, as a new Alaskan, these locations were magical, fabled places, attainable in summer by boat and during winter over solidly frozen water via dog team. Great interior river trails were connected by the establishment of many all-important overland trails. A display of provincialism, no doubt, that I should become smitten mainly by one of these, the Iditarod Trail. That intrigue, that allurement, has evolved into a lifetime of volunteer service in an effort to reestablish the trail on the Kenai Peninsula and to promote what now is the Iditarod National Historic Trail. Its primary artery, of something less than one thousand miles, stretches from the year round Pacific Ocean port of Seward to the short season Norton Sound port at Nome. Numerous connecting and secondary trails associated with mineral locations account for a lion's share of the two-thousand-three-hundred-mile trail network.

I learned that the Seavey's newly adopted hometown of Seward was founded for one principle reason—exploitation of natural resources to the profit of the exploiters. That was how it was with all "rush towns" of the North Country, be it Juneau, Dawson, Nome, Fairbanks, or Iditarod. Of necessity, that was how it was, how it had to be, whether a great industrial region like Prudhoe Bay oil fields or a small, temporary native fish camp. There had to be a reason for people to show up and stay. In Seward's case, it was an ice-free harbor location, offering relative ease of ingress to the territory's great interior, with its vast, proven coal reserves. Seward began its life as the natural child of a stock company formed to construct a railroad from saltwater to, at first, the Matanuska coal fields, near present-day Sutton.

Mr. Lee Poleske has been the volunteer curator of Seward's Resurrection Bay Historical Society's museum for more than thirty years. I had the pleasure of serving with Lee as Seward High's two-teacher social studies department for twenty of those years. On August 28 of every year, reaching back a bunch of them, Lee and members of our society celebrate Seward's Founders Day. Doors of our museum are flung open to all, tea and crumpets are served, and our old pump organ once again is caused to accompany us in some fine, old, nostalgic tunes of our youth. Before the prospect of another year's rest, the old girl is coaxed into a final number, "Alaska's Flag", our hauntingly beautiful state song. Unlike our national anthem, Alaska's anthem is non-martial, with lyrics dedicated instead to the praise of creation and an uplifting of the spirit. Eats, drinks, and songs on August 28, the day of the month that our pilgrim railroad fathers came ashore at Resurrection Bay to begin their quest for riches. The year? Lee Poleske had that covered as well. Every year, a shiny 1903 silver dollar is awarded as a door prize in commemoration of that all important date to our little town and, as it turns out, extremely important as well to the Territory of Alaska, and later, the state.

From Files: (Press Release, Feb. 26, 2008, Iditarod Historic Trail Alliance.)

The Trail at 100

Iditarod Historic Trail Centennial starts with celebration at Mile 0 Seward. On the first weekend of February, one hundred hardy souls, including Alaska Governor, Sarah Palin, came together in the face of the icy ocean winds in Seward to launch the Iditarod Historic Trail Centennial.

The celebration included a historic reenactment of the departure of the 1908 scouting expedition to Nome by Seward's famous mushing family, the Seaveys. Dressed in period garb and leading two dog teams pulling historic freight sleds, the expedition reenactors gamely answered questions from a period newspaper reporter [Mike Brittain]. Dan Seavey, one of the founders of the Iditarod Sled Dog Race and a board member of the Iditarod Historic Trail Alliance, played the role of Colonel W.E. Goodwin, the historic expedition leader, while his grandson, Danny Seavey, played the role of the dog handler on the expedition.

It was fascinating to learn that Seward was not yet five years of age when, in January 1908, an Alaska Road Commission team, headed by Walter Goodwin, landed there to undertake a preliminary survey of a winter mail route to Nome.

In truth, Goodwin pioneered the route as directly as possible from Seward to Kaltag on the Yukon River. The remaining stretch over the Kaltag Portage, and along Norton Sound to Nome, was well established at that time. The Portage itself was a centuries-old native route between the Yukon Athabascan and Norton Sound Eskimo. In more recent times, it saw mail teams traveling between Whitehorse, Yukon Territory, and gold rush Nome. Following the great Yukon River ice trail, a major portion of the route traversed Canadian domain, a condition lending double importance to Goodwin's 1908 winter survey. One of these was an attempt to reduce mail travel distance by some four hundred miles. The other, and perhaps as paramount, was the desire to establish an "all-American" route and severance of United States dependency on Canadian good will where mail delivery was concerned. In addition to the Seward to Nome route, improvements on a rudimentary trail from Valdez to Fairbanks were under consideration by the Alaska Road Commission.

Goodwin and three assistants arrived at Seward via steamship from Seattle on January 25, 1908. Their assembled "outfit" accompanied them. This included three dogs, two basket sleds, eighteen sets of dog harnesses, provisions, and camp outfit. Five days were spent in Seward, purchasing and test driving dogs. Sleds were packed in readiness for a January 31 departure.

From Files: Copy of Goodwin's report on survey to Alaska Road Commission Headquarters, Skagway,

(April 6, 1908)
The route traversed, briefly described, was as follows: The Alaska Central Railway was followed to its end at Mile 54, thence via Turnagain Arm, Glacier Creek, Crow Creek Pass, Eagle River, across country to Old Knik, [later Eklutna], across Knik Arm to New Knik [the present one] across country to Susitna Station, up the Susitna three miles, up the Yentna, Skwentna, and Happy Rivers, Pass Creek to Rainy Pass, down the Dalzell, Rohn, and Kuskokwim Rivers to near the Ozona, across country to the mouth of the Tacotna at McGrath's up the Tacotna and across country to the Tacotna Slough, over rolling hills to Gane Creek, down Gane and across country to Ophir Creek (the Innoko district) across country to Dishkaket and thence across country to the Kaiyuk Slough to the Yukon, and then up the Yukon to Kaltag and by the Overland Mail Trail via Unalaklik. [Goodwin's spelling] to Nome.

This was quite a trek by any standard when one considers much of the travel from Susitna Station to Kaltag was over trackless topography, without benefit of even a trail, much less one marked and packed. Snowshoes were the order of the day.

From Files: (Goodwin report continued)
Resume tabulated data. Winter reconnaissance.
Seward to Nome. January 31st to April 5th, 1908.

Seward to Kaltag	**Seward to Nome**
Days consumed to Kaltag: **49**	Days consumed to Nome: **66**

Days lost on account of weather: **6**	Days lost account of weather: **12**
Days actual travel: **43**	Days actual travel: **54**
Miles traveled: **563.08**	Miles traveled: **875.08**
Average miles per day: **13.09**	Average miles per day: **16.20**

When all was said and done, Goodwin reported the entire route to be feasible as a mail route, with the exception of Crow Pass in the Turnagain region, due to its extreme steepness and elevation. He speculated that a possible alternate might be Indian Pass farther west, or elimination of the problem altogether by extension of the railline around Turnagain Arm into the Matanuska Valley. Even so, Goodwin, the professional engineer, concluded: "It would take infinitely more travel than is in sight at present to break a fast or feasible trail over the route, even were a trail cut out through the timber the entire distance, and unless the new Innoko District shows up well or some big strike is made along the route, it would be entirely impracticable to send Nome mail by the route…"

As if to order, the Innoko District did show up well. Very well, indeed. During waning months of that fateful year, 1908, as Mother Nature turned the Innoko country from green to gold to white, a pair of determined miners picked and shoveled a couple of dozen exploratory shafts at a location on Otter Creek, tributary to the Iditarod River. At the twelve-foot level of their twenty-sixth shaft, John Beaton and Bill Dikeman received the present of a lifetime. Gold! Gold in unmistakable abundance. It was Christmas Day. Predictably, this rich discovery precipitated yet another gold rush—destined to be Alaska's last.

The Seward Commercial Club was organized in 1909 for the purpose of promoting Seward in general and the Seward to Iditarod route in particular. Through its nurture, Seward was publicized as the "Port City," and the "Gateway to the Interior," destined to become the "San Francisco of the North." This early chamber of commerce hired, during the winter of 1909-1910, Jujiro Wada and local musher, Alfred Lowell, to traverse the route from Seward to Iditarod. Wada, of Japanese descent, was, by that time, renowned for his mushing prowess across much of the Northland. Hope was that the Seward route would, in fact as well as in word, prove to be advantageous over the one treading north from rival city, Valdez. Not surprising, Wada and Lowell submitted a most favorable report upon return. I recognized their desire to "keep the boss happy" as being closely akin to my own situation of agreeing to teach an Alaska history course when, at that particular time, I was totally unprepared.

One would expect such exuberance from a commercial club, but, fact was, the desire to "put Seward on the map" came from many quarters. That is, given a freight dock and lengthening railway, Sewardites pitched in to build an infrastructure of trail support, which assured its prominence in territorial matters and those of the nation. The more I learned of Seward's vital relationship to the Iditarod Trail and of its importance in matters of state in general, the more I became convinced that this great chapter of our history should not be lost to later generations. In the future, somehow, there needed to be signposts planted, pointing to that wondrous era when our thriving little ocean side settlement was indeed the gateway to Alaska's vast interior, the hub of important events. Seward was, indeed, a place that had the potential to become another San Francisco. How could I have known then that most of my adult life would be spent attempting to plant those signs along an abandoned trail leading from an all but forgotten community by an archaic means, a dog team?

Seward and the Iditarod Trail were to become inseparably linked in Alaska's history. The human infusion into the Innoko District started as a trickle over the summer and fall of 1909. Locals, mostly miners, from wound-down districts like Nome, Fairbanks, and Dawson. Floodgates were opened wider over the year 1910 with arrival of the prospector hordes from "outside." Like mushrooms following rain, the towns of Iditarod, Flat, and Dikeman appeared. Iditarod, for a brief time, sported more souls than any other community in the territory. The year 1910 also saw the Alaska Road Commission begin work on what was then deemed feasible, the Seward to Nome Mail Trail, with a branch off to Iditarod and Flat. Since all trails led to Iditarod at the time, the title, Seward to Nome Winter Mail Trail, never stood a chance for general acceptance. Common use had it to be simply the Iditarod Trail unless, it appears, you lived in Iditarod at the time, where the route south was commonly called the Seward Trail.

It was that route south, beginning with the winter of 1911, that witnessed the first of many "gold trains" traveling from Iditarod to Seward. These trains were actually huge dog teams of huge dogs pulling huge loads weight-wise, over one-half ton at times, of the yellow stuff. It has been estimated that sixty-five tons of gold were taken from the Iditarod area alone, most transported out behind sturdy commercial dog teams owned and usually driven by professional dog men. Back haul consisted of passengers, mail, and sundry freight items.

As events unfolded and the calendar advanced month by month toward March of 1973 and the First Great Race, the Seavey family of Seward had maintained the lone sled dog kennel on the Eastern Kenai Peninsula. What had begun as a Minnesota kid's fantasy became reality: An almost magic carpet move to Alaska. Homesteading. Dog teams. A community that tied it all together historically for one immersed in history. The stage had been set for the greatest adventure of my life.

17

Who's the Mother?

Dorothy Page, Mat-Su Valley historian. The question persists:
Does she deserve title "Mother of the Iditarod?"
(Photo: Jeff Schultz Photography)

If it were not for the past, our private and societal history, there would be little for us to celebrate in life. Birthdates, various anniversaries, even death dates provide us with milestones of order for our stay on earth. I became aware of one such celebration during the summer of 1967. Ted Sires, a member of our church congregation, had talked this landlubber into a summer fishing job aboard his newly acquired commercial troller, the *F/V Sword*.

The plan was for me to connect with Ted and the boat at Bellingham, Washington, once school had ended, mid-May 1967. We would fish the Alaska coast en route to Seward, which meant ten days on the fishing grounds, delivering to the nearest processor, then on to the next likely spot north. Our final delivery of the voyage would be at home in Seward. That is pretty much what happened, with the remaining summer spent trolling the waters of Middleton Island, guardian to the rich fisheries of Prince William Sound.

One of our ports of call on the homeward voyage was the former Russian-American capitol, Sitka. Poor Ted had a difficult time prying me away from the place. All that history! We visited Sheldon Jackson's huge collection of native artifacts, and the beautiful Russian Orthodox Church. Sitka gave reminders aplenty of Russia's glory days in America, all made possible by Mother Nature having decked out her sea otters in such luxurious, coveted coats. Most fascinating of all, however, were the efforts of two native men, transforming a fifty-some-foot cedar log into a genuine—the real thing—Thlingit war canoe. Why? It was, I found, one of Sitka's many projects, commemorating the Alaska Purchase Centennial. The transfer of Alyeska, the Great Land, from Russian to American ownership occurred at Sitka on October 18, 1867. The two talented carvers were working feverishly under pressure of a midsummer deadline. Soon, I was to discover that events were being staged across Alaska in observance of that momentous historic occasion. Not the least a sled dog race over a segment of my favorite trail.

Thlingit war canoe being carved at Sitka as an Alaska Purchase Centennial (1967) project. In Southcentral Alaska, a special sled dog race was being planned.

Modern revival of both long-distance sled dog racing and the Iditarod Trail began with an idea for celebration of the Alaska Purchase (1867) Centennial. While a war canoe would be fashioned for that purpose in Southeast Alaska, appropriately, plans for a special sled dog race were laid for the South Central region. Dorothy Page is generally credited with getting things started in that direction. At the time, in 1964, Dorothy was chairperson of the Wasilla-Knik Alaska Purchase Centennial Committee and, providentially, secretary for the Aurora Dog Mushers Club. It was this resident Wasilla historian who first conceived of and began to promote the idea of a showcase sled dog event, among like-minded local history buffs and dog mushers. What better way of reliving, though briefly, the glory days of Territorial Alaska than to stage a specially billed race over an existing segment of the old and mostly forgotten Iditarod gold rush trail?

Page realized a cooperative effort would be required to carry such a scheme forward. During the winter of 1966, she discovered eager allies in the persons of Joe and Vi Redington, who, at the time, lived beside the Iditarod Trail on their Flathorn Lake homestead. The Redingtons were already recognized sled dog folks and were prime movers of the Aurora Dog Mushers Club. In what was most certainly a marriage of convenience, the Centennial Committee and Dog Mushers Club joined forces to get the job done. Wasillan Ed Carney, president of Aurora Dog Mushers, appointed a committee whose job it was to accomplish all tasks necessary to conduct a successful celebration. Included in Ed's "Iditarod Trail Committee" were the likes of Dorothy Page, Vi Redington, Bob Fleming, Jack Hale, Al Hibbard, Lee Twing, Ed Carney, and Joe Redington, chairman. The trail had to be cleared and marked, and publicity and advertisement undertaken. Public relations had to be developed, in particular with the mushing community, volunteers, and with potential event sponsors. Fundraisers galore were held. As events would unfold, this original committee, responsible for pulling off that single sled dog race, would become progenitors of the present Iditarod Trail Committee, with four decades of successful one-thousand-plus-mile races to its credit. In the end, herculean efforts by a cadre of dedicated volunteers carried the day. A purse of $25,000 was raised to pay down twenty places. The course was to be fifty miles total from Knik to Big Lake and return. Date? February 11 and 12, 1967. Isaac Okleasik of Teller won the race with a time of three hours, fifty minutes, fifty three seconds; he earned seven thousand dollars for his efforts.

It is noteworthy that only nine miles of actual Iditarod Trail were used in that first Iditarod, those just outside Knik. Just a few miles, for sure, but they were oh so important. Not in number obviously, but important because they were the first to be singled out and given public recognition. Those nine miles were the few to be spotlighted, written about, talked about, and given historic importance, a dim beginning of what would amount to an Alaska Heritage Renaissance. A renaissance to such an extent that the words "Alaska" and "Iditarod" are inseparable today throughout the world. In 1978, the Congress of the United States decided that those piddling nine miles of old Iditarod Trail needed company and created the Iditarod National Historic Trail. It is not "a trail" at all. Rather, it is a trail system totaling 2,300 miles of primary, secondary, and connecting routes. I can think of no greater legacy for us to hand over to future generations of Alaskans.

Of this small, but all-important, first step toward today's Iditarod Trail Sled Dog Race, I was mostly oblivious. I had at that time neither dogs nor interest in racing. I read news articles the 1967 race generated, clipping some for my files. Frankly, references to the old Iditarod Trail held way more interest for me at that time than the race itself. Many of the fifty-four finishers of the '67 Centennial Race were well-known sprint circuit mushers, the only variety of sled dog racers at that time. Four veterans of the Centennial Race would join us in 1973 for the first run from Anchorage to Nome, namely, Isaac Okleasik, George Attla, Herbert Nayokpuk, and Dick Mackey.

The 1967 event appears to have had identity issues. In various places, reference is made to Iditarod Trail International Championship Race, Iditarod Trail Seppala Memorial Race, and Iditarod Trail Centennial Race. On its official program cover, the committee settled on the latter, Iditarod Trail Centennial Race, while on the actual program page, Seppala Memorial is used. The latter, no doubt, was occasioned by the death of that legendary musher, Leonhard Seppala, just prior to the Centennial run. His widow was guest of honor at the opening ceremonies, and start position number one was held open for Seppala as the honorary musher. This name confusion was carried forward into the early 1970s Iditarod races as well, until Iditarod Trail Race was officially settled upon.

The Centennial Race, its name notwithstanding, was scheduled to fall between the World Championship in Anchorage and the North American Championship in Fairbanks in order to allow most sprint team drivers to participate. Nor did the $25,000.00 purse dampen their enthusiasm in any way. A complete compilation of entrants represented a who's who in Alaska sled dog racing at that time, including my personal heroes, George Attla and Roland Lombard (see Appendix I Starting Order-1967 Centennial Race).

Always the promoter and sled dog advocate, Joe Redington donated one acre of his Flathorn Lake homestead to the Iditarod Trail Centennial Race Committee, of which Joe Redington was president. Carved into one foot square parcels, they were peddled to the general public for $2.00. Each was accompanied by a decorative souvenir deed of the Alaska Purchase Centennial. Proceeds went to the race effort. Regrettably, most remained unsold. In 1987, the modern Iditarod Trail Committee, Inc., Joe Redington, president, again sold land, 1/998,600th interest, this time, in an unspecified, undivided lot complete with warranty deed for ten dollars. I purchased one. To this day, I do not know the location of my estate. Since I have not, in all the intervening years, received a tax bill, I assume the tax collector is also ignorant of its whereabouts.

One would expect interest in further sled dog races by the Centennial Committee to have waned after the one-hundred-year mark of Alaska's purchase was dutifully and adequately celebrated. And so it did. In modern lore, Dorothy Page is recorded as "Mother of the Iditarod," meaning the modern Iditarod Trail Race. This relatively minor myth had been and is perpetuated not by Page or successive race officials, but mainly by folks ignoring "the facts of the case." There can be no argument that a sled dog race over some of the nearly forgotten Iditarod Trail was the idea of Dorothy Page. There can be no argument that this astute, tenacious local history addict (I can relate) awoke interest and action in Joe Redington and the Aurora Dog Mushers. There can be no argument that combined forces of Dorothy's Centennial Committee and Joe's Aurora Dog Mushers Club pulled off a successful centennial celebration event. That Dorothy Page planted a seed for a much grander race event must also be allowed.

Debate, however, is alive to this day over how deserving a person is of the title "Mother of the Iditarod" when she had very little, if anything, to do with staging the first Big One in 1973. Indeed, according to early organizers of that event, Tom Johnson, who was my partner in crime, and Gleo Huyck, Dorothy Page wanted absolutely nothing to do with it. Beginning with winter 1970-71, I personally attended many brainstorming meetings on a future race, which involved Aurora Dog Mushers and associates. Page was absent from them all.

Mr. Lee Poleske, fellow teacher and Seward Museum curator, and I attended an evening meeting at the Wasilla home of Von and Dorothy Page in the autumn of 1983. Also present were Joe Sr., Iditarod artist Bill Devine, and Susan Butcher, who had finished that year's race in ninth position. Already a tough competitor, Butcher was just three races away from initiating her amazing championship career.

The purpose of our meeting was to organize a statewide, blanket Iditarod Trail Blazer nonprofit to coordinate efforts of local trail groups we hoped would spring up along the Iditarod route. Only two such clubs had been organized and actively involved with trail matters at that time: Nome Kennel Club and Seward Iditarod Trail Blazers, the latter of which I was instrumental in founding and, for some thirty years, have served its membership as president. As meetings go, the one at Wasilla was a flop. No lasting blanket organization emerged. The most memorable occurrence of that gathering was an offhand comment made by Joe Redington to Dorothy Page. With that trademark devilish smile, Joe remarked, "You know, Dorothy, if you are the mother and I am the father of the Iditarod, as people seem to think, that makes the Iditarod a real bastard, doesn't it?"

Perhaps when that last T is crossed and the last I is dotted on a given chapter in history, it is what "people seem to think" that gives any event of the past a measure of importance and credibility. Did Dorothy forsake her motherhood role by not jumping in with both feet to organize the first full-length race in 1973? In my opinion, "no!" She performed an invaluable service by devoting her all to the 1967 event, planting the seed for something more grandiose. One should not forget that even the "Father of the Iditarod," Joe Redington, was first teased into his role by this remarkable woman. What is more, her love for Iditarod Trail history, even things pertinent strictly to the first of many Iditarod races, was unfaltering. For nearly twenty years, Dorothy was writer, editor, and publisher of that unique, history-filled *Iditarod Trail Annual*, treasured now by collectors of Iditarod memorabilia. Both Pages served the Iditarod Trail Committee, Dorothy as treasurer and husband, Von, as president. Dorothy Page had made an indelible mark on the Iditarod Trail Sled Dog Race, not to mention trail history in general. Upon reaching the end of her life's trail in November of 1989, lasting honor was paid to Mrs. Page by renaming the Wasilla Museum, The Dorothy G. Page Museum.

To the general public and casual peruser of things Iditarod, that period between the 1967 Centennial Race and our first public announcement of the 1973 event, most likely, seemed void. A time when nothing significant happened. Not so. Those closest to the action at that time—the Redingtons, Johnson, Huyck—assured us that the event was forefront in their thinking and a main topic of their discussions. Much of 1968 found Aurora Dog Mushers scraping up money to reduce debt incurred by the '67 event. For many, scant snow conditions of the '67-'68 season was looked upon as a blessing. No race that season. No need to go looking for prize money.

The slim purse and fizzled musher turnout for the 1969 attempt indicated to all but true believers that an ongoing Iditarod Race had been pigeonholed in the dead letter office. The race of 1969 was skimpy on purse, a total of $1,000.00, and skimpy on trail. The most recent of a string of "Huslia Hustlers" and World Champion sprint racer, George Attla, took first. Joe Redington, Jr. (Joee), second and 1967 champ, Isaac Okleasik of Teller, Alaska, third. But dreams died hard, remaining vivid and unaltered of a "big race" in the near future. A few members of the Aurora Dog Mushers Club dreamed on.

18

Straight Scoop

L-R: Joe Redington Sr., Gleo Huyck, Tom Johnson, chief conspirators in the plot to stage the First Great Race, 1973.
(Photo: Gleo Huyck)

My involvement with the Iditarod Race, as things progressed, first came about in 1969, via the back door, namely, commercial fishing. By spring following the feeble 1969 Iditarod Race attempt, Tom Johnson had talked me into partnering with him to lease Joe Redington's boat, the *F/V Nomad*, for a season of Cook Inlet gill netting. Tom, recall, had been a fellow Seward High School faculty member and entry level dog mushing partner. After leaving Seward, he joined the Palmer High School staff and, soon, the Aurora Dog Mushers, his connection to Redington.

Beginning in1969, Tom kept a dog team on the corner of Hollywood and Vine Streets, off the Knik Road, midway between Wasilla and Knik. Gleo Huyck, a transplanted plainsman from South Dakota, musician, and music teacher, had become Tom's friend, mushing buddy, and, consequently, a member of the Aurora Dog Mushers. Thus, for me the stage was set for a lifetime involvement with Iditarod. It evolved that my acquaintanceship with Joe and Vi Redington was occasioned by a commercial fishing deal, brokered by friend, Tom Johnson, which, in turn, led to my 1969 membership in the Aurora Dog Mushers Club, which has resulted in my forty-plus years of friendship with Gleo Huyck and other Iditarod Race pioneers.

Over the course of those many years, I was cognizant of the important roles played by both Johnson and Huyck in launching those first sled dog racing teams toward Nome. I have had much closer contact with Johnson over those years than I have with Huyck. Consequently, I was gratified and honored when Huyck consented to my recent request for a taped reminiscence session with him in an effort to capture permanently, facts and observations concerning the staging of the first Iditarod Race, only casually spoken of by us in the past.

From Files: (Compilation of main thoughts from: Reminiscence of the First Race, recorded interview, Gleo Huyck with Dan Seavey, November 15, 2009). Transcribed and edited by author.

Race founder, Gleo Huyck, is a native of South Dakota. Born in 1940 at Clark, a small farming community located east-centrally, some sixty miles west of the Minnesota border. With several years' teaching experience under his belt and a music degree from Ball State University in hand, Gleo, together with wife, Pam, and infant daughter, Heather, arrived in Alaska in 1970. As eager as he was to begin his music teaching duties with the Matanuska-Susitna School District, even more so was he anxious to fulfill his own Sergeant Preston-induced dreams. In rather rapid succession, Huyck had met the Seward transplanted Tom Johnson, purchased sled dogs, joined the Aurora Dog Mushers Club and struck up a felicitous acquaintanceship with Joe Redington, Sr.

Seavey: How about the first Iditarod, how did you come to be involved with it?

Huyck: Probably the year '71-72. In talking to Joe (Redington) about long-distance races and other mushers, they all seemed to be keen about long-distance races and copy it after the sweepstakes races...The summer of 1972, Joe asked me if I wanted to go to work up north in Unalakleet to buy fish from local people in Unalakleet and Shaktoolik. I went up there and spent the summer...Joe talked a lot about dogs and long-distance mushing...Joe really wanted to have a long-distance race to try to bring back dog mushing into the villages...At that time, most of the dogs were in decline in the villages and snowmachines had pretty much taken over winter travel.

Seavey: So what you are saying, Gleo, is that as late as the summer of 1972, there were no concrete plans for a race, we were still in the talk stage?

Huyck: That's right.

Seavey: And we were only months away from 1973?

Huyck: That's right.

Seavey: Let's get into where you guys actually start serious planning. You are up in Unalakleet to the end of summer, you come home. As far as the race is concerned, what happens next?

Huyck: To lead up to this a little bit, Tom (Johnson) and I would drive to Anchorage once a month to buy a truck load of dog food at Don's (Alaska Mill and Feed) to take back to feed our dogs. One of these trips, in October of 1972, we stopped off at a hotel to have a cup of coffee before heading home. In our talk over coffee that evening, we got really, really excited about having a long-distance race... Since, in the past, we had talked primarily to Joe about such a race, we decided to call him from the pay phone in the hotel lobby. "Hey, Joe, we think it might be a good idea if we are going to have a long-distance race to get one started this year." And Joe said, "Do you really think we can do it this year?" Of course, we were naive and dumb young kids, we said, "Sure we can do that." So we agreed to meet with Joe in a couple of nights and, of course, we started meeting three, four, five times a week to plan what eventually got to be called the Iditarod Trail Race.

Huyck relates original talk was of a race from Knik to Iditarod and back, roughly the distance covered by early 1900s All Alaska Sweepstakes mushers running from Nome to Candle and return, a total of four hundred and eight miles. Joe Redington championed the route until won over by arguments from Howard Farley, who was tagged by Redington to be the Nome "race coordinator." Farley managed, however, to escape Nome and run the first race. It was his sensible argument that at Knik, there would be no one to see us leave, and at ghost town Iditarod, no one to see us come in. He reasoned it would be best to start in Anchorage and end in Nome. A stamp of approval was placed on Farley's idea by those involved. This catapulted the proposed race course an additional five to six hundred miles across the face of Alaska.

Soon, others were recruited, mushers in particular, mostly members of the Aurora Dog Mushers Club. Steve Schmirnof of Anchorage was recruited to handle publicity aspects of our operation. With an eye toward keeping us somewhat legal, Anchorage attorney, Terry Aglietti, consented to join the effort. Kathy (Lanman) Johnson, Tom's wife, suggested that Bill Weimar, head of the Young Democrats ad hoc committee in Anchorage, be contacted. Huyck states, "Weimar was quite excited about the whole idea. They were looking for ways to raise money and saw how association with our organization might help them. The Young Democrats lived in a warehouse at 15th and Karluk (Anchorage). It was a place that didn't cost us anything. So we started meeting at The Warehouse, as it was called."

Huyck went on to say, "When Terry Aglietti came aboard as our volunteer lawyer, one of the first things he insisted we do was to become a legal corporation to protect us individually from lawsuits that may come. One night, on our way home in Joe's truck from The Warehouse, we elected officers. Tom nominated Joe as president, so we elected him as president. I nominated Tom as vice president, so we elected him as vice president, and then they nominated me as secretary/treasurer and voted me into that office. So these were the first officers of the Iditarod Trail Race, Inc."

Seavey: How frequent were the meetings at The Warehouse?

Huyck: Usually, three to four times per week. We drove in to Anchorage to have these meetings and we kept inviting other volunteers to come and join us. Basically, though, it was Bill (Weimar), Joe, Tom, Steve (Schmirnof), Terry Aglietti, myself, and one or two other mushers.

Seavey: How about Dorothy Page? She is given credit as being the Mother of the Iditarod. Where did she fit in this organization?

Huyck: Very, very early in the planning stages, Joe suggested we go talk to Dorothy Page to see if she is interested in being part of this, because Dorothy Page had been instrumental in getting the Centennial Race going back in 1967. Joe thought it only courteous for us to call on her about becoming part of the Iditarod Committee for this race.

Seavey: Okay, you are back from Unalakleet at the end of August, you and Tom got the idea (race) in October. The Warehouse meetings were in October or November, or when?

Huyck: They started in October.

Seavey: Then your meeting with Dorothy would have been roughly the same time?

Huyck: The latter part of October, first part of November, somewhere in there. We went to meet with Dorothy and explained our idea of having a long-distance race of three hundred to four hundred miles. She wanted nothing to do with being any part of this race and washed her hands of it. She said, "I don't think it can succeed and somebody is going to get hurt, and I just don't want my name associated with it." Those were just about her exact words. She wanted nothing to do with it, so we (Redington and Huyck) left there... That was our meeting with Dorothy. That's the last I saw of her for all the months we put in planning the first race.

Seavey: Before we get away from that initial serious planning, let's call it, what would you define as the deciding moment when you said, "Hey, it's actually going to happen?"

Huyck: I don't know if I can point to a certain place. When you plan a big event for the first time, just saying publicly, "It's on," gives impetus to its happening. I think once we set the date for the first race, we were fully committed to seeing it through.

Seavey: There are many folks even nowadays who think there is some connection between the first Iditarod and the famous Serum Run of 1925. When we were planning this first race, did we ever deal with that issue?

Huyck: We never talked about it being a reenactment of the Serum Run.

Seavey: So how do you account for its part in the Iditarod mystique?

Huyck: Probably through the newspapers that have done so much about putting names on things in this race. We did give out bib Number One for the first race in honor of Leonhard Seppala, because he had been the most famous dog musher back in the days of the Serum Run and during the Sweepstakes races.

Seavey: Dorothy Page, "Mother of the Iditarod," true or false? Joe Redington, "Father of the Iditarod," how did those titles come about?

Huyck: These titles came from newspaper writers. There was one article that came out, I think, after the first Iditarod was run. They were interviewing Joe and somebody in the article said, "Joe is the father of the Iditarod." That name stuck to Joe from then until today. To us planners, he was just one of the co-founders. Tom and I wanted to put Joe into the forefront of our group because Joe was a very, very fine, persuasive speaker. We called him the Silver Tongued Fox. He was also very well known. People did not know the names Gleo Huyck and Tom Johnson, so we decided to put Joe up front as spokesperson of our committee. He was not agreeable at first. He kept saying he was too shy. Well, we knew better. Joe loved to talk in front of people and, as I said, he was very persuasive.

Seavey: What about the almost magical $50,000.00 purse, which awestruck all mushers, being more money than most made during their entire racing career at the time, how did that come about?

Huyck: That was Joe's idea. We were talking about it early in our planning and Joe said we had to have an attractive payoff and suggested $50,000.00. All present agreed it sounded good. That's how that figure was chosen.

Seavey: Did you consider a lesser amount?

Huyck: No, we didn't.

Seavey: So now, we (Seavey had been on board as the Kenai Peninsula PR person and fund-raiser since winter of 1969) are well along with day-to-day planning and, eventually, invitation letters go out and mushers send in our entries of $100.00.

Huyck: You see, the primary purpose for having such a low figure was that we really wanted to attract native mushers to come in and race, and there was not a lot of money in the villages. We had no idea what it was going to cost to run this race. We were really naïve.

Seavey: So all this planning was going on, volunteers being lined up, all the logistics, and so forth. Dates are being set and, finally, on Thursday, before the race starts, everybody is assembled for the first mushers' banquet and drawing in Anchorage at the old Gold Rush Hotel (located between C Street and Arctic Blvd. on Northern Lights Blvd; at this writing, vacant and boarded up).

Huyck: There were some interesting things that happened before even that point. About a week before the banquet, we started getting calls from the airport that a musher had landed with all his dogs, unannounced. All of a sudden, we were spending almost all of our time, up until the race started, trying to find places to go with their dogs. Many had no money, no food, trusting we would somehow take care of them. Eventually, we found places for all these mushers and their dogs, but it was really a hectic time.

Seavey: Saturday, March 3, do you recall how we settled on that particular date for the race start?

Huyck: We looked at all other dog races in the state… The only date we found that wouldn't conflict with other races was the first weekend in March. We also decided that would be the date for all future Iditarods, the first weekend in March.

Seavey: We were talking during our break about how Joe actually wanted to run that first race.

Huyck: He was packed and ready to go.

Here, Gleo revealed some rather interesting insider information, much of it new even to me. He stated that he and Johnson knew by Anchorage banquet time that there was not nearly enough money for the payoff at the end of the race. Joe was needed for fund-raising. Their problem was how to approach him in a persistent manner in view of what Huyck calls "Joe's temper" when riled, and knowing Redington had planned to race all along made the task doubly difficult. Finally, Gleo screwed up enough courage and, in the lobby of the Gold Rush Hotel, race headquarters for that first year, he took Joe aside and broke the news. He had to stay behind to help raise the $50,000.00 promised for the purse. There simply was no way he and Johnson could possibly do it on their own. A crestfallen Redington finally acquiesced to Huyck's argument and agreed to cancel his personal race plans.

Previous to that episode, the race committee had gotten a promise from an "Anchorage politician" that he would front the $50,000.00 prize money. A couple weeks before the race, he reneged on his promise. Colonel "Muktuk" Marston had given the race $10,000.00 during the early planning stages, which was used as seed money to get things going and had been all but spent by race time.

Finally, after aggressively pursuing several fruitless money sources well into the first week of racing, committee members, in company with the mayor of Anchorage, paid a visit to the fellow who had backed out of that prize money promise. Huyck recalled, "We were very straight with him. We needed the money and didn't want to cause harm to anybody, but we probably would have to publicize the fact that he had reneged on the prize money for the race. Well, he was not happy with that, wasn't happy with the meeting, but finally agreed to countersign a loan from the first National Bank of Alaska for $40,000.00, and that would give us most of the money for the finish." The politician in question was not revealed by Huyck during our interview. However, without question, he referred to Bruce Kendall, a past Speaker of the Alaska House of Representatives.

Seavey: At the drawing and banquet prior to the first race, that would have been Thursday, March 1, 1973, in the evening at the Gold Rush Hotel, do you recall the concern raised by a representative of the native community of mushers regarding uncertainty of purse funds?

Huyck: Yes, I do. It was Jim Huntington, one of the most respected men of the native community in Alaska and a fine musher in his time. Apparently, an earlier race had been held where considerable prize money had been promised. Native mushers came from the villages and the prize money was not there to pay them off at the end. Jim Huntington got up and asked Joe directly whether the money was in escrow for the finish of the race. I don't remember his exact words, but Joe promised that the money would be there at the end of the race. Joe, being the Silver Tongued Fox, a great orator, convinced everybody that everything was on the up and up, that we were honorable people and the money would be there.

Seavey: Redington completely diffused a potentially volatile situation. Thirty-four mushers, whose honored representative directly challenged him: "Is the money there?" Joe had to admit, "Well, no, it's not there, but upon my word of honor, it will be by the time mushers arrive in Nome!" A tense, dramatic point in the history of the Iditarod.

Huyck: Yes. It really was. And thank God, with Joe's skills, he was able to bring that off. If for no other reason, we have to respect Joe for saying the words he did that evening.

Seavey: Ten a.m. Saturday, March 3, 1973, teams began leaving for Nome from Tudor Track in Anchorage. We, the mushers, are off and running, but there must still have been real headaches for the nuts and bolts organizers like Joe, Tom, and yourself. We were a long way from the finish line and the race equally a long way from a success.

Huyck: It certainly wasn't an assured success. Frankly, we didn't know if it could be done. We had no idea if a musher could go that distance. The more we got into the race, the more we realized how dangerous it was. There were special problems that came up daily. One was communications. Then, we relied on shortwave radio operators moving along from checkpoint to checkpoint, relaying information back to the Gold Rush Hotel in

Anchorage. We were glued to radio sets the entire time. Our "Iditarod Air Force" was born during that first race. All were volunteer pilots who donated their planes, themselves, gas, the works. They flew gear from commercial hubs like McGrath to smaller villages, which were checkpoints. They flew radio people along the trail and flew out dogs left behind by mushers. Those pilots deserve a lot of credit for making the race a success.

Seavey: Dick Tozier, how did he become race marshal for the first one?

Huyck: When Dick accepted the role of race marshal, we were truly grateful. Committee members, Orville Lake and a couple of mushers, met at Dick's house to ask if he would accept the job. At first, he was reluctant because of the start-up problems we were having and rules he would have to enforce, which were quite different than he enforced as marshal for sprint races. With Tozier's help, we drew up a workable set of rules for the first Iditarod.

Seavey: And Orville Lake, he seemed to be everywhere during the race. What was his job?

Huyck: He was hired by one of the radio stations to report on the race. Thus, his presence along the trail. He was not a really great promoter of the race when we started. We got a lot of negative vibes from Orville.

Seavey: How were those first checkpoints established? How did we know where we were going and if we would be welcomed at, say, Galena or Kaltag?

Huyck: Our committee had communicated in advance of the race start so as to have at least one contact at each village selected as a checkpoint. We started the great tradition of village volunteerism for the race.

Seavey: What about trailbreakers?

Huyck: The army took on the role of breaking trail for us, plus some local mushers, Don Rosevear being one. He ended up having to leave his bogged-down snowmachine several hundred miles out on the trail. The army was helpful; however, mushers in a couple places resorted to snowshoes for making their own trail.

19

Captured—Put to Work

Kids race sponsored by Aurora Dog Mushers Club.
A small group destined to bring about an Alaska Cultural Renaissance. L-R: Kathy Johnson, Mitch (musher) Tom Johnson, Shirley, 1972.

As noted earlier, active scheming for an endurance sled dog race did not cease with the completion of the abbreviated 1967 Alaska Purchase Centennial run. My involvement with the whole business came via the Aurora Dog Mushers and somewhat prior to events related by Gleo Huyck in his interview. My first awareness of such an idea would have been in December of 1969. During that month, I made the first of many trips from Seward to Knik in order to participate in local races sponsored by the Aurora Mushers.

Included in club membership at the time (1969) were Joel Kotke, Bill Cotter, Dave Olson, Jerry Crum, Tom Johnson, Keith Poppert, and Joe and Vi Redington. There were many other members, but these folks stand out in my memories. Local races generally included kids' races—one, two, and three dog events—and various adult sprint-type races. Start and finish of all events took place on Knik Lake. Longer club races were run over segments of the old Iditarod Trail. Invariably, when the day's activities were over, participants would squeeze into Joe and Vi's tiny log cabin, located across the way from today's Knik Museum. Here, Vi would serve coffee to most everyone present, and tea with honey to Joe. Once chatter generated by races just completed had subsided, inevitably, conversation turned to the "Big One." We visualized an endurance race to rival or even outshine the granddaddy of all dog races, the All Alaska Sweepstakes of a half century past. The Sweepstakes Race was held in Nome during its gold rush days and featured a four-hundred-and-eight-mile course.

Files I kept over the years pertaining to things Iditarod, fat in their present state, are quite thin when it comes to mention of conversations that took place after those club races. I do, however, recall discussing purposes behind such an event, which could be boiled down to two main ones: preserve dog mushing in Alaska, and reestablishment of the gold rush era Iditarod Trail.

There were questions and opinions as to where the race should start and finish. Should it be Knik to McGrath? Knik to Iditarod? When should it happen? How long in planning? How much purse and how to fund it? What name to give it? Talk! Talk! Talk! But it was good talk. Exciting talk. As it turned out, important, profitable talk.

Toward spring (1970), we even got around to some preliminary action of an exploratory nature. Various tasks were taken on by those of us with high interest levels. Joe Redington agreed to contact high-profile persons who were thought to be in a position to lend support in one form or another. Tom Johnson, given his supposed and apparent English teacher skills, undertook some letter writing. To me went the task of drumming up interest and support on the Kenai Peninsula.

After all, it was reasoned, I was a history teacher and Seward and the Iditarod Trail were practically synonymous. Right? Other club members pitched in to lend assistance as their circumstances allowed. It should be added that we operated under a decidedly loose, impromptu, voluntary, committee system until the fall of 1972. As brought to light by Huyck in his interview with me, the decision to end the talking and take positive, determined action toward realization of our dream was made in October 1972, just five months before the actual race start. Hundreds of tasks needed attention. Thousands of details looked to. Not the least was the whirlwind creation of a legal, private, nonprofit corporation with the State of Alaska, thus creating the Iditarod Trail Committee, now over four decades old.

Some of that groundwork, fortunately, had been laid as early as 1970 by our impromptu, grassroots committee. A first ever, heads-up-type letter was sent to all known mushers and mushing clubs, under a date of March 23, 1970, authored by Tom Johnson. Mention was already made of a $50,000.00 purse, a 1973 start date, and the importance of the Iditarod Trail. Likewise, that first letter was instructive of our ignorance and naïveté. We had the race going from Knik to the ghost town of Iditarod, and back. Tom stated: "We intend to construct cabins approximately fifty miles apart the entire length of the trail…" And the race title? We had a whopper: Leonhard Seppala Memorial Iditarod Trail International Championship Race (see Appendix II, Johnson Letter, March 23, 1970).

During this early time, Redington began his pursuit of influential business persons, politicians, and key public servants. Once under Joe's spell, there was no escape. His power of persuasion was such that we, close to him, were sure he had been a most successful used car salesman in a former life. In house, he was the "P.T. Barnum of dog mushing." He personified the first principle of successful salesmanship: believe one hundred percent in the product you sell. But he went a giant step beyond. With uncanny charm and a most believable demeanor, he convinced total strangers that not only was their support (money, labor, or whatever) absolutely vital to our success, but the person, and his or her emotional commitment to our undertaking, even more so. I personally observed several incidents in which a new contact under Joe's sway went, in just one face-to-face session, from, "What in the world is this Iditarod?" to "Count me in. What can I do to help?" Such was the way of our SilverTongued Fox.

Soon after the 1969-70 winter break-up in April, I went to work as the committee's Kenai Peninsula representative. Although fund-raising was part of my job description, my chief function was public relations, to bring about some level of race and trail awareness in my neck of the woods. Letters went out to persons and organizations across the peninsula who I thought ought to be interested. Most effort, however, was expended in the Seward area. The old history teacher in me kicked in. "By gum, if folks in this town don't realize the importance of the Iditarod Trail in their history, they will when I am through with them." I wrote letter upon letter, editorials, and spoke to local groups until my welcome was, I suspect, worn thin.

From Files: (Sample letter sent by author on behalf of race committee, April 2, 1970)

Dick Kirkpatrick, President
Seward Chamber of Commerce
Seward, Alaska

Dear Dick,

The Iditarod Trail Committee (Joe Redington, Sr., Chairman) is asking the Seward Chamber of Commerce to join with it in promoting the longest, cruelest, but richest sled dog race in history, the Iditarod 800. The accompanying copy of our letter to over 100 mushers' clubs in the United States and Canada is enclosed for your information.

As you perhaps know, the Iditarod Trail started in Seward and served as the main transportation artery to the Iditarod mining area during the early 1900s. With proper promotion, the 1973 Iditarod Race can become not only a mushing success, but can serve to arouse Seward's pride in her historical significance as the southern terminus of that great trail. I believe this event can also generate substantial commercial activity for Seward. If you are interested, you can help in several ways... sending a letter of endorsement...

> your letter will be used to aid us in securing an underwriter for the $50,000.00 prize money...purchase for resale...our reprint souvenir booklets of the famous and historic Nome All Alaska Sweepstakes...perhaps most importantly, we need your ideas for tying Seward into the overall race activities....

Be it in written form, as in letters, such as the above, or in speaking opportunities, my theme was pretty standard. There was going to be a race over the Iditarod Trail, and due to its historic prominence, Seward needed to become engaged. How can you, your organization, our community best do this?

At that time, the Kenai Peninsula was served by state legislators Senator Bob Palmer and Representatives Clem Tillion and, Seward resident and merchant, Irv Metcalf. I wrote directly to Senator Palmer with copies forwarded to the two representatives. On behalf of the Iditarod Trail Committee, I made those public worthies aware of our existence, what we were up to, and reminded them of the trail's importance to Seward and the peninsula. I stated that my personal interest "lies mainly in publicizing the peninsula and especially Seward as the southern terminus of that historic trail."

And an additional new twist: "Also, it has occurred to me that attention given the trail can aid those who are working for its inclusion in the nation's system of historic trails." It is significant that this letter was written on April 10, 1970. Obviously, the topic of creating a nationally recognized Iditarod Trail had been discussed by our first pioneer committee, with feelers, such as mine, going out as early as the spring of 1970. From the beginning then, our two chief missions as a committee, were expounded: an event to give purpose for sled dogs and preservation of a trail over which to drive them.

One of my most treasured file items is a copy of Representative Irv Metcalf's letter to the committee in response to what I had written in my letter. In it, Sewardite Metcalf not only expressed his pleasure and approval, but gave good argument why the "Dog Sled Derby," as he labeled it, should have its beginnings in Seward. What an encouragement for those of us just getting our feet wet with this whole affair (see Appendix III, Metcalf Letter).

The notion that the Iditarod deserved national recognition and prominence did not lie dormant for long. As early as the winter of 1972, letters started to go out to those thought most likely to give wings to the idea. Recipients were made aware that a gala sled dog event was in the making. At the same time, the historic importance of the trail was emphasized, and a plea for assistance was made in one form or another. My letter to Alaska's U.S. Senator Ted Stevens had a rather fruitful, if slow in coming, result.

During the year of 2000, Seward Iditarod Trail Blazers, Inc., with assistance from the United States Forest Service, Seward Ranger District, sent to Senator Stevens's Washington D.C. office a request for four million dollars to fund the start-up phase of what amounted to reclamation of the Iditarod Trail on the Kenai Peninsula. Stevens, at that time, was thirty-two years into his amazing thirty-eight-year stint in the U.S. Senate. Forester and, longtime Sewardite, Patrick O'Leary had helped with the Trail Blazer proposal, providing cost estimates and pertinent information to which the Forest Service was privy.

As president of the Seward Trail Blazers, I made a couple of follow-up calls to the senator's legislative office. We waited. Then, in May of 2001, we learned that a $1,400,000.00 appropriation had been made for what came to be called the Seward to Girdwood Project. It wasn't enough to do the job, but it was a start. In these days of governmental economic stimulus, I am happy to report that the overall project is well funded and moving nicely toward completion.

The point being is that Senator Stevens had bought into the concept of turning the Iditarod into some sort of national trail upon receipt of my February 8, 1972 letter. Stevens's heartening reply, dated March 9, 1972, gave assurances of his interest and support (see Appendix, IV, Stevens's Letter). "Uncle Ted" later gave his nod of approval, as did Senator Mike Gravel and Representative Don Young, to the 1978 federal legislation designating the two-thousand-plus-mile Iditarod trail system as the Iditarod National Historic Trail. Senator Stevens also became a life member of Seward Iditarod Trail Blazers shortly after its 1982 founding. From conception to construction, Alaska Senator Ted Stevens was there for Iditarod.

20

Clutching at Straws

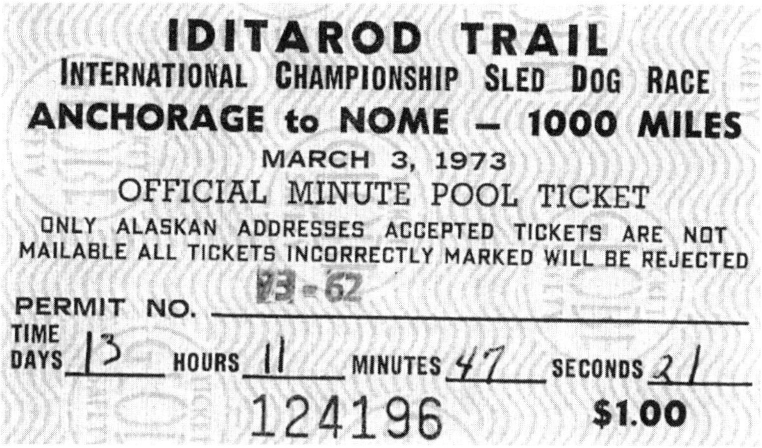

IDITAROD TRAIL
INTERNATIONAL CHAMPIONSHIP SLED DOG RACE
ANCHORAGE to NOME – 1000 MILES
MARCH 3, 1973
OFFICIAL MINUTE POOL TICKET
ONLY ALASKAN ADDRESSES ACCEPTED TICKETS ARE NOT MAILABLE ALL TICKETS INCORRECTLY MARKED WILL BE REJECTED
PERMIT NO. 73-62
TIME DAYS 13 HOURS 11 MINUTES 47 SECONDS 21
124196 $1.00

Ticket number 62. Prerace hype touted a state wide lottery authorizing a half million tickets with a potential payout of $195,000.00.

For me, the winter of 1972-73 winged by at an ever-accelerating pace. Workload at school, family, and community responsibilities all clamored for their fair share of my time. They all took a backseat to training my dog team. Likewise, the closer race day loomed, the less time I had for trail committee chores, so that those three months prior to the race, I had begged off almost completely. Meanwhile, Johnson, Huyck, Redington, and, by then, many others forged ahead with preparations.

A short time before the arrival of 1973, probably during December 1972, the Iditarod Trail Committee sent to all who cared, and a lot who didn't, I am sure, a teaser written by Gleo Huyck, extending an invitation to receive further information and to enter the "Big One." Printed blue on white, this flyer had a detachable mail-in portion, on which the deadline for registration was stated as February 28, 1973. I mailed it off immediately (see Appendix V, Huyck Letter and Flyer).

Soon, there arrived an impressive seven-page bundle of eagerly studied information. My intent here was to treat this material rather lightly. Dig it out of its file, summarize it, and move on. Problem is that my revisit after nearly forty years left me fascinated by its content anew. Much has remained unchanged, race-wise, over the years. Dissimilarities between then and now are even more pronounced. Examples abound: The total fifty-thousand-dollar purse of 1973, is taken home nowadays by the first place champion alone, plus a lot more. In 1973, we ran physically all the way from Anchorage to Nome. We did it again in 1974, and that feat has not been duplicated since. Checkpoints have moved around over intervening years. Today's rules amount to a small book—twenty-one pages in total number—while back then, the whole lot easily fit on one side of one legal-size page. Perhaps the most glaring shocker was found on the last page, the entry form. Among provisions agreed to by an entrant was, "To pay the sum of one hundred dollars ($100.00) as a nonrefundable entry fee on or before February 17, 1973, and if payment is made between February 18 and February 28, the entry fee shall be $150.00…" In 2010, mushers paid an entry fee of four thousand dollars. Without further comment, I commit the lot to the reader's perusal (see Appendix VI, Race Sign-Up Information and Entry Form).

Another, and perhaps long forgotten, endeavor of that first race committee was establishment of a lottery. Albeit a financial sinker, its attempt illustrates desire and creativity on the part of the committee to render the race a monetary success. Keep in mind, the decision to, in fact, make the first race happen, came just five months prior to its kick-off. Because of this time crunch, almost every preparation was hurried. Our lottery was no exception. Legal research had to be undertaken. Legal opinions sought. Tickets, advertising, and sale outlets procured. All in double-quick time.

One would not be disappointed if he expects to discover the hand of Joe Redington in that lottery business. Dated January 4, 1973, the committee sent a letter to several score prospective lottery ticket sales outlets. In that wistful dispatch, which began, "Dear Friend," all were invited to participate in what was likened to a modern gold rush, a rich lottery inspired by Alaska's great gold rush trail. A comparison was made to the venerable Nenana Ice Classic, where just guessing the correct time the ice goes out on the Nenana River each spring earns the lucky guesser about $100,000.00. The reader was assured of our legality to conduct a lottery, but cautioned that each person who actually sold a ticket needed a federal tax stamp, suggesting that the committee could assist with information on its procurement. Rather detailed instructions were given for exchange of a lottery ticket for coin. Ticket sales were to end on March 4, 1973. "Brochures, race rules, mileage sheets (between checkpoints), and other data, as well as posters, will be provided to you for promotional purposes…"

Most likely, this letter was the product of a cooperative effort on the part of Joe Redington and Tom Johnson, not an unusual occurrence with the early committee. Joe, the big idea P.T. Barnum of our operation, and Tom, the English teacher, who gave those ideas a degree of literary respectability. Finally, the letter stated: "Thank you for your assistance in making this the truly greatest race in the history of dog mushing." Signed: Joe Redington, Sr., Chairman, Iditarod Trail Committee, (see Appendix VII, Redington Lottery Letter).

No sooner was the Johnson-Redington letter in the mail drumming up ticket salespeople, than the hurried committee shot off a press release to Anchorage's two daily newspapers, going all-out public with the lottery. There was a short, to-the-point article announcing the lottery with an accompanying photo and caption.

By January 1973, Tom Johnson was serving as the committee's treasurer and it was he who was responsible for that news announcement: A statewide lottery with a potential payout of $195,000.00. The winner will be the person guessing exact arrival time of the first team into Nome in days, hours, minutes, and seconds, or closest to it. The pot was to be split in case of a tie. One-dollar tickets were going on sale in every town and village in Alaska. The winner was to be declared within seventy-two hours of race completion. One-half million tickets had been printed.

Quoting Tom Johnson: "We decided to have the race and lottery to raise money for the committee so that it can begin work on preserving the trail, restoring some of the historic roadhouses and portions of many gold rush towns that have begun to deteriorate with time." In addition, the committee was taking on the task of lobbying for federal recognition of the Iditarod Trail as a National Historic Trail. All was not lottery hype on the part of Johnson. The Iditarod Trail Committee (ITC) would become the banner carrier to the U.S. Congress, agitating and no doubt aggravating, until the Iditarod became a National Historic Trail.

A companion photo to the Johnson article titled "Lt. Governor Tries Lady Luck" featured Lieutenant Governor H.A. "Red" Boucher and ITC treasurer, Tom Johnson. Below the photo, we were informed that Mr. Boucher had purchased the first thirteen lottery tickets, donating them to the Alaska Crippled Children's Association. Here again, mention was made that "Tickets are on sale at towns and villages all across the state."

Not quite so. The February 28, 1973 *Great Lander Shopping News*, a very popular newspaper insert of the time, published a full-page lottery souvenir poster. It included basic race information with route map. It listed lottery rules, gave distances between established checkpoints, and pinpointed ticket outlets "throughout Alaska." Fact is, there weren't all that many and they were noticeably localized. Fifty-six was the total, of which, thirty-four were located in Anchorage, at the likes of Chilkoot Charlie's, China Doll Bar, and Dance Den. Big Lake, Kenai, Palmer, Soldotna, Wasilla, and Seward, each with but a smattering of outlets. Seward, for instance, had but four ticket outlets: Werner's Family Store, the Pioneer Bar, Solly's, and Seward Skill Center (Alaska Vocational Technical Center, nowadays). I must admit, I was so involved with training my dog team that I remained completely oblivious to any ticket sales in Seward. And, for shame, I purchased none.

Later news reports had only 4,450 lottery tickets sold a full three weeks following the lieutenant governor's purchase of those first thirteen. Still, lottery tickets sales manager, Gene Lambert, remained hopeful of selling at least two hundred thousand by race time. In this, he was disappointed. In a piece dated March 21, 1973, two days before the first place finish in Nome, Terry Aglietti, ITC legal adviser, announced gross one-dollar-per-ticket income at a mere $13,417.00.

The payoff to be $6,037.00. Now, the hope expressed was that there would be enough money for the ITC to help pay off a growing stack of printing bills. By that time, Aglietti claimed 133 outlets had sold lottery tickets.

And a final lottery twist—perhaps a last gasp. Because ticket sales were poor, Aglietti said the committee decided to hold a "Last Chance" lottery on the final thirty miles of the race from Solomon to Nome. "Last Chance" tickets also cost one dollar. It is of interest to note that a lasting result of that first end-of-the-trail lottery is the present-day tradition of keeping record of the fastest team between Port Safety (Safety) and Nome for a given race.

Before leaving the lottery topic, let us declare its winners: First, Kathy Snow of McGrath, Alaska, came within just eleven minutes and nineteen seconds of Dick Wilmarth's completion time of twenty days, zero hours, forty minutes, and forty-one seconds. Snow's winning ticket read twenty days, one hour. It was worth six thousand dollars to her. Racer Bud Smyth had the fastest run of all between Solomon and Nome. Phyllis Fields of Anchorage was just thirty seconds off Bud's time with her guess, winning $294.74 in the "Last Chance Lottery." Tom Brown, Sr., a White Mountain, Alaska, resident, had the second best guess. The third place winner was Vicky Horton of Nome. Their respective earnings were $220.80 and $147.87 for a grand payout of $6,662.21, a bit shy, to say the least, of the $195,000.00 lauded on our prerace poster.

Earlier, mention was made of Joe Redington's personal pursuit of key Alaskans in an effort to bring them in tow and into an active support of our first race. Redington's answer was formation of an Iditarod Trail International Championship Sled Dog Race Honorary Committee. Quite the mouthful, but it got the job done. This pure but sincere promotional stunt brought out the best of P.T. Barnum in Joe, Sr. A February 6, 1973 article published in the venerable *Nome Nugget* said it all: Race Aides Named by Race Head… Names of (Honorary) members were released by Joe Redington, Sr., general race chairman, who said, "I am pleased that so many prominent Alaskans have agreed to assist with the race. The thousand-mile sled dog race over ice and snow from Anchorage to Nome should be the greatest sled dog race ever held. The race has the potential of becoming the greatest sporting event in Alaska and will result in both national and international publicity for the race."

He listed the committee members as follows:

Vide G. Bartlett of Fairbanks, widow of Sen. E.L. (Bob) Bartlett and a member of the board of regents of the University of Alaska
Lt. Governor, H.A. (Red) Boucher
Alvin O. Bramstedt of Anchorage, president of Midnight Sun Broadcasters
Edith Bullock of Anchorage, businesswoman and a member of Alaska board of regents
Governor William A. Egan
U.S. Senator Mike Gravel
Albro B. Gregory of Nome, publisher of the *Nome Nugget*
State Senator Willie Hensley of Kotzebue, president of the Alaska Federation of Natives
Bruce Kendall, Anchorage hotel proprietor
Howard Pollock of Anchorage, former member of the U.S. House of Representatives
Elmer Rasmussen of Anchorage, banker
Mayor Robert Renshaw of Nome
Jack Roderick, mayor of the Greater Anchorage Area Borough
U.S. Senator Ted Stevens
Mayor George Sullivan of Anchorage
Don Wright of Anchorage, Alaska, native leader

That so many Alaska notables were willing to allow their names to be associated with a bunch of dog mushers—of all people—and their hare-brained, addle-headed scheme for racing dogs across the state is ample proof of Joe's power of persuasion. Most folks from all walks of life simply found it very difficult, if not impossible, to say "no" to Joe.

One factor working in our favor, when confronting both the movers and shakers, and Alaskans in general, was that dog mushing had been proclaimed Alaska's Official Sport by our legislature in 1972. In February of that year, State House Bill number 652 had been introduced by a geographic cross section of thirty state representatives and referred to the State Affairs Committee. Entitled: "An act establishing the official sport of Alaska," it was amended by adding a new section to read: "State Sport. Dog mushing is the official sport of Alaska." I like to believe that through my efforts as the race committee's Kenai Peninsula agent, both Keith Specking and Clem Tillion, Peninsula members of the House of Representatives appeared among the measure's willing sponsors. It passed both houses, was signed by Governor Bill Egan, and passed into history as part of the proceedings of the Seventh Legislature, Second Session, of the State of Alaska.

Lottery, entry fees, accelerated hype, dignitary approval, and donations notwithstanding, the nearer to the race start we moved, the poorer we became. Certainly, Jim Huntington's concern, voiced at the Anchorage prerace banquet, was justified. Would there be a $50,000.00 pot of gold awaiting mushers in Nome? Or any for that matter? And race committee debts continued to grow with each passing day.

Thinking back, it seems providential that nearly three weeks were required for the front-runners to arrive at their Norton Sound destination in Nome and not the ten days estimated so casually by Joe, Sr. in some of his prerace hype. As it was, we were just two days out from Nome when the Race Committee announced that the purse had been funded—for sure. Well, as we will see, most of it anyway.

Joe and his committee found themselves undertaking some very frenzied fund-raising activities as soon as the last team disappeared down the trail toward Nome. Fact is, when I and my thirty-three trail mates struck out for Nome on that memorable date, Saturday, March 3, 1973, a major portion of our eagerly anticipated pot of gold was mostly—empty An estimated seven thousand dollars, that's all. Stacked alongside our "accounts payable," it was a pitiful trifle—and all that public bluster, ballyhooing, and promises given. Many reputations were on the line. A healthy portion of Alaska's elite had come out in support of this untested affair by becoming honorary members of Joe's equally untested race committee. Redington had stood before thirty-four trusting mushers at their prerace banquet two days previous and proclaimed to them and the world that, upon his honor, the money would be waiting for them upon their arrival at rainbow's end. One has to believe that Joe, Tom, Gleo, and others, concerned with financial success of the race, counted their blessings daily as each passed and the race dragged on and on. One more day of grace. Another day to beat the bushes in quest of desperately needed cash. Another day of clutching at straws.

There was a promise by British Petroleum of one thousand dollars, later bumped up to a whopping twelve hundred and fifty dollars. B and C Auto Supply supplied seven hundred fifty dollars, while the City of Nome initiated its unending tradition of Iditarod cash support with a donation of one thousand dollars. Our ill-fated guess-the-finishing-time lottery was expected to make another four to five thousand available by race end. This was pretty much our financial picture, glum though it was, two weeks into the race and only four days before the winning team would trot down Front Street in Nome.

Finally, the dogged treasure seekers struck pay dirt. First in the person of Marvin "Muktuk" Marston. Marston was no newcomer where traveling by dog team was concerned. A retired colonel in 1973, during his active military service, he is credited with organizing the Eskimos of the northwest coast of Alaska into scouting units during World War II. Inter-village travel for that purpose, and subsequent training was via dog team. He chalked up thousands of miles in performance of official duties before war's end. Marston chronicled his adventurous sojourn among our far north defenders in his book, *Men of the Tundra*. Later, he established a successful real estate business in Anchorage. He cut quite an imposing figure even at age eighty-four in 1973. Marvin R. "Muktuk" Marston died in 1980 at age ninety-one.

Joe, Sr. and other stay-at-home committee members accosted Marston several weeks prior to race start for a ten-thousand-dollar loan. He refused them flat out—"no loan!" But he was most happy, indeed proud, to donate that amount toward our efforts. For Muktuk's vast and important experience driving sled dogs and his generous financial assistance, which helped the first race down the path to reality, he soon would be inducted into the Mushers Hall of Fame.

A second pay streak was found in Anchorage, over at Alaska National Bank of the North. It was announced in local papers, on March 21, 1973, that bank president, Frank Murkowski (later Alaska U.S. senator and governor) had approved a thirty-thousand-dollar loan to the Iditarod Trail Committee.

Banking being banking, certain provisos affixed themselves to that lifesaver loan: One-year payback, proceeds to go to prize money only. Loan agreement to be co-signed (repayment guaranteed) by financially capable individual(s). Actual funds to be disbursed by Alaska National Bank's Miners and Merchants branch in faraway Nome.

In turn, those signing on the dotted line, thus cinching the loan, tied their own strings to the deal. It was to be understood that in return for their support, they would have the loudest voice in the selection of manager for the next (1974) race and race lottery.

Of all key players in that crucial transaction, none was more critical than Anchorage businessman and former Speaker of the Alaska House of Representatives, Bruce Kendall. In a sense, Kendall was of the Muktuk Marston mold. He was strong-willed, and had firsthand experience with old time Alaska through trapping and mining. He was a self-made, successful Anchorage hotel owner and promoter of Alaska's future. Like Marston, he became caught up in the Iditarod Race extravaganza. As it turned out, Kendall was the only "financially capable" signatory to that bank loan. As such, he, after the dust settled on our inaugural race, handed over thirty thousand dollars, plus accrued interest, to Frank Murkowski's bank from his own funds. Apparently never regretting his generosity, the visionary looked upon the whole affair as a well-spent investment in Alaska's future. He believed then that the race would grow to become what, in fact, it is today, an international sports event highlighting his beloved state.

Kendall, Murkowski, and Marston came to an eleventh-hour rescue of Joe, Sr., our race committee, and their twenty-five or so mushers still wending their way toward Nome. They, in fact, rescued the Iditarod Race concept itself. They saved the day. The top twenty mushers could expect to be paid upon arrival in Nome. In addition, "Herbie" Nayokpuk of Shishmaref was assured of receiving the one thousand dollars promised for driving the fastest team on opening day between Anchorage and historic Knik. However, as we will see later, even with all the foregoing financial scurrying about, we were found wanting to fully fund that purse.

Here, perhaps, is a good place to shed light on the recurring fable that Joe and Vi Redington lost their Flathorn Lake homestead in support of Joe's dream of a long-distance sled dog race, that it was offered as security for the Murkowski bank loan and lost due to default thereon. That story persists to this day, in my estimation because it is "oh, so noble." "A dreamer gambles all in pursuit of his dream." Then there is confusion of facts. It is true that Joe offered his Knik home and property in support of the 1967 Centennial Purchase Race, but it was not lost by the Redingtons. Truth be told, Joe did offer his Flathorn Lake homestead to secure Frank Murkowski's loan, but Murkowski declined the offer. Raw land was just too risky. Besides, there was a public relations factor at work. What kind of black eye would the bank sport if it had to foreclose?

Another possible item of confusion in this regard may be Joe and Vi's donation of an acre of land to the Iditarod Trail Committee. A true Redingtonian promotional: For a mere ten dollars, one could become the proud owner of 1/998,600th interest in "that portion of Government Lot 5 U.S. Survey Number 1726, Palmer Recording District." Official title passed via an impressive, artsy warrant deed. Mine is number 1068 and was issued on May 20, 1987, duly signed by Lavon Barve, Iditarod Trail Committee president, at the time, and Joe Redington, Sr., "Father of the Iditarod," and notarized by Violet E. Redington, notary public, bearing a gold corporate seal of the ITC, and certified by McKinley Title and Trust, Inc (see Appendix VIII, Redington Land Deed).

21

Helping Hands

Dody Nesbit of Tulsa, Oklahoma, a personification of the Iditarod Race Volunteer Corps. For 15 years she kept a cold, lonely vigil on night shift at the Nome dog lot. Here she mushes a team in northern Minnesota. (Photo: Dody Nesbit)

The word "volunteer" is synonymous with success where modern Iditarods are concerned. That vital necessity had its beginnings with the First Great Race. It makes no difference if we are talking a fifty-thousand-dollar budget race in 1973 or the modern multimillion-dollar budgeted race, its success hinges on our volunteer corps. Nowadays, volunteers number around eighteen-hundred strong, coming from virtually all over the globe.

The importance of those pioneer race volunteers cannot be overemphasized. Some two hundred homegrown Alaskans from all walks of life and conditions gave freely, generously of time, money, machines, knowledge, and enthusiasm in support of a few nutty mushers who wanted to drive dog teams to Nome. Had it not been for those dedicated, true believers volunteering their all toward a successful culmination of that first race, the whole show would have resulted in a big flop. We, in all probability, would not be nudging into five decades of Iditarod today.

Whenever a list of persons to be thanked or recognized for parts played in any event, the danger of omission lurks. To my knowledge, there was never a complete accounting made of 1973 volunteers. Although unfortunate, it was inevitable due to the far-flung nature of our event and self-effacing nature of most pioneer volunteers. Native checkers, for example, in the many villages visited by the race, didn't care for the limelight, didn't want it. They volunteered to assist the race, while serving as village goodwill ambassadors. Those unsung and now mostly forgotten folks made us welcome. They found us housing and dog food. They fixed sleds and patched our wounds. When asked, they gave invaluable advice on local trails and weather. Villagers and miners alike treated us as visiting dignitaries with a generous hospitality customarily given dog team travelers of Old Alaska. Those warmhearted Alaskans were our life support system, extending over one thousand miles of rugged and unforgiving Alaskan terrain.

Many first race volunteers are, of course, known. Many have, by now, snuggled comfortably into race history. Logically, the first volunteers and cause of it all were members of the original race committee and close associates. The visionary people: Joe Redington, Sr., Tom Johnson, and Gleo Huyck. Closely associated with this core was Vi Redington, seemingly a most willing partner in most of Joe's schemes, myself, as history buff, friend to Tom, Gleo, and the Redingtons, and coming in the back door, so to speak, via Aurora Dog Mushers Club. Other club members who were contributors of ideas and plans, as memory allows, were Dave Olson, Bill Cotter, and Joel Kotke.

With this core, there emerged a plan, a concept really, of a Big One, a long-distance sled dog race of the dream weavers. With the decision to go ahead and organize a race came the sobering reality—how? Though out of character, lofty-minded Tom Johnson, at one of our meetings, posed the question, "How in the world will we ever pull this thing off?" A bunch of ideas and suggestions were offered amid a goodly portion of friendly banter. It was agreed that to sell the race, it would be necessary to get all sorts of people emotionally involved. Get them to volunteer, to buy into the race. Joe, Sr., never one to think small, brought our task down to nutshell simplicity when he stated, "We have to get the whole darn state involved."

This was our message: Look out, Alaska, here we come. We are going to buttonhole you and ask for your help. We believe in our product, now we want you to believe, too. To become involved in our dream. You, the musher, politician, lawyer, army, air force, event organizer, banker, merchant, recreationist, publicist, publisher, miner, villager, pilot, radioman, and a myriad of others, are needed. Together, we can relive our glorious past and provide something positive for Alaska's future. Without you, all is lost and we are doomed to failure.

That was our basic approach in rounding up volunteers for the first race. It was an easy sell. Be the motive for joining us that of reliving an illustrious history or to get in on the ground floor of something exciting, or both, folks signed up in abundance. Many remained willingly ensnared for life in the race's volunteer web.

Beyond volunteer committee members and their close allies, the next recruit list was made up of those willing to assist with a thousand and one organizational chores being undertaken by the committee. Again, keep in mind, the decision for a race was made in October 1972. Soon after, race day was set for the first Saturday, March 3, 1973. Organizers had only five fleeting months, at best, to put it all together. A prodigious amount of work was performed in short order. To my knowledge, no list of things to do was ever compiled. No master plan developed. The first race was organized and run by common sense, seat-of-the-pants methods. Each active committee member agreed to undertake and oversee specific tasks, recruiting volunteers for the job. Every day brought a new crop of hurdles to surmount, crises to handle, problems to solve, and the clock kept running.

It was considered necessary to establish race headquarters in Anchorage and begin our event there as well. Anchorage provided more spectators, more volunteers, more potential sponsors, more of you-name-it than any other starting point. We had discussed a Knik Lake start, but feared we would draw very few fans and spectators to such a remote location. There was also the matter of a prerace banquet, where mushers traditionally drew for starting positions, met one another, and mingled with race fans. Those kinds of problems were solved when managers of the Gold Rush Hotel volunteered three rooms for use as a headquarters and provided a banquet room as well. Volunteers were set to work organizing headquarters and arranging the banquet.

Since we dived into the affair with no real planning budget and a negligible treasury, it was of utmost importance to chase down every dollar possible. Fund-raising and public-awareness building were inseparable. The hope was public awareness would equate with financial support for our event. Steve Schmirnof, Anchorage public relations consultant, came aboard to generate as much race excitement as possible through state media, newspapers in particular. Radio was important, generally using an interview format to disseminate race information to listeners. I have no recall or file items relative to the use of TV to spread the word. We hadn't gotten started, much less "arrived," where TV was concerned. Another name in connection with fund-raising and promotion is that of Terry Aglietti, an Anchorage attorney who gave able and certainly needed advice while getting us legally incorporated and keeping our lottery "on the level." Schmirnof and Aglietti started as hires to be paid "later." This arrangement, due to lack of payment, resulted in both evolving into donor/volunteers in support of the race.

At every turn, a discovery was made, calling for more volunteers. In a sense, the largest single group of volunteers was the mushers. Not the hundreds predicted, but a much more modest thirty-four who signed up for the race. Volunteers were needed to correspond with, find transportation and housing for, and generally accommodate dog drivers and their teams arriving in Anchorage. Several mushers from off-the-road system showed up at the airport with not much more than themselves, dogs, and sled.

Elected officials of the Municipality of Anchorage had to be convinced that an Iditarod Race would be a plus for the community. That expenses incurred for snow hauling, traffic control, sanitation, and other public facilities somehow would be worth it all. Dog races through Anchorage were, in fact, old hat. The World Championship sprint race had, by 1973, a nearly two-decade history as the paramount feature of the annual Anchorage Fur Rendezvous winter celebration. The general attitude of city officials was, "Oh well, it's just another dog race, let's go for it."

When attention turned to the actual trail between Anchorage and Nome, and the task of physically driving dog teams along the route, the absolute necessity of volunteer help became apparent. Had we bit off more than could be chewed? This race would be through a thousand-plus miles of remote wilderness—hundred-mile stretches that were uninhabited. Lonely mining locations and decaying roadhouses of a bygone era. In places, mushers would be three hundred miles from the next phone. Places where temperatures of minus forty, fifty, or sixty degrees F were commonly recorded and one human error could eliminate all future prospects. The route coursed its way from Anchorage to Knik, Susitna drainage through a high pass in the Alaska Range, Rohn to Ruby, down the Yukon River to Kaltag, Kaltag to Unalakleet on the Bering Sea, and the final three hundred miles of windswept Bering Sea coast to the finish line in Nome. Much of the trail route had been left unused for decades and lost to modern travelers. We definitely were going to need help. Tom Johnson's earlier question seemed apropos: "How in the world will we ever pull this thing off?"

Organizational challenges seemed endless. We needed a location and personnel to start the race in Anchorage, route and road crossing personnel north around Knik Arm to Knik itself. Checkpoints along the entire route were essential for convenience, but mostly for musher safety. Tons of dog food, people food, and supplies of all kinds had to be distributed. Some sort of communications system setup was necessary. Transport of race officials along the trail and evacuation of possible disabled mushers and their canine charges demanded consideration. Racers' arrival at Nome, if indeed they did arrive, created yet another set of challenges, all begging for more volunteers. Race organizers expected Nome folk to blithely provide for race officials, mushers, dogs, and all associates. There was also the matter of a finishers' banquet.

Nome residents came through admirably for the first Iditarod. Everyone, including fans associated with the event, was made welcome in the "City of Gold," and treated as if visiting dignitaries. Mushers, for sure, were. One grand banquet wouldn't do. Every musher was a hero of the trail and deserved a banquet. Consequently, several were held as "Kings of the North" trickled down Front Street over a nearly two-week period. Many fine race traditions observed to this day were initiated by race volunteers of Nome, beginning with the first race in 1973.

It appears the closer one was to Anchorage and its various media centers—newspapers, radio, television—the more aware the general public became of one's part as a volunteer. Take, for example, fellows such as Dick Tozier and Joel Kotke. Both were well-known figures in sprint-racing circles as participants as well as various officiating capacities. That they should become race marshal and race judge, respectively, for of-all-things a slow, long-distance race, is decidedly newsworthy. Subscribers all over the state learned of those two prestigious volunteers from articles published in Anchorage's two daily papers. Naturally, given the importance of their duties, Tozier, Kotke, and others, who were involved intimately with affairs of the race for its duration, got the most press.

A thorough account of Iditarod Race founders and volunteers would have been impossible without inclusion of John Norman. I had the pleasure of engaging Norman in a telephone interview during January of 2011. This was done more to confirm what I already knew of his vital role in creation of the Iditarod than to gain new information.

In the early 1970s, that quiet, studious man had just begun a lifelong Anchorage legal practice. He, like so many of us, became involved with the first race through an innocent interest in sled dogs and mushing. John told me, "I did some mushing with Con Bunde, who, of course, knew Joe, Sr., who contacted me for free legal work for the infant organization."

And work he did. "I took over the incorporation process from Terry Aglietti. But my biggest job was damage control. I handled various legal matters resulting from the first race, such as unpaid bills, suits, and threats of suits." Norman stated. John Norman did it all for free.

To this day, John Norman is an Iditarod volunteer. In 1976, he established the Iditarod Trail Race Foundation, a legal entity, completely separated from the Iditarod Trail Committee. The foundation's chief purpose is to pad the race against financial disaster by providing emergency loans to the race committee. The idea of such a foundation was, according to Norman, "Prompted by four hundred anti-race letters to the *New York Times* and a consequent pull-out of Arco as a major sponsor." He was an original incorporator of that race-saver organization and continues to serve as secretary for its five-person board of directors. John Norman is an Iditarod lifer. Dedication comes in no greater measure.

The world had heard of, and maybe history has recorded names like Tozier, Kotke, Redington, Wilmarth, and maybe even me. Few, however, had an acquaintance with the likes of Tex Gates, a miner at interior Alaska's Bear Creek. On the heels of our snowmachiners, I and other front-runners arrived at Bear Creek, unexpected, unannounced. Race checkers were unable to get to the mine to oversee the race passing through. Ever have thirty to forty unexpected strangers drop in on you? Strangers who asked for and expected to get food for each person, and for scores of dogs, plus heated housing, snowmachine repairs, and fuel to get them on up the trail? Tex and his wife did. Out of the clear blue, the race began to arrive. One can only speculate on the outcome of the race had Tex Gates refused to become an Iditarod Race insta-volunteer. There are many fascinating stories involving unsung volunteer heroes resulting from the first race. People all across Alaska doing what needed to be done to make it happen. Tex, I don't remember if I even thanked you way back then for the rescue. I do now.

Volunteerism, Iditarod style, has come a long way over the years. The number of people who volunteered for race number one, in 1973, is estimated to be "around two hundred." The volunteer force grew to a whopping 1,800 for race number thirty-nine, in 2011. Basic needs, however, have remained essentially the same: Start and finish personnel, race officials to conduct the race itself, transportation, communication, housing, and dog care. The same needs, but on a much grander level. An example serves to illustrate. For the first Iditarod, we employed one volunteer veterinarian, Dr. Terry Adkins, who was actually on loan from the air force. Adkins, who would later carve an impressive Iditarod racing career, covered the entire one-thousand-plus-mile race course by means of a volunteer plane flown by a volunteer pilot. Today, the Iditarod Trail Committee hires a chief veterinarian, who oversees up to forty, mostly volunteer, vets along the same extent of trail. With the first race, both the volunteer vet corps and what would become a thirty-plane volunteer Iditarod air force were launched.

Motives of Iditarod Race volunteers have always fascinated me. Why? Why does a person, at great cost in physical comfort, not to mention fortune, willingly, happily, indeed eagerly, sign up to become one of the chosen eighteen hundred? Present-day volunteer extraordinaire, Dody Nesbit, a Tulsa, Oklahoma, educator, personifies such an individual. She is a true blue, diehard Iditarod volunteer. A perpetuator of that let's-make-it-happen spirit set in motion by those, long ago, first race supporters. As astonishing as it may seem, she has been among the select for the past fifteen years.

Nesbit first became smitten with Alaska in the early 1990s, when she ventured north to volunteer at the Fairbanks Environmental Center. She fell head over heels for the Great Land that summer. Alaska continued to brew in her mind, but being a high school counselor, a job she loved above all others, precluded a permanent move north. Then one day, while thumbing through an outdoor magazine, she ran across a diminutive ad encouraging her to become an "Iditarod volunteer."

Problem was, the ad did not come equipped with a phone number. So, by enlisting help from a long-distance operator, Dody was placed in contact with one of the two remaining residents of the near ghost town of Iditarod. No, they really didn't need volunteers there, she was informed. She was given the Wasilla phone number for the Iditarod Trail Committee, who, her informant revealed, is always in need of free help. In contacting personnel at race headquarters, Nesbit made it amply clear she did not want to volunteer for just any job. She wanted to work with the sled dogs. Period! Yes, that was possible, she learned, there was an opening for the Nome dog lot starting the second week in March. That was the summer of 1995.

Every second week in March, beginning in 1996, with the exception of one, due to a hiking accident, Nesbit has made an annual pilgrimage north, to the Nome dog lot. She has paid her own travel, her own board and room, and shelled out for decidedly necessary Arctic clothing, of no use in Oklahoma. To put the frosting on the cake, the time given so freely to the Iditarod is her hard-earned spring break vacation from school, with a few personal leave days thrown in when necessary. This sprightly, captivating woman donates it all, plus sixteen years of accumulated knowledge and hard-earned experience to the race "for the dogs."

She likes the dog lot night shift best of all. Looking after scores of canine veterans just off the trail from Anchorage is fulfilling. She assigns bed-down locations to incoming teams. She pays special attention to the few who may be under veterinarian care, while keeping a sharp lookout for unwelcome strays, both human and canine. Dody never sleeps during the long night's duty. Anyway, how could she? A constant wind whips through the block-long dog lot, lying as it does beside the Bering Sea, stirring up the minus twenty degrees temperatures into a flesh-freezing unpleasantness. No lounging there. An unheated windbreak offers little in the way of enticement to linger. Nesbit keeps moving in order to keep "kind of warm" during her all-night vigil among the huskies.

During our mid-January 2011 interview, I asked Dody, "Why do you, winter upon winter, end up on graveyard shift, volunteering for a duty most of us wouldn't perform for all the tea in China?"

Without a second's hesitation, she exclaimed, "I do it for the dogs. I love the dogs. When I am alone with all those wonderful animals, I feel grounded. My spirituality is grounded. I look at the whole business as an exercise in commitment."

Commitment, indeed. Seventy-six years of age at the time of our interview, this remarkable lady would put many a younger folk to shame with her future-oriented zest for life. A life she cannot imagine without her once-a-year fix of Iditarod sled dogs in her care at Nome. To my query as to how much longer she planned to continue her volunteer service to the race came her casual response, "Oh, until I turn ninety-nine."

Dody Nesbit and hundreds of her devoted confederates give assurance of a future for the Iditarod Trail Sled Dog Race. They confirm that the spirit of giving, born of the first 1973 race, is alive and doing quite well after four decades of "The Iditarod."

22

Can We Get There From Here?

Army to race rescue. General Charles Gettys on trail inspection tour (fourth from left). Col. "Muktuk" Marston (fifth from left) race benefactor accompanied him. (Photo: Terry Adkins)

From the musher standpoint, perhaps most prerace anguish had to do with trail matters. Specifically, was there going to be a trail on which to run? If so, how will the thing be marked? What will it be like going through the Alaska Range? Down the mighty Yukon River? How can a trail possibly be kept up on Norton Sound, where hurricane-force winds and driven snow could roll a dog team into a tangled ball? Mushers were keenly interested in all prerace information regarding the alleged trail and its reported volunteers. For mushers close to the inner circle of preparations, the word "skeptical" should be added to the "keenly interested" bit. Given Joe, Sr.'s propensity for media bluster, it was justified.

From Files: (News clipping, January 1, 1973. Volunteers Blaze Route on Iditarod Race Trail)

> With the thousand-mile Iditarod Trail Classic less than sixty days away, the task of preparing and marking the trail has begun in earnest with hundreds of volunteers across the state lending a helping hand.
>
> Primarily, the race sponsors want to make certain that the trail is clearly marked between all of the 18 checkpoints along the route…
>
> The preparation of the trail is of considerable importance, according to Dick Tozier, the recently appointed race marshal and longtime supporter of sled dog racing… "We are making sure that every foot of that trail is marked." According to Tozier, more than two hundred persons will be involved as officials during the race itself… Joe Redington, chairman of the Iditarod Trail Committee, has spent dozens of hours in the air surveying the route, then returning to the scene with dog sleds to break and mark the trail. "We are responsible for every man and every dog that's on the trail… and it is a responsibility that we take very seriously. Several hundred entries from Alaska, other states, and Canada are expected."

At the time the above article made its appearance, several mushers, including Joe Sr. (as time allowed), Ron Aldrich, Dick Mackey, and I were having quite a go at locating, clearing, and marking the trail between Knik and Susitna Station, some twenty-five to thirty miles. This was a minute distance when considering the length of the whole trail. Nonetheless, it was exhausting, frustrating work. "How in the world, with only two months remaining, could volunteers possibly have over one thousand miles of trail ready for use?" That question was asked often among us as we labored over our short local section.

But the wheels of trail progress had begun to turn. Backing up to the winter of 1972, a snowmachine party of four Anchorage men became the first known snowmobilers to travel from Anchorage to Nome via Ptarmigan Pass (Hell's Gate.) In 1973, the intrepid Sam Bowman, member of the 1972 trek, organized another machine trip in the hope of traversing the Alaska Range by way of the much more challenging Rainy Pass route. In addition to Bowman, Rich Holsema, Bob Groeneweg, and Art Dittbrender, all Anchorage residents, made up the adventurer's club. Joe, Sr. had a finger in this endeavor, as he did with most all aspects of first race planning. He agreed to fly cover for the machine expedition. Yes, Joe had a private plane, too. That arrangement was in exchange for breaking out Rainy Pass ahead of the race. By that means, the Iditarod gained five more volunteer workers.

That party of snowmachiners took off for the pass during the waning days of January. A February 23, 1973 news article reveals that with a week to go before the race start, only twenty-three mushers had plunked down their one-hundred-dollar entry fee. And that a route change was necessary. Mushers would be going through Ptarmigan Pass after all. An earlier snowmachine expedition (Bowman's) failed in its attempt to reach and breach the four-thousand-foot Rainy Pass, due to extraordinary snow depth.

We were not yet "dead in the water," to quote a nautical expression. Enter nothing less than the United States Army, Fort Richardson, Alaska. Race committee members contacted Major General Charles M. Gettys, who was commander of all army forces in Alaska. "Was there any way to get the army involved? We are in desperate need of trail-breaking volunteers. In particular, for work on those sections not traveled and maintained since the 1930s." On first thought, it may strike the uninformed as a preposterous idea, thinking the military, the federal government, could, much less would, assist a civilian endeavor. That endeavor, when all is said and done, boiled down to a fun and games opportunity for a very few sled dog enthusiasts. Not so. As with all the frontiers in our nation's fulfillment of Manifest Destiny, the military had been assigned to protect civilian persons and property since the earliest days of the republic. Alaska, "the last frontier," was no different. Following its purchase by the United States from Russia, the new acquisition, one-fifth the size of all the rest of the country, was placed under the Federal War Department. There it remained in control by the army between the years of 1867 and 1877. Since then, the military has been an important feature in development of the Territory and State of Alaska. Be it trail and road construction, telegraph lines, radio stations, law enforcement, disaster relief, search and rescue, or a host of other activities, Alaskan civilians have undeniably profited from having the military in their midst.

In view of the above, it was not surprising that no one cried collusion, or accused the trail committee and army of being in cahoots, when it was publicly announced on February 22, 1973, one week before race time, that the army was planning a winter maneuver from Fort Richardson in Anchorage to Nome. In the spirit of cavalry to the rescue, Major General Gettys saw an opportunity to assist a civilian enterprise while accomplishing a military objective. He set the wheels in motion.

Gettys soon revealed that on February 26, four days prior to race kickoff, twenty members of the 172 Arctic Light Infantry Brigade, stationed at Fort Richardson, would begin a training run to Nome. General Gettys stated that plans for such an exercise had been in the works for months, that the team would be driving twin-track snowmachines and be commanded in the field by Captain Harry F. Lockhart. A fourteen-day completion was estimated. By this means, General Gettys, in fine military fashion, volunteered twenty "volunteers" who, as we would soon discover, turned out to be—well, the cavalry to our rescue.

Like Bowman's earlier party, deep, loose snow of Rainy Pass forced the army to divert the trail through Ptarmigan Pass, which lengthened the distance to Nome by about thirty miles. That Captain Lockhart and troops arrived in Nome was truly an important factor in the success of the race. A trail route had been established and a trail base laid down, greatly easing our passage to Front Street, Nome.

As important as the army's contribution was, even more so was that of trailbreakers from the inhabited locations along the trail, such as McGrath, Ruby, Kaltag, and Unalakleet, who saw to it that local, and often untraveled stretches of trail, were marked and otherwise made ready for the race. Bearing in mind that the army team was about a week ahead of the front-running dog teams, when Mother Nature tricked us with something more cruel than a simple practical joke. On the heels of military trailbreakers, over the vast expanse between McGrath and Ruby, came a fierce, most inconveniently timed winter storm. Two feet of new snow fell. Strong winds stacked it shoulder deep on open, treeless sections of the trail, completely erasing all evidence that Uncle Sam's army had passed that way just a few days before. As the storm subsided, skies cleared, and a newly whitened world was bathed in brilliant sunshine by day and partial moonlight by night. The bottom fell out of the thermometer, stopping in the minus fifty degrees F range. We front-runners in particular would have been in a world of hurt had the race committee not provided us with an "ace in the hole."

Again, volunteers came to the rescue. Civilian snowmachiners this time, in the persons of Carl Fritzler, Don Rosevear, Bill Copeland, Bob Stone, and Joe Smith, who got talked into breaking trail. Their job was to stay ahead of the leading dog teams from Knik Lake, on to Nome. That job would become monumental. The storm that wiped out the track laid down by Captain Lockhart's team south of Ruby would have to be reestablished at civilian expense in toil and perseverance. Of the five men, Bob Stone, driving a used Scorpion machine, was destined to arrive in Nome ahead of race winner, Dick Wilmarth. He, Joe Smith, and Bill Copeland had the dubious honor of getting us through no-man's land, south of Ruby, before they quit. Fritzler and Rosevear, both Mat-Su Valley drivers, experienced machine breakdowns, benching them early in the game. I will have more to say in another place about how it was Stone, Smith, and Copeland, for several days, held the fate of our inaugural race in their hands.

Eight days after the race started in Anchorage, on Sunday, March 11, the second annual Nenana to Nome Snowmachine Race began its seven-hundred-mile charge down the Tanana River toward Nome. There were nine teams of four machines each, representing a pretty fair cross-section of both Alaskans and machinery available in those early years. These pioneer motor heads wound their way down the frozen Tanana and Yukon Rivers to Ruby. There they joined the dog trail coming up from the south. From Ruby, motor teams ran down the Yukon to Kaltag, over the Kaltag Portage, and on into Nome. Machines and dogs ran generally a common trail. Most machiners had completed the course in about five days, well ahead of the front-running dog teams' arrival at Ruby. The point being, drivers in the mechanized event benefited the trailing dog mushers by running their machines over sections of the trail. This was most evident on the ninety-mile portage between Kaltag on the Yukon and Unalakleet on Norton Sound's shore. Worthy of mention is that these early 1970s snowmachine races would become precursors to the now famous annual Iron Dog Snowmachine Race, run between Big Lake, Alaska, and Nome. In 2011, organizers announced a $90,000.00 purse for that motor extravaganza.

23

Diving In

First Seavey long distance race team training for the "Big One," 1973. Many will follow, driven by other members of the clan over the next 40 years. Leaders L-R: Kiana and sister Eska.

After that fateful October 1972 decision, spurred on by Gleo Huyck and Tom Johnson to proceed in earnest with the "Big One," my involvement with the race committee inner workings waned considerably. I turned, instead, to preparations necessary for entering my team in that totally captivating event.

Where to start? Only five months remained in which to accomplish all tasks necessary for arrival at the race start line. There were other concerns, too. Would my wife approve? Her life most certainly would become more complicated and demanding with my lengthy absence from home. How would the kids do? Could we truthfully afford this thing financially? Besides, I had a job. I was under contract to teach through mid-May 1973. How in the world could I realistically walk out of the classroom for a month or more and expect that job to be waiting upon my return? Fears and doubts flooded in.

However, what an opportunity for a once-in-a-lifetime adventure. A chance to truly go somewhere consequential, somewhere distant by dog team. What a thrill it would be to soak in the very essence of a trail known only vicariously through book and legend. How overpowering the thought: To ride runners over a pioneer's boulevard, where august spirits of old time dog men sit in watch. Here was an occasion where all the noble qualities of a noble animal could be demonstrated to an ever-growing remote and mechanized world. Dare I hope that such an event would excite a renewed interest in the historic trail? That my adopted hometown, indeed all the communities along the way, would begin anew, an appreciative relationship with that heritage treasure? Yes, I just had to do it. There could never be another first Iditarod Race, and for that matter, the first could well be the last.

One by one, early obstacles lying between Nome and myself were overcome. My wife Shirley, who had been hearing about the Big One for a couple years by then, gave her resigned but wholehearted support, not only to the idea but to the preparations as well. The children were excited at the thought of the race. They expressed an eagerness to chip in and help out with additional work and shoulder new responsibilities brought about by their father's latest bright idea. Even our financial picture wasn't all that glum. Close scrutiny by Shirley and me of income versus outflow, occasioned by estimated race expenses, revealed that things were going to be—well, a bit tight. But if we could raise a few hundred dollars in cash to support our race effort and if we had a decent commercial fishing season the next summer, we could manage even with a couple months' loss of teacher's salary. Also, there could be some prize money forthcoming. A final, but formidable hurdle still remained, however.

Offhand, I do not recall the exact process entailed in procuring a leave of absence (without pay, of course) from the Kenai Peninsula

Borough School District. I do remember raising the topic with my principal, who wasn't a bit more surprised than Shirley that I wanted to run the first Iditarod. I was unprepared, however, for his reaction. He said, "I think it's a good idea! We can justify it from the standpoint you are a social studies teacher." He promised to send my request over to the superintendent in Soldotna with his approval, which I could count on, provided I was able to find a competent substitute to cover my classes at Seward High. My next breath, I remember, was one of relief. So committed was I by that stage that I was willing to tender my resignation on the spot and let the chips fall where they may. I was going to drive a dog team to Nome come hell or high water.

In due time, a letter from our superintendent arrived, which granted leave from mid-February to mid-March 1973. One month. My teaching duties fell into the very capable and experienced hands of Dorothy Knighten, a family friend since her arrival in Seward a few years prior with husband, Keith, who took up his duties with the coast guard, and young sons, Kimo and Gilbert. Dorothy had substituted for me many times, generally while I traveled with the Seward Seahawk wrestlers. Her presence in my classroom during the race was a source of certainty that learning would progress in an enjoyable, productive fashion.

By December of 1972, race preparations had taken on true meaning out at the Seavey homestead. A nonbeliever could have justifiably doubted the race's inevitability right up to its March 3 start date. But there were no doubting Thomases at the Seavey place. We forged ahead with hearts of true believers.

It would be a stretch to state that Seward is a dog mushing paradise, because it isn't. Marine (soggy) climate and rugged, mountainous terrain conspire to keep even the most "doggy" of mushers in a constant state of anxious frustration over snow and trail conditions on the few, relatively short trails available to them. Since I had the only team on the Eastern Kenai Peninsula during that decade prior to the first race, I can state with certainty that there was no such thing as off-season cart training. The kids had a couple cobbled-together contraptions that saw little use. So I did sled training predominantly. I waited out with gritted teeth the rainy fall season. I tolerated emotional ups and downs of late autumn's cat and mouse games of now you have snow, now you don't. Finally, around Thanksgiving time, snow visited with intent to stay a while. Jack Frost huffed and puffed frigid air, mostly from the northwest, turning lake and river surfaces to dog team thoroughfares. In the case of beautiful Kenai Lake, eighteen miles north of Seward, he folded back a wintry curtain, welcoming teams and drivers to the very heart of Alaska's magnificent Kenai Peninsula. As in years past, I checked the thermometer out the back window, looked at the sky, and hoped it would be an early winter. "Please, God, this of all your winters, can you send this one a bit early?"

Not that there wasn't plenty to do without snow and frozen trails. I took a long, hard, critical look at the twenty-five or so dogs in my kennel. Which were too young, old, or lazy to warrant spending my very limited time training? What sort of performance records do those who survived my first cut have? By consulting my shoebox file system, determinations were made, which reduced my "lucky dog list" to fifteen individuals who would hit the training trail, come snow.

Author frolicking with Kiana. Only 2 years of age, she led most of my first race. Her sweet disposition was equal only to her rawhide toughness.

A perusal of breeding records brought me up short. I expected most animals on my lucky dog list to be products of my own exacting selection program, dating back to Chignik II, and many of the better arrant rascals saved from a dogcatchers noose some eight or ten years previous. Not so. When the final dozen "Nome dogs" were subjected to a thorough parental accounting, just one, Crazy by name, went to Nome bearing a questionable birth certificate. Poor dog. Even the first part of his entry in my Dog Diary was rather dreary: "Crazy, male. No background, received for board bill. First used 1971 -1972 season (1 ½ years of age est.) 1973 and 1974 Iditarod races – very good. Sold to Jerry Mercer 7/76." The fact that all other eventual Nome dogs were direct descendants from proven stock goes to demonstrate the value of a thoughtful breeding program. All remaining eleven were direct products of breeding assistance from kennels of well-known Alaskan greats, Earl Norris and Joe Redington, Sr. Likewise, three of my very best to reach Nome came from crossings with animals owned and driven by former Chistochina musher, Dick Gilliand.

In my son Mitch's recent book, *Lead, Follow, or Get Out of the Way*, starting with tried and proven stock is emphasized:

> That's one of my big gripes with some kennels. A new guy comes along, just getting started, and they dump dogs on him that are not going to help him, dogs that will retard the development of his kennel, and may discourage the guy so bad he doesn't stick with it. Meanwhile, the new musher feeds these critters for a year or more before he even figures it out. It's even worse when they do it to junior mushers.
>
> "This isn't much of a dog, but he will be good for a junior team." That's the perfect way to discourage the future of our sport. Put a young musher on a long race with poor dogs and tell them to go have fun. If anyone doesn't need to have worries about the performance of the dogs in the team it's a junior musher. [Pg. 24]

Another early autumn concern was that of canine nutrition, in particular, just how and what to feed dogs in training for the Nome trek. So much about the first Iditarod was a trail-breaking effort, an experimental belief in past attainments mixed with a good dose of foolhardiness. Old time dog-men quietly worked on trails, managed dog teams, and generally left little in the way of how-to-do-it manuals. To my knowledge, there had never been, in all of history, a sled dog race of Iditarod magnitude. So the question remained: "How does one feed a dog for and during a one-thousand-mile race?" I didn't know. No one knew. We all had unproven ideas sticking out our ears. Perhaps the one agreed upon understanding was an everyday diet for a working dog would, in the end, be grossly inadequate. Available were fifty-pound bags containing Friskies for $3.10, Don's for the same, Purina at $4.50, or the king of dog food for the time was Iams at $6.25. That was about it. I know of no serious endurance racer nowadays who would even consider feeding any of the above foods. Not for off-season maintenance, and definitely not for serious work. Mushers now prefer, at around $50.00 per forty-pound sack, the modern, super foods scientifically compounded with high-performance nutrition, which partially justifies the price. These super foods, I am sorry to report, have been judged by the grueling demands of the nine- to ten-day Iditarods and found wanting. At this writing, there is not a single, ten-thousand-plus-calorie diet per day that gets a top twenty finisher's team to Nome. All must be shored up with natural canine fare, such as red meat, fat, and fish.

Back to the dietary no-man's land, my dog lot of 1972. Frankly, my dogs had been fed just about every food imaginable: Bear, moose, porcupines, caribou, horse, deer, chicken, varieties of fish, Friskies, Don's, Purina, Iams, you name it. In the end, for both training and racing, we decided on a Purina base, with the oiliest fresh fish available, augmented in cold weather by beef fat. Given my level of knowledge and what was available, it seemed right. Previously, many of my Nome dogs had stood up well to demands of extended winter expeditions on such fare. But ten to fifteen days, seventy to eighty miles per day in race mode? Well, I figured I should have an inkling by the time training was complete just how suitable that diet would be.

Norman Rockwell, the famed American illustrator of a bygone era, created a wonderful depiction of a typical family, piled into the family car, loaded obviously for a family vacation. Off they went, the family home in the background made to appear quite bedraggled, tired. In his second illustration of the set, the family returned. Everyone appeared worn out, done in, ready to be home. And the family house took on the appearance of a new, happy, welcoming castle-like dwelling. As I sorted through my "dog gear" in the way of an assessment that last Saturday of October, I chuckled at the similarities. Before being bitten by the Iditarod bug, my gear was fine, okay. It got the job done, like Rockwell's house. Now, being off on a vacation with my dog team, my gear looked bedraggled, and sad. Lists were begun: Repair items. Replacement articles. Old Oak, my main, old faithful sled would have to stay home. I needed to build a new, flashier "Iditarod sled." Look at those harnesses, nothing but a pile of rags. Order new ones. Every item, from snow hook to collar snaps, was held up to scrutiny in light of its fitness for the Iditarod journey.

Our pickup truck, a 1968 yellow Dodge Power Wagon, served as the dog truck and didn't warrant but a moment's reflection. It ran well and had carted dogs, mushers, and equipment all over south and north central Alaska. For the time, it was pretty standard. Home built plywood, flat roofed box, somehow painted green. Ugly green. Affixed to the interior of this box was a continuous tethering chain to which traveling dogs were snapped. By laying a sheet of heavy plywood inside the box and atop the sides, an additional tier of critters was accommodated for a total of up to eighteen. Sleds and gear went above on the roof. In 1973, most dog trucks answered closely to the above description. Today, it is a whole different scene. Forty-thousand-dollar pickups sporting ten-thousand-dollar dog boxes are common. Folks would think I had been towed in from Slumsville if I were to show up at a present-day sled dog event with the likes of my first race dog truck.

Clothing, too, came under pre-training season investigation. But not much. At the time, I believed myself to be well haberdashed, thank you! My haberdashery was 5th Ave. Army-Navy Surplus Store in Anchorage. I had, however, splurged the past winter and ordered a forty-sixty rip stop nylon, down-filled parka from REI in Seattle, red in color. It needed a fur ruff, another item for my "to get" list. I probably didn't have more than three hundred dollars in the whole kit and caboodle, unlike the nearly fifteen-hundred-dollar Northern Outfitters "cold weather system" that I purchased prior to my 1997 Iditarod.

And, I hasten to add, discarded a few days before race start in favor of my old, familiar layers of musher's togs.

Thinking back, I cannot fathom how on God's green earth I got every necessary thing done. Responsibilities, commitments, family, home, teaching, coaching, church. "Oh, to be young again." Amid it all, I somehow found time to work myself out with weights, run, and wrestle. I also revisited, for the umpteenth time, old Iditarod Trail literature in my possession, memorizing various terrain features and, with the aid of topographic maps of the route, fixing the country in my mind to the extent possible. I began to think of means of raising money to lessen the race's economic shock to the family purse. And, of course, I talked up the Iditarod to anyone who would listen, or pretend to, as the case may be, local and peninsula civic groups mostly.

Nowadays, one hears frequent reference to an enumeration referred to as a "honey do" list. I have had friends point to this item with a staged fear and trembling, occasioned in the old days only by the approach of a hangman or perhaps the undertaker himself. It has been employed to abort the best laid plans for a weekend of fishing and weeklong hunting trips up north. I had one. It seemed to grow and become more persistent as days drifted away and the race grew closer. Only my list didn't have the romantic ring of "honey do." In reality, it was a "you need to get these things done if you want to run that race" list! Omitting details, my assigned tasks, I am sure, included most all those that fellows around the country get assigned prerequisite to weekend football games. To my list was added cut, haul, split, and stack eight to ten cords of firewood, and haul about as many thousands of pounds of dog food fish from Seward Fisheries to our walk-in freezer.

24

Don't Hit the Trail Without It

Tether chain, an essential piece of equipment for early Iditarod Racers. Now, thankfully, replaced by steel cable towline that does it all.

November 1972 rolled into December and the pace at the Seavey place quickened. The woodpile grew. Fish got hauled. Faucets fixed and weather stripping placed as bulwarks against those miniature but persistent Arctic invaders. Catalogs were studied as if knowledge of their contents would determine success of one's college finals.

Orders were placed. Orders were eagerly received. Piece by piece, my Iditarod "outfit" was assembled, contributing to a growing heap in a basement corner.

As it turned out, my trail-ready pack for both the first and second Iditarod races weighed an estimated one hundred and twenty pounds. Experience later deemed many items either superfluous or archaic. Accordingly, the burden was reduced by nearly fifty pounds for my 1997 Iditarod. The 1997 race marked the twenty-fifth anniversary of our event (see Appendix IX, Gear List -1973).

At this writing, the Iditarod Race has entered its fifth decade. It has evolved in many aspects far beyond the imaginations of most of its founders. Mine for sure. Every category of my 1973 gear list has been face-lifted to such an extent as to be but vaguely recognizable today. A few select items serve to demonstrate my point.

Take snowshoes for instance. Mine were the long "trailer" type, heavy hickory wood frames and rawhide (babiche) lacing, weighing six and one-half pounds. Lighter ones could not be found in the common marketplace. George Attla sported a wonderfully light pair made of birch wood by his brother, Robert. To put them on, all he had to do was insert his foot in the binding, twist the snowshoe 360 degrees, and George was set to go. Ingenious. My type are now found mostly adorning cabin walls, replaced by aluminum-framed, synthetic-laced shoes weighing but a few ounces. And, it should be added, rarely used. Twenty race Iditarod veteran, Bill Cotter of Nenana, Alaska, remarked to me once that he hadn't used his snowshoes in nineteen races and he guessed they were still somewhere in the bottom of his sled bag. A statement, no doubt, tongue in cheek, but it illustrates the vast trail improvement in recent years. Without snowshoes, the 1973 race would likely have stalled somewhere south of Poorman. And that may have spelled an end to the whole Iditarod business.

Personal illumination, too, has seen unbelievable improvement. In 1973, my little pocket flashlight, featuring two C-size batteries, was seldom called into service during my twenty-plus days on the trail. Unless you were Dick Wilmarth tailing snowmachines to Nome on your last night of racing, mushers relied almost entirely on natural light, of which there was an abundant fourteen to fifteen hours. For all practical purposes and for as many practical reasons, the race stopped at night to resume come morning. I do not recall a single headlamp being used in 1973. That device is standard equipment now. Because of its universal use, a modern Iditarod race never sleeps. Lithium battery packs with head-mounted space age reflectors and bulbs penetrate the darkness, pushing it aside and driving it beyond a team a hundred yards or more. There can be little doubt that this modern marvel in lighting has been a prime factor in slicing overall race time in half, and then some.

Added to my dogs' burden was a five-and-one-half-pound cassette tape recorder with spare tapes and batteries. I accepted the extra weight and inconvenience because I wanted an audio record of my first race. It was heavy and awkward, but it got the job done, if I kept cold-blooded alkaline batteries warm. Many of today's Iditaroders pack audio devices over the trail, not for the sound they want to put in, rather for the sound those technological masterpieces put out. Diminutive, they fit in a shirt pocket, where they are constantly warmed. Plug in unobtrusive ear buds and away you go. Hour upon hour of one's favorite tunes. Some mushers prefer to have a book read to them as they glide along the Old Iditarod Trail. Total weight? About that of a cell phone.

In time for his 2009 Iditarod Race, my grandson Dallas purchased the most up-to-date dog sled possible. It cost him 4,500 hard-earned dollars. Constructed of aluminum and fiber carbon components, it came equipped with a custom made sled bag, a sit down musher's seat, and a quick change runner plastic system. Away went my old wooden, stand up, bolt on plastic model, together with my clunker snowshoes to the Seward Museum. Four-time race champion, Jeff King, one of the first men to adopt the "lazy boy" sit-down-style sled, figures it has added ten years to his racing career by greatly reducing back strain caused by prolonged standing on the runners of earlier models.

There is yet another bit of early mushing paraphernalia, thankfully gone, namely, the tethering chain. Prominent in the first race and a few more of the earliest, its purpose was to secure an entire dog team off the trail. Mine was made of light, twisted wire chain with short, eight-inch tags affixed along its length every two and one-half feet—twelve dogs, twelve tags. Ends were attached to solid, immoveable objects: sled, tree, bush, or extra snow hook set for that purpose. The notion to use my towline (the one that connects each dog to the sled) to tether the team for the night never entered my mind. Too many times in the past, one or more fish burners decided to play chew toy with the light plastic rope towline, in vogue at that time.

But miracle of miracles, somewhere along the way, racers began to use aircraft tie-down, plastic-coated steel cable for towline set ups. Light, very strong, and not fun on which to chew. Bingo! What an innovation! Another developmental milestone in race history. No more one dog at a time, laborious hookups to a chain secured off the trail. Indeed, no more tethering chain. When a team is stopped for any length of time, the snow hook is set. Then the front of the team is secured by another anchor, usually a second snow hook. Traces (lines running from harness to towline) are unhooked, and that's it. Team secured. Each dog remains fastened to the cable towline by its neckline. Huge, huge savings in time and effort.

Cable towline affords a large measure of protection against injury and even death, which not uncommonly occurred when plastic lines were chewed, releasing perhaps a major portion of the team to fall victim to all manner of unpleasant mishaps. Why, oh why, hadn't someone thought of steel cable towline before our inaugural race?

Three items on the "cut list" by the 1997 race warrant some explanation—the whip, lamp black, and can with paintbrush.

There exists a well-circulated, thus well-known photo of Dick Mackey (a first race veteran), whip in hand, outrunning Rick Swenson to the finish line by one second and, as a consequence, becoming the 1978 champion. A heady picture, sure to excite even the slowest-pulsed member of the Bleeding Hearts Club. Maybe well meaning, but for sure ignorant of the whip's use in modern dog mushing, these "humaniacs" point an accusing finger at one of the most dramatic photos in dog mushing history. Convinced, as they are, that a mother lode of self-incriminating evidence had been discovered, and, for all the world to see, is proof positive of blatant dog abuse condoned by the "Iditarod Race." Hogwash! Whips were banned from the race a few years back without the slightest whimper from competitors. For good reason. In my nearly fifty years of dog mushing, I can truthfully state that I have never witnessed dog abuse by a whip. Like the rattler commonly employed by sprint racers, the whip of our era was essentially a noise-maker. Its sole purpose was to excite the dogs into additional speed, more exertion. Over the course of the past couple decades, race records time after time, have been shattered in absence of a whip. A simple whistle or particular voice sound does the trick.

Perhaps the most dramatic mushing moment ever captured on film. Dick Mackey, pioneer Iditaroder, whip in hand, drives his team to a one second victory over Rick Swenson. Nome, 1978. (Photo: Jeff Schultz Photography)

I carried lamp black (soot) in my sled pack both in 1973 and 1974. Somewhere in my preparatory reading, I had stumbled across an account where, in Arctic exploration, light-colored dogs, those without dark hair about their eyes, had this powdery blackener smeared around their eyes as protection against snow blindness. At the time, it made sense. After all, an item of required musher's gear was sunglasses—for the same reason. I must confess, I carried that darn stuff on the first two races, never once thinking about it or remembering I had it along. Nor have I ever heard of a snow-blinded dog. As for myself, I foolishly went without my "shades" for most of one mostly cloudy day during the first Iditarod, with dire results. I stumbled and fumbled around the White Mountain checkpoint, paying for my less than brilliance with burning eyes and about zero depth perception. I lived and learned.

Finally, why in the world should a paintbrush and tin can show up on a list of necessary gear for dog racing? Let me explain. They were for the benefit of my dogs' feet. Among the folks I pestered for information on dog mushing was Sewardite Ernest Blatchford, who originated in Nome and whose children I taught at Seward High. Blatchford was a quiet, handsome, native man with what seemed a perpetual smile. Ernest had my undivided attention from the moment he let it be known he was the son of Percy Blatchford of Nome's All Alaska Sweepstakes fame. Albeit a Sweepstakes driver in years 1908 through 1911, Blatchford actually made his living, like Leonhard Seppala, driving teams commercially. Sons Ernest and Percy Junior, who also moved from Nome to Seward, assisted their father many times in his work. So when Ernest spoke of neats foot oil and pine tar as an effective dog foot ointment, I listened and took note. It was Blatchford who first made me aware of such things as dog boots or "muttluks" as he humorously called then. Up on the coast, dog boots were made of sealskin and used only when the foot preparation failed to do its job. For the first race, I thought it necessary to carry with me a can to hold the foot ointment and small paintbrush with which to dab dog feet. By the second race, I had smartened up a bit, forsaking the messy paintbrush operation in favor of a neater squeeze bottle application.

Pre-Iditarod Race days were the dark ages of sled dog cart training. I knew no one who actually used a cart of any description to get a jump on the arrival of snow when sled training began. "Four wheelers," all-terrain vehicles, had yet to make their appearance. Therefore, I longingly awaited that most blessed event of the year 1972, our first consequential snowfall. This marvelous, white, lifeblood of the mushing world arrived a few days before Thanksgiving and, as good fortune would have it, resolved to stay until spring. Inland mushers to our north, away from the warming influence of the Gulf of Alaska, predictably, were handed their winter anywhere from two to six weeks earlier. Lucky dogs—guys, too.

From Dog Diary:

> Thanksgiving vacation (from school). Hooked up and ran two small teams up Resurrection River Valley on the day after Thanksgiving. An onlooker would be hard pressed to tell who is more excited, teams or driver. Seven dogs each team. First runs of the season. "Nome, here we come."

Inaugural fun runs over, our training charged forward in an aggressive, progressive manner. All stops were out. Every available minute was snatched and handed over to training. Small five-to-eight-dog teams, on ever-lengthening runs, with increasing amounts of weight being piled onto sleds, were mushed over taxing mountain trails and across lakes and flatlands. Daylight, moonlight, or no light, if an hour, a day, or a vacation was at hand, it was converted to dog team trail miles. More hurriedly than wise, perhaps, small teams were scrutinized, combined, reexamined, and finally boiled down to my twelve "going to Nome" dogs. They, in turn, were put to task during the final weeks before the race. I was satisfied that, in view of the abbreviated prep time available, we had made every one of the 1,100 plus training miles count. Given my personal circumstances, I was as ready as it was humanly possible to be.

25

An Affair

The best support crew this musher ever had.
L-R: Shirley, Darian, Mitch, Tracie, 1973.

Immersed in the entire business of getting me to the start line of the first Iditarod race was my family. My wife, and my personal race director, Shirley, together with eleven-year-old Darian, twelve-year-old daughter, Tracie, and Mitch, halfway into his thirteenth year, all put their shoulders to the wheel in pursuit of my dream. All were my most loyal fans throughout. Each a justifiable reason for pride. Each contributing immensely to what had became a Seavey family affair.

Shirley and I are now into our sixth decade of togetherness and our fifth decade of sled dogs. The undisputed matriarch of the Seavey clan, she has provided a loving acceptance and unfailing calmness of spirit for what is now four generations of Seaveys in Alaska. Our son Darian, with an artistic bent, and wife Siri (daughter of Iditarod Race veteran,

Jim Strong), a conscientious, hardworking couple, have grown our family tree by a granddaughter and grandson, plus, to date, a great-granddaughter. Our daughter Tracie, "animal crazy" from the beginning, has dedicated her life to the worthy cause of animal health and wellness. A certified animal therapist, her successes with seemingly hopeless cases is truly uncanny. Tracie is married to a former high school student of mine, Louis Audette, a dyed-in-the-wool mariner, they have contributed one daughter to our gang. Then there is Mitch.

For me to reminisce first race training is to recall the inseparable role Mitch played in preparation of my original Iditarod team, genesis of Seavey entrenchment in the world of endurance sled dog racing. Of all mushing memories collected over the past half century, those of Mitch and I, and our experiences while training for Iditarod number one, stand out the strongest, most vivid in my mind.

Once, we were side-hilling our way up the Resurrection Pass Trail between Swan Lake and Devil's Pass. Mitch, driving a five-dog team, brought up the rear. There occurred a comic mishap in which I happened to look back to see Mitch, sled and team doing barrel rolls off the trail, collecting themselves in an upright position and proceeding untangled and as if all in a day's work.

We spent frigid campouts and moonlit night runs of eighty miles or more. Shirley, burning the midnight oil, sewed special and rather peasant-looking clothes to help keep Mitch warm. The downright rescue of his dad and team from the bottom of a glaciated avalanche chute also comes to mind. There was a time we drove and broke trail until 2:00 a.m., seeking a cabin that should be "just over the next hill." Out of sheer exhaustion, Mitch and I decided to camp in a stand of spruce alongside the trail. A five-star hotel would not have appealed more to our weary bodies. Later, after a few hours under a frigid, starlit sky, we went through the laborious routine of hooking up, we traveled not more than one city block, and there it was, the cabin with gas heat, gas lights, and real bunks. The works. Through it all, Mitch never uttered a complaint. He was always willing to utilize his out-of-school time for the good of my cause. Ever eager to hit the trail on the next mush, quickly forgetting, or more correctly, forgiving, all accumulation of experience with cold, wind, wet, fatigue, and, no doubt at times, a cranky, unreasonable traveling partner. He was only thirteen and one-half years of age. Do they make them like that anymore?

The family tree has not wilted under Mitch's care, either. His wife, Janine, and he have given us four grandsons and via them, to date, three great-granddaughters, all of whom are most certainly brag worthy in the eyes of the planters of that tree in Alaska soil a half century past.

For Mitch's unflinching support, I am truly grateful. For the wonderful trail memories of our shared experiences, I am most thankful. Recently, I asked Mitch if he had chipped in and helped out of duty, or if he had honestly enjoyed doing so. Without hesitation, he said he enjoyed the whole affair. If nothing else came of his involvement with the first one, he most certainly got bit by the bug. Over the long succession of years, he and his boys—my grandsons, I'm pleased to add—have helped elevate endurance sled dog racing to a plane only dreamed of by the prophets of long ago 1973.

Mileage charts were religiously kept for each dog that remained in training. Since I was looking for a dozen good dogs, individuals were dropped from training freely, sometimes, perhaps, too freely. December, with early freeze up and a nice accumulation of snow, turned out to be unexpectedly fruitful in terms of accrued miles and hookups. Mitch and I took full advantage of our Christmas/New Year vacation from school to put miles on our dog teams. Take the dog named Crazy (that's how he acted while being hooked up) for example. He is the one of unknown parentage who survived all training cuts to become one of the chosen twelve. Crazy was, at fifty-five pounds, a beautifully marked gray-and-white male. His chart indicates he was hitched up eighteen times during December. Early runs were of six miles, building to four runs, twenty miles in length, with the last two for that month, twenty-five miles.

Notes taken on Crazy's performance show effects of progressive training:

12/5/72 - 6 miles "petered out last mile"
12/10/72 - 16 miles "loose line last 4 miles"
12/23/72 - 20 miles "gave out after 15 miles"
12/28/72 - 20 miles "in there, ok"
12/30/72 - 25 miles "good, all the way"

Distance, while obviously an important training consideration, was not an end in itself. Weight on the sled was, like distance, increased on a progressive scale. By the time of final dog team cuts, I had piled on 250 pounds as standard equipment, so to speak. The sled never moved without that amount (sacks of dog food and weights from a barbell set) tagging along. In training I rarely stepped off the runners or pedaled, not even on the steepest of hills. Considerable and herein unrevealed weight was added to training runs by me doing so.

"Crazy," one of twelve in my pioneer Iditarod team, out for a prerace skijor with son Darian, 1972.

December, of 1972 faded into January of the New Year, 1973. I went back to school following the holidays and returned to the hectic, not-enough-time dog training routine. Until mid-February, when my leave from school would begin, my available time amounted to weekend long runs and Wednesday night modest-length runs. On weekends, I usually had Mitch's assistance in pulling off seventy- to eighty-mile treks, often camping out to hone those skills while constantly shaking down gear and equipment. Trails of the northern Kenai Peninsula, such as Mystery Creek, became familiar. One of the more rewarding journeys, in terms of dog workout and natural beauty for the beholder, was that from Primrose, on the south shore of Kenai Lake, to Hope, and return. We (Mitch, the dogs, and I) traveled west down Kenai Lake, crossed the Sterling Highway at Cooper Landing, and followed Bean Creek and Resurrection Pass Trails north to Hope on Turnagain Arm. A time or two, we camped for a few hours near Hope. More commonly, we wheeled teams around, fed fish or tallow (fat), depending on how cold it was, pulled the hooks, and headed for home. Round-trip distance was very near one hundred miles. Both Mitch and I have fond memories of our runs among the Kenai Mountains along that route on moonlit nights. There were minutes, hours, and whole nights we wished would not end for the beauty of it all.

As far as the shorter, mid-week practices went, a look at my Dog Diary and the mileage charts show all were done at "the cabin" and were sixteen-mile runs. Our 1923 vintage cabin was located adjacent to the old, abandoned Sterling Highway, near Quartz Creek, in the Cooper Landing neighborhood. This hand-hewn log cabin, together with a tin-roofed woodshed graced our 20 acre mineral claim, turned mushing camp. Training Wednesdays were busy days: I hurried home from school, gobbled something to eat, and loaded the old, yellow power wagon with dogs and gear. Then off for a fifty-mile, in the dark, drive to the cabin. I parked, unloaded, and hooked up for two enjoyable hours behind the team on a trail that used to be a road. Mitch didn't accompany me on those night forays because of school the next day. If all went well or even mostly well, I arrived back at the cabin and truck usually about 10:00 p.m. Then it was load up and head for Seward, an hour distant. Unload, feed, water dogs I had driven. Mitch had, in my absence, cared for those left behind. With luck, I was in the house by midnight. Lots of tomfoolery for a puny sixteen miles. But it was better than nothing.

January miles tallied a few shy of four hundred, with the very last an eighty-mile marathon completed in nine hours, including a couple dog snack stops. Pulling Old Oak, my steel shod beater of a training sled, we were getting there. My goal was to work the team down to a tireless eight-mile-per-hour trot, sustainable for twelve hours under a load of two hundred fifty pounds, plus me riding most of the time. Interestingly, my note for Crazy on that eighty-mile dash read, "In there, has arrived."

If Crazy had arrived, we—the teams, Mitch, and myself—weren't too far in the rear. Each new run was completed with fewer glitches. Dogs not measuring up were left at home. Remaining individuals were moved about within a team until the best niche was found. Increasingly, more was demanded, more expected of us all. We spent more time on the trail, and did more trail-breaking. My lead dogs were put through more intense training, under more difficult conditions. More of everything with the exception of rest vacations. There was no time for such luxury. The March 3 race start was peering over a near horizon.

Part Two

26

The Gentle Bully

A man of letters and an author in his own right, Doug Capra has energetically encouraged this account of the First Great Race. (Photo: Doug Capra, Adak, 1972)

That second month of the year 1973 remains fixed in my mind as my busiest ever. February left only one month until race time—and so much to do. Without huge amounts of enthusiastic help from family and friends during that final push for readiness, March 3 most likely would have found me at home in Seward, filled with remorse and in wonderment as to what had gone wrong. One such enabler was a brand new friend at that time, Doug Capra, a newly arrived English teacher at Seward High.

Douglas Capra was first introduced to me in the autumn of 1972. Our high school principal performed the ritual as a prelude to our first teachers' meeting of the school year, which took place a couple of days before arrival of the untutored horde. Doug was a young man of medium build, with a full head of dark hair surrounding a youthful face. He wore dark-rimmed glasses, and had what seemed to be a perpetual smile, but would be hard pressed if called upon for even a short stint of belly laughter. Voice clear, crisp. Diction precise, as one expects from one licensed to profess our sacred tongue. Albeit not without blemish, it would appear. Perhaps an east coast tinge. And so it was.

Doug, I learned, as our acquaintanceship, indeed our friendship, grew over the passing months, had been born in Boston twenty-four years previous, in 1948. He was raised and received his early "school housing" at Worcester and Westboro, Massachusetts, and, in 1971, graduated from Northwestern University. That very summer, he and friends arrived in Anchorage on a lark—and broke. Doug's ace-in-the-hole was his English teaching degree. Haunting the State Education Office in Anchorage during the waning days of August, an offer was tendered to teach English at Adak. Capra signed on the dotted line "Without knowing where in heck I was heading," he reflected. "I was able to borrow money for an airplane ticket at the Credit Union on the strength of that signed contract."

Bidding Aleutian fogbanks adieu after a school year's sojourn, Capra arrived on the doorstep of Seward High. His continued tenure, except for a couple years for professional improvement, resulted in a noteworthy elevation of standards for English and drama studies at Seward Schools and the community in general. It is with pride I state that my children learned their English from Doug.

As fate would dictate, Doug arrived on the scene while I was in the throes of preparations for the first Iditarod. A pair of introductory runs behind a dog team, though daunting, served to tease Doug into wholehearted, and without question, invaluable support of my preparative efforts for both the 1973 and 1974 races. He went to work for my benefit with skills and knowledge he had won as a news reporter, DJ, newscaster, and classroom teacher. He tirelessly did trail research, investigated trail foods, and made photos to compliment an unending stream of promotional articles and audiotapes. He helped me record hours of tapes, both prerace and postrace, further insisting I cart a recorder on my sled in order to have an audio record of the race in progress. Of course, a tape recorder would probably fail in subzero temperatures, so he encouraged me to have means of keeping a written record as well. A man of letters and an author in his own right, Doug has energetically encouraged this account of the First Great Race.

At this juncture, when I have at last sat myself down to write what I fervently hope to be an account worthy of that first grand undertaking, I have come face-to-face with the astounding realization of my indebtedness to Doug Capra. Human memory being what it is—of short duration for most of us—Doug insisted that as complete a record of events as possible, surrounding the first Iditarod, be made and kept. In truth, this book is making its debut some forty years after originally intended, a tribute to a certain unnamed person's propensity for the sluggish art of procrastination. Good fortune only weakly describes Capra's persistence, or better, insistence, that we tape and write down everything possible about the First Great Race.

Capra sat me down and conducted three taped prerace interviews, covering all facets of our training program and race preparations. In short order, his English students had those vital interviews transcribed with copies for my files. Further, Doug insisted I carry a tape recorder to Nome, and that filled tapes be mailed back from post offices along the historic route. Transcriptions of those, with many cold battery and sleep-deprived slurs, were awaiting me upon my arrival back home. No sooner had my dogs returned to their private housing at Seavey's "Dog Patch" when Capra called on me, recorder under one arm, pen and pad in hand for his end-of-the-race interview. Transcripts of that particular interview were truly priceless, inasmuch as there was considerable dwelling on things of the mind. Thoughts, impressions, fears, elations, and the like. They, too, found themselves languishing, patiently waiting for the light of day, there in my files. Seemingly indefatigable when it came to promoting my race, Doug made photographs, wrote newspaper and magazine articles, and conducted local radio (KRXA) interviews. And he pestered me to get going on my "Iditarod book" for several years before succumbing to conditions commonly referred to as exasperation and resignation. Passage of years and the fleeting of memory have only served to impress upon me how valuable Doug's taskmaster friendship has been.

As useful as I found all the Capra-Seavey interviews to be, nothing in those dusty archives fascinated me more than Doug Capra's transcript of his taped, in-person coverage of the first Iditarod Race start, March 3, 1973. Capra, speaking into a recorder, saw all pioneer Iditaroders off to Nome and, in a unique and colorful manner, painted vivid word pictures of the entire event. I am unaware of the existence of any other complete commentary on the start. Featured several times on Seward radio KRXA, Doug, with a historian's presence of mind, saved it. That wonderful bit of Iditarod Race history and Alaskana is resurrected in Chapter 29 of this narrative.

What follows here is an edited combination of Capra's transcripts with the intent of spotlighting first race preparations, thoughts, both wise and naïve, insightful and ignorant.

From Files: (Edited and combined transcripts of Capra-Seavey interviews, February 26 and 27, 1973)

C: How's the trail? Is it a snowmachine trail?

S: I know the lower end (Knik – Susitna) is in. I just got back from working on it. It should all be snowmachine trail. There is kind of a Jeep trail between McGrath and Placerville that would be snowmachine trail in winter, I'm sure. (In a few days, we front of the packers would be wandering hungry and lost north of McGrath without a trail of any kind.)

C: How many do they have (signed up) so far in the race?

S: I'm sure it is over thirty. Seems it was thirty-five last time I heard from Tom (Johnson), who should know. (A bit shy of the one hundred Joe Sr. predicted.)

C: What is your prediction as far as the number that will finish?

S: Ummm, half.

C: What will be the factor that will eliminate half?

S: It is just a hunch, but I would say it would be driving the dogs too hard. Some drivers I know have got this figured down to where they can save seconds by not un-harnessing their dogs, that sort of thing, just for the idea of keeping then on the road longer. There ought to be some surprised guys. I plan to run mine only twelve hours a day.

C: Only? That's a lot.

S: That is a lot actually. But I know guys who are planning on sixteen. Maybe they have the dogs to pull it off. I don't know if I do and I'm not going to take the chance. (My last run of the race was an eighteen-hour grind from White Mountain to Nome.)

C: How many days were you out on the trail last week?

S: Five.

C: What was your best mileage in one day?

S: It averaged out to seventy-five. We worked on the trail between Knik and Susitna Station with side trips up the Yentna and Skwentna Rivers.

C: You were at the beginning of the trail. From there, does it get better or worse?

S: It gets better. On the map, the terrain gets better except over the pass, which will take a day however you cut it. If the army ends up going the Ptarmigan Pass route rather than Rainy, there will be an additional thirty miles added to the race.

C: Even if Rainy Pass wasn't open, you could take it?

S: Yes, but 3,500 to 3,600 feet! Nobody in his right mind is going to take that if there is a trail another way.

C: Well, a lot of people are going to say nobody in his right mind would be on the trail, period!

S: No comment.

C: There is a lot of trail activity now?

S: For sure. Knik to Susitna is well marked and Knik to Anchorage is in the process.

C: What signs have they out there?

S: We made up over three hundred one foot square plywood signs painted white and stenciled with a red figure of a dog, sled, and a musher. The rest of the trail, I don't know about signage. Probably, the army team will mark as it goes north.

C: Army team?

S: Yes, the army is going out now, starting today, Monday, February 26th in fact, heading to Nome. They will go through Rainy Pass if possible. If not, through Ptarmigan. We are relying on them and it just happened they were planning this mission anyway. They juggled things to correspond with the race. (Ptarmigan route was selected.)

C. Are they going by snowmachine?

S: Yes. They bought some ridiculous number, twelve, I think, just for this excursion. They will get the trail in, no question about that. They have everything to do with, including helicopter support. Also, a separate civilian volunteer group of machiners will be going ahead of the racers, come Saturday. They will do a final check of the trail and, if there is new snow, pack the trail again. This isn't for public consumption, but I personally think that last bunch detracts from the spirit of the race. But they are a fact and we might be real thankful that they are there if we get new snow. (Those civilians became saviors of the race, bogged down south of Poorman.)

C: Weather will be a factor, then?

S: Absolutely. Another point of strategy is to check with the Weather Service just prior to the race for a long-term prediction. There is a heavy snow belt on the south slope of the Alaska Range. The whole show could come to a sudden end if we get hammered with snow on the approach to the mountains. Maybe, if we saw it coming, we could push to stay ahead of a whole lot of snowshoeing. (I forgot to check.)

C: Changing the topic, how are you liking your new sled, the one Bob (Hill) built for you? Is it lighter?

S: Not much lighter, except for weight saved switching from iron shoes to plastic. It is patterned after Old Oak, a sled I have run for nearly ten years. It has hickory wood, a strong, springy wood, used for axe handles, weighs about the same as oak. The new one is designed after the old, although we did curve the runners more to better get in and out of dished-out trail left by heavy snowmachine travel…Minor joints are bolted, major ones are tied with rawhide, which is strong but flexible. That looseness takes up shock. Eventually, I should be able to walk it ahead while standing on the runners…Oh, the plastic strips used on the runner bottoms are new to Alaska, just last season. Guys who have used it are sold on it.

C: Did you use it last year?

S: No. This is my maiden voyage with the stuff. I don't know how it will work out. Metal adds strength to a sled. Plastic won't. Of course, plastic will reduce friction, I am guessing by 75 percent at most temperatures. Another bad point about this white plastic is it wears out fast and could break completely, I would guess.

C: Do you think it will make it all the way to Nome?

S: I don't know.

C: Do you plan to bring any extra with you?

S: No. We have to run on bare wood if the plastic goes. (I ended up with a plastic-less runner from Unalakleet to Nome.) I am going to run my old iron-shoed sled from Anchorage to Knik. That will be a gritty, grimy run. Road crossings, bridges, lack of snow will be rough on plastic. I will carry just surplus mandatory gear and catch up with the hickory sled at Knik basically packed and ready to go, required equipment and all.

C: Shirley is making dog booties, right?

S: Yes, here they are.

C: Have your dogs ever worn them?

S: No. I think what I will do is break them (dogs) in a few at a time on the lower end. I hope I don't have to use them, but imagine I will have to on rivers where there is overflow and lumps of wet, frozen snow. That condition is murder on the feet.

Shirley: I talked to an Eskimo lady from up on the coast. She told me about what they call muttluks. She helped me with the pattern.

C: Do you think anyone else will use them?

S: My guess is that all the Eskimo racers know about them.

Shirley: They do use them up there. Especially in spring time, when that real hard, icy snow is left. She said when the guys see blood on the trail, they will put the muttluks on the dogs.

S: Shirley is making a dozen dog coats as well. The material is high-count nylon I got from Recreation Supply in Anchorage. I doubt many racers will have dog coats, but reading about the old races, they were standard gear on the coast. I know from experience in cold, cold wind, some dogs will just lie down and curl up for self-preservation.

C: Are you liable to run into such conditions?

S: That's what I am told. One of the traits we look for in puppies and in breeding animals is well-furred bellies. Still, if conditions are extreme, they will lie down and refuse to budge. Self-protection is a law of nature.

C: Booties, coats, harnesses, lines, and dogs like to chew. Is this a problem?

S: Oh, yes. Fortunately, by this stage in training, very little of that goes on. About one good chomp on the mainline (plastic rope) and it can be severed, transferring all exerted force in front of the cut to the necklines and dogs' necks nearest the cut. This can be injurious or fatal to those dogs. That is the main reason I use very light snaps on very loose collars. Either the snap will fly apart or the dog will slip the collar. This saves the dog, but now, that section of team ahead of the chewed place is free to go their merry way. Not good.

C: So what is to be done with chewers?

S: You have to catch them in the act; it does no good to discipline a dog after the fact. I merely give the offender a slap on the nose with a sharp "NO." Normally, they chew because they are nervous or excited, waiting to get going. They saw around there with their teeth on anything handy. The more worked down a team is, the fewer the problems all around.

C: How about harness chewers?

S: Knock on wood, but so far so good with the bunch going to Nome. Again, harnesses get chewed when a nervous dog is harnessed and has to wait too long to be hooked in the team. I do think racers planning to leave harnesses on for the duration, as a couple have indicated, better have along a bunch of spares. In my experience, most harnesses were shredded by dogs trying to get comfortable in bed.

C: Have dogs ever chewed on your sled?

S: I hate to admit it, but, yes, a few years back, on one of my earliest treks, I, of necessity, tied two dogs overnight to my sled. Next morning, I saw vivid evidence of just how much dogs love rawhide.

C: But still you use it. Why?

S: I haven't, in all my experience with rawhide, seen it break. As a fastener, it's almost indestructible if one keeps the dogs at bay. As pointed out, key joints of my racing sled are fastened with it. My snowshoes are laced with it, so, consequently, a couple spare strips are included in my gear pack. It is easily made. I have made it from moose, caribou, black bear, and horse. If you buy it in a shop, it's most likely to be cow hide. Hair and flesh are removed and the green (raw) hide is cut into convenient widths—thickness is determined by location on the hide, thin on the flanks, thickening toward the back. It is used for tying while wet and stretchy. It tightens as it dries and remains flexible even after a few coats of varnish is applied to keep it from getting wet and going soggy on you, and as a dog repellant. Way better than bolts in view of the beating a sled takes.

C: I see candles here. For inside your tent?

S: No, they are real handy for starting a fire. I have used them for years. Light a candle—one match—lay it down, arrange your tinder, when it ignites, remove the candle. A one-match operation. My matches are the waterproof type, kept in small, waterproof containers in various places. I never want to be without matches and a candle, so I have them in parka and shirt pockets, and different locations on the sled.

C: What kind of tent?

S: A double-walled, lightweight mountain climber's tent. On sale, Recreation Equipment store for seventy-two dollars. The tent, a foam pad on top spruce boughs, plus a down-filled sleeping bag with wool liner is pretty much my trailside roadhouse.

C: Have you tested your sleeping bag at all?

S: Many times this winter. It is a mummy type. I think three-pound down filled. I have slept fairly well at minus twenty-five degrees in this bag on spruce bows under the stars, no wind. But I have one of these wool liners for a GI mummy bag. Put that inside the down bag and you really have something. You are ready for some good sleep in extreme cold. The liner serves two purposes. First, it boosts the comfort range of the down bag and it collects body moisture. Controlling sleeping bag moisture is of little concern for the weekender. But if you are sleeping out for who knows how long in very cold temperatures, like we will be doing, it's a whole different ball game.

C: And you don't have time or place during the day to dry them.

S: Right. You can beat that rap in two ways. One is to turn your bag inside out every other day. The other, when the wool liner is used, is to remove it from the bag and carry it outside your pack, assuming a clear, cold day. Exposed to cold, dry air, moisture crystallizes. Shake the thing like mad to get rid of the ice crystals, thus at least most of the night's body moisture. This method works with a nylon bag also, but to a lesser degree.

C: Are you taking extra clothing, warm clothing?

S: Except for my parka shell, no synthetics, pretty much down and wool. There won't be a whole lot in the way of extra clothes. An extra suit of ninety-eight percent wool long johns to be used like pajamas. Conscious of moisture accumulation in the bag, I do not want to get into it with sweaty clothes. Also, several pairs of wool socks will be packed.

C: What kind of food are you taking for yourself?

S: I like fat in cold weather. It gives you the fuel you need. Shirley cooked up some fat hens into soup and dumplings. Also, some moose stew. Another item that is a complete, hard work, cold weather ration is Shirley's trail cake. In training, I have eaten several pounds already and love the stuff. I think one could get by just fine for weeks on it only. Boy, she uses gobs of good ingredients. It has protein from nuts, different dried fruits—raisins, dates, citrus. The works. Eggs and honey, too. Then slathered with butter a small loaf, say about 2 ½ inches by 4 inches by 8 or 9 inches weighs 2 ½ pounds. Solid. I kid her that any leftovers, she can market as boat anchors (see Appendix X, Shirley Seavey's Trail Cake Recipe).

C: How many food drop stations and where are they located? Do you know yet?

S: As far as I know, there are five for people things—food, extra gear, and supplies. We (the Race Committee) decided on places served by commercial flights. I am not yet sure of the final decision on the where part. The last we talked, it was to be McGrath, Ruby, Kaltag, Unalakleet, and, yeah, Koyuk. Those places for people needs.

C: Dog food goes to different places then?

S: Well, yes, but in reality, several additional spots. Let me check here…Okay, dog food drops at Knik, Rainy Pass, Farewell, McGrath, Placerville, Ruby, Kaltag, Unalakleet, Koyuk, and Nome. (If only it would have worked out that way.)

C: Will your team get fed differently than at home?

S: On the race, they will be fed about the same as around here except more, no doubt. I have over three hundred pounds of fish (halibut heads) stashed among those drop points, also several bags of high-protein Purina, topped off with thirty-plus pounds of beef suet divided up along the way. Of course, there will be one full feeding—maybe more—on my sled at all times in the event I get stalled between supply points. What I picture is, breezing into a checkpoint, feeding dogs from my drop sacks there, resting them if it's time, moving on. Should I arrive at a checkpoint in the middle of a run, I will grab enough to feed them where I do make camp further up the trail. I will have to keep an eye on the amount of people food on board since resupply is at only five locations. A day's supply of both people and dog food are mandatory—required items by our rules.

C: People food, dog food, what additional required items?

S: Let's see…snowshoes, Arctic-type sleeping bag, matches, axe or saw, tie-out chains for dogs, and either sunglasses or goggles as protection against snow blindness. By the way, adequate dog food is to be considered two pounds of dry food per dog. In my case, with twelve dogs in harness, I am required to have a minimum of twenty-four pounds of dog food with me at all times. That is, unless it was fed to cover an emergency situation between check stations. We don't have a gauge of adequacy for people food.

C: Today is February 26, that means…that means we are only five days from race day. What happens between now and then?

S: Boy, things really get wild now. Busy! Yesterday was my last run, a short one, twenty miles. As far as the dogs go, I am going to feed them up, fatten them up some by race day. I need to clip their toenails and candle the feet.

C: Candle feet?

S: Yup! I actually use a lighted candle to singe the hair between the toes to reduce the collection of snow between toes and forming little, hard snowballs, under certain snow conditions. If not removed, they can cripple up a dog. It sounds brutal, but it isn't if done right.

C: What else?

S: Well, we have to go to Anchorage on Thursday for the start position drawing and prerace mushers' meeting. Back to Seward that evening. Friday morning, load dogs, sleds, everything needed, and head back up to Anchorage so we are close by for Saturday's start at 10:00 a.m.

C: Where is the start, by the way?

S: I talked to Tom Johnson yesterday and he said the committee was negotiating with the sprint racing club to start at their track on Tudor Road. Also, there is an unfinished stretch of highway out near Fort Rich we have been eyeing. So, right now, your guess is as good as mine. Regardless where, I feel there won't be much in the way of attendance with the Rendezvous just getting over.

C: I bet there will. I think you are in for a big surprise. What starting position do you want?

S: Toward the front—even first would be okay. I have good leaders so I am not worried about leading the pack. It gives me a better chance to arrive in Knik before dark. Generally, the trail is less punchy for the front teams.

C: Did you say start time is 10:00 a.m.?

S: Yes, with a team leaving every two minutes.

C: That's good. At least all thirty-some teams will be off by noon.

S: Still, it will be dark by the time we get to Knik. It is over fifty miles, more like sixty over there. I don't expect to arrive much before 8:00 p.m. Then on the trail to Susitna Station by five the next morning.

C: Do you plan to help the dogs by pedaling?

S: In training, I don't help even on the steepest hills. Racing, I will help all I can, pedaling and even running up hills where needed and possible. Besides, after, say, eight hours on a sled, I will be looking for things to do.

C: After eight hours on a sled, I would be looking for a place to lie down!

S: My longest stint training was fourteen hours, but for one day only.

C: From our mush that day, we did sixteen miles. I got the impression it was really warm for our teams.

S: As I recall, it was warm. Warm temperatures slow the dogs down, which can be good at times. Temperatures between zero and minus five degrees F, that's just right. You have to work a little to keep warm, but don't have to worry about your face freezing. Dogs can function in colder temperatures, minus twenty to thirty degrees; people start having problems, though. Travel by dog team below minus thirty-five degrees is foolhardy.

C: Speaking of travel, what does your race travel schedule look like?

S: Day one will be spent getting out of Anchorage and over to Knik, a straight, pretty much nonstop trip. If there are to be typical trail days, they would start after leaving Knik. Set the alarm for 4:00 a.m.—on the trail by 5:00 a.m.—still dark, but not for long. Stop for about fifteen minutes every two hours, throw snacks to the dogs, continue until around twelve noon. For sure, if the day is warm, rest with harnesses on until around

3:00 p.m. Back on the trail until semi-darkness, enough light to make camp. Camp until 4:00 a.m. next morning. This schedule gives me around twelve hours on the trail. Good, long rest for dogs, and even if I don't get done with evening chores until 8:00 p.m., eight hours' rest for me.

C: Dan, you mentioned dog snacks. What are they and when do the dogs get their main meal?

S: Snacks amount to roughly a half-pound chunk of fat or fish. Fat if it's cold, fish if it's warm. Serious eating will take place at night, after the day's work is over. This entails melting snow for plenty of water for dogs to drink and to mix in their dry feed. They will also be fed fish and or suet. I expect to feed them at least twice the amount fed even in training. I've never run dogs, really run them steady, like is required in this race, before. When run six or seven days hard in a row, they lose weight fast. Maybe my schedule is too ambitious—twelve hours, seventy-five miles per day—even over rough trail. One thing certain, there is a heck of a lot to be learned about long-distance dog racing.

27

Trail From Somewhere – Will Mush for Money

Along Knik Arm on the first Iditarod Trail from Anchorage.
Only mushers in the 1973 and 1974 races have run the complete distance between Anchorage and Nome.

My last day in the classroom leading up to the race was Friday, February 9. Dot Knighten attended classes that day, as well. She was an old hand at filling in for me, due to my frequent and lengthy absences while traveling with the wrestling squad. I had made lesson plans to cover each class through the month of March—just in case.

And a good piece of foresight it was, too, as the race ground to a snail's pace midway through. Dot and I went over daily and weekly objectives with students of each class, informing them what was expected both academically and in the way of behavior. This routine was repeated again in 1974, when Knighten covered for me while I completed the second Iditarod. The fact that learning proceeded uninterrupted both years, that not a single disciplinary action was necessary during those personal leaves speaks volumes, not only for Dot's kind, steady, intellectual approach in the classroom, but to a fine and wonderful quality of each and every one of those unforgettable kids. That school day over, with profuse exclamations of gratitude, I handed my keys, lesson plans, and grade book to Dot, and wished her well. A feeling of unleashed freedom overtook me as I left for the homestead to load the team and head out for training over the Knik-Susitna section of the Old Iditarod Trail.

A full week of vigorous dog training and needful trail work ensued. I located my camp on the far end of Knik Lake, close to where the trail leaves the frozen lake and disappears into a heavy stand of mixed birch and spruce. Camp, perhaps, is a misnomer since the spot was actually a cache, a depository for surplus food and equipment, while all manner of the same was stacked high on my sled for use as our work and travels took us farther afield in the direction of Skwentna. Word had been put out by the race committee that some serious work needed to be done on that particular section of trail. Brushing and marking mainly, but location and reestablishment of the old trail over a rough obstacle called Mile Nine Hill, too. Several musher types answered the call.

Dick Mackey of Wasilla was one. "Ruggedly handsome," as they say, a bit older than I, Mackey exuded the confidence of an experienced outdoorsman and dog driver. He, like most who had a part, large or small, in that first great adventure, had fallen under the spell of Joe Redington's persuasive power. He, too, was preparing a team for the race to Nome. If that wasn't sufficient unto itself, he had taken on the responsibility for providing racers a trail between Anchorage and Susitna Station. A most difficult, one-hundred-mile portion it would prove when it came to signage.

The race committee had caused to be made hundreds of one square foot, three-eighth inch ply board trail signs. Painted white, a figure of a sled dog pulling a musher on a sled was stenciled on each with red paint. Following his work and training with us out of Knik, Mackey and a small crew put in place over three hundred of those unique markers between Anchorage and beyond Susitna Station a few miles. By race day, however, all but perhaps ten had been stolen, much to the chagrin of drivers navigating teams through the Anchorage maze. I cannot recall seeing a single trail marker the entire run to Knik on start day. A few did remain upriver from Susitna Station.

Mackey and I reminisced over the phone in mid-January of 2011. Dick told of living in the Mountain View area of Anchorage, and driving his team out along the two-lane Palmer Highway in the early 1950s, rarely meeting a car, especially at night on his way to and from Palmer. Daytime traffic was somewhat more evident, but hardly in the commuter category of today. Dick did not become involved to any degree in the business of the Iditarod Race Committee, but was sucked into the race vortex as a result of his Aurora Dog Mushers Club association.

He, like I, was unsure how it came about that the first Iditarod had a veterinarian attached when it was unprecedented in sled dog racing. A plausible explanation is that from day one, the Iditarod has had its detractors, some public resistance, and a modest amount of negative press. It takes only a small leap of faith to conclude that Joe Sr., with his military connections through General Gettys, saw a means to combat the bum publicity threat. As will be seen later, that was pretty much the story. We shared a laugh at Dick's understanding that the veterinarian we did engage for our race was, in real military life, a meat inspector. Turns out it was true.

Mackey thought the most trying aspects of putting in the trail out of Anchorage was dealing with Eklutna villagers for permission to cross their property. Likewise, our State Department of Transportation (DOT) officials needed an inordinate amount of convincing that crossing Knik and Matanuska Rivers on their bridges was a good idea after all.

Dick Mackey, beginning with the inaugural Iditarod, went on to a lengthy eight-race career, which was climaxed by his thrilling 1978 one second victory over that era's toughest competitor, Rick Swenson. Neither before nor since have finish line spectators been treated to such a heart-stopper. That lead dog length triumph produced, in my opinion, the most dynamic photo taken in sled dog racing history. Pictured is Mackey, whip trailing, after a thousand miles of racing, calling on that final ounce of reserve hidden there, somewhere in himself and his noble trail companions. One has to wonder if there can ever be another photo taken—as that one by Rod Stapleton—that will capture such a magnificent mushing moment. Not satisfied with his own race achievements, Mackey proudly claims bragging rights to two of his sons, Rick and Lance, race champions both. Lew Freedman's 2001 book, *One Second to Glory*, is an excellent source of insider information on Mackey's 1978 championship and his lifetime of Alaska adventure.

Mackey wasn't the only new acquaintance made while training and doing trail work out of Knik prior to the 1973 Iditarod. Ron Aldrich, ex-military man from Willow, was there. His team was led by a large, light-colored dog named Cucumber. Upbeat and positive in all trying situations, Ron's "can do" attitude was contagious, and sustaining. Another Aurora Club member was Dave Olson. He paid his sweat dues working on Mackey's trail gang, and like Mackey, Aldrich and I would have a go at the race.

Individually and collectively, we reestablished the old trail over Mile Nine Hill, brushed and signed from Knik Lake to Susitna Station and twenty or more miles along the Yentna and Skwentna Rivers. As busy as Joe Sr. was with race organizing, he drove a team out there on several occasions during our sojourn. Fact was, Redington was snatching every available hour to "train up" his dog team in preparation for the race to Nome. It was only through the persuasion—insistence may be a better term—of Tom Johnson and Gleo Huyck at the eleventh hour that Joe decided to stay behind. With little money for the purse and a thousand and one loose ends fluttering about as race day rapidly approached, he bit his lip, rolled up his sleeves, and stayed home to mind the shop.

Whenever Joe came out among us, he drove a very large team, probably eighteen or twenty dogs, in order to get as many dogs trained as possible during one run. Generally, he had his sled loaded to the gunnels with supplies either for us workers or to be used in fabrication of a race checkpoint at Susitna Station. One day, I left Knik behind Joe, who had a mammoth team hitched to a mammoth homemade, mostly of aluminum, contrivance sporting no less than a half ton of freight, all kept together with a steel cable towline the size of one's little finger. We crested a small but steep hill at wide-open speeds. On the downhill side, Joe lost it. His sled left the trail on the right side, collided with a five-inch-diameter birch (I measured it later), sheared it off clean as a whistle, and, for considerable distance, continued to mow down botanical obstructions of a lesser order. Regaining the trail, off he went, neither slowing down nor looking back. Another time, a huge, double-track snowmachine was stuck, spinning out on one of the formidable slopes of Mile Nine Hill. Along came Redington, again with a huge sled and load. He whipped around the yellow, fuming trail obstruction, and brought his team to a smart halt. In some fashion, he gained purchase on the front of the machine with his snow hook, "hiked up" his team, and, without hesitation, the whole assemblage marched over the crest, out of view. All in not much more time than it took to give this account.

For Redington, a stunt such as towing a machine over a hill represented a coup for sled dogs in general and for those who adhered to the then-dying art of dog mushing. Be it running to Nome, pulling heavy loads on sleighs, a Greyhound bus, or scaling Mt. McKinley, the Alaska husky was capable of it all. To some degree, a measure of a person's worth for Joe, Sr. was decided by the degree to which a given person was "into dogs." To be dubbed "doggy" by Joe was to have arrived. "Oh, yes, old George is real doggy, a good man, he has a nice team." For a novice musher to be accepted as "doggy" by Joe was like being—well, knighted in days of yore.

From Dog Diary: (Dated February 20, 1973)

Home yesterday from Knik. Gone one week, excluding a day going, another returning. Run dogs, work on trail…12 race dogs,

> did runs 35, 36, 71, 70, 40 miles, Genghis and Kiana in lead. Team clicking, no injuries. Good.

Sled dog racing has a long history of sponsor dependency, where team owners seek financial support from individuals and businesses. This practice was well established and accepted as common in the heyday of the early 1900s All Alaska Sweepstakes races at Nome. Sled dog people, it seems, have always been strapped for cash. I did fund-raising in a halfhearted way, as time permitted. Not that I was flush with money by any means, but rather, because available time was being stretched in all different directions. Part of my duties as Peninsula Representative for the Trail Committee was distribution of reprinted All Alaska Sweepstakes souvenir annuals to various businesses. These booklets were either sold outright or consigned as a benefit to the prospective race. By no means a hot seller, the annuals did serve to promote awareness of the hoped-for race and provided opportunity for me to solicit sponsors in the process. That solicitation met with but modest success. Businesses and individual contributions supporting my race effort amounted to $1,025.00.

However, I had another monetary scheme, which resulted from my study of trail history. The chief purpose of the original trail was to provide means of mail transport to remote mining settlements scattered across the vast Alaska Territory. Why not carry real mail to Nome by dog sled—for a price—and mail it from the Nome Post Office upon my arrival? Local artist and race advocate, Dot Bardarson, created the first "Iditarod Race Mail" ever, in the form of a souvenir letter that could be written upon, folded, stamped, addressed, and sealed, ready for my sled mailbag. Printed on Dot's artistic rendition was this note: "This message was carried from Anchorage to Nome, Alaska, a distance of 1,000 miles over the historic Iditarod Trail by a dog team owned and driven by Dan Seavey of Seward, Alaska. The Iditarod Trail began in Seward and served as the main winter trail to the great interior of Alaska in the early Gold Rush days." (See Appendix XI Souvenir Letter)

Souvenir letters sold for $5.00 each and purchasers supplied the eight-cent stamp. From letter sales, I raised $417.00. Combined with the $1,025.00 received from sponsors, my grand total was $1,442.00.

That seems a puny sum in light of today's inflated prices. But I recall thinking it was substantial since the one-month pay loss it was to replace came to exactly $1,428.00. In 1974 (second race), Iditarod Trail Committee adopted my concept of trail mail, making it mandatory for each racer to carry cachets—up to ten pounds' worth—to be later sold to benefit the race in general. An Iditarod tradition was born.

That first trail mail tallied eighty-three of my souvenir letters, sealed in plastic as to be waterproof. They were lodged in the bottom of a small pack attached to the rear of my new hickory sled. There they remained, mostly forgotten for the duration of their long, slow journey to the City of Gold. Postmarked from Nome, on March 24, 1973, the letters were flown off to thirty-eight different states and four foreign countries. Nowadays, collectors search the most remote recesses of Alaskana, hoping to find one of these rare relics of the First Great Race.

By my return home from that week of training and trail work out of Knik, I had settled on the dog team destined to be the third Iditarod team to arrive on Front Street, Nome. We human pioneers of the "great camping trip," as George Attla would dub it, will remain incorporated, as it were, in the fabric that weaves our history. But what of the four hundred pioneer dogs? Those wonders of God's creation, who weathered Arctic gales, slept in snow banks, suffered exhaustion, sore, raw feet, and, to some degree, human ignorance and neglect. What of them? Leaders Genghis, Kiana, and Sonny. Others, who strained in wheel, team, and swing positions, and at times, in lead as well, were Kuchik, Koyuk, Snippy, Eska, Shiak, Flame, Bandit, Casper, and Crazy. Names listed on a sheet of paper seem such a hollow tribute to twelve of a person's most loyal, tested friends. And hollow that tribute would be, if all twelve of them were not imprinted indelibly in my heart. Those twelve devoted, steadfast trail companions bestowed upon me the one true adventure of my life. In so doing, they became the pathfinders for all ensuing generations of endurance race dogs. Genghis, Kiana, Sonny, Kuchik, Koyuk, Snippy, Eska, Shiak, Flame, Bandit, Casper, and Crazy—a renewed and heartfelt salute.

The chosen twelve made four final runs before race day. We traveled sixteen, fifty, eight, and twenty miles on those runs. The sixteen-mile run entailed a trip to our Quartz Creek gold claim while the fifty-miler was a run down Kenai Lake to Cooper Landing from Primrose, located at the south end of the lake, and return. A brief eight-mile jaunt up Resurrection Valley was followed on February 25 by a final durability test of my Iditarod sled. Some two hundred fifty pounds were lashed to the poor thing. I hooked the twelve to it, and charged up a segment of the Iditarod Trail north of Moose Pass. Ten miles each direction, all stops out, slam bang, "damn the torpedoes, full speed ahead." The sled survived. The dogs were ready. Six days were allotted the team to laze about and fatten up for the ordeal ahead.

There had been no respite for the Seavey clan during those waning days of the countdown to race day; much was accomplished. Thanks to Shirley, kids, and friends, all needful tasks were finalized. Lists checked, gear packed, sled loaded and secured, dog gear rechecked, last-minute purchases made, missing buttons sewed on, late-arriving souvenir letters received, and much more begged our attention. But as day follows night, the clock ran out on us. What was done was done. What remained unfinished was probably not so important. We would sink or swim with the bulk of preparation completed.

28

Silver Tongued Fox—Musher Herding

In Nome at completion of the 25th Anniversary Race, 1997.
L-R: Photographer Jeff Schultz, Shirley, me, Joe Sr.,
Vi Redington, Janine Seavey with infant Conway. It was
the Silver Tongued Foxes' last Iditarod.

Thursday, March 1, 1973, found Shirley, kids, and I stuffed in our pickup cab, heading for Anchorage. Upon arrival, we would rid ourselves of the dog food and personal packs frozen solid in back, which were to be flown out to supply points along the trail toward Nome. The main event of that day, however, was the musher meeting and start position drawing held that evening at the old Gold Rush Hotel, race headquarters for the 1973 Iditarod. We wound our uncertain way to its Northern Lights Boulevard site, and arrived with time to spare.

With publication of *The Iditarod – Most Demanding Race of All* in 1974, George Attla became the first participant to give an account of our first race. As may be expected, there are elements of his narrative that I question. However, he has my concurrence on many descriptions of events and situations mutually experienced on our trek. Certainly, I agreed with Attla when he wrote that he knew very few of the mushers who showed up for the drawing for the Iditarod race. "This was a new crowd altogether," he remarked. Of the thirty-five [thirty-four] mushers there, Attla claimed he knew Bobby Vent, Isaac Okleasik, Bud Smyth, Dick Mackey, and Raymie Redington. Not being a racer in any circle that was more than I recognized. Again, I nod knowingly when this legendary sprint musher states, "I didn't know who was who…I didn't know them when we started, and never met them on the trail. Then we came home before they got into Nome…But I tell you some of the other guys, I got to know them pretty good before the whole thing was over."

Dick Mackey's photo of his 1978 triumph over the race's winning expert, Rick Swenson, may represent a high drama point in race history, but scarcely more than the exchange of words that took place between Jimmy Huntington and Joe, Sr. that night in Anchorage. Essentially, Huntington cornered Redington with a point-blank question: "Is the prize money in escrow to pay the mushers?" Huntington, a native spokesman from Galena on the Yukon, then recalled some race event dating back to the 1940s, when native drivers ended up short-changed on prize money. The Silver Tongued Fox rose to the occasion, answering, "No, it is not. But upon my word, one man to another, I promise it will be there by the time you boys get to Nome." Had Huntington expected mushers to desert en masse, he must have been totally disappointed. Fact is, not a single individual gave the matter further comment. Joe had nipped the insurgency at its bud. Personally, I remember thinking, "Where in the world is this guy (Huntington) coming from?" I was so committed to going to Nome by dog team that, frankly, I could not have cared less if there had been no end of the trail payoff. So it must have been with all my new trail-mates, for when Joe, Sr. asked, "Do you men still want to go to Nome?" With one voice, we exclaimed in the affirmative.

It was a low-key undertaking, that first Iditarod ingathering of the public. Held in an average-sized hotel conference room, it was attended by perhaps a hundred people, mostly race officials and racer associates. The visiting dignitary was Mayor Robert Renshaw of Nome, who promised us an enthusiastic welcome upon our arrival in his city. The couple of newspaper reporters in attendance had no competition from the non-attending radio or TV media. The prerace meal was simple, thus inexpensive. The drawing for start positions was the high point of the evening. Mushers filed up in traditional fashion—according to sign-up order—and drew a number from the traditional mukluk. Mine was number fourteen. A good number. With a two-minute departure interval, I figured I would be in Knik before dark (see Appendix XII, Starting Order – 1973 Iditarod Race).

A brief, to-the-point mushers' meeting followed, conducted by our race marshal, Dick Tozier, who resided in Anchorage. That evening was the first time I laid eyes upon Tozier, although he was well known in sprint-race circles, both as a breeder and sprint-race official in various capacities. Bigger than average size, with dark hair and heavy brows, Tozier presented a gruff, pugnacious, no-nonsense demeanor, which, to me, seemed contrived since at the same time, he appeared constantly on the verge of breaking into a genuine smile, maybe even a laugh. In view of the fact he represented something akin to the Supreme Court, duly sworn to interpret our race rules, we listened with rapt attention to his interpretation thereof.

Noteworthy is the fact that all twenty-one rules of the first race could be fitted on one side of a legal-size piece of paper. That's right—twenty-one rules, one page. In way of comparison, the fifty-one rules governing the thirty-ninth Iditarod demand—indeed require—fifteen pages to accommodate their growing modern sprawl. Our rules were the All Alaska Sweepstakes rules—modified to suit our anticipated set of circumstances. For instance, two mushers were allowed to drive one team, but in no case shall a driver accept assistance from a motorized vehicle. The last, rule twenty-one, gave the race marshal broad authority based on his judgment. Otherwise, most were common sense race rules, many of which have survived to help swell our modern set (see Appendix VI, Rules Section).

Not much interest was shown the rules by mushers, only a few "what-ifs" for Tozier to answer. The main topic of concern was the trail. Was it in? What condition? Were the checkpoints in? Will our food bags be placed where promised? What kind of problems will we have getting out of Anchorage? Answers to all were reassuring and positive. If everything questioned wasn't up to snuff that Thursday night, it would be by race day or most certainly before arrival of racers in need. "Yeah, right," I thought, doubting that all could be taken care of. Time would prove my skepticism was well founded. Finally, Race Marshal Tozier provided us with a few housekeeping details. He informed us that the first Iditarod would start at Alaska Sled Dog Racing Association's track off Tudor Road at 10:00 a.m., Saturday, March 3. Teams would leave at two-minute intervals. A team unable to leave at its designated time would leave after all teams had departed. The trail from Anchorage to the Skwentna River was well marked. At that point, Tozier held up one of Dick Mackey's red-and-white dog and musher signs. "Oh, by the way, the trail committee is awarding a special purse of one thousand dollars to the fastest team arriving in Knik, our first checkpoint."

Meeting over, the Seavey gang made a mad dash for the pickup. We had a one-hundred-thirty-mile drive home that night, only to load the team and head back to Anchorage the following day. Shirley and kids managed a healthy nap on our way back to Seward. Driving and wide awake, I rehashed the thousand and one details related to race preparations that had occupied me over the past several months. And then there was that one thought, a realization actually, that wouldn't leave me. It thrilled me, affecting me physically with goose bumps and heart palpitations. The idea, the awe-inspiring comprehension that I, Dan Seavey, was really going to drive a dog team along our great artery of history—the Iditarod Trail.

Early in the afternoon, Friday, March 2, 1973, the Seavey family was packed overly snug in the power wagon, and again headed north over the Seward Highway to Anchorage. Lashed securely atop the pickup's shell were two dog sleds with gear for the tasks before them. Under the shell, in a mountain of straw bedding, reposed the first Seavey Iditarod team. Nobody back there was overly excited, off to who-knows-where for yet another training run, most likely. Little did those twelve dogs know what was in store for them in the weeks to come.

Old Oak, my iron shod training sled was packed for Saturday's run between Anchorage and Knik. All required gear, mostly borrowed or second-string items, and twenty-five pounds of dog food to meet the letter of the law, were stuffed in a couple of duffle bags. These, in turn, were tied to the sled in such a manner and with such disregard for proper knots as to cause a yachtsman to weep. Certainly not a really great image builder when compared with the truly beautiful, artistically crafted "sleighs" that were sported by some of the native drivers. Still, I would be more than thankful for that old beater with its iron shoes and relatively light load as I ground my way over rutted, rocky trail and concrete bridges barren of snow on the way to Knik.

Bob Hill's hickory creation, equipped with white plastic runner shoes, was pretty much packed. Heavy, bulky items were wrapped in a canvas tarp with lines and knots borne out of careful consideration for ease of use and convenience. A small day pack also came along to hold small items for ready use, such as my camera, dry gloves, and, of course, a loaf of Shirley's trail cake. This most-used pack was strapped to the rear of the handlebar, above the brake claw. Arrangements were made with Tom Johnson to get this sled to Knik by day's end for use from there to Nome.

Our Friday night Anchorage destination was just off Jewel Lake Road, at the home of Gary and Twilah Bernhardson. I had met Gary via high school wrestling. At the time (1963-64) I introduced the sport to Seward High, there were but four Alaska schools with wrestling programs. They were Fairbanks – Lathrop, Kenai – Central, and Anchorage – East and West. Seward became the fifth. Bernhardson coached the East Anchorage squad. Mild-mannered, sincere, soft spoken, and above average in stature, one would naturally wonder how Gary could possibly fire up enough of the sixty-plus boys out for wrestling each season to build a winning team. He did, though, much to the chagrin of his competition, me and my Seahawk mat men included. During my thirteen coaching years, sitting on opposite sides of the mat from Coach Bernhardson, I never once heard him even raise his voice to a contestant, referee, or opposition coach. His actions were far and away louder than his words.

Pre-adolescent son Eric, daughter Britta, and a bouncy, overly exuberant black Lab named Soot completed the Bernhardson family. We enjoyed wonderful family outings aboard the Bernhardsons' pleasure craft, the *Berganser*, for fishing, hunting, and sightseeing. Accustomed to the exchange of lodging privileges, the whole Seavey gang's arrival on the Bernhardson doorstep was not extraordinary. The twelve dogs? That hadn't happened before. But their large, wooded lot was ideally situated to accommodate those canine visitors, bordering on a small lake as it did. There was plenty of space to string out a tethering chain, all within sight and sound of the house. Quiet—no through traffic—ideal.

The team, having grown accustomed to campouts, was fed early in the evening and, quickly, in a resigned manner, settled in for the night. Likewise, Twilah served an early dinner, which was followed by an hour, or more, of inevitable race talk. In due time, my alarm was set for 7:00 a.m. and the light extinguished. I was tired, but my mind took a long time to slow down. "Had I done all that was necessary? Wonder how it will be getting out of Anchorage. Hope the dogs will be okay out there. Yes, I did arrange for my pickup to get back to Seward. Shirley may need it to get out to the highway. Wonder where the army trailbreakers are by now. I have to bum a couple of sandwiches from Twilah for the run to Knik. Did I put that .22 revolver in? I need to get to sleep. Big day tomorrow. The Great Adventure begins. Did I? Where did I…? How will…?

"How will I get that noise to stop? Please, someone, stop the noise!"

Another second and I realized it was my alarm clock, ushering in one of the most consequential days of my life—Saturday, March 3, 1973. Indeed, the first race was about to begin. Or had it begun years ago with a country school geography lesson on Alaska? Perhaps the great adventure had roots in that decade-old telegram, inviting me to come to the Great Land and teach. What about the first cuddly husky pup, Chignik? What about my total fascination with our state's past? Who's to tell? My hunch, though, is that a seed for such an adventure had found fertile ground in my being long before my first kitchen table dreams at the Redingtons' cabin.

The day that was upon us was mostly gray, warm—around fifteen degrees above zero. It didn't take long for the whole household to spring into action. Dogs were checked, fed, and watered. A hearty breakfast was consumed and the pickup repacked as needed. Planning to arrive at the Tudor track by 9:00 a.m., the kids volunteered to load the dogs, going outdoors to do so at about 8:30 a.m.

"Dad, Genghis is gone!" Mitch yelled, charging into the house at full throttle.

And so he was! After his breakfast, the old rascal slipped his collar and left for an extended inspection of the neighborhood.

We were all thrown into an instant state of near panic. For my part, I was counting on Genghis to get us out of Anchorage. I had one hundred percent confidence in him. We had been through so much together, he being my chief leader for the previous eight years. We fanned out, Seaveys and Bernhardsons, searching on foot throughout the subdivision, which encircled the small lake. No luck. The clock had run out. We had to leave immediately or we, for sure, would be starting at the back of the pack. Kiana, a green leader, not yet two years of age, would have to substitute. Then another fear engulfed me. What was to become of a stray country dog on the loose in a city? All manner of possible misfortunes flashed through my mind. Should the waif return to the scene of his escape to find things familiar vanished, he, for sure, would be lost. I must admit that with the clock ticking and engine running, I stood paralyzed with indecision. A glance at the clock revealed 9:15 a.m. The race would begin at 10:00 a.m. and we still had to drive across town. With a rather weak resolve, I hoisted myself into the driver's seat, popped the four speed into first gear, looked up, and there the scamp came, trotting down the drive toward his thankful, relieved entourage. Not a tinge of remorse or shame did he display, but rather conveyed an attitude of something like, "Hey, what's the hold up? Let's get going." Off we raced to the race; euphoria prevailed, for the prodigal had returned.

29

…Last Words Just Before You Go

Shirley and I wait for my countdown to begin at Tudor Track that historic day. March 3, 1973.

To my knowledge, there is in existence no complete narrative of the first race start except that provided for us by my friend, fellow educator and mentor in this work, Douglas Capra. Capra was in attendance that historic day, March 3, 1973 at the Tudor Race Track to produce an audio tape to be aired on KRXA radio, Seward's one and only station in those days. Eventually, Doug's tape was transcribed and he passed the result on to me. Its fate for the next thirty-five years, or thereabout, was to languish in a box of files marked "Race 1973."

Shamefully, I admit, I had not read the KRXA transcript until recently. But, WOW! When I did, I discovered a jewel of historic originality. Since then, I have read and reread the piece and offer it to my readers here for the first time with but minor editing. Read it as a sportscaster would—an excited sportscaster.

From Files: (March 3, 1973) Taped and transcribed by Doug Capra for radio broadcast, start of first race—complete.

"Well, we're here at the Iditarod Trail Race. Beginning of the race down on Tudor Road in Anchorage. And it's quite a sight. There must be about three hundred people here. Three hundred spectators and the thirty-five mushers that are going to make the race from Anchorage to Nome. I think we have about four minutes, four minutes they just said, four minutes before the race is going to start. They're asking all the spectators to clear the holding area, and so everyone's starting to clear out. It's quite a colorful sight here. You can imagine thirty-five mushers with anywhere between ten and twenty dogs apiece. The noise of barking is all over the place. Some of the mushers spent the night here. They just camped out and were up early this morning. I got down here at nine o' clock and people started coming, but now with only about three or four minutes left to go before the race starts, it's really crowded. I was going to meet Dan Seavey down here; of course, you all know Dan from Seward is going to be in the race. I was waiting for Dan at nine o' clock, I was going to meet him here, and then I found out he wasn't here at a quarter past nine, and he wasn't here at twenty after. We were wondering what was happening. Finally he showed up at nine-thirty, just as relaxed as anything, no problem, and I asked him what happened, and he said that at the very last minute, one of his dogs got loose; he had to chase him all over the neighborhood to catch him before they came out here. That was Genghis or (Jenges) as he calls him, his old time lead dog, ten years old, that he is using as one of his wheel dogs, just bringing him along in case. By the way, Dan is bringing twelve dogs, and he's got two lead dogs; he plans to use two out front, and he's keeping old Genghis as one of his wheel dogs in the back just in case he needs him. Well, two minutes before starting time and the first position mushers are starting to bring their sleds and their teams up to the starting point. They've been marking the dogs so that when they get to Nome, they will know that they are the same dogs that started out in Anchorage. Bud Smyth from Fairbanks, Bud Smyth from Fairbanks they're announcing. He'll be the first one to start the race, with twenty dogs, and they said it's one of the largest teams they've seen around here in a long time. He's coming up to the starting position. There were a few minutes there when we were wondering whether Dan was going to make it at all, I think it's kind of amusing, the way he pulled in here so nonchalantly about half an hour late, and just went to the business of getting ready. Two minutes before the race, now there's only one minute. One minute, I wonder what those mushers are thinking right now. In one minute, they'll be on their way to Nome, a thousand miles through the Alaskan wilderness. I wonder what the dogs are thinking now. I wonder if they know how many miles are ahead for them. It's quite a colorful sight, reminiscent of the Fur Rendezvous, which is just about over up here in Anchorage, lots of parkas and mukluks and so forth. Thirty seconds, they said, which should make it about twenty seconds or fifteen seconds to go. They're bringing the team up there, what a team, twenty dogs; it's the longest team I've ever seen. Ten seconds left and they're going to start, and the Iditarod Race will be on its way. Five seconds. Here's the countdown, and he's gone. There he goes. The first Iditarod Trail Race from Anchorage to Nome, first one, 1973, has begun with the first racer from Fairbanks [Houston], with a twenty-dog team. I think they're going to have intervals of about, about two minutes, that's what I was told not too long ago, intervals of about two minutes between mushers. They'll be announcing them as they go, and Dan Seavey is number fourteen. I'll keep you informed as they start. You can hear the dogs in the background; they seem to be very excited. They know something's going on, but I bet they don't know how many long, grueling days they have ahead of them. Dan's still hitching up his team right now, and I'm walking in that direction; maybe we can talk to him if he's not too busy. I'm sure he's got a lot on his mind. There he is.

"Hey, Dan, as you're walking along, I'm making a tape for KRXA in Seward, so say something to the folks in Seward."

"Well, after a long, long time here, we're finally going to get under way."

"Yeah, you got here a little late."

"Yeah, we got here a little late, chasing the dog around for a half hour. We finally caught him."

"The number one racer started, had twenty dogs."

"That's right, and we're just going to get hooked up here ourselves."

"Yeah, I'll let you go. You've probably got a lot to do."

"Okay, Doug."

"We'll see you."

"Hello to the folks in Seward."

It's a little chilly here in Anchorage; it's probably about fifteen degrees and it's cloudy, and I guess they're going to start five minute intervals between racers. The number one musher has already gone with a twenty-dog team. One minute to go now before number two starts off, and they, I'm sure, announced his name [Dr. Hal Bartko], number two, because I heard them say he had eleven dogs, but I'm not sure who he is, we'll wait to see if they tell us again. We just talked to Dan. Dan told you he was a little late getting here, and it didn't seem to faze him a bit, he just nonchalantly came up here. Thirty seconds before the next musher starts, five seconds and this is the third musher, we must have missed the second one, and there he goes, eleven-dog team, John Schultheis from Knik. John Schultheis from Knik with eleven dogs, and that was musher number three, number four coming up. One minute before number four starts and he's from Point Hope. I don't know what his name is [Ron Oviak] they said it, but I wasn't concentrating at the time, they haven't told how many dogs he has. The crowds have started to gather around the starting points. The dogs, and of course all the other dogs waiting in line, are all excited. Thirty seconds to go. It's going to be a long morning; we have thirty-five mushers altogether taking off here. Ten seconds for musher number four, there he goes.

Well, they're telling the spectators to move back. I didn't get that last musher's name, but he's from Point Hope, and as he left, they said on his way back to Point Hope. That's the interesting thing about some of these village mushers that are coming down. Some of the mushers from around here are just saying they're just on their way home. Evidently, the spectators are getting too close to the start, so they've sort of held up the action here until people have moved back a little bit. They're telling especially young children to move back. Everybody seems to have a camera down here. They just told spectators not to use flashbulbs. During Fur Rendezvous races, too, they were telling people not to use flashbulbs; they can really distract the teams. Well, we've probably got about thirty seconds left before the next musher goes. Yeah, thirty seconds. They're lining up. John Komak from Teller, number five. Number six is Ron Aldrich from Montana Creek, he's moving up into the starting position now. He's got four men on his dogs. It looks like he's got two, four, six, eight, ten, or twelve, I couldn't count. Ron Aldrich. One minute before musher number six starts off along the trail, Ron Aldrich, he's got two, four, six, eight, ten dogs; no, he's got twelve, I didn't see those two. It's a little chilly here, and it's overcast here in Anchorage, probably about fifteen degrees. We must have about four or five hundred people here to watch the first Iditarod Trail Race, a thousand miles from Anchorage to Nome. We just had the thirty-second announcement for musher number six, and all the dogs look like they're ready to go. These dogs are anxious. Ten seconds. There he goes. Musher number six. See you in Nome. George Attla, George Attla is musher number seven, and boy his dogs don't want to stop. They don't want to wait. Two, four, six, eight, ten, twelve, fourteen, sixteen dogs it looks like he's mushing. George Attla, of course, was in the Fur Rendezvous races, former champion, I believe. Oops! A couple of his dogs are getting tangled up here, but he's got four men on them, getting them straightened out. It was quite a sight down here just before the race, watching all the mushers put their dogs into harness, and, of course, with so many dogs down here, everyone was watching where they were stepping. He's got a pretty big team. The biggest team to leave so far was a twenty-dog team, and boy did that look long. This is sixteen dogs. Of course, you know that the mushers can drop any dogs along the way if they want. They can leave them off at the way station and they'll be sent back, they will be flown back—all right. Fifteen seconds before George Attla starts. He's number seven. There he goes. Riding along on one runner there as he started out. People are lined up all along the starting way, and it seems that in the last ten or fifteen minutes, the crowd has increased. A lot of latecomers here who are here to see the mushers off. A lot of encouragement given the mushers. You can imagine the stamina necessary for a trip like this. Dan Seavey from Seward is number fourteen, so we're going to sit here and wait for Dan. There are about thirty-five mushers, thirty-five or thirty-four, I'm not sure, are going to be in this race. Number eight musher has come up into position now, and he's running two, four, six, eight, ten. He's running ten dogs; ten dogs seem to be about an average. Boy, his dogs don't want to wait, either; most of these dogs are all psyched up by now. They all look in good shape. They're not going to wait. It's interesting; one of the spectators is talking about the lead dog. There goes number eight, [Ken Chase] and I don't know who he is, they didn't announce it, and I don't have the list here. As they were waiting to go, the lead dog was sort of talking to them, saying, 'Wait a minute guys; we've only got a few minutes left.' Number nine, double team Robert and Oliver [Owen] Ivan, coming up into position now. They're moving along quite on schedule here. About ten minutes to ten it looks like—let's see, we have two, four, six, eight, ten, twelve, thirteen dogs in this team, musher number nine. One minute. They're moving along on schedule, as I was saying about ten minutes before ten o' clock, ten before starting time it looked like complete chaos out here. Mushers were showing up late, dogs were running all over the place, people were harnessing dogs, men were running around with paint, marking dogs; it didn't look like this race was ever going to get going, but here we are, we're already up to musher number nine. Thirty seconds. It's interesting how the lead dogs seem to be talking to the rest of the dogs. Just waiting to go, the lead dog is looking around, waiting for that start. Ten seconds. Oh, I see what they were saying. This is the first double team, they said. He's got a rider, there's someone riding in the sled, too. It's a two-man team here. Musher number ten is now on the starting line, Darrel Reynolds of Anchorage. Ten seconds now before Darrel Reynolds of Anchorage gets off. He gets a kiss good-bye. There he goes, little whistle there and he's off. Musher number eleven, waiting for musher number eleven to come to the starting line, and he's not here. Isaac Okleasik is the next musher, number eleven. He might not be here. They're wondering if Isaac is here, musher number eleven, but he hasn't come up to the starting line yet. One minute, they're going on with the countdown anyway. Here he comes, he's here, he's here. Here they go, there they are. Just getting there in the nick of time. Probably about thirty seconds now before musher number eleven is going to start out on the thousand-mile trek to Nome. To Nome, that would be something, a thousand miles from Anchorage to Nome in a dog sled. Now that would be a race. Fifteen seconds. Well, they said go, but he's still here. I guess they have some problems up front there, there he goes, he's off, number eleven. Musher number twelve coming up here now. He's mushing two, four, six, eight, ten dogs, he's mushing ten dogs. The spectators are getting in the way around here, so they're pushing people back. The spectators, of course, can affect the dogs. They were warning people about that during the Fur Rendezvous, too. They've already warned the people about using flashbulbs. Herbert Foster from Kotzebue is the number twelve musher in the race. He's all packed up and set to go, mukluks and parka, ten dogs. Of course, the dogs are nervous, so many people watching them. Thirty seconds. These village dogs, too, are just not used to crowds, and I imagine what it does to them when they get into the city here. Fifteen seconds and then Herbert Foster from Kotzebue will be on his way. There he goes, little whistle and he's off. Number thirteen [Bill Arpino] coming up, mushing two, four, six, eight, ten, twelve, thirteen or fourteen dogs he's mushing, I think. Number thirteen. I don't know his name yet; they should be announcing it. He's pounding his snow hook into the ground right now. The snow hook is a hook that is attached to the lead line; it stops the dogs.

Instead of holding the brakes, you just pound the snow hook into the snow, and of course, you can always wrap it around a tree if there's a tree available. Dan Seavey's team is back there waiting, he's on deck. There he is and Dan's got his number on, number fourteen. Bill Arpino from Tok is number thirteen. One minute before he's going to start. Boy, he's got some lively-looking dogs there. As I said, Dan is coming up next, who we're all rooting for down in Seward. There he goes, number thirteen, and here comes Dan. Dan's on his way up and I'll see if I can get a couple of words from him before he goes. Okay, I'm going to talk to Dan now.

"Well, hello, Dan. What are your last words, just before you go?"

"Well, I'd like to say thank you to the folks in Seward for giving me this opportunity to go up the trail."

"Okay, fine, I didn't want to say your last words, that didn't sound too good."

"My last words are, 'We'll see you in Nome.'"

"Okay, we'll see you. Good luck, Dan."

"Thank you, thank you."

"So, Dan Seavey, number fourteen, from Seward, is on the line now and he's mushing twelve dogs. He got here a little late; he got here a half an hour late. We were waiting for him at nine-thirty and when he finally got here, he told the story of his old lead dog Genghis who got loose just before he was ready to put him in the truck, and he and his kids went chasing Genghis all around to get him. One minute to go, and Dan looks like he's ready to go, he's in a new sled, a custom-made sled built by Bob Hill of Seward. He's all packed up, and of course, all his kids, all Dan's kids, are out there, holding his dogs. He just asked Mitch to tighten them up a little bit. He's got a good-lookin' team, Dan does; he's got a good chance. His wife's here and his kids, holding his dogs for him. Thirty seconds to go. Fifteen seconds.

"HIKE, HIKE, HIKE, HIKE, HIKE!!!"

"Oh, gee, there he goes. Ah, that's interesting. Just as Dan was starting, they said Dan Seavey from Seward on his way to the Seward Peninsula, and that's right, he's on his way there now. We'll stick around here and watch the other mushers on their way. Down here in Anchorage at the Iditarod Trail Race, thousand-mile race from Anchorage to Nome, and Dan Seavey just took off, and he had a few words to say before he left; he looked all set to go. Number fifteen musher stepping up there, and I didn't get his name. I was busy putting my cartridge on the other side. We'll try to get his name in a minute, number fifteen. Musher number fifteen, Dick Mackey from Wasilla. Sixteen coming up now, mushing one, two, three, four, six, eight, it's hard counting these dogs. It looks like he has about twelve dogs. Musher number sixteen and we're almost halfway through, and they're moving along at a quick pace. There aren't too many delays. One of the mushers got here a little late; oh, it must have been musher number eight, or nine. We were wondering whether he was going to show up, and they kept the countdown; they keep the countdown whether they show up or not, and he showed up here with just about thirty seconds to go, stopped his dogs, and they sat down to rest, then he started them again and they didn't want to go. One minute to go. Rod Perry of Anchorage, number sixteen, Rod Perry of Anchorage. It's kind of interesting, as Dan brought his team up, he sat them down and his lead dog just sat down and he was a little bit worried; he was looking at them, wondering whether his lead dog was going to get up, but when they said go, Dan just said, 'Hike!' and his lead got up and just took them on the way. It's cold here. Ten seconds for number sixteen. There he goes, a little bit of trouble, he got off to a bad start, something happened here. Musher number sixteen had a little bit of a problem getting going here, but he's on his way now. Musher number seventeen. A lot of excitement down here, a lot of newspaper men and radio men and camera men. One minute to go. Those dogs are whining—they want to go to Nome. That was close, that was close; he's on his way. Herbert Nayokpuk from Shishmaref, and that was interesting, as the countdown was going from ten, he was up with his lead dog, and as they were going ten, nine, eight, he was running back to get onto the end of the sleigh, the sled to get going. He just made it back on number one and he was off. The crowd starting to clear out it looks a little now. We're more than halfway through. About thirty-five mushers going to

Nome. The next two teams, we've been informed, aren't ready yet, but their times will start, we are told, when their official times start. I'm not exactly sure what that means, but let's wait and find out. Team number eighteen coming up now. Let's see how many dogs we have now. Oh, I see what we're doing. Teams number eighteen and nineteen aren't ready. Teams eighteen and nineteen aren't ready, but they're counting them down anyway, because they're still hitching up, evidently. Okay, team numbers eighteen and nineteen are not ready, but they're counting them down anyway and they will just have to leave after everybody else, so team number twenty is here, waiting, and it's Slim Randles. One of the dogs had a problem just before we were going to start off, and of course, Mother Nature called and the dog wouldn't start that way until he answered Mother Nature's call, so we all sat here and waited. Number twenty is on the line now, waiting for number eighteen and nineteen to have their countdowns. Eighteen has already been counted down, and nineteen is being counted down right now, and then twenty. Some of the dogs are just being marked now as they're coming up to the starting point. Slim Randles from Talkeetna. Now we've just been sitting around and waiting for the countdowns of teams eighteen and nineteen; they're not ready and they're going to have to leave at the end of the race, after everybody else is finished. Team number twenty is here and he's been waiting, Slim Randles of Talkeetna. His team's been patiently waiting here. Team number twenty has been sitting here about five minutes now. The dogs are probably wondering what's going to happen, but they'll be off in one minute. It's a little chilly here in Anchorage. You'll probably be listening to this; well, you might hear it Saturday night or Sunday. Of course today is March the third, the start of the Iditarod Trail Race, a thousand-mile race from Anchorage to Nome. Chilly here. It's probably about ten or fifteen degrees, cloudy skies; it seems like a good day to start the race, a little bit of trouble with the spectators. Fifteen seconds for number twenty, Slim Randles of Talkeetna. There he goes. Team number twenty-one coming up now. Looks like a small team, under ten, in fact. His lead dog is an unusual dog. It doesn't look like a husky or a malamute, can't tell what kind it is, though; it's not Great Dane. Redington is number twenty-one, and his lead dog is a cross between a husky and a Belgian sheep dog, and it does look rather unique out there. Raymie Redington from Knik is number twenty-one. The variety of dogs around here is something else. You see huskies and you see malamutes and every cross in-between. Number twenty-one, Redington from Knik, is ready to go. He's mushing nine dogs. He's got about fifteen seconds to go. Raymie Redington from Knik is on his way back to Knik, of course; he's going to go the rest of the way up, I hope, to Nome. Terry Miller of Palmer, number twenty-two, is getting ready. Terry Miller of Palmer just took off. I took a little break. I guess people from all over the place are out here. I just met an old friend of mine from an island out in the Aleutians, from The Rock, good old Adak. We're waiting now for the next musher to come up to the starting line. Terry Miller of Palmer just left with a small team, I think he had only nine dogs, but I'm not sure of that. Nobody has come up here yet. I guess they're still marking the dogs. We're running a little bit behind schedule on that. What they're doing is marking the dogs with a special type of paint down here so that when they get to Nome, they will know that they are the same dogs. Bruce Mitchell from Ester Dome, number twenty-three, and they're still marking the dogs; they're marking them with this kind of paint down here so when they get to Nome, they'll know they are the same team—the same team that has been running from Anchorage to Nome, just to prevent a little hanky-panky from going on along the way. We're waiting now for Bruce Mitchell from Ester Dome; thirty seconds to go and he's not up here yet, so he might have to leave at the end of the race, like mushers eighteen and nineteen. They're probably marking his dogs. They might be doing that. Okay, well, Bruce Mitchell of Ester Dome had his countdown and he wasn't up here; he's number twenty-three. Well here he is now. Is that him? Some team's coming up now. Maybe this is twenty-four. No, this is twenty-three, Bruce Mitchell of Ester Dome; here he comes and he's already had his go, so he's probably going to go right through. He's got nine dogs and he's stopped up here at the starting line, but he's already had his go.

What are they doing? I think they're marking his dogs. They're marking his dogs, and they're marking them, well, wherever they can find a white spot. All right, number twenty-three's off. Now Mitchell, he's about a minute behind schedule. John Coffin, team number twenty-four. One minute to go and he's on his way up to the starting line, too. They must be behind him, marking his dogs, that's it, because they're just marking his dogs about twenty, thirty feet from the starting line, and he's got one minute. The crowd has thinned out; there aren't as many people. I suppose people came down to see certain people run, and then they watched him and they left. Fifteen seconds and John Coffin will be on his way. Oh, look at that, he got himself a running start. John Coffin, number twenty-four. He started about thirty feet from behind the starting line as the countdown went five, four, he was off, and by the time it hit one, he was over the starting line. We're waiting for musher number twenty-five; we've got about nine or ten more to go after this. Here comes team number twenty-five. Let's see who this is, mushing ten, John Luster from Chickaloon, team number twenty-five. John Luster's got no brake on his sled, some of the other mushers were commenting on that, and someone said he doesn't need a brake; he's not going to stop. I bet it would be real interesting to talk to some of these mushers and ask them the type of equipment, type of things, they're bringing and how much it weighs, and so forth. Fifteen seconds, ten seconds now before musher number twenty-five gets along the way. He's off. There are still quite a few people here, lining up at the starting line here on the sides. Conrad Killigruk from Point Hope, number twenty-six. They're still marking the dogs; that's why it's taking these mushers a little bit of time to get to the starting line. Killigruk is just getting his dogs marked and he's up here now with probably about a minute to go, then dogs. The largest team we've seen here was one of the first teams to race, twenty-dog team. This is a ten-dog team. Conrad Killigruk from Point Hope, number twenty-six. I was just told that he has some of the biggest dogs around here; now that I look at them, they do look a little bigger than some of the others. Of course, when you're seeing by now with twenty-six mushers, we've seen quite a few dogs, and you don't start looking at personalities. He's off. Conrad Killigruk of Point Hope, on his way. Musher number twenty-seven with a yellow tarp over all his supplies. I'm trying to find out who number twenty-seven is; they'll tell us in a minute. Bobby Vent from Huslia, number twenty-seven. A lot of encouragement from the crowd. Of course, the number one musher is going to get twelve thousand dollars, and that might be enough motivation right there, and the first twenty places take money, even the twentieth place gets five hundred dollars. Of course, a lot of these mushers have a lot of money tied up in their dogs. They're talking to him about the signs right now, following the signs. The trail is marked and, of course, the first section of the trail is to Knik, and there's a special prize for the first musher to reach Knik; there's a thousand dollars in gold waiting. He's off. What's his last name? Vent, Bobby Vent from Huslia. It's an Indian village up north and he's an old-time musher. He's been mushing dogs for a number of years. He used to come down to the Rendezvous years ago, but he hasn't been down recently, and this is the first time he's entered a race for a number of years. He's got a lot of fans and a lot of people who remember him from the old times, and he's going to get out there and give her heck this time. That's good. Who's this that just came up here, do you know? Alec Tatum, number twenty-eight. This is actually the first time he's been in a dog race. He just started mushing dogs this year. He's a real game guy; he's a real sport, because he's never really been involved in any dog mushing until this year, and he's going to start out with a big one. He's working for the Park Service. He's a young fellow. That's the one to start out with, I guess. He has said that he looks forward to this as an adventure, not so much that he wants to win the race, but if he can make it, he'll be happy. Oh, my coffee has come. I'll take it black. It's a little chilly here in Anchorage. It's probably around fifteen or twenty degrees. He's off now, that was musher number twenty-eight. Someone started telling me that they saw a team go out wearing dog boots, little booties or mukluks for dogs. Of course, they wear those to protect the dogs' feet from sharp stones or ice, but I don't think there have been many teams wearing those out of here. They're saving them for up north, when they do run into that sort of thing. I know that talking to Dan. Dan Seavey has made up forty-eight mukluks. Dave Olson from Knik, number twenty-nine, is starting now. Dan was talking about these forty-eight mukluks that he made for his dogs, and he's worried about having to put them all on. That would be a problem, because his dogs aren't used to wearing them. That's Dave Olson, number twenty-nine, on his way to Nome. Musher number thirty should be coming up next, but I see number thirty-three or thirty-two, but let's wait and find out. We've only got thirty-four or thirty-five mushers. Evidently, at the end of the trail, the starting line must be like a funnel and the spectators are moving closer and closer in out near the end. We were just told that if they get run over, it's going to be their fault. Another double team coming out, number thirty. I got one of the names, Mike Schreiber of McKinley Park, but I don't know who the other one was [Ford Reeves]. He's got a big team, thirteen or fourteen dogs. I was just told that in this double team, some of the dogs are wearing freight-style harnesses, and it is a freight sled. There are a lot of different types of sleds here, and the freight sled is a really long sled. Sleds used in the old days to carry freight up the trail, which was one of its purposes. He's got some big dogs here, and they're off, double team again, two double teams so far. Howard Farley, number thirty-one, from Nome, and he's on his way home. Fifteen dogs. One of the questions has been, "Are all these mushers going to make it?" But I suppose there's no question about Howard Farley. He lives in Nome, so he's going to get there sooner or later, I suppose, with fifteen dogs. He's got a big sled, too; he's got a freight sled. Boy, it's a long one. There he goes. Howard Farley from Nome, on his way home with fifteen dogs and a big freight sled. They said he had a little tangle starting out, but he looks all right; he's gone. Musher number thirty-two coming up, Tom Mercer from Talkeetna; he has fourteen dogs. Tom Mercer, Talkeetna. Musher number thirty-two, Tom Mercer from Talkeetna. Dick Wilmarth from Red Devil, musher number thirty-three, and we're getting near the end here. And musher number thirty-three is on his way (Phooy). We're waiting for musher number thirty-four.

We should be getting down to the end here. There are either thirty-four or thirty-five in this race, and just before the mushers go, they're being given directions to Knik because the trail is marked. Victor Kotongan from Unalakleet, which is on the western coast, just below the Seward Peninsula, Unalakleet, it's one of the stops so he's on his way home, too. It's not far from Nome. There's musher number thirty-four on his way; he's from Unalakleet, he's going home, too. Casey Celusnick and John Schultz from Delta, double team, they're number eighteen and they didn't make it off in time. Number thirty-four was the last team in the race. Now number eighteen is getting ready to go, double team and a big freight sled. Team number eighteen has another problem now; one of their dogs, named Sam, has got a cut and so they're going to take him out of the team. Number eighteen's on its way now and they've had a couple of problems now because they didn't make their position because of problems. Berry McAlpine, who is number nineteen, from Goat Creek, is going to be the last musher, and number eighteen, another double team, had trouble just before they left and they had to leave one of their dogs that had a cut, and that was about one minute before starting, so they're one less dog now. The final musher, number nineteen. Barry McAlpine from Goat Creek, having a little trouble here. What's the matter? Won't his dogs go? He was supposed to go, number nineteen, but he wasn't ready, and so now he's last and he's having problems now getting started, some of his dogs. Soon as he goes, the race will be over, as far as the start anyway. He's on his way, Barry McAlpine from Goat Creek. The Nineteen Seventy-Three Iditarod Trail Race is underway, all thirty-four mushers have started on a cold, cloudy day here in Anchorage, March third, Saturday, and this is Doug Capra in Anchorage for KRXA in Seward."

30

OK, Hike!

Our race committee provided over 300 of these trail markers for the Anchorage-Susitna Station segment of trail. Nearly all fell victim to souvenir hounds before race day.

Day 1: Saturday, March 3, Anchorage to Knik

As observed in the Capra narrative, the Seaveys made their appearance at the Tudor (now Tozier) Track in a tardy fashion or, at best, later than we had hoped. Nobody seemed to notice or care, if they did. Nor did I, for that matter, as we had nearly an hour to hook up before my 10:30 a.m. countdown.

Our none-too-glamorous power wagon rolled to a stop before overrunning a lath bearing a paper plate with a none-too-glamorous number fourteen scrawled upon it. All hands hit the deck running as we undertook to contribute our one-thirty-fourth part to the growing bedlam and make up for time lost in our attempts to locate Genghis. Dog teams already assembled in the staging area gave our arrival a loud, excited welcome.

What a scene greeted us. It was one of semi-organized chaos, bordering on near pandemonium. It was not a large crowd of spectators by today's standards—perhaps three hundred as Capra has it—but it was a highly charged and excited crowd mingling freely with dogs and drivers. They were well-wishers mainly, family and friends of the thirty-four Iditarod Race trailblazers, there to witness history in the making. Dogs, 396 of them, produced the most commotion. From low bass repetitive barks to high-pitched operatic-like screams, each, in turn, informed the world it was ready and eager to hit the trail. Mushers chased loose dogs, strung out towlines, checked sleds and gear. Fans shouted out questions and took pictures with cameras requiring photographic film to do so.

Race officials traveled from team to team, dabbing a green, long-lasting paint on each dog. The idea here was to provide security against replacement of worn-out dogs with fresh ones during the race. As a security measure, it was a flop, because little green paint ever arrived in Nome. Most had been rubbed off during frequent and violent snow baths taken by the gaudily decorated during the long journey there. Officials, strangely, did not check sleds for mandatory gear.

As an aside, one day in February 2011, an animal control person (formerly dogcatcher) contacted my grandson, Danny, age twenty-eight, wanting to know if he had lost a dog in the Wasilla area. In fact, he hadn't, and he asked why he had been contacted. It was revealed that an old stray husky-like dog had been turned in to the Wasilla Center. Using a special electronic scanner, an embedded, under-the-skin microchip was discovered and checked against Iditarod Race records. Indeed, it was Danny's former dog, named Checkers. He had run Checkers in his 2001 team, the year he, Mitch, and I became the first and only three generations of one family of mushers to participate simultaneously in an Iditarod. By use of this modern means, the aged veteran, then fourteen years old, was identified. He had traveled to Nome ten years prior and was sold to a second party two years later. Now that's long-lasting ID.

Even at this distance in time, I have a vivid recollection of my fascination for all the dog men, gear, and dogs. Of the thirty-three other mushers,

I was acquainted with just four: Dick Mackey, Raymie Redington, Ron Aldrich, and Dave Olson, all were Aurora Dog Mushers Club members. All others were complete strangers, seen two days earlier at the mushers' banquet or, in the case of George Attla, blazing down the Fur Rendezvous sprint trail behind twenty dogs at twenty-five miles per hour. I was pretty sure Attla wouldn't be traveling at that pace over the trail lying before us. By reputation, only I knew the fearless competitor and winner of the 1967 Alaska Purchase Centennial Race, Isaac Okleasik, an Eskimo driver out of Teller, Alaska. That was it.

Such a collection was never seen before or since. I was immediately fascinated by the Eskimo drivers of the Bering Sea Coast. Most were short, stout pleasant fellows sporting knee-high sealskin mukluks with tough oogruk bottoms. Knee-length, fur-lined parkas abounded, protected by resilient white canvas shells crowned with polar bear, wolf, or wolverine fur-trimmed hoods. An Eskimo parka is a product of centuries of Arctic living, truly the wearer's home away from home. Large, lightly loaded, mostly freight-style sleds were in evidence among those intriguing figures of the treeless tundra regions. Handsome, stoic, confident. Their dogs were not large, but well furred with heavy undercoats and long guard hair without any apparent preference as to color. Sleek, well-fed animals, like their masters, they were the amazing handiwork of an unforgiving, ruthless northern environment. If I were awed by any mushers, it was those real, honest-to-goodness Eskimos as they prepared to mush north to their homes, to a barren wasteland, as I naively imagined it to be.

The remainder of us was a cosmopolitan bunch of interior Athabascans, a black man, and plentiful Caucasians, with and without beards. Uniform, likewise, was without uniformity. Mine being typical—air force surplus footwear, pants, trigger-finger wool gloves, army surplus great mittens with long cuffs, wind-breaker pants, down-filled parka from REI, hood trimmed with fur ruff, and a surplus navy watch cap just about completed my mushing ensemble. There were a couple additions: a medium-weight, all-wool jacket and a union suit of heavy, all-wool underwear. To be sure, many exhibited beautiful, artistically-sewn fur caps of leather, beaver, martin, and mink. Several army surplus parka hoods were adorned with rather scruffy coyote ruffs.

My dogs were a mongrel lot when compared with those of my Eskimo trail-mates. Somewhat larger than their Eskimo counterparts, they were most certainly ten to twenty pounds heavier than the wiry endurance dog of today. Heavy protective coats were evident in most all dogs there that day, without regard for color or markings. They were, in fact, prototypes for what would become known simply as the Alaska husky.

Sleds—or sleighs, as interior people called them—varied in form according to, I would guess, availability. We used what we had or what we could manufacture, the result being a hodge-podge. I remember a delicate, almost fragile-looking light-freight sled, beautiful, and made of birch. Another defying identity, was banged together from two-by-six-inch lumber. There were, also, sprint-stanchion style sleds, with a vintage look that suggested a preference for a return to retirement rather than a strenuous trip to Nome. Added to those a couple of huge, perhaps twelve or fourteen feet, authentic freight sleds from a bygone era, and one gets the picture.

"My people" were there to greet us latecomers, obviously elated that we hadn't decided on a last-minute race withdrawal, as rumor already had it. Genghis, you old scoundrel. With the exception of our Anchorage hosts, the Bernhardsons, all were Sewardites. There, for the start of the first Iditarod, were lifelong friends Bob and Shirley Hill, Don and Ruth Mai, and Joanne Hoogland, all fellow educators at Seward High School. A light smattering of Seward High students, including Dale, Joanne's son, turned out. Good friend and congregation member, Rae Elde, was also there. Microphone in hand, tape recorder churning that gray morning, Doug Capra was present to give words to history in the making.

Harnessing and hookup were both smooth and speedy due to able assistance from Darian, Tracie, and Mitch, the latter serving as pit crew boss. We had rehearsed on the way to the track the hookup order and position of each dog in the team—lead, swing, team, or wheel. The day was relatively warm and working at a fever pitch, I soon was in bare hands and had shed my red parka in favor of a wool jacket. Together with my days' supply of sandwiches, the parka was thrown, without further thought, on the front seat of the pick up—and forgotten. This oversight caused me endless anguish during the run to Knik as I contemplated the absurdity of venturing into the Great Frozen

Unknown parka-less. The reality of the situation was that I would have to somehow acquire a parka before proceeding beyond Knik or scratch from the race before having a respectable go at it.

In a spur-of-the-moment decision, I placed Kiana, who was less than two years of age, in single lead. She would remain there for most of the trip to Nome. Next, in the swing pair, I placed Snippy and Crazy. The first set of team dogs was Bandit and Sonny. Sonny was destined to become one of my crackerjack leaders of the second Iditarod in 1974. Next back, Eska, hitched singly in team position. Third set back were team dogs Flame and Casper. Genghis, my old and tested leader and partner, Shiak, made up the fourth pair of team dogs. Lastly, the kids harnessed and hooked in two extraordinarily strong, aggressive pooches, Koyuk and Kuchik, in wheel, just in front of the sled. With the team complete, I made last adjustments to my sled pack and we were ready to sail—before the first team's countdown began. It is worthy of mention that as far as I could observe, not a single bootie left the start that morning on a dog's foot. Unlike today's races, where just about every dog foot in the entire race is protected via the laborious process called "bootying." For the first race, I used two booties only on two occasions. Religious care of feet with an assist from my "old Eskimo foot ointment" did the trick. The old adage—"no foot, no horse"—rings doubly true for dogs. By comparison, the first few races were slow races—twenty-two days, let's say; modern ones are very speedy, nine to ten days for front-runners. Our slower pace, no doubt, contributed to better overall feet condition without use of booties. Joe, Sr. once remarked that he wouldn't own a dog that had to be bootied on the way to Nome. As race times began to shorten in the mid-1970s to seventeen, then fifteen days, even Joe adjusted his dog standards, giving in to the bootying procedure routinely throughout his many treks to Nome.

The first two-minute countdown began promptly at 10:00 a.m. A battle between an excited crowd and the race track's public address system to be heard was decidedly won by the latter. Present was the race marshal, Dick Tozier, wearing his signature ruffed red parka and black baseball cap. Race judge, Joel Kotke, clipboard in hand, was also present, reminding me of a slim, sophisticated Western movie actor of the day. There, too, at one end of the official start line, was honorary race marshal, Colonel Muktuk Marston, who, in the past, was organizer of Alaska's Territorial Guard and, at that time, a key benefactor of our first race efforts.

Looking smug and confident as the countdown continues on the beginning of the adventure of my lifetime. That demeanor would change. I left my parka and lunch at the start line.

Bud Smyth was the very last of thirty-four mushers to draw his start position from the traditional mukluk, Thursday evening. The Huston, Alaska, driver waited all evening to discover that he would be first out the chute on race day morning. So he was, with twenty super-charged huskies, the largest hitch in the race. Bud would become a lifelong friend and avid supporter of the Iditarod, even to the extent of siring two tough competitor sons, Ramey Smyth and Cim Smyth. Bud Smyth, a husky, no-nonsense type of man, became first ever to "pull the hook" and head off toward distant Nome as an Iditarod race competitor.

In a measured cadence, teams came to and cleared the Tudor Track starting chute. Palmer medical doctor, Hal Bartko, would become tired of bringing up the rear of the race and scratch at McGrath. Third musher, amiable John Schultheis, plagued with illness, called it quits upon reaching Knik, our first checkpoint.

Numbers four and five, seasoned Eskimo dog men, Ron Oviak, down from Point Hope, and John Komak of Teller, both drove teams of thirteen dogs. I spent a good bit of time traveling with the stoic but friendly Komak. Ron Aldrich, with whom I became acquainted, and grew to admire and respect while working and training on the trail out of Knik before the race, was number six to leave, with his big, friendly Cucumber in lead. Fairbank's George Attla, already a sprint mushing legend among fellow mushers and with John Q. Public, pulled away with fourteen sleek, short-haired racing machines, causing me to rethink my expectations for a top finish in Nome. Number seven, Attla, was followed by Anvik native musher Ken Chase driving ten dogs. Chase would eventually rack up a sixteen-race career, including sharing the trail with me during the 1997, twenty-fifth race anniversary run. Ninth up caused quite a stir among race fans, the Ivan brothers, Robert and Owen, in from Akiak. With a huge freight sled, thirteen dogs, and two drivers, they were the first of three "double teams" to leave Anchorage that day. Those three doubles were unique in Iditarod race history, never to be repeated after 1973. Unique, too, were the Ivan brothers, the only double team to hold together and arrive in Nome. Number ten in line, Darrel Reynolds, an Anchorage musher, would have a short Iditarod career, ending it upon arrival at Knik. Another six minutes and numbers eleven, twelve, and thirteen—Isaac Okleasik, from Teller; Herbert Foster, from Kotzebue; and Bill Arpino, from Tok—were on their way.

"Number fourteen," barked the announcer as my handlers—my kids—escorted our team to the start position. "Dan Seavey of Seward, on his way to the Seward Peninsula—one minute to go." I do not remember much about that final moment before my great adventure, my personal odyssey, began. What I do recall was a feeling of a most calm serenity enveloping me, an at-peace well-being filtering into my very core. All was done. All was right with the world. All was going to be just fine. Come what may during the next one thousand miles, we—my dogs and I—could handle and profit from each and every one of the experiences awaiting us. Indeed, my dogs had settled way down from their excited carrying-on exhibited upon our arrival at the track an hour earlier. Kiana, the sweetest natured leader I have ever trained, stood in an attitude of quiet anticipation, as did most of the twelve. My team size for the first race was near the 11.65 dog average, with teams ranging from seven to Bud Smyth's twenty. A grand total of 396 furry ones were entered in that race.

"Thirty seconds!" Hugs all around. Sincere good-byes as kids, Shirley, and I had no reason at that time to think we would be reunited before my return to Seward at race end. That Shirley and the children would travel to Nome for the finish hadn't been discussed, nor occurred to me. As events unfolded, however, I would again see my family that very day and to my great joy, some one thousand miles and twenty-two days later in far-off Nome. Hearty handshakes all round with well-wishers. And "Five, four, three, two, one! Go!"

"OK, HIKE!"

Kiana lunged forward, Snippy and Crazy took up the slack in swing, and the team lined out nicely. Then a final glance back, a quick wave, and we were on the way. Mixed birch and spruce soon edged the trail, muffling crowd noise back at the chute. The last I remember hearing was, "Next up, number fifteen, Dick Mackey of Wasilla with a beautiful team—a team of sixteen dogs," blaring out of what seemed more than ample speakers.

Behind me, nineteen remaining teams departed to the rhythm of a two-minute clock. Well, most teams, that is. Number nineteen, Barry McAlpine, for reasons known only to him, was not ready when his turn rolled around, so he was allowed to proceed down the trail at the tail end of the pack. With but seven dogs in harness, McAlpine left the chute, traveled perhaps one hundred yards, where they became ensnarled in a seven-dog ball of fighting fury, bringing their own as well as their distraught master's Iditarod bid to a calamitous halt. Alec Tatum did better, being disqualified at Knik. Seems he arrived two dogs short of the eleven in his team at Anchorage. We were allowed to "drop" dogs, but only at designated checkpoints, where they could be cared for and flown back to civilization. In all, nearly one-third—twelve of the thirty-four starters—would lose out in their quest of the Iditarod Trail. A further look at drivers leaving after me shows Rod Perry, who would become an author with Iditarod as his theme. Another was Herbert Nayokpuk, on his way to becoming the "Shishmaref Cannonball," and one of the most colorful and popular mushers of all times. Raymie Redington, filling in for

Joe, Sr., was destined to contribute two sons to future race competition. Bobby Vent, considered at age fifty-nine to be the "old man" of the event, would become a travel companion. We mushed halfway across Alaska and finished in Nome together. For Howard Farley, number thirty-one, Nome was home. He has been Mr. Iditarod there since finishing his one and only Iditarod, in 1973. John Schultz of Delta Junction lost his double partner due to injury and continued to Nome alone—literally—to become the all-time record holder for the red lantern—spending thirty-two grueling days plus five hours en route. Nowadays, race officials can withdraw a musher who falls too far behind. Schultz has that record, it seems, in perpetuity. With the unfortunate exception of Barry McAlpine, all first Iditarod hopefuls, by 11:15 a.m. that historic day, were underway over the first segment of their long march to Nome. We were off to the first checkpoint, "New Knik," a gold rush relic town situated on the west bank of Knik Arm. Every single one of us was a rookie in the sport of long-distance, endurance, sled dog racing.

Our route along the Tudor Race Track and beyond to the Eagle River vicinity was not the historic Iditarod Trail. As designated in 1910, the Seward to Nome Winter Mail Trail coursed its way north from the Gateway City, of Seward, rounded Turnagain Arm and climbed over Crow Pass, connecting Old Knik (Eklutna today), Cottonwood, and New Knik while skirting Knik Arm. Then, off it headed toward the newly discovered Iditarod gold fields. Sewardites, of that time, liked to point out that Anchorage was but a mariner's note at the mouth of a rivulet known as Ship Creek.

Within three miles of the Anchorage start line, the team settled into an easy eight to nine miles per hour trot for which they were trained. Folks lined the way by the hundreds, unlike the thousands of today's Iditarods. But the encouraging shouts were heartfelt, duly acknowledged, and much appreciated. From some, an impression was conveyed that they believed we were off to meet our untimely and unnecessarily foolish demise. "Hope you make it," "You guys are nuts" or exclamations to that effect were common. One fellow had the nerve—gall, really—to suggest I would have better luck "making it" if I were driving a snowmachine.

Toward the end of our first hour, we were smoothly gliding along a subdivision frontage road. Homes nestled among birch stands were generously spaced with a drive for each joining our frontage road trail.

Approaching yet another of these drives, Kiana, without courtesy of an advance notice, whipped a ninety-degree gee turn into it and, with no noticeable hesitation, the rest of the team followed. We were, in fact, on a hot trail of a wayward dog team. That team being wrapped every which way amid birch and spruce, plus a porch post or two, carrying on with the most profound dog racket possible. I managed to get stopped just short of becoming actively involved. Judging from the large number of canine participants in the growing tumult, I rightly suspected that it was Bud Smyth who had led me astray. No problem, really. For the past five years, I had been perfecting a maneuver for just such occasions—turning the team around in its tracks. With all the commotion, it took a bit of doing to get Kiana's attention and that of the swing dogs. Once I had it, I issued a rather calm, non-urgent command, "Haw-haw-haw!" The front three then stood facing me. Next, a sharp, "Come!" was given, and the front three and each pair of team dogs, in turn, peeled off to my left, retracing their steps to our rear, executing a very nice u-turn. As the wheelers were passing my position, I simply gave the "hike" command and off toward Knik we flew once again.

Bud Smyth pulled into the Knik checkpoint on late Saturday night with a badly broken sled. He remarked that he had "made every wrong turn possible between Anchorage and Knik," complaining of an absence of trail markers. According to Dick Mackey, who, in fact, personally marked the trail extremely well, "There weren't three of the three hundred markers left on race day; souvenir hounds got them!" George Attla, too, found markers to be scarce and became lost several frustrating times. Personally, I do not recall seeing a single marker over the entire course. That I avoided the grand detour maze speaks more of my good luck than any special trail-sniffing ability I may have possessed. Trail conditions between Anchorage and the Palmer Highway weigh station were good with adequate, compacted snow. Volunteer trail guards were strategically placed at road crossings and thinning crowds, which equated to fewer distracting flashbulb photos being taken, contributed to our ease of travel. We crossed to the west side of the two-lane Palmer Highway at the weigh station. There, our good luck went sour. The trail north, after making the crossing, ran mostly in the road ditch, skirting the east boundary of Fort Richardson on its way to Eklutna. It was terrible. Two two-foot wide, one foot deep tank tracks with a hump between, some five to six feet in width. A mixture of churned-up dirt and gritty snow for the running surface confirmed my wisdom in selecting Old Oak, shod with iron as it was, for use under such conditions. A great amount of fancy footwork with resulting perspiration was required to successfully negotiate several miles of that roughed-up trail—in an upright position. Was the army trail to Nome going to be like this? A sickening thought, if but a fleeting one.

As the team neared Eklutna, located between the Alaska Railroad and the east side of upper Knik Arm, a gnawing feeling that I had forgotten something back in Anchorage overtook me. Was it the chill I began to feel through the wool plaid jacket I wore as we neared the predictably breezy Knik Arm? Or could it have been those little reminders of hunger that welled up from time to time in my stomach? Regardless, in a flash of realization, I knew I had left behind both my parka and that day's food ration—Twilah's sandwiches. No need to check my load for them. I remembered placing them on the dog truck seat to be loaded at the last minute—and forgotten. What to do? "There was no way," I reasoned. "I could leave Knik the next day without a parka; to do so would be, without doubt, suicidal." This newly discovered plight was having its way with my imagination as we neared the graveled road to Eklutna, where it joined the highway and crossed the railroad track both in just a few feet.

To my surprise, there, serving as a road and railroad crossing guard, was my fellow race organizer, the music man, Gleo Huyck. George Attla had, a short distance back, flown by me for at least the third time, having taken time consuming wrong turns along the way. He was just then, with Gleo playing lead dog, making his way over the combined road and rail crossing onto the dog trail, which skirted Eklutna Village toward Knik Arm flats, some half mile beyond. Since George's team was up and running, my outfit sped through the rather difficult crossing in chase mode without incident. As I passed Gleo—and to this day, I do not know why—I hollered, "Gleo, I left my red parka in Anchorage!" Bear in mind this was the Dark Age of Great Disconnectivity. It was that far-off time, devoid of matchbook-size cell phones, a time when only the select had even citizen band two-way radios. It was an era when darkness of the time was illuminated by a lighted pay phone booth on a windy street corner. An epoch punctuated by rows of sit down pay phone booths lining long stretches of air terminal walls worldwide. Anyway, it was a dumb utterance and I knew so as soon as it was out of my mouth. What in the world did I expect Huyck to do, stuck as he was, at his duty station without means of communication? What is more, Anchorage, even at that time, was a pretty fair-size place to be searching for something as small as a parka, identified only by color. Gleo must have thought I had already gone "trail wacky."

With Knik Flats in sight, and an obscured sun high in the heavens, I pulled to a stop to straighten a tangle and rummage through my "small pack" for something edible—for me. This was our first real stop since the countdown.

> From Files: (Tape Transcript) And the other funny thing (in addition to the Gleo-parka incident) was, not long after that crossing, before we got to the Village of Eklutna, some fellow, a complete stranger, informed me that George Attla was "broke down," as he said, farther down the line.

A hulk of a guy, deep-set eyes that seemed to drill right through me, instantly brought to mind my high school football coach. Odd as it may seem, he even had the demeanor of a coach, or was it a drill sergeant? "Come on, there's a thousand dollars waiting for you at Knik. Wind those dogs up and go get it." I crammed the last of a mushy, once-frozen apple in my mouth, pulled the hook, and off we marched. I half expected that intriguing character to burst into our high school pep song—"You can win, you Rangers, you can win…" as a final encouragement. He didn't.

George Attla was far from "broke down." He had obviously taken another minor detour and was back on the trail, straightening out his team as I whizzed by. However, while dropping down a mud bank onto the Eklutna (Knik Arm) Flats, Kiana did a left turn onto a fork, which led back to the village instead of forking right toward Knik. I was getting things squared away when George—again—blew by, not to be seen again on my side of the Knik checkpoint.

Eklutna Flats, Knik Arm Flats, the Hay Flats are general and usually synonymous terms for a wide band of low, mostly treeless land that surrounds the head of Knik Arm. Much of the area is subject to flooding at extreme high tides, or from two major rivers—the Knik and Matanuska—which empty into the northern arm. The area is characterized by violent seaward winds, sled-wrecking tussocks (or hummocks, if you prefer), sandbars, and gritty snow. Or, as was the case during the first race, no snow at all. During the coldest of winters, the Knik River does not freeze below a power-generating plant located some distance upriver from our course. Accordingly, race volunteers made arrangements for the teams to cross on the Palmer Highway bridge. The year 1973 being some distance from today's four- and six-lane Anchorage-MatSu commuter craze, the Knik Bridge and the highway were but two lanes. Snow had been dumped and spread along the guardrail of the southbound lane. Traffic was stopped, giving teams right-of-way while traversing the bridge. Once across, we dived down the road embankment to continue our way over the ever-trying and physically-taxing flats.

The warm days leading up to race time had forced a last-minute—literally just minutes before arrival of the first team—decision to route our race trail over the Matanuska River Bridge as well. Wisely, no one wanted to take unnecessary chances by running teams over thinning ice of that formidable waterway. So, on to the bridge we went without benefit of any strategically placed snow. I ran alongside my sled whose iron shoes shot sparks against a mostly bare, dry concrete surface.

As with the Knik Bridge, once across the Matanuska Bridge, we scurried down the left highway embankment through the ditch and out onto what valley folks call the Hay Flats. Almost immediately, I picked up a faint trail outline on the still snowless ground. As we rounded the Arm, and headed west in the direction of Knik, it grew wider and more distinct. Here and there, slick ice stood in lower parts, producing a welcome hope of better sledding ahead. Then it struck me. I had come to an important junction in this most fascinating of all trails. Here's where a well-trodden trail from the Palmer area intersected with that from Seward, forming a main artery of commerce into the golden heart of a vast territory. My steady team of twelve was now fast trotting over a true historic segment of Iditarod Trail, as it came to be known. To the south lay my adopted hometown of Seward, to the northwest, Rainy Pass, the mighty Yukon, and the Bering Sea. At last, I had struck the trail of my history book giants. Over this very ground, runners ridden by the likes of Goodwin, Wada, Lowell, Griffiths, Dikeman, and Beaton had passed many years ago. Thrilling, heady thoughts. Oh, if those tussocks, now standing sentinel along this beaten way, could speak, what marvelous stories could they tell? Truly, we of the present generation do stand on the backs of giants. Patchy ice gave way to solid ice as we progressed toward that first day's goal. An indented way among mute hummocks soon became indistinguishable, buried under a welcome deepening snow cover on toward Knik.

From near Eklutna, where Attla passed me—probably five or six miles from Knik—I was alone on the trail. Then, peering back, I saw a team coming on strong. A few minutes later, I relinquished the trail to Isaac Okleasik by coming to a complete stop upon his shout, "Trail!" Passing etiquette was not addressed in the flimsy rule book of our first race. First race Iditaroders simply, on their own, followed established procedure commonly used in other races. That etiquette, with variation allowed, went something like this: Driver of overtaking team demanded the trail only when within one-team length of musher ahead. Driver of overtaken team stopped, secured his team (hooked down), and cleared the trail of his sled, as much as practical, allowing the passing team and driver to get by. Before proceeding, the driver just passed, allowed at least two team lengths to be gained by passing team, before .proceeding. In modern distance racing, a passed team must travel at least one-half mile before a driver can re-pass. In actual practice, however, an overtaking long-distance musher simply lets his trail-mate know that he wants to pass, and in the next wide, practical spot, the front driver "pulls over," and stops. The pass occurs, and away both go—simple, where seconds are of little consequence. Dick Mackey and Rick Swenson would, no doubt, argue that point. Sled dog races both fast and slow have a "no-man's land," which is a zone near the finish line where a pursued musher need not yield the trail to an overtaking team. It is a free-for-all zone, if you will. For sprinters, it is generally a couple of blocks. Presently, the Iditarod's no-man's land begins at the Fort Davis Roadhouse, roughly three miles east of Nome's iconic burled arch finish line.

It took veteran driver Okleasik but two or three seconds to clear my team and flash one of those inner-soul Eskimo smiles, accented with a friendly wave of a gloved hand. On our run over from Anchorage, it never occurred to me to race to Knik in the hopes of posting the shortest trail time and claiming one thousand dollars offered by the race committee for the effort. Even had I thought of it, I would not have pushed my team so early in the race, taking poor trail segments and warm temperature into consideration. From all indications, Isaac had no such reservations—he was out to win the early prize. As things turned out, he was first to Knik, but not with the fastest team. That honor went to Okleasik's Eskimo kinsman, Herbie Nayokpuk, who came in just behind Okleasik but posted a faster time.

It was about 6:15 p.m. when I parked the team in front of our first checkpoint, the Knik Bar. I took just a couple of minutes to check in. I noted our time over from Anchorage, an estimated sixty-five miles, wasn't all that great—seven hours and forty-five minutes. Imagine my surprise, as I came out of the checkpoint, to find a good number of Seward well-wishers encircling me. Imagine even more my delight in seeing Shirley and the kids there, parka and lunch bag in hand. Old home week all over again.

From Files: (Tape Transcript) **Knik Lake,** Saturday, March 3, 1973; 10 p.m.

I came in here to Knik in sixth place. Trail rough on dogs …heat not so bad as it keeps them slowed, preventing injuries …I believe. Waiting for me were the Hills, Shirley and our kids, Rae Elde, and her children, plus others from Seward …well-wishers here to greet me, which was so nice of them. One reason for following the race out from Anchorage was to bring my parka. I left the two most important items at the start … my lunch and my parka. I was a little hungry on the way over here, but was really worried about that all-important coat. Sled, Old Oak, held up pretty darn well for an old beater coming across. Tom Johnson met me here with a bucket of water and kibble and a box of halibut heads. Also my hickory sled with plastic shod runners. A good thing I didn't drive that one over here; it wouldn't have any plastic at all left on it. Tom helped me finish packing the new sled for its long journey.

We are required to have on board several items and everyone carried those things from Anchorage over here. They include a day's rations for man and beasts, snowshoes, axe, tethering chain for dogs, matches, sunglasses, and sleeping bag. Of course, when I leave here tomorrow, I will have a lot of non-required items, plus extra dog food, just in case, around one hundred fifty pounds, I suppose. Weight not all that bad, I don't think, because with plastic, friction is reduced tremendously, over steel. Tom told me that next week has been proclaimed Iditarod Trail Week by Anchorage mayor, George Sullivan. Neat!

Everyone left. Moved dogs to my old cache spot on far end of lake, alongside outgoing trail. Teams still arriving camped mostly around north edge of lake. Few native teams out on trail beyond lake.

Got dogs settled in. Chain out, harnesses off, fed dry dog food mixed with water plus halibut heads. Good campers, being tired, no noise, considering there are hundreds of dogs hereabout. I didn't put up the tent. Put a couple of sacks (empty) on the ground, then my pad, sleeping bag, and sled tarp over all. It is snowing. I had dinner in bed … sandwiches. Snow coming down pretty good, in fact.

My plan for tomorrow is …I have my alarm set for 4:00 a.m., I hope to be on the trail by 5:00 a.m. I will run until about 8 a.m., stop, make coffee, and rustle up some breakfast. From there, play it by ear. After it warms during the morning or early afternoon, then we'll take a long break and run up close to dark.

There's not a whole lot more to be said for today. I was truly gladdened over so many Seward people up for the race start. We are generating way more interest than I predicted. People are really excited over the thing. I am so proud of and happy with my dogs. They handled crowds and trail confusion like old pros. What few minor problems came up were invariably due to their musher's sleeping at the switch. They are fine. No cripples. No detectable health issues. Am camped next to Ron Aldrich, the "Montana Creek Flash," as he likes to be called.

That being all, I will say "good night" to you all this Saturday evening, ending my first day on the Iditarod Trail.

I turned in that first night tired, for sure, but also with a conviction that the most nerve-wracking and least-intriguing section of trail was behind. Tomorrow, the real adventure would begin.

Some folks may wonder about halibut heads as dog food. By 1973, I had already eight years of experience feeding it, not as a main course for canines, but as a supplement. Results were satisfactory. Fish, of course, had been fed exclusively to dogs for centuries. Usually dried. They don't call them "fish burners" for no good reason. And don't forget the salmon species called Chum, or "dog salmon." The ultimate fish for dogs and humans is the chinook, or king salmon. Per one hundred grams, king salmon packs two hundred and three calories, whereas halibut has one hundred twenty-six. The king's percentage of protein is nineteen and seven-tenths compared to halibut's eighteen and six-tenths percent. Finally, one hundred grams of king contains thirteen and two-tenths percent oil, with halibut rendering five and two-tenths percent. Halibut, then, compares quite favorably with king salmon in protein. The oil and calories produced, being about half that of king salmon. Oil is the key. Generous amounts of oil are stored in the head portion of that great, flat, delicious fish. To the seafood processor, heads are essentially waste, converted to fishmeal or offal to be dumped into the ocean. In sum, for me, halibut was cheap or free, available and nutritious, and best fed raw. Combined, pioneer Iditaroders provided their teams with a veritable fish smorgasbord. In addition to halibut, trout, sheefish, white fish, herring, and dried dog salmon appeared on the canine menu.

While I slept fitfully "in my robes beneath the snow" at Knik lake, Shirley and kids had undertaken an adventure of their own. They, of course, had ridden to the Anchorage race start with me. Fellow musher, Bob Hill, had taken our pickup from the Tudor track to Con Bunde's home, to be parked until needed after the race. Bunde, also an educator and novice dog musher at that time, would become involved in local and state politics.

Arrangements had been made for Shirley, Mitch, Tracie, and Darian to ride home with Joanne Hoogland. Joanne shared English department duties with Doug Capra at Seward High and was a member of our church congregation. Shirley and I are godparents to her daughter, Carol. Growing up, Joanne's son, Dale, and our Darian were good buddies, who managed to stay just on the safe side of trouble most of their time together.

After leaving Knik, all, stuffed into Joanne's brown sedan, stops were made in Anchorage for—that's right—food. They purchased groceries to take home and restaurant food for immediate consumption. After the meal, they made a final stop to fill the gas tank, and then headed off to Seward, one hundred and thirty miles distant. It was dark; snow fell along Turnagain Arm, driven by a strong facing wind. In those early years, traffic flow on the Seward Highway south of Girdwood, after midnight, dropped to near zero cars per hour. Ascending into Turnagain Pass, Shirley became aware of a growing engine noise, a sort of metallic clatter of which Joanne seemed unaware. The kids slept. Not knowing if Joanne was also asleep, deaf, or both, Shirley asked, "Do you hear that noise?" Joanne answered that she did and kept driving. By then, the old engine was producing a whole chorus of sounds, but not of a melodious nature. A new feature was added, the odor of scorched motor oil.

About then, their driver displayed a glimmer of concern, expressing regret that she hadn't checked the engine oil back in Anchorage or thought to carry an extra can in the car. So there you have it. It's the middle of the night, snowing like blazes, no traffic on the road, car full of kids, and an engine telling you it's going to fly apart like—right now. Oh, yes, they were also traveling through uninhabited national forest. No cell phones then. No lighted public phone booths along the way. The only thing to do was hope the thing held together and limp into the only spot where there may be help—the Silvertip State Road Maintenance Camp, a few miles north of Hope Junction.

Good thing the last several miles were downhill. The old sedan clattered, coughed, and smoked its way to the Silvertip Camp bunkhouse door and, as if to say, "Enough is enough," it quit. A sleepy, coat over nightshirt guy, not unfriendly, was coaxed from his warm bed, talked out of five quarts of state property, and waited to see if the old engine had remaining life. It did. They made it home, albeit not until experiencing two close encounters with middle-of-the-road moose. The Silvertip Good Samaritan went back to bed.

It was a good thing I didn't know about their troubles getting home. As it was, sleep didn't come much at all that first night on the trail.

Why? Maybe it was the excitement of the first day, dogs moving about, snow falling, or racket coming from the distant Knik Bar. Maybe anxious anticipation for what tomorrow would hold kept my mind spinning too fast for real sleep to come.

The next day, I reasoned that the early part of the trail would be familiar since I had trained and done improvements on it in the direction of Skwentna, less than a month before. It dawned on me that ascent through the Alaska Range via Ptarmigan Pass would, in fact, begin when we started up the Susitna, since that water originates in high country beyond. After the Alaska Range, there would still be two more mountainous obstacles, the Kuskokwim Mountains and Nulato Hills. Somewhere along the route to Nome, we would pass from Alaska Standard Time Zone to Bering Sea Time. We would gain an hour, so to speak.

Several misconceptions, as it would turn out, plagued me. One involved the climb through the Alaska Range. My map had the pass at 3,350 feet. Now, that is close to the height of Mt. Marathon at Seward, the one raced up by hundreds of runners every July fourth. In my mind's eye, I falsely pictured struggling teams and sweaty, laboring mushers, giving it their everything to achieve the last grueling mile before topping out in Rainy Pass, followed by a sled-crunching, bone-breaking, out-of-control descent down the other side. Another falsity was my idea that the coastal trail would be devoid of wood, a barren wasteland. Truth is, it was that notion that caused me to pack the Coleman stove and fuel for it—items found on my gear list. As it turned out, wood is to be had over the whole course, except on sea ice from Shaktoolik to Koyuk—if you know where to look. Finally, akin to the woodless myth was that our coastal run would be, by and large over flat, featureless, even dangerously shifting sea ice. That one was really a doozey. Some of the toughest hill climbing encountered was on the inland trail along Norton Sound. Such were my thoughts prior to my little travel clock's alarm announcement that 4:00 a.m. had arrived. Time to get up and hit the trail.

31

National Historic Trap Trail

Joe Delia opened his home and served as race checker for 35 years starting with the first one. He has been honored by induction into the Iditarod Hall of Fame. Trapping was his chief source of income. (Photo: Joe Delia)

Day 2: Sunday, March 4, Knik to Skwentna

From Files: (Tape Transcript) Beyond Finger Lake, Monday, March 5, Midnight.

This is Monday night, so I will try to fill you in. I didn't use the tape recorder yesterday, Sunday. Got into and through Skwentna some distance before camping. It was pretty late by the time I camped and dog chores were done—toward midnight.

Going back to Sunday morning, I left Knik about 5:30 a.m. It snowed overnight there about three inches, which I thought was an improvement to the trail. Ron Aldrich from Montana Creek and I camped together where trail left the lake. I woke him when I got up at 4:00 a.m. Haven't seen him since leaving the lake ahead of him.

The original intention for Sunday was to run about twelve hours and call it a day. I was first to be on the trail, no fresh tracks. About seven miles out, I literally ran into the camp of Isaac Okleasik, Johnny Coffin, and John Komak. Tents pitched right on the trail. They were up to help me get around them with no problem. Not long after Mile Nine Hill, George Attla came upon me and passed, moving at too-fast a pace, I judged. We tagged on for a few miles before he disappeared. Instead of burning my team out, I thought I'd make one long day of it today and slack off. In other words, I will be up close to the front when I start to back down. This might even things out a bit for me with drivers pushing too hard this early. It is a long way to Nome.

Both Okleasik and Nayokpuk passed me before reaching Susitna station—flying. Herbert, I think they call him Herbie, stopped to rest up the trail. I pulled over, we chatted a bit. He took off. I tagged on until he called it a day around 6:00 p.m., short of Skwentna.

No pictures Sunday; Grey, cloudy, snowy day… So we came to Skwentna, 7:30, Sunday evening… A long, hard trip on me. Dogs held up well, Kiana keeping them moving. Joe Delia is the race checker for Skwentna, at his cabin. Mushers were fed by Joe and wife Carlene, delicious, and much-appreciated, chili, prepared for the taking.

The Delias were, in a word, wonderful. Joe Sr. had counted on Joe Delia to have a trail for us extending many miles both north and south of his Skwentna home. In this, he wasn't disappointed. Delia quipped, "I have the only national historic trap trail in the country." A heartwarming memory to this day is little seven-year-old Christine Delia's insistence on feeding my team for me. Like, stand back and I will show you how this should be done. Don't get excited, racers; outside assistance of this nature didn't have a rule yet.

Day 3: Monday, March 5, Skwentna toward Rainy Pass

Monday, left Skwentna around 8:30 a.m., traveled pretty steady until 6:00 p.m. tonight… Now camped somewhere between Finger Lake and Rainy Pass Lodge. Tomorrow we go over the hump.

Herb Foster, a Kotzebue Eskimo, left Skwentna ahead of me this morning driving a very nice nine dog team… Caught up with him about noon. We melted snow, made coffee, snacked dogs. Foster an interesting guy, married with four kids. The team he is driving is his hunting team. Gets on a polar bear track, pursues, sometimes for a couple of days. After catching up to the bear, he turns the front three of his team loose. They chase and bring the bear to bay on an ice hummock. Herb drives up, sets his hook, and dispatches the bear.

Herb says, "It doesn't make sense to push a dog team in the mountains because the going is much easier on the coast." He thought Isaac is already done in and doubts we would see him again… "Isaac hasn't quit yet, but should," he said.

This guy (Foster) is super efficient around camp. Last night at Skwentna, he had his tent up, dog chores done, and in the sack before I could get my tent out of my pack… Very efficient. Took a couple of pictures of Herb snacking his team… Whacks off small pieces of fresh, frozen sheefish… Some for himself. I tried some, ended up eating maybe a half pound. Takes care of both hunger and thirst. Foster tipped his sled off the trail… Rolled it a couple times. Trail not good coming up to Finger Lake, hanging on side hills, bushy. He lost both his axe and fish supply. Axe not easily replaced out here—McGrath maybe—fortunately he had dog food waiting for him at Finger Lake.

My camera wouldn't work this morning, shutter froze, left it out on the sled overnight… Would operate at Skwentna… Put it under my jacket for a couple hours… Used it for photos of our approach to the Alaska Range… Beautiful, beautiful!

Having a little problem with feet. Both Shiak and Koyuk with sore front wrists. Pads are good. Will keep up with pine tar and neats foot oil for everybody and move those two to middle of the team… Less work there. Team not as tired tonight as last. I am not going to drop anybody if I can figure out how to keep them on their feet without undue injury.

Mention should be made that Herb Foster and I practiced passing one another for most of the run from Skwentna to Finger Lake checkpoint, Gene Leonard's cabin. Very hospitable man. Due to snowy weather, planes did not fly yesterday to Skwentna with supplies… So my package didn't catch up with me until today at Finger Lake. Joe, Sr. (and his plane) came through with my moose stew and trail cake. He also came through with Colonel "Muktuk" Marston, honorary race marshal, General Gettys, who dispatched army trailbreakers, Orville Lake, radio broadcaster, a major whose name I didn't catch, and a small assortment of others. Orville Lake handed us a newspaper with a good display of race hype, took photos, and put me on tape. Poor Herb Foster… Came in right behind me and got caught, too. We ran for another hour in the direction of Rainy Pass and camped… A little excitement shortly before going into camp… Chased a wolverine up a short hill full out, dogs and wolverine really made tracks.

Herb Foster snacks team along the Skwentna-Rainy Pass stretch. Back home in Kotzebue, Herb used that same team to hunt polar bear and on a 250 mile trap line.

Hands and lips are getting dry and cracked. Have to dig the old Bag Balm out of the sled pack. Things going well… What a beautiful day. If I am dreaming, don't wake me until I get to Nome. Tomorrow (Monday) will probably be a tough trail day. Then things should start to get easy, or easier anyway, from then on. I'll try to fill this tape up in the next couple of nights and mail it at McGrath. That's all then, through Monday on the historic Iditarod Trail.

A few days prior to the 2011 Iditarod Race kickoff, executive director Stan Hooley emailed our musher corps, informing them that the Delias would be retiring as race volunteers after an incredible thirty-nine years. This would be their last. "Will each musher, before leaving Skwentna, please make a special effort to thank these most dedicated, loyal friends of the race and wish them well?" So ended an era,one that began with that first pot of chili given so freely to the first racers of the first Iditarod. Oh, but Father Time is as relentless as he is patient, never knowing the taste of defeat.

A short time after returning home following the first Iditarod, I shot letters off to persons who had manned the sixteen checkpoints along the way, an inquiry really. "Can you please tell me something of the community, and provide some personal information? What were your impressions of the race? Of the racers?" One of the most fascinating replies came from Joe Delia, at the time a twenty-three-year resident of Skwentna. In 1997, Delia was inducted into the Iditarod Hall of Fame in recognition of his outstanding volunteer service to the race. By 2011, when advancing age forced the Delias to give up their wilderness lifestyle, Joe had lived out sixty-two of his eighty-one years in his log cabin home in Skwentna. Trapping was his main occupation. For anyone who has even dreamed of a subsistence livelihood, Alaska style, Delia's biographic information will be of great interest. Perhaps more so when placed in the context of the inaugural Iditarod race four decades past. Delia's May 1973 letter, transcribed and edited for clarity, is included herein (see Appendix XIII, Delia Letter). Gene Leonard of Finger Lake is another checkpoint original. In 1973, the Hayes River Lodge on Finger Lake was owned by Dennis Branham, while Rainy Pass lodge on Puntilla Lake, owners were Bud and Mike Branham. Gene Leonard was the caretaker at Hayes River Lodge. He greeted and treated royally mushers of the first race. Indeed, he would continue to do so year upon year until his recent retirement and move to a warmer clime.

32

Genghis to the Rescue

Tough sledding on the upper South Fork of the Kuskokwim. Kiana in lead. The evening before, Genghis lead us out of a tight spot back up in Ptarmigan Pass.

Day 4: Tuesday, March 6, south of Rainy Pass through Ptarmigan Pass

On Tuesday, March 6, I made a run from an estimated twenty-five miles south of the Rainy Pass checkpoint, through Ptarmigan Pass, and down Hell's Gate. I made camp in a nice stand of spruce timber a few miles above the South Fork of the Kuskokwim River. Tape recording for the following transcript was made on the morning of Wednesday, March 7.

From Files: (Transcription of Tape) Hell's Gate, Wednesday, March 7, 2:30 a.m.

We, Herbert Foster and I, decamped from our overnight spot between Finger Lake and Rainy Pass Lodge. We were on the trail by 8:30 Tuesday morning.

Probably five or six miles out… Dogs warming into their seven- to eight-mile-per-hour trot, we came to a steep downhill with a sharp left turn at bottom… missed the corner, sled rolled, settling among tops of alders. Heck of a job getting out from twisted brush and very deep snow, I guessed to be five to six feet. By the time I had worked up a good lather attempting to extricate my sled, who should come roaring down the same hill but Isaac… his dogs all piled into the rear of my team and the little bit of sled I had wrestled back on the trail. Isaac and sled shot at least twice as far off the trail as I into a fresh patch of brush and landed handlebar down. Isaac provided comic relief by flashing a big smile and shouting "I beat!"… He did by two sled lengths. Later, I noticed I had broken a sled stanchion above the basket… made a splint and repaired it while held up at Rainy (Pass Lodge)… Nothing serious, no dogfights, we got out of the ditch and straightened things up. Okleasik tagged on to me for the last twenty miles up to the Rainy checkpoint… The climb up to the pass was steady but nothing dramatic like I expected… Sky, high overcast… warm… at Rainy Pass the timber is gone, only patches of brush here and there. Completely surrounded with rugged mountaintops of the Alaska Range. We finally came upon the lodge.

A big disappointment greeted us. Rainy Pass was to be a dog food drop… no food… no planes in yet. Found out that lodge is owned by the Branham family, who owns the Finger Lake (Hayes River Lodge) cabin as well. A very helpful and concerned young fellow named Allen Budinski is caretaker there… he used the lodge radio to try to locate our dog food.

My wait was four hours right in the middle of our daylight. I had maybe one feeding on the sled so couldn't see heading off to McGrath two days away in hopes of maybe our food bags would be there so we all waited. I took the downtime to repair that broken stanchion… snacked the mutts and worked on all the feet… After four hours to the minute, a plane arrived, landed on the lake at some distance and dumped out maybe a dozen bags and took off… Thankfully, one of the few bags was mine.

Teller musher, Isaac Okleasik, prepares to depart from the Rainy Pass checkpoint after a wait of nearly 4 hours for dog food to arrive.

Any teams I might have thought I had the jump on arrived during our four-hour hiatus. Bobby Vent, who I think is from the interior… a native Athạbascan more than likely, has a small team, six if I remember, but nice, large, racy-looking animals. Vent is the elder of us all at fifty-nine or thereabout… a lightweight guy with a light, racy-looking sled compared to some of us. Attla has dropped another dog… think he is at ten now. John Coffin, a classic Eskimo driver out of Noorvik… his team looks best of all of us, I think; like myself, he still has all the dogs he started with back in Anchorage. He himself impresses me… stuffs his really beautiful mukluks with straw for insulation… like the old days I guess.

Got away from Rainy Pass checkpoint shortly after 4 p.m. There wasn't much snow up there, stunted bushes poking up everywhere… a few puny spruce… whole pass obviously subject to heavy winds… scary… no trail markers. As it turned out, I had to run for over eight hours before finding suitable timber for camping on the Kuskokwim side.

Before I forget, I wanted to record an observation. Just as this whole business of long-distance dog racing is experimental with this first race, so is the feeding of the dogs for such an ordeal. There sure was a variety being packed on sleds back at Rainy… after the plane arrived. A lot of dry kibble… mine, too. I think someone will need to figure out how to put a lot more nutrition in those bags for it to be useful for this business… All manner of meat and fish, it seems, is being fed… some of it not good. One musher was feeding dried king salmon. Only problem, it is the leftovers, what little meat is left on the ribs and backbones, which clogged up his dogs, causing a whole lot of problems for him, not to mention his poor dogs.

That delay… waiting for dog food those four hours really screwed up the works. It forced me to decide to camp before dark up in the barrens with the wind building, or to hightail it down Hell's Gate to some timber after dark… I decided to continue over Ptarmigan Pass and run down the other side until I came to a camping spot. We were on a good snowmachine track… figured, why not?

When I was up at the head of Ptarmigan Pass… and it was starting to get dark, I heard wolves singing. It didn't last long, just two or three howls. Made my day… thrilling. At Rohn, Herbie Nayokpuk later told me that he and Isaac came upon a wolf-killed moose in that area some distance off the trail… They chased four wolves off and went into camp for the night at the kill site. They gorged their dogs and carried off the rest on their sleds.

Certainly was glad Genghis was in the team for our run down Hell's Gate… Ran for some distance on top of what seemed to be a frozen creek… could hear water running under the ice in places… on good trail when rounding an outcropping of rock on my right, we were forced out onto what I mistakenly took to be a large, open meadow. Ran for maybe a quarter of a mile… things happened fast in the dark. Front of team bunched up, front six or seven in water up to their bellies. Poor little Kiana was actually treading water… bewildered… I waded in, hauled Kiana and swing dogs to better footing. No luck trying to get her to lead in an effort to pick safer route. Genghis to the rescue… Old faithful, the one I drove through the high school and over parked cars. I switched Genghis to lead from mid team and replaced him with Kiana. In front, a long, narrow ribbon of ice had caved into slow-running water, which must have been a small feeder creek flowing into Sheep Lake from the west. I had steering now… the old guy swung the team sharply to the left, I brought him back to the right, staying maybe twenty yards from open water… went fifty to one hundred yards beyond the broken ice… while attempting to cross back toward the right side of the pass, my front end broke through ice again. This time Genghis found good footing, towing swing dogs with him. Decided to backtrack and run over to the right side of the valley on the Rainy Pass side of where I first broke through. So I decided on the turnaround-in-our-tracks trick we did to get away from Bud Smyth in that Anchorage yard. Fearing another break-through into perhaps deeper water, I had the front tighten up the team while I hauled backward and set the brake as best I could. I gave Genghis my calmest "Haw" and then "Come" command… worked like a charm. The team "turned-on-a-dime" backtracked,

> and we crossed over as planned and were soon on our final climb up to Ptarmigan Pass.
>
> It was quite late and very dark by the time we got through the Gate to a spot with good camp timber on the right bank of the creek… Ptarmigan Pass route added about thirty miles more than had we gone the Rainy Pass way. Sometime later, John Komak, a native driver out of Teller, showed up… he has been pushing his dogs hard. He was very tired… half asleep. Brewed him a cup of tea and served some of Shirley's trail cake. He camped next to me… learned a lot traveling with Eskimo mushers, including Herb Foster and Herbie Nayokpuk, whom I traveled with yesterday… he is from Shishmaref… a real nice fellow, a Christian man… he remembers us being up to Nome from Seward with our church congregation… a good dog man.
>
> Right now, I am camped out under a tree with no tent, which is fine on nice nights. Weather has been good to this point, a little warm if anything. I still haven't learned to set my double-walled tent up, it's always night when I'm trying to do so. End up spreading the inner tent on the ground as a ground cloth and using the outer tent as the shelter. That being all, I will end this recording through Tuesday, March 6, on the Iditarod trail.

My on-the-trail camping routine was arduous for sure, but probably typical for racers in those first few Iditarods. What I prefer to call our "great adventure," George Attla, somewhere along the way, dubbed our inaugural event the "great camping trip," not without reason. Monikers aside, an exhausting day behind a dog team, added to laborious camp procedures, rendered it unnecessary to count sheep in order to achieve sleep when it was all over for the day.

For both the 1973 and 1974 races, my camping routine—though certainly not set to script—played out in rather routine fashion. It was usual to drive only to a point where enough daylight remained for use in setting up camp. About two hours were allowed for this, which meant I started looking for a good location between 5:00 to 6:00 p.m., the main prerequisite being an adequate stand of timber. Incidentally, I figured fourteen to fifteen hours of useable daylight for that time of the year—early March.

The reader may justifiably wonder if pulling in for the night suggests an aversion for, even a fear, of darkness. For my part, I harked back to my "great adventure" mind-set for the first race. Most things, with some imaginative exceptions, are best experienced in light. I wanted to soak it all in. That new Alaska I hadn't seen before. It was a new trail, going to new and wondrous places with new people, and new dog teams. I had so much to experience, to photograph, to absorb, to drink in, all best done in daylight, where feasible. A new trail, going to new places, but, an old and a fabled trail, going to old and storied places, as well. Every day on the Iditarod Trail ended for me as one more day of a grand adventure.

A practical reason for setting up camp before dark was, we humans do not see well in the dark. This was pre-mega headlight days. The batteries that I left Anchorage with, in my little pocket-size flashlight, were used so little that they still had life upon their arrival at Nome. I do not recall a single dog team being driven by use of artificial light. Most mushers simply preferred making a daylight camp to stumbling about, trying to do so after day had turned to night.

In days before corralling was written into race rules, a musher arriving, say at Ruby, had been chosen by a villager who wanted to house that particular musher. Dog teams either were parked in a designated location or in the host's yard. The corralling rule now requires all teams be parked in a common area and that the mushers be in attendance of his or her team at all times. That is to say, in the first and several subsequent races, teams generally camped between occupied checkpoints only out of necessity, preferring to take advantage of whatever amenities a given place had to offer. What this all meant was very little camping was done once the Yukon River was reached. Villages became checkpoints along that mighty waterway. The same is true of the Bering Sea Coast villages. However, as race speeds increased over the years, that picture changed. Racers running on a time schedule—for example, run six hours then rest six hours—began to ignore their position in relation to a checkpoint. In essence, then, there is much more "camping out" in today's races than in the early days. Corralling, it should be noted, came about due to abuse by some top-end mushers of the village host program. Race officials, by the mid-1980s, became aware that certain mushers, race after race, were receiving kingly accommodations at certain checkpoints—as were their dogs. Often, a team would be driven to a host's house, right into a heated garage. The musher would shower, eat, arrange for a wake-up call, and go to bed. Meanwhile, the team was rested in heated surroundings, fed, watered, and given first aid where necessary. Before being awakened from an undisturbed and peaceful repose, the friend-host had another hot meal waiting, dogs harnessed, bootied, and ready to roll. All this pampering gave "pamperees" a huge unfair advantage over competitors and teams forced to sleep in a snow bank. There has, regrettably, been a downside to axing musher hosting by villagers. I believe this system has reduced Alaska Native villagers to mere race spectators, for the most part. Naturally hospitable, friendly, and eager to give help, interior and coastal folks have been denied real meaningful participation in, and ownership of, the Last Great Race since the corralling rules were put in place.

But back to race, camping, 1973 style. Stopping beside a serviceable timbered site, I would shed my parka, strap on snowshoes, and grab my axe, two items that had prominent places atop my sled load. Snowshoes were worn from the time I left the sled trail until crawling into my tent to sleep. With snow depths up to five feet, it was virtually impossible to move about without them. First, a dog trail in and out of the site was stomped down. This loop had an extra-wide spot compacted where the tethering chain would be strung out and secured, usually between two trees. More snowshoe dancing was required to stomp down spots for the tent and the fire pit. I avoided the chore of tent pitching whenever possible. Strong winds and/or wet snow would drive me indoors. Whereas moderate cold temperatures, say, down to minus twenty degrees F by themselves, did not, thanks to my excellent sleeping accommodations.

Still wearing my snowshoes, I cut armloads of spruce boughs and placed them bow side up as beds in each dog's spot, with several trips more required to do the same for the tent area. I used my axe for chopping a small green (growing) tree, limbing it, and chopping it into lengths of about three feet. These were laid corduroy fashion across the snowshoe-compressed fire site; they formed a platform on which my campfire was built. Without the green wood barrier between fire and snow, one's fire quickly descended toward ground level, assuring its own watery demise. Some wise guy has said, "He who burns wood is warmed twice." Quite so. Thus, the parka shedding. Several small, dead, dry trees had to be cut from the stump, dragged to the fire pit, and hacked into useable pieces.

A snowshoe trail notwithstanding, the team had to wallow its way to its night's lodging. Come morning, the outgoing stretch of the loop would most likely have set up enough to make our exit much easier. Having not mastered the art of riding a sled while wearing snowshoes, they had to come off and were donned again once the team was parked. Off came the harnesses. Each dog was then led to and secured at its awaiting spruce bed. Twelve trips for me. Camp chores from thereon were performed with an eye on hitting the sack as quickly as could happen.

This meant building a fire first. I carried, as indeed I do to this day, several "fire kits," as I call them. They are simply a plumber's candle and waterproof matches in a water-tight container. Small, pocket size, I had one each for my jacket and parka, and at least two aboard my sled. The idea being, should I become separated from my team, there is still a high probability of avoiding death by freezing. I lit the candle, a couple hands full of crushed spruce twigs, and I was in business. Larger pieces of wood were stacked on and the snow-filled dog bucket set to heat; occasionally, more snow was added until I had four to five gallons of hot water. To this was added dry kibble, set aside to soak and cool to eating temperature. Another important item of my "outfit," as the real old-timers called their camp gear, was my combination kettle and coffee pot, a three-pound coffee can. This, too, was set to melt snow and, eventually, heat a frozen chunk of moose stew or chicken soup. Once its contents had been devoured, that lowly vessel was sort of rinsed, refilled with snow, and given the task of brewing my coffee or tea. After evening beverage, a partial can was brewed anew the size of three football fields, bordered with alders, in or near the dying camp fire. Rarely did it freeze solid overnight, and by means of a small blaze, I came by hot morning coffee and a thermos for the road. Breakfast and lunch for me were in the form of Shirley's super nutritious, and extremely palatable, trail cake. One of the best things about the trail cake was that it did not freeze. A quarter-loaf washed down with a hot cup of morning coffee, and I was ready to tackle the trail ahead.

The last of the major concerns demanding my attention was my sleeping arrangement, which, at the core, was as simple as it was satisfactory. As mentioned earlier, I spread a thick layer of spruce boughs first. They were followed by the inner tent of my double-wall tent, which had been relegated to the unglamorous role of ground cloth, topped with my two-inch-thick insulated pad. Finally, my goose down-filled mummy style bag with an added wool liner was spread out. Should there be a threat of snow, as at Knik Lake, the sled tarp went over the works. During the first race, the roomy, bottomless outer tent was pitched over everything, perhaps twice, and that during our "wandering in the wilderness" south of Ruby due to extreme cold temperatures. Mindful of carbon monoxide poisoning, my little Sterno burner was operated just long enough to make my tape recording or write a few notes.

That tent saw much more use while being carried with me on the second—1974—race. Participants in that one witnessed not only extreme cold but also fierce winds. Not wishing to overdramatize things, let it be said that George Attla and I drove teams in minus fifty-eight degrees F near McGrath, that seven of us survived gale-force winds atop Ptarmigan Pass by literally and most willingly digging into snow banks and staying there until morning. Joe Sr., on his 1974 inaugural run, had strayed off course toward Rainy Pass. By use of his thermometer and wind gauge, he calculated the wind chill that fearful night to be at a quick-freeze level of minus one hundred and three degrees F. Except for that snow bank experience, my tent saw use at just about every camp south of the Yukon that year.

Somewhere in the routine, I fed my dogs. Aluminum one quart pans were distributed and the steaming contents of the cook pot were portioned out to always eager and deserving eaters. Halibut heads were axe-cleaved into generous pieces, and I fed a couple of pounds per dog. Next, I cut up enough fist-sized pieces for three snacks per dog for the next day's run. The next day's breakfast, when available, consisted of another two pounds of fish. An all-important dog chore was saved for the last. I inspected every wrist, foot pad, toe, and toenail, and administered first aid as needed. Before hitting the trail the next day, every foot received its pine tar and neats foot oil treatment.

Eventually, all was done that needed to be. With tape recorder, flashlight, and alarm clock within reach, boots and dampened clothes removed, I stoically shrugged off the first cold contact with my sleeping bag, knowing warmth was on its way. I recalled events of the day on tape, set my alarm, and all too soon, it was—morning.

Striking camp required less than half the time needed to establish it. Again, most every task had to be performed on snowshoes. I built a small fire over which to heat coffee and warm the dogs' foot ointment; all forty-eight dog feet needed ointment. The twelve dogs were fed, harnessed, and then hooked up. The sled was packed. I figured two hours for setup and an hour for the decamping process. Is it any wonder then, considering time -consuming camp procedures, food supply delays, and an uncertain trail, that it took even the front-end racers the better part of a month to reach Nome?

Few would argue that en route camping wasn't time demanding and fatiguing. For me, nonetheless, an important outcome of the many forced and lengthy halts was the blossoming of genuine comradeship among mushers. This wonderful feeling of togetherness was fostered, honestly, by our common inability to resist light, in particular, light produced by a wayside campfire, as darkness set in. To camp alone was rare with most encampments, including—I'm guessing—two to four teams and drivers. They were times of sharing and fire circle friendship building. Camp chores were divvied up. Just about everything was shared, including people food, dog food, clothes, and dog gear. All, I might add, with the exception of dogs. Those, too, I suspect, would have been loaned to assist a fellow musher getting low on dog power had it not been forbidden by race rules. Those remarkable displays of mutual support would become even more commonplace during our ordeal south of Ruby. The beginning of many enduring, lifelong friendships can be traced to that string of cold and, by now, mostly forgotten campfires of the First Great Race.

From Files: (Notes taken during race) Camp Partners—South of Yukon River

Camp partners in Skwentna were Foster, Wilmarth, and Luster. Beyond Finger Lake was Foster. At Hell's Gate was Komak. With

> me at Rohn River were Nayokpuk, Okleasik, Foster, Luster, Coffin, and veterinarian Adkins. I camped alone south of McGrath. At McGrath, we were housed in private homes. At Ophir camp, partners were Attla, Wilmarth, and Coffin. At Bear Creek were Attla, Wilmarth, Coffin, Vent, and the trailbreakers. South of Poorman (night one) were Wilmarth and the trailbreakers, and on night two were Wilmarth, Attla, Vent, Coffin, and the trailbreakers. At Poorman camp, partners were Wilmarth, Attla, Vent, Coffin, and the trailbreakers. At Ruby, we were once again housed in private homes.

I noted earlier that modern, top race contenders run more by the clock than checkpoint to checkpoint. As a consequence, a large number of "rest stops" by a given musher for a given race, take place outside of checkpoints. Several noteworthy changes, innovations, and improvements have resulted in faster, less labor-intensive races than of old. Pioneer Iditaroders, for the most part, were developed woodsmen with survival skills who knew how to pack the right stuff for that job. But we were not equipped or even programmed for fast racing. So, what has transpired over ensuing years that enabled modern mushers to ignore checkpoints and take rest stops just about any old place, breaking race speed records in the process?

There are, in fact, several such enablers, the first of which concerns the dogs themselves. Forty years of selective breeding have elevated today's canine endurance racers far above the capabilities of their ancestors. Where fifty-mile days were impressive in the early 1970s, one-hundred-mile days are routine for recent races. With more running and less resting, many checkpoints become just that, check-in and check-out points. At best, checkpoints are places to drop a tired dog and pick up straw in preparation for a stop somewhere up the trail. Musher motivation has also undergone an evolution. With a total race purse knocking at the door of one million dollars nowadays, there is an economic incentive absent certainly in the first few races. True, the fifty-thousand-dollar total purse of our pioneer race was unprecedented, but sixty-nine thousand dollars cash, plus a fifty-thousand-dollar pickup truck for today's winner only was then totally unthinkable. Increased remuneration has led to a growing professionalism within the musher corps. Greater trail certainty is another vital factor playing into the conduct of the race. No more "wandering in the wilderness"—as I like to term it—for nearly three days, as front-runners did in 1973. Today, there are more trail volunteers and better trail-building equipment, allowing the trail to be established well and more adequately marked for both day and night use. Improved trail conditions were followed by drastic musher-friendly changes in sled design. Gone is the necessity of driving dogs from Anchorage to Nome in a standing position only. First came the sit down, bicycle-type seat, which has evolved into the now popular sit down and drive "lazy boy" tail dragger model. Price tag? In the neighborhood of $4,500.

By the way of a footnote, only those of us who completed the first and second races have bragging rights to have actually, physically, every step of the way, driven dogs the complete distance from Anchorage to Nome. That total number of us braggarts is forty-eight, the twenty-two finishers of 1973 plus the twenty-six in 1974. After 1974, I like to kid the younger generation Seavey mushers, with a wee exaggeration, "Dogs get to ride halfway to Nome in their dog trucks." The fact is, the ceremonial start and the restart, as they are known today, were separated with the latter marching from time to time farther away from Anchorage to its present location at Willow.

Continuing the race changes theme, leaving PETA out of it, no rational person can possibly believe that today's Iditarod dogs do not receive the very best, top-notch care ever. Early racers fed what was available and it got us to Nome in twenty-two or more days. Today's drivers feed what is available and arrive there thirteen days sooner. Years of research and experimentation have gone into that fifty-dollar-per-forty-pound bag of dog food, which, by itself, is but a dietary foundation on which to build. Then come costly supplements and equally pricey natural canine foods, such as red meat and fish. Prerace medical checkups assure today's four-footed athlete's medical condition is not ignored. Even the sixteen-dog maximum team size is designed so that each dog gets a fair share of driver and veterinary attention. Frequently spaced dog-drop opportunities are provided. Medical attention during a race is paramount, with thirty to forty veterinarians spaced along the race route. In sharp contrast to the above is the fact that no medical exam of any kind was given to dogs prior to the first race. There was but one volunteer veterinarian, Terry Adkins, who monitored dogs as best he could over the entire race course. One veterinarian, period. With an eye out for dog welfare, there have evolved, over the years, two eight- and one twenty-four-hour mandatory stops. Without doubt, mushers forced into a nearly three-day vacation among snowdrifts, south of Ruby on that first race, would have scoffed at an idea as absurd as a compulsory rest for man or beast.

Present-day logistical support for the race is nothing short of amazing. Ton upon ton of supplies, people, and dogs are flown along the race trail by upwards of twenty-five private airplanes, by private, volunteer pilots of the Iditarod Air Force. For an event spread over a thousand miles of Alaskan landscape, good communication is vital. Where pioneer mushers of 1973 relied on ham radio operators, overseen by the tenacious and capable Roy Davies, state-of-the-art everything is available to present-day race participants. Picture-taking cell phones, satellite phones, G.P.S. locators, and dog team trackers are all commonplace gadgets on the Iditarod Trail of today. There are limits, however. The Iditarod Trail Committee has outlawed night vision devices—so far.

Finally, some nuts and bolts innovations that have contributed in no small way to the changing face of the Iditarod. Elsewhere, attention was brought to bear on the beneficial role played by powerful musher's headlamps, which, in essence, has pushed aside darkness of night as a deterrent to dog team travel. For most serious mushers, the state of darkness has ceased to exist in setting a race schedule. And, I reiterate here, the huge change wrought by universal adoption of the steel cable towline, by so doing, mushers' axe need for the tethering chains as well as their accompanying labor. Gone, too, is the danger inherent back when poly rope was the towline of choice and dogs often chewed them apart. Used for both towing and tethering, one cable setup does it all, making it one of the most valuable time and labor savers to make an Iditarod appearance.

As with poly rope towline, so too, have bolt-on plastic runner shoes, the bough bed, campfire, and double-walled pup tent been relegated to fading memories of those who knew of them firsthand. In their stead has cropped up bales of imported straw from Oregon State, pint plastic bottles of alcohol for dog food cooker fuel, and coolers filled at checkpoints with hot water for feeding dogs during a rest stop, a couple hours down the trail. Slick, fast, efficient, and when held in light of the camping procedure I used on my first run to Nome—easy. But not camping. Indeed, the quest for speed has done everything imaginable to eliminate camping per se. Even race jargon no longer has use for the word "camping." In truth, I haven't heard of it for years. We do not camp any longer. We take a "rest stop" or we "give them (dogs) four"—or six hours' rest, or however many "between Ruby and Galena." Mushers with fifteen or more races under their belts have told me that they have never seen a campfire during any of their races, or had to use snowshoes for that matter.

In 1982, my son Mitch, on his first Iditarod, together with six others, including Joe Sr., was pinned down on sea ice just short of Shaktoolik. A violent blizzard of gale intensity rolled sleds, buried dogs under two feet of insulating snow, blew gear away, and drove Mitch and others into their sled bags for an interminable eighteen hours. During that long entombment, fierce wind drove snow through Mitch's sled bag zipper, packing it around him. Body heat went to work melting the snow. As the wind began to subside, weary, wet mushers emerged as if from cocoons. They were beat up for sure, but survivors. A sled bag large enough to fit its musher was the answer to the hassle and time wasted pitching a tent. Of course, to set up a tent in Mitch's situation would have, undoubtedly, resulted in its being taken by the wind, to be seen no more, whereas a sled bag saved the day. An inspection of items carried by the modern driver, reveals items not found among those thought essential by mushers of the first Iditarod. Most relate directly to dog health, safety, and comfort, with an eye toward increased efficiency and speed. Here is a good sampling: dog booties—lots of them, sixty-four are needed to boot a sixteen-dog team, plus the complete set required by the rules as reserve. Booties become lost, worn out, or are changed after driving through water in below-freezing temperatures. Mushers have a healthy resupply of this article stashed at upcoming checkpoints. Dog coats for unusually cold weather and windy conditions are carried. Shoulder coats with sewn-in pockets to hold chemical warmers for sore shoulders. Wrist wraps, most often of a lightweight foam material, to hold heat in on medicated sore wrists. Carried also are groin (male) wraps for protection against severe temperatures and wind, and a special small bag for dog "meds." Except for a few booties the first year—I used only two the whole trip—and lightweight coats, I was unacquainted with most of the above before running in the 1997 race after a twenty-four-year hiatus.

I have rambled on over the past few pages in an attempt to answer the oft-asked question: "How has the race changed since the first one?" I hope that this explanation will suffice. My customary short answer is, "It's gotten faster." In timely fashion, Iditarod veteran musher, John Baker, has provided the period to my short answer on race changes.

> *Anchorage Daily News*, Wednesday, March 16, 2011 – Record Breaker Baker [Headline]
> John Baker arrives in Nome on Tuesday morning, winning the Iditarod in a record time of eight days, nineteen hours, forty-six minutes, thirty-nine seconds – three hours faster than Martin Buser's record run in 2002. [Caption below photo]

Ramey Smyth, son of my old trail-mate, Bud Smyth, was reported by the *News* as having crossed the finish line in second place, also in record-breaking time. "With just five hours of sleep in the previous six days," not much camping going on there.

33

Buffalo Chase

Remains of by-gone days at Rohn. There was also a well used BLM cabin. Here I prepare for a run down river toward Farewell and, as it turned out, a buffalo chase.

Day 5: Wednesday, March 7, Ptarmigan Pass to Rohn

I drove from Hell's Gate to Rohn River Roadhouse. A rough passage prompted me to overnight there. Next day, Thursday, March 8, found me battling terrible trail conditions in the direction of Farewell Station, camping for the night some four hours beyond that place.

From Files: (Transcription of Tape) North of Farewell, Thursday, March 8, midnight.

Well, I messed up—again. Didn't get to record yesterday (Wednesday), but will fill you in on as far as I have gone… Backing up, I camped at the foot of Hell's Gate with John Komak and Wednesday morning struck out ahead of Komak for Rohn River Roadhouse following the river. Going real good until maybe, ten miles upstream from Rohn. As the river valley (South Fork of the Kuskokwim) widened, a strong tail wind came up and sledding conditions became the worst I have ever experienced. What had been a beautiful trail deteriorated into a trailless waste of rocks, gravel bars, snags, windswept patches of glare ice and nearly knee deep open water. I got wet. I got repeatedly flipped over. Wind wrapped sled and team around snags. One big worry was if my plastic runner shoes would stand up… Thankfully, they did, but I don't know why… whole stretch I wished for iron runners… Took several pictures of the mess. Kiana was at first dumbfounded, having to lead without a definite trail to follow. I spelled her off with Genghis, once, I think it was… By the time we reached the Rohn checkpoint she was working like a little champ… Proud of all of them. They got wet, overheated, tangled, whipped off their feet, and plain sick of it, but bore up like the good troops they have always been for me. Their determined performance to be part of it all made my rough day at the office, well, worth going to work.

Arrived at Rohn River Roadhouse about 4:30 p.m. yesterday, (Wednesday, March 7). What is left of the old roadhouse operation is a small, falling down log cabin, filled with ice from river overflow nearly up to its window ledges… big disappointment, as I was hoping to see a real roadhouse of the trail's heyday… but Fish and Game (actually Bureau of Land Management) has a cabin that we were using as a checkpoint… very small… I, and most drivers there, camped in surrounding timber. Tough decision to stay or not. Still had two to three hours of daylight… There were no supplies of any kind at the Rohn checkpoint. Thought if I could make it to Farewell yet that day… then on into McGrath on Thursday, my dogs wouldn't be any worse for wear. I decided to stay there (Rohn) and rest the dogs and me. I just did not want any more of that river… it's a good thing, as it turned out, I didn't go because the run between Rohn and where the trail left the river toward Farewell, Egypt Mountain it's called, was not a place to be driving dogs after dark… Plus I was wet over my knees and needed to get dried out in case the weather decided to turn cold.

The vet (Terry Adkins) was at Rohn… following the teams along the trail… He looked my bunch over and said, "That's the best-looking team that has made it this far." Incidentally, he took a picture of me painting dog feet (pine tar and neats foot oil), he is going to try to follow this foot care along and see its results in Nome… While there, several mushers who had been in our loosely formed group arrived: Nayokpuk, Foster, Luster, and Isaac Okleasik, whose dogs looked much better. He has slowed down now and keeping up with us, so he might still be in this race. Maybe the moose meat from Ptarmigan Pass has taken effect… I admit I am in awe of these Eskimo drivers and their teams. Crackerjack leaders, beautiful parkas and skin boots… They drive their teams effortlessly, it seems.

Lots of good timber at Rohn, so had a big, roaring campfire… mostly dried out… Put dogs on half rations because there was no food to be had and I doubt any will show up anywhere before McGrath, which, for all I know, could be two days away, or more… For the dog's sake, I hope we get there sooner. Other guys in the same short-of-dog-food boat. We had hoped with an airstrip here, some of our supplies would have shown up… I was able to find in my sled "fix-it" bag, a bolt Isaac could use to repair a runner. Knowing I was getting short on dog vittles, a bit later he came by and insisted I accept maybe six to eight pounds of dry dog food. I consented only after he convinced me he had "plenty moose" to get his team to McGrath. I made soup of about half of it and fed it to my gang before leaving Rohn this (Thursday) morning.

Day 6: Thursday, March 8,
Rohn to between Farewell and McGrath

Forgot to check departure time from Rohn checkpoint, though must have been around 8:00 a.m.… Eskimo drivers left ahead of me downriver toward Egypt Mountain and on to Farewell… except for Isaac, who was behind. When I got out on the ice, it was not a very inviting sight… No rocks or sandbars or snags, but an entire valley, probably wider than Resurrection Valley (near Seward), flooded with overflow, frozen and glare ice in spots, weepy wet in others… hung to the left side of the valley, sometimes hitting stretches of decent snow and good going on short, un-obliterated sections of trail. I never caught up to any of the teams in front, nor did Isaac overtake me… Running along on perhaps a half-mile patch of overflow ice, my whole outfit—sled, team, and all just slowly sank down into the water—a real sinking feeling, believe me, not knowing if we would stop short of the river bottom. Thank God, we did. But once again, I was up nearly to my knees in icy water. Fortunately, the ice ramp out of the mess didn't give way or I would have had a real problem. Stopped on next patch of snow. Dogs rolled, shook themselves, and looked back as if to say, "What's next?"… Sure am glad I stayed in Rohn last night; that overflow business would have been spooky in the dark. I had Kiana in lead and probably wouldn't have had such a bad time of it if she were better on her commands… But like yesterday, she just got better, the longer she was at the head of the team, picking up on gee – haw commands without benefit of any trail to follow… The last couple of days on the river have been a good lead dog training session.

I missed the trail to Farewell, where it left the river (south fork of the Kuskokwim), ending up adding about an hour's extra travel time with no gain for the day. Darndest thing, five buffalo… I had no idea there were any up in this country… anyway, five of them, all of a sudden, showed up on the trail from behind a small, wooded point to my left. They took one look at us, the dogs went for them, no way could I hold them on the ice… They saw us bearing down and away they went ahead of us down the trail. No way could we gain on them, so I just let the team pursue… The team stayed in a fired-up mode for maybe a quarter hour before excitement of it all wore off and we went back down to a fast trot… In a bit, the shaggy critters wheeled up a steep embankment off the river and disappeared from sight… I ran for another half hour before I realized we had passed our landmark, Egypt Mountain… No runner marks to be found. Backtracking, it became obvious that in the excitement of the buffalo chase, we had whipped right past our poorly marked turn… a bit of pink ribbon about twenty-five yards after the turn. I still wonder if I dreamed about those buffalo, or something.

About five miles off the south fork, following a small, well-frozen stream, I came to Farewell, which appeared to be a former weather station or something on that order… the checkpoint was in a cafeteria sort of place, manned by a middle-aged fellow—a volunteer, I assume. Close by was a huge, old, one-story log building, which must have had some importance in years gone by… maybe a roadhouse… I feel I cheated myself by not spending time there and get more information on the place. But I had hopes of making McGrath, due to the dog food situation. All the Eskimo drivers, including Isaac, had arrived ahead of me and were ready to take off, and did, as I arrived… I very much appreciated the two bowls of chili I wolfed down, but even more so, the half sack of dog food that somehow arrived at Farewell with my name on it. Boy was I happy to see that… A quick checkpoint—in 1:00 p.m., out 1:30 p.m. I drove on, then, until nearly dark, by which time the sky had begun to cloud over… By mid-afternoon, I had passed all the Eskimo teams… Coming up the trail these last two days, I have managed several good pictures to show what things are like… No buffalo shots. I was too busy hanging on for dear life to even think of my camera.

Right now, I am camped alongside the trail some miles short of Big River Roadhouse… I like that name, denotes something grand and bustling, I do wish something remains from bygone days. I have the dogs fed and am drying out my boots by a fire which is mostly coals. This morning was rough going… dogs seem in good condition, no injuries, feet looked good tonight… Of course, we didn't travel all that far today, fifty to sixty miles, which means it still is a long day's mush over to McGrath. Plan to get out of the sack bright and early and on the trail. It is snowing right now, wet snow in fact. If the trail plugs, I might just go back to bed…The plan, anyway, is on to McGrath tomorrow.

It seems most of the miles between places have been messed up. They (mushers around me) talk about the "Redington mile," which is apparently shorter than the actual mile. By ham radio at Rohn, I am trying to get some neats foot oil and pine tar sent to McGrath, where I hope to intercept it. I was ninth out of Farewell and passed four teams during the afternoon, so there are teams ahead… I'm going to try to stick around fourth and not be out in front. It is too early for a race to get started.

This venture has most certainly been blessed so far. The race has had great weather, a little on the warm side maybe… I think how I went over the pass at night and still avoided a particularly nasty situation… The dogs are in fine shape and to travel with them is pure joy. I tell you, it's really hard to express in words what a really great undertaking this has been. I cannot believe it is actually happening… That I am out here in this beautiful country with a fine dog team, going someplace big, instead of around in little circles.

Probably won't have another tape until after McGrath because I will be running until late tomorrow to get there. Big River Roadhouse is supposed to be twenty miles this side of McGrath, but don't know if they are normal or Redington miles… Will try to get underway around five or five-thirty in the morning, push the team pretty hard and make it to McGrath tomorrow. There, I hope for provisions… I am down pretty low on both dog and people food. I have one package of dried soup and about one-third loaf of Shirley's trail cake… Shouldn't be any problem if the trail doesn't get plugged with this snow. It could be a little tight, especially if I have to sit around here more than a couple days.

Mention to Bob Hill that I think his sled has held up over the worst of it. When you see my slides, you will know what I mean. Some real sled tests have been run on that sled, which, so far, has passed them all. One criticism is that the plastic is so slippery that the wind has actually blown me to the side and ahead of the team, dragging them along, coming down the south fork the past two days.

I do think the worst of this journey is over. They say the trail between McGrath and Ruby is excellent. I am not going to try for any real long runs until I get on some of that good trail.

Well, I am just about at the end of this tape. I am guessing much of what is taped will not make a whole lot of sense to you, but will serve as a reminder to me… I can fill you in with pictures and details. So far, taping has worked out pretty well except I am most often so darn tired by the time I get to the recorder, that it is extremely difficult to arrange my thoughts. It would help to come up with some pattern, say trail, dogs, people and pictures. Something of that nature… It has been, up to this point, a hard, hard, tough trip… But a wonderful one at the same time. Worth it all and then some. That will be all, through Thursday night, March 8, on the Iditarod trail where it appears a blizzard is in the making.

There wasn't anything new or specifically race prompted about my camping routine. Use of snowshoes, tethering chain, bough beds and a campfire to make water were all comfortable standard operations for me. They had been perfected by scores of prerace dog team outings, dating back as far as eight to ten years. Most race mandatory gear, of necessity, had been discovered and adopted years before the 1973 Iditarod. When all was said and done, camping with dogs was old hat by race time. Not so, however, of physically running, driving a dog team day after day for three weeks. All first race participants were rookies where that was concerned.

To this day, the reward for owning a dog team—with all that implies—is driving it through wintertime Alaska. The beauty of it all. Words have always failed me in an attempt to describe the inner and predictable feeling that wells up each time I pull the hook, allowing my team to rocket down a new trail. Put the two together, dog team and winter Alaska, and you have created nothing short of magic. Pure, wand-waving magic. With absence of both conceit and embarrassment,

I can, in truth, state that I never express gratitude more fervently or more closely feel the presence of my Creator God than when riding the runners behind a well-tuned dog team.

As with the camping aspect, I had a good bit of runner time prior to the Big One but not three weeks' worth, one day upon another. It is doubtful any of the finishers had firsthand experience traveling such a distance with dogs in race mode. Because we were all beginners in endurance racing, our expectations, presumptions, speculations, knowledge, and our high hopes all came to be poured into an experimental test tube. All, in turn, were held to the flame of a thousand-mile, three-week-long trail.

For me, the learning curve for long-distance sled dog driving was huge. I learned something of sled dogs in that connection, but vastly more about myself. Truth is, one can get by with a good deal of slipshod team management when that team may be run two or three days in a row and then put to rest for the same or longer span. I learned early in the race that a bruised pad or torn toenail will heal on the run if cared for properly. Consequently, I learned to almost constantly monitor each dog while on the run. A slight limp, a loose trace, signs of diarrhea, all took on a greater significance with no lengthy downtime in my race plan. I became more in tune with each dog, a more alert, aware musher than ever before.

From Files: (Transcript of Tape) South of McGrath to Galena Friday, March 9 through Friday, March 16.

Day 7: Friday, March 9, a Camp between
Farewell and McGrath, to McGrath.

The first part of this tape is coming to you from Bear Creek Mine and I am told it is March 12, a Sunday. A lot has happened over the three days since the last one (tape) done the Anchorage side of Big River checkpoint…Blizzard didn't happen overnight as I expected… Just a little snow. That morning was gray, snowy with wind…Threatening like bedtime, night before. Slept well from midnight to 4:00 a.m. …Up, did morning chores, and was on the trail toward McGrath not long after 6:00 a.m., if I remember correctly…with dry feet and boots…those air force mukluks. Once we get cranked up and we, the team and I, that is—are eager for what lies ahead. A wonderful feeling of adventure overwhelms me…Trail into McGrath and beyond to around the native village of Takotna is pretty flat… Lots of small river bottom traveling… Vague in places due to drifting. About two and one-half hours into the run, I came to a cabin; I think the permanent home of a native man whose name was Petra [Pitka]. We stopped for a bit to chat…nice, friendly guy—middle age I would guess…said we're on the Salmon River. He told me the distance from his place into McGrath, but that escapes me now…Also, how surprised he was when all the army machines came blasting through his yard a couple of days before.

In what seemed like another two hours (I didn't carry a watch on the race), we arrived at the checkpoint of my dreams…romantic-sounding Big River Roadhouse checkpoint. Boy! What a disappointment. It consisted of a blue pup tent occupied by two young fellows…Volunteer checkers…never got their names. I didn't see anything of a roadhouse except maybe a fallen-in building, mostly buried with snow. The checker's tent was pitched right next to an old log cabin…with a good roof and all…that a native family…a young couple with children were using while trapping beaver… had coffee…Inquired if that cabin was part of the old roadhouse operation…nobody knew. The trapper's name was Philip Esai. Ma Nature began to deliver the storm she had been promising…soon after leaving Big River.

Dashed dreams. I had hoped to see something grand at Big River Roadhouse. This pile of past Alaska, a checker's tent and trapper's cabin was it.

Pushed on to McGrath…A real town…storming pretty good by the time I reached McGrath around 5:00 p.m. (5:09 p.m.. official time) in second place behind George Attla, who pulled in the night before…Let's see…the checker's name was Jim Schroeder. He had my fish heads loose in bed of his pickup. The checkpoint was at the airstrip…race marshal Dick Tozier and Orville Lake were there. He (Lake) was conducting musher interviews for radio audiences. I don't recall all of what he had to say, but he did complement the appearance of my team and made mention that I still had all twelve of my dogs in harness. He referred to me as "that kooky school teacher from Seward"…and gave his in-depth analysis of my performance up to that point as "One hell of a job."

Dick and Audra Forsgren took me in for the night…the team spent the night on the school playground…no boughs for bedding. They were buried under snow by morning, so did fine… Forsgrens were great hosts…What luxury!…huge dinner, bath, and a good night's sleep on a real bed…breakfast of bacon and dried eggs, too…I should mention that I took several pictures yesterday…hope they turn out.

34

...A Woman in Here

Tex Gates at his Bear Creek Mine. His generous hospitality contributed immeasurably to the success of the first Iditarod.

Day 8: Saturday, March 10, McGrath to Ophir

There were three of us who left McGrath for Ophir Saturday morning...Attla first, after a day and a half rest, left at 8:50 a.m., then me, five minutes later, and Johnny Coffin five minutes behind me...Storm backing off...Trailbreaker machines left before us, but trail blew in behind them so we battled the entire way. Not much going on at that place called Takotna…did not stop…the people I stayed with at McGrath (Forsgrens) flew over to Ophir…opened up their mining claim cabin and made an unofficial checkpoint there. (Placerville, eighty-eight miles from McGrath, was supposed to be next.) Very slow going…dogs, what I call swimming through drifts a good bit of the time…didn't seem like we made many miles today…but dogs had enough by the time we arrived at Forsgren's cabin in Ophir…which is strictly a mining location, no permanent residents.

What great people…cabin warm…bunks to sleep in…Dick flew over dog food for us and beat us all, Audra brought a roasted turkey, with everything that goes with it, for our dinner…We (Attla, Coffin, and I) are getting spoiled. Great people is an understatement.

My team parked at Dick and Audra Forsgren's home in McGrath. Next day they flew to their Ophir cabin to set up a "temporary" checkpoint that has been in operation for over 40 years at this writing.

The Forsgrens went on to host their spur-of-the-moment Ophir checkpoint for the rest of their active lives. In recent years, the job has been turned over to family members, who carry on a tradition begun with our first race.

Day 9: Sunday, March 11, Ophir to Bear Creek Mine

Everyone was up early at that unofficial Ophir checkpoint. Mrs. Forsgren had a swell breakfast…sourdough pancakes, bacon, eggs… coffee for there and to go in my thermos…that's roughing it, huh? Dick Forsgren said it is fifty-two miles from his cabin to Poorman… Machines are ahead of us somewhere…didn't stay in Ophir with us.

Attla left shortly after 6:00 a.m. Coffin and I not too much later… heading for Bear Creek Mine and on to Poorman, that is if trail conditions allow. As it turned out, storm conditions continued, and even with machines ahead, the dog trail was drifted and buried in most places…a long day got us only forty-two miles up the trail. Not long after leaving Ophir, maybe an hour…an hour and a half, we all passed Wilmarth's camp… who passed us at Ophir during the night…It made me wonder if he has already started to race…I later learned that Attla had run head-on into our trailbreakers …They had missed their turn. They and Attla backed up a quarter mile and where they left a cardboard sign tacked to a tree that read something like, "Wrong way, but cabin one half mile." By… mid-morning, I caught up with George who had stopped for lunch…I joined him…He commented on the good appearance of my team and said he was having trouble with diarrhea in his dogs and worried about weight loss…was hoping things would improve now…since he managed to get some beaver meat…I think back in McGrath…forty-two miles from 6:00 a.m. to probably 6:00 p.m. when we arrived at Bear Creek, some twelve hours of continuous snow plowing and battling wind and flying snow… Dogs tired, I am tired.

Strange deal… out of the blue three or four days ago, the miner here, Tex Gates and wife, said a half dozen or more army snowmachines came roaring into the yard…the first they had heard the race was to come through there. No one for sure seems to know how Placerville got missed altogether… Nothing belonging to the Iditarod Race is here (Bear Creek)…no food, no gas, no checkers, due probably because planes haven't been able to fly last couple of days. Gates had no idea we would show up today—or any day, I suppose. An amazing couple, they hustled around, got heat in a cabin for us…Mrs. cooked up a big pot of stew…unexpected company of over a dozen by time night was over…Let's see if I can remember who all is here:

Trail Committee volunteer snowmachiners are Carl Fitzler, Bill Copeland, Joe Smith, Bob Stone, and Don Rosevear. With them is a woman hitch-hiker, doing stories for one of the papers (Pam Randles—*Anchorage Daily News*) Mushers—Attla, Coffin, Vent, Wilmarth, and myself…Attla and I got there in daylight…The rest after dark. Dick Wilmarth's arrival was announced by his long and loud string of cussing. Seems nothing was going well for him and he wanted to share his misery with his trail-mates…One of the snowmachine guys…from somewhere in the darkened cabin, hollered, "Hey! Why don't you shut up? There is a woman in here." …meaning the news lady… The camp got quiet early as everyone was pretty well rung out.

The fate of the first race was, for several days, in the hands of ITC volunteer trail breakers south of Ruby. Here Bill Copeland persuades his machine to start at Bear Creek Mine.

George Attla provided much needed stature to our first race by entering and his wholehearted participation. Here, he readies his team for departure from Bear Creek.

Day 10: Monday, March 12, Bear Creek Mine toward Poorman

> No one was in a big hurry come morning to leave this place. The snow had let up some, but very strong gusts had it whipped into a whiteout condition… Had some camp coffee and filled my thermos…One-third loaf of the trail cake and I am ready to go…I am recording now, waiting for the machine gang to leave…They have a tough job compared to the mushers. Bill Copeland worked for an hour to get his machine started…Tex Gates…what a great guy!…helped us, helped the machiners, including giving then gas to see them through to Ruby. Five machines' worth.
>
> Looks like the machines are fix'n to take off from Bear Creek here heading toward Poorman…it's 10:00 a.m. by Bobby Vent's watch. I doubt we will make it to Poorman if the trail over there is anything like conditions here at Bear Creek. It will be tough going for sure… high wind, huge drifts five to six feet high around the buildings here. Army trail will be buried across miles of open country. Gates said a normal trail position in this hilly open country is along a contour above what he called the "drift zone" down in the bottoms.
>
> Well, that's what roughly has happened to this point on the Iditarod Trail. With my notes and photos I should be able to fill in more detail. Most of us—me for sure—are out of dog food. I shared the last of my fat with Bobby Vent, who I grow increasingly fond of the more I associate with him…Will end for now and pick up again the next chance I get…And get on the trail.

As that day, Monday, March 12, unfolded, my prediction that we probably would not see Poorman that day, proved sound. As evening set in, I was running, it seemed, as if on a magic carpet. A partial moon showed through a thinning cloud layer. The wind was down. The trail was in place and setting up. I thought I had at last been set free of restraints, that the trail was mine to run all the way to the Yukon if I desired. A wistfulness that came abruptly to an end as the front end of my team began to pile up against a squad tent pitched where the trail should have gone.

Okay, I'm recording this tape segment the same day (Monday, March 12)…I am talking this time in regard to the area between Bear Creek Mine and roughly six miles south of Poorman. Plan was for the race to go through Placerville, a deserted mining location off to our west…The army, for whatever reason, had broken it to somewhere in this neck of the woods. Our problems came about due to this storm, really…It was still snowing with strong wind when we left this morning from Bear Creek. I believe I mentioned before that the machines left Bear Creek ahead of us mushers… Our order leaving was—Bobby Vent, George Attla, then myself. Wilmarth and Coffin followed.

I passed Vent just a couple of miles out. Attla stayed ahead of me, but decided to call it a day about 7:00 p.m. His dogs looked beat, really bad, I thought…After making the pass, I cranked the team up, heading, as I hoped, for Poorman, maybe twenty-five miles away. The sky was high overcast with plenty of light from a half moon… With the machine trail well set up and temperature dropping, my dogs, Kiana in lead, seemed to have a new lease on life. That old seven to eight miles per hour trot seemed to have returned…We were clipping along beautifully…me half dozing on the runners when—just like that—we are in a big ball against a large tent with machines scattered about. Even in a half moonlight, I could see a large willow thicket just beyond…Not good.

They (trail crew and reporter, Pam Randles) were in the tent, asleep…Had run out of light and army trail…like I said, there was new, deep snow, especially down here…Very hard to find the trail…Of course, after dark, it was impossible…A hard, tiring job without doubt. So here I am, the only musher up here ahead and at the end of the trail, at least until morning…Not much progress in two days past.

The dog food situation is getting critical. I've got to—even if on snowshoes—get over to Poorman tomorrow…Late afternoon today it cleared some and I heard planes flying, and I am supposing there is dog food placed at Poorman. If you look at a map, you will notice it (Poorman) isn't far from Placerville…straight north as I remember. Now that the army saw fit to cut Placerville out of the race, I assume Poorman will be supplied as a check station in its place. So my hope is to get over there first thing tomorrow...I have shortchanged these dogs on food the last two nights, which I hate to do...that business will catch up to me and hand me its bill...Eska is out of it, she had given up so will drop her as soon as I can...at Poorman or Ruby when we get there...I suspect she may also be coming in season...This is some of the worst terrain so far...hard on dogs...just rolling hills, up and down, up and down. It hardly seems we will hit the Iditarod Trail between McGrath and Ruby. The army, with its dozen machines, or whatever, put their trail in as quickly and as direct as possible, and it's not good...All aside, we are now in the very heart of the historic Iditarod gold discovery...to me that's good, very good.

As far as the race goes, it is impossible to race without a dependable trail. I really do think Attla is out of it. His dogs just don't seem to get enough rest...even with an extra day in McGrath... beaver meat, too. Should we ever get a chance to race, there will not be time for his team to recuperate...I don't see how he is going to finish the race. Vent, same way. Just six dogs and just dragging. Our dogs, most likely, will slow down also under real racing conditions. For now, they are eager...except for Eska...they are in better shape than when we left Anchorage.

One team here in front that concerns me is Dick Wilmarth, the guy from Red Devil. He has a very good-looking team that, so far, has stood up to being pushed hard. Then again, he is having some problems with feet, as I would guess we all are. I think I will do as I have with Attla...whoever is in front, just hang around by him... follow...avoid any more than my share of trail breaking...If I can just keep them fed up and keep working on feet...Looks to me like there is no problem to go on ahead in this race...I am confident, barring accident, this team will look pretty darn good coming into Nome...After Ruby, we will begin to open it up a bit, which, I think, will mean longer days, as I believe we are at full throttle on a run now. Flat running down the Yukon should allow for longer days when compared with this hilly country...Flat going, but for one more hump over there between Kaltag and Unalakleet. I don't think it is time yet to make a race of it…Watch who is coming up from behind and keep in this front bunch…conserve my team as much as possible.

Can't think of much more that's happened today. It must be pushing midnight…Dog chores are done and I am in my tent…tired. Overall, I feel I am getting stronger and more eager, especially once on the trail each day. It is as neat as ever. I know I am losing weight…Weighed myself at Forsgren's in McGrath and weighed in at one hundred seventy-five pounds, so am getting down where I should be.

I am rambling. I know…Again our dogs look in good shape, though losing weight, these past couple days—some food will remedy that situation. Attla and others remark on how good looking they are, best they have seen so far. Until I drop Eska, I will be the only one up this far who hasn't dropped dogs…If we can find the trail out of here tomorrow I might be able to make Ruby in one run. That's doubtful. More than likely will be another night. I will try to fill this tape and mail it from Ruby. That's all for tonight from what may be the Iditarod Trail. Camped approximately six miles south of Poorman.

"Lost Trail Camp" south of Poorman. We front runners fell victim to a terrific blizzard that raged over the area completely erasing trail made by the army team days before. Dick Wilmarth in foreground.

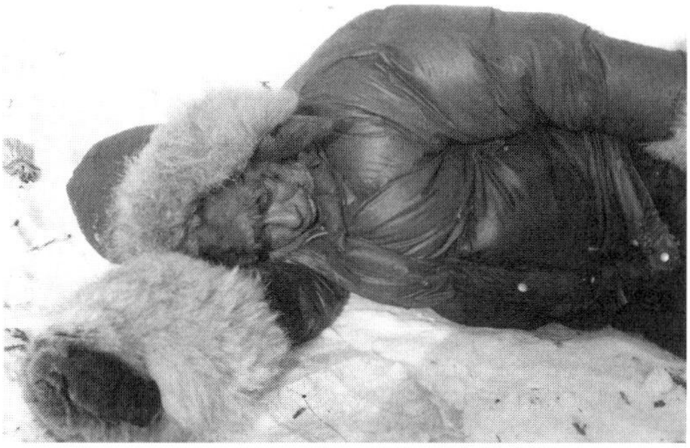

Race day 11, Bobby Vent takes an afternoon snooze, map by his side, at Lost Trail Camp. A minus 20 degree F temperature was not a deterrent to sweet repose.

Noorvik musher, John Coffin, takes our down time at Lost Trail Camp in stride, as indeed he will in an unfortunate personal difficulty further up the trail.

Summit meeting at Lost Trail Camp resulted in the conclusion – "We are lost." L-R: Don Rosevear, Pam Randles, George Attla, Bill Copeland, Joe Smith, and Bob Stone. We decided to go into a creek bottom camp 2½ miles to the rear.

A growing accumulation of trail days brought to the fore the necessity of close attention to each dog's care and maintenance, thus assuring the team's overall well-being and, in the end, that of the driver, as well. In view of the fact that a one-thousand-mile endurance race in itself was an experimental endeavor, it logically followed that dog care, to some degree, would be experimental as well. And so it was.

A common, routine question put to finishers of the first one was, "Well, was it worth it?" And, with uncanny predictability, would come an answer such as, "Oh, yes, it was a great adventure for me." And in the next breath, "I learned a lot about taking care of a dog team, I'll tell you." We all brought to the table, so to speak, a bit of knowledge gleaned through our personal long or short association with the sled dog. Added to our frontline wisdom were gift insights that came to us, as eager learners and attentive listeners, when others of greater knowledge of the subject wrote or spoke. Eternally neutral, Mother Nature, the trail, the Great Land, handed each his measure with absolute impartiality. Those twenty-three masters of the first long trail challenge employed what skills each brought to the task and by adaptation and perseverance, laid down indelible runner tracks stretching from Anchorage to Nome.

By McGrath, my dog care routine had been fairly well established. Beginning at rise-and-shine time and assuming it was on hand to feed, each dog received up to two and one-half pounds of fish and fat. The amount of fat itself was increased on very cold days. Next, I would check feet and brush neats foot oil and pine tar on each foot. If there was a foot with a cut pad or pulled nail, I would additionally treat it with the thick, popular salve Bag Balm and bootie it, which was necessary on but two feet the entire race. Imagine my pleasant discovery that a foot wound actually healed on the run when treated in this manner. Now came harnessing. As far as I was aware, the Fishback, X-back harnesses were the only commercially marketed harnesses at that time. However, had they been available then, my team would have been harnessed in either the H-back or the Seavey spreader style. Had it been possible, I would have happily traded my old poly-rope towline for what now is referred to as the Seavey spreader steel cable towline. Attention was given to cross positioning dogs for each run. If, say, Shiak ran on the right side of the towline yesterday, he would go for today's run on the left side, and Crazy, his partner, switched accordingly. This, in an effort to prevent sore shoulders. Often, but not necessarily routinely, I switched dogs along the length of the towline. On long hauls, I found my team would eventually slow to the pace of the slowest animal. Not wanting those slower dogs to set an even slower pace, dogs with remaining gas in the tank would be rotated toward the front. Also, to assist either Genghis or Kiana up front and provide company, I doubled them with usually my budding leader, Sonny. From this, I learned that one's speed can be significantly increased by use of double lead over the single arrangement.

I came to expect, early in a run, a bit of limp here, stiffness there, even a slack tug on occasion, but all usually disappeared as the dogs warmed into the day's work. Frequent stops became part of the picture when our runs became ridiculously long (fourteen, eighteen hours) after hitting the Bering Sea Coast. There, in particular, I made it a point to stop every hour, give or take, go forward, pet and play with each dog. Yes, and talk baby talk to each. Perhaps by so doing, I transport that wondrous creature, if but briefly, to a happier time, of puppyhood. I gave special attention to the leader, who had, if you think about it, the loneliest job of all. When available, at about two-hour intervals, I gave snacks—fish or fat. Kibble comprised the bulk of the evening ration, augmented with fish and fat when possible. All kibble was fed as a very watery soup with an eye on maintaining hydration at a high level. Water came by way of laboriously melting snow or from a convenient open creek in a couple instances. By today's standards, the kibble I fed my team didn't have much to recommend in it, but it was all we had.

Dick Mackey spoke for most of us regarding trials and tribulations encountered on our way to Nome that first year. In an *Anchorage Daily Times* article, published ten days into the race, at the time we were floundering in mountainous snowdrifts of McGrath and beyond, Mackey is quoted to have said:

"None of us expected a red carpet out here. We knew there would be problems when we started. Many things have come up which we hadn't counted on and there have been some rough times, but without running the race the first time, there was no way to ever have a precedent set as far as planning for the next one and eliminating some of the problems. I am sure everyone from the committee, the snowmachiners who are helping break trail, to the mushers and the many pilots and check station people involved, have all learned a lot so far."

35

Day We Went Backward

The day we went 2 ½ miles backward, south of Poorman. Dick Wilmarth (foreground) and volunteer snowmachiner cut brush in an effort to regain the lost trail.

Day 11: Tuesday, March 13, South of Poorman to South of Poorman

Okay, I have found time to record again, this being just after dark on Tuesday, March 13, I think it is…This is the day we actually went backward about two and one-half miles…That's all we did for the entire day…two and one-half miles back toward McGrath… Remember, I said on the last recording I camped at the dead end where our trail crew had lost the trail short of Poorman…

We got up bright and early this morning, got the machines running…it was our coldest morning so far, though cloudy with not real heavy snow, but wind…broke camp after machiners left to scout out the trail. Incidentally, last night I had only about half a honey can of food for each dog and a little bit of fat and about a tablespoon of halibut…These dogs are getting hungry.

We (five mushers) waited, killing time after the trailbreakers took off into the valley in front of us…to the north…where they thought the army trail went. No luck…They came back to camp toward evening, beat, very tired…Did have some good luck, though. A break in the weather allowed a plane to locate us about…the time…the machiners had returned to camp. Whoever the pilot, saw our situation… being way off the trail…and pointed us in the direction of the trail by doing two or three flyovers…about forty-five degrees to the west from our location.

It is only about fifteen miles to Poorman, but we sure are having our share of troubles getting there. What happened was the army went ahead of the race to put down a trail base and mark it for our trail crew to follow just ahead of the front-running dog teams. This big storm that we are in put a big crimp in our operation. Where there are trees, the army crew tied red ribbons, but in this mostly wide-open country, they simply dropped ribbons on the ground…Of course, there is no way our crew can find the ground markers when a large number of the trees with ribbons are buried in new snowdrifts…Our poor snowmachine crew, all day staggering around out there, looking for a trail that is way over on the opposite side of the valley…west of here…Anyway, from the Lost Trail Camp, we dropped back today to a small creek bottom (Fourteen Mile Creek)…Lots of nice timber for a good camp.

Our Fourteen Mile Creek Camp. Pam Randles was designated camp cook, which she did using a dog food bucket. She concocted a kind of stew from an assortment of meager food items each contributed. It was minus 38 degrees F the following morning.

We have set up a community camp here…One big campfire… Pooling our people food for a common larder…dog food as well…set up pretty well by early evening…I put on my snowshoes and stomped out the words "DOG FOOD" in about ten-foot letters in hopes that we would get another plane fly over…which happened…and sure enough, we managed to get some dog food out here tonight…Air dropped a bag for each team before dark…big relief…Strange how it happened, but just before the airplane showed up and the pilot wiggled its wings to let us know he understood the dog food message…George Attla was getting his rifle out of his sled pack and I began putting on snowshoes…to go hunting for a moose for dog food and camp meat… Others were preparing to help with the hunt as well. There is plenty of evidence of moose in this bottom so I would have to say there is one lucky one today…saved by an airplane.

Things are looking up…good camp…air-delivered dog food… and with the help of that pilot this morning, we are now back on the trail. The fellows on the machines just don't quit…before dark tonight they broke a trail over to on old cat trail used for freighting, which is supposed to get us into Poorman in the morning. Mushers in camp here are Bobby Vent, George Attla, Dick Wilmarth, Johnny Coffin, and me. Plus the snowmachine party, which includes Mrs. Randles…her husband, Slim Randles, also a writer, entered this race, but dropped out because of an injury...She is doing a news story for the *Times* (*Anchorage Daily News*).

Tonight it has cleared off and getting colder...tonight a pilot landed on skis with news that no one has reached Bear Creek yet...My guess is they are lost out in those tundra flats north of McGrath...Hope someone comes to their aid.

I have my tent set up and a sterno fire going...It is cold...I will check the temperature in the morning, which will be the first time to do so on this trip. It was cold last night as well...maybe minus thirty degrees... about what it seems now...A clear moonlight, beautiful, beautiful night. Dogs are losing weight, but, thanks to the air drop, were fed well tonight...If the trail conditions allow, I am at least thinking of burning it on into Ruby tomorrow...I think we have been on the trail now ten days. I am not sure. Someone tonight had it figured that Placerville is the halfway mark to Nome. Of course, we are not going there, but are about opposite that now. I think.

One of the snowmachines was wrecked today and was abandoned up in that dead end valley beyond Lost Trail Camp, as I call it...I will be able to show you on my map what went on here when I get back to civilization. The machine guys are going to talk the army team into coming out and hauling it into Ruby for repairs. One of the snowmachine fellows is disgusted. He is going to quit when he gets to Ruby.

A positive outcome of all this wandering in the wilderness is I have had lots of time to take pictures...some significant ones, I think. To this point, I have gone through three rolls of thirty-six exposure films on various subjects. We all are eagerly anticipating arrival at Ruby, because that's where we hit the mighty Yukon River...flat going until Kaltag, then a ninety-mile stretch with a hump in its middle...that won't be too bad. Then along the Bering Sea Coast...I am looking forward to seeing how that country looks and to what the mushing will be like up there.

That's about it for this time from Fourteen Mile Creek, somewhere south of Poorman on the Iditarod Trail. Tuesday, March 13.

It is noteworthy and of some importance to this narrative that my enthusiasm for tape recording events of the day was in a steep tailspin by my arrival at Ruby. By conclusion of the tape which took my race to Galena that zeal had, for better or worse, crashed. Not to despair. In Anchorage I had stuffed a thick, pocket-sized notebook in my jacket pocket. Throughout, I had recorded therein mostly inner, personal thoughts and emotions as they came to me along the way. Some of these, I confess, when read at this great distance in time, come across as being downright gushy. Entries more befitting my old, poetic dog mushing partner, Tom Johnson. Others, without apology, have been written into this account of the First Great Race. To some extent, from that wonderfully historic village of Ruby and for sure from Galena, on to our final goal on Norton Sound, that notebook sufficed as first depository of daily observations from the trail, accommodating, at the same time, those rare flights of my mind's fancy. Returning home at race end, I sat myself down and undertook a thorough, critical editing of that overstuffed tablet. The result, I transcribed to paragraph form, and laid the results to rest for nearly four decades in my cardboard box file. I am truly indebted to Mr. Doug Capra for his pertinacity, which resulted in completion of those all important race transcripts, while details were yet un-fogged by the veil of time. Should praise be forthcoming for any latter portion of this account, it should be directed to Capra's insistence that written material be preserved in useful form. It has proved invaluable in completion of this work.

At the time I fell asleep, there in that snug but frigid camp at Fourteen Mile Creek, on the evening of Tuesday, March 13, I believed completely that evening of the next day would find us in Ruby. Ruby is an old gold rush town on the Yukon, the iconic river of the North Country. There to resupply, break the restraints of bad trail, and fly unencumbered down that great frozen thoroughfare. But that was not to be.

Day 12: Wednesday, March 14, South of Poorman to Poorman

When we got up (at Fourteen Mile Creek Camp, ten to twenty miles south of Poorman) in the morning, it was minus thirty-eight degrees F by my thermometer inside my pack...the morning of Wednesday, March 14. Yesterday morning was about as cold...That was the first time I looked at the thermometer. So much for a daily record of weather conditions…It was a joke to think the trail into Poorman would be easy due to colder weather to harden things…a real joke. The machines took off, maybe an hour ahead of the first team…we soon caught them…Those machine drivers had a terrible time due to soft drifted snow…huge drifts eight to ten feet in places…Those poor guys…They pushed, shoveled, and unstuck machines over and over... it is little wonder that it took from 9:00 a.m. to about 6:00 p.m. to cover certainly no more than twenty miles…ending for the night at the Poorman mining camp.

Snowmachiners set their tent up…By the way, Don Rosevear's machine died for its last time and was left behind in one of the endless successions of drifts encountered…We mushers requisitioned a cabin with a good stove…After dog chores, settling in pretty snug on another cold night…No more asleep when some machiners roared in from the north…Caused lots of excitement…Don Stickman drove all the way from Galena, talked Emmitt Peters and Albert Kangas, who live at Ruby, to go south with him to meet up with us…They arrived about 9:00 p.m., making trail all the way. They left Poorman to overnight in a cabin back toward Ruby a few miles…I thought our luck at last was changing for the better. Boy, it is really a good feeling to be on a defined route (actually, a summer road) with a well-packed trail… Such luxury!

Day 13: Thursday, March 15, Poorman to Ruby

We made it to Ruby…Hill upon hill from Poorman. Our musher group remained the same. Vent, Wilmarth, Attla, Coffin, and myself on one another's heels all day. Bobby Vent led the pack out of Poorman. Attla, Coffin, and I stopped about noon and made up a pot of coffee before continuing on. Further up the trail toward Ruby, there is a mining location I believe called Long.

Albert Kangas, one of the guys who showed up at Poorman last night, has a claim at that place (Long) and must have stayed at his cabin there last night. Daughter Nerylen and son Ivan were there also…had the coffee pot on…chili pot, too. Had one of the guys take a picture of some of us having coffee. Kangas told us he had mined two hundred ounces of gold there last summer. An airplane landed as I was about to get on the trail out of there…Kangas knew him…a wolf hunter who lives in McGrath. He was proud to inform me he had three animals in his plane, shot, I guess with a shotgun, while in the air…That whole business is sickening to me.

Bobby was first of the drivers to leave Long and the first to arrive at Ruby, as I remember it…I was either second or third…A distance, I am told, a bit shy of sixty miles…Checked in late afternoon, Harold Esmilka is the checker here…nice, accommodating man…Owns the one and only trading post.

I was taken in for the night here at Ruby by Emmitt Peters and his large and most helpful extended family…I think I have this right… With Emmitt, there are three boys and five girls…ranging in age from late teens to upwards toward forty…Emmitt is one of the older ones at thirty-two…Mother's name is Mary and Paul is the dad. Emmitt has sled dogs of his own…mushing since very young…entered the Fur Rendezvous race in Anchorage this year…sounds like he is interested in doing this race in the future. I stayed at the family home and was treated to my first-ever barbequed beaver…had a good night's sleep… cornflakes for breakfast. Emmitt helped me hook up and escorted me down a river bluff trail onto the Yukon with his little yellow Ski-Doo… pointed me down the river toward Galena.

On the road again. Good conversation and a much appreciated meal, compliments of miner Al Kangas at Long. L-R: Wilmarth, Attla, Kangas, Vent, and Seavey.

My Ruby host, Emmitt Peters, first stop on the fabled Yukon River. Peters was destined to run 14 Iditarods earning the championship in 1975 and title – the Yukon River Fox.

Hey, Kids (mine), the highlight of my stay at Ruby was that letter from you and Mom, which was waiting for me at the trading post… Love you guys…Thank you all for making this adventure possible.

Day 14: Friday, March 16, Ruby to Galena

On the trail (out of Ruby) this morning, Friday, March 16, about 6:45…Arriving at Galena something after 5:00 p.m. (no watch). Pretty slow going…couldn't get the team cranked up to speed the entire run of, I guess, around fifty miles…all were fed and ate well at Ruby… Maybe getting tired of it or maybe the wide-open spaces of the wide Yukon have them freaked out…I do have some foot problems, which I need to keep working on… I used one of those muttluks (bootie) on Snippy with bag balm…was improving by Galena. Mushers are beginning to push us from the rear. Isaac is back in the race, a day behind and a couple others coming up. Like us, they had their fair share of storm-related problems.

Checking feet on way down the Yukon.
L-R: Bandit, Casper. Good foot care paid off.

Break time on the Yukon. In my imagination I picture summer steam boats heading for the Klondike and historic freight teams traveling my direction toward new gold discoveries at Nome.

Hope we can stay in here and keep plugging away…Still a long way to Nome…Tomorrow, I will run downriver to Nulato only about thirty-five miles…from there to Kaltag, another…about the same… then it is ninety miles to the coast at Unalakleet.. . I don't know how far it is from Unalakleet to Nome, but she's a stretch for sure…Guess I have already mentioned that I can't get the dogs enthusiastic. That stay in the woods hurt us because I had such little fish to feed. Wilmarth had his Piper Cub buddy, Bobby Vanderpool, or something like that, drop fish for him south of Poorman.

I am staying with Gordon Cruger and wife out at the Galena Air Force Base. Very nice folks, as every single person along the trail has been. Like Cruger, cannot do enough for the mushers. A plain, old dog musher, a celebrity. Even an honorary membership in the Galena Sports Association was given me, and a patch to boot. What is this world coming to?…When I end here (recording), I will be walking over to the trading post and see what's there in the way of trail food and to check on the dogs…Sidney Huntington is the checker for the Galena checkpoint. OH! Gordon Cruger told me that someone is working up a charter plane to Nome, in case we show up there…just joking…That's great. Hope some Seward folks can make it up…I plan to make it there even if I have to use the last patch of snow to get there… George Attla's dogs are pretty well burned out. He says he is going to lay over for two or three days at Galena and work on getting them nursed back on the trail. I hope he does get back. He has gone through too much to not finish this thing.

So, that being all, I will sign off here at Galena, the evening of Friday, March 16, on the Iditarod Trail.

36

Good Checkpoint That Wasn't

Perched as it was, high on a Yukon River bluff, Koyukuk took a bit of effort of visit. However, it was a most rewarding side trip.

From Galena on into Nome, my saga was recounted without further use of audio tape recording while en route. I could fabricate a story wherein my recorder broke down or perhaps a more believable prevarication, like frozen batteries rendered it inoperative. But I will have none of it. Plain truth be told, I simply tired of the operation. I was tired of being tired, falling asleep while attempting to record three days' worth of happenings. And then, I reasoned, if there was to be a race made of our trek to Nome, it most certainly would start on the Yukon. Race mode would result in much longer runner time, greatly increased dog care demands, and in a lot less sleep than what I enjoyed during our recent respite south of Poorman. Besides,

I had become increasingly handy using notebook and pencil since about Rohn.

That's what was done. Notes on my observations increased many fold per day. The recorder took the fast way home via the Galena Post Office. Once a semblance of coherency returned after reaching Nome, I edited my handiwork. A clarification was done here, a corrected spelling there—okay, lots of spelling corrections. I made notes in places where more information was desirable. Back home, I shot off letters to most checkpoint villages, seeking answers to my race note questions—and from most, I received helpful answers. I was, with aid of photos and maps, prepared to meet friend and mentor, Doug Capra, with his myriad of organized questions and once again talk to a recording machine. Transcripts of those tapes are herein—after used to navigate this narrative along its serpentine way.

Galena, I learned, traces its beginnings, as did so many present-day Yukon Valley communities, to an Athabascan fish camp. By 1918, it had become a supply point for lead ore mines of the area. Soon, a sizable collection of native families had congregated there, working chiefly as wood cutters, supplying boiler fuel for an average of two steamers per day during the 1920 navigation season. Galena was selected by the U.S. Air Force as a site for an airfield installation, part of a network utilized in ferrying WWII lend-lease warplanes to the Soviet Union. A fellow at the trading post told me that in the spring of 1945, an ice jam below town backed Yukon water into town and flooded the air base. A whole squadron of B-17s dropped thousands of pounds of bombs, which persuaded the blocked ice to move along. One wonders what the Environmental Protection Agency would have said about that. In more recent years, a communication station and fighter jet interceptor squadron were located there. My Galena host, Gordon Cruger, was a civilian employee operating the air force water purification plant. I found him both hospitable and interesting. He and his wife lived in a spacious, modular home, situated on base some distance from the town site. The main part of town was essentially lined up along the north shore of the Yukon.

Gordon had several intriguing hobbies, among which was taxidermy and rejuvenation of antiques. At the time, he was in the midst of spiffing up several old trophies for dog races, which dated back to 1920s Galena. Before going out to the Cruger home, I arranged to stake my team out at a Native fellow's place near the trading post. His name was Eddie, a friendly guy with a perpetual smile, who insisted he help with dog chores, including working on dog feet. Eska, Kiana's sister, and sometimes lead dog, wasn't all that great coming down from Ruby. Not working. I decided to take her on one more run before a decision to drop her was made. She could have been coming into heat. I noticed she was garnering increased attention from the boys. With chores completed, I went off to the Crugers' for a wonderful hot shower and just as hot and even more wonderful wild game feast.

It was near 11:30 p.m. when I walked back to where my team was located near the trading post for a final check on it. Lights were still on and three or four locals were seated around one of the two small tables placed near the door. Sidney Huntington, our checker, was one of the patrons. In 1993, Huntington would author *Shadows on the Koyukuk*, a descriptive personal account of Alaska Native life along a major tributary of the Yukon, our next stop downriver. In a spur-of-the-moment decision, I bummed use of the phone to call home.

It didn't work. Being a radio-telephone, I assume the air had to be just right with all stars in proper alignment for it to perform its expected function. I couldn't even make contact with the outside world. Only loud, Rice Krispies-like snap, crackle, and pop. Good thing, really. There was no phone installed at the Seavey place. That high-tech convenience would be another five or six years in making its appearance at our homestead. My thwarted, near-midnight call was directed to friend and fellow teacher, Don Mai, who lived in Seward. Poor Don. He would have most likely had to get out of a warm bed, driven four miles in a cold car to our place, and wake Shirley up. She, in turn, would have had to drive into town to Mai's, and call back. You get the picture. And me, planning to get up at 5:00 a.m. and hit the trail? How does that go? God looks after fools?

Before leaving the trading post, I inquired into purchase of a pair of wool pants. As with the phone call, no luck. That ended my hope of a complete change of clothes before heading downriver and over to the coast. Soiled, moisture -saturated clothing, and cold air temperatures make for a most uncomfortable condition. It could, in dire circumstances, be downright life threatening. The more one perspires in cold weather, the greater and faster the rime—or what is called hoarfrost by some—built up in clothing. Moisture from perspiration is driven outward by body heat, collects, and freezes. This outer frost travels slowly inward, greatly reducing the insulation qualities and benefits of clothing. Without new pants, the old ones went back on. I had wanted a complete change in Galena with an eye toward being more prepared for what Norton Sound could hurl by way of adverse travel conditions—cold and wind. Assault on my olfactory sensitivities was a consideration as well.

There was an occurrence at the Galena checkpoint that, though unfortunate in nature, should be recorded. In my trail notes, I referred to it as the "Johnny Coffin Affair." Johnny Coffin was a first-race musher from Noorvik, Alaska. Come to think of it, all first-race mushers were from someplace in Alaska and it was an all-male show. Coffin left Anchorage with thirteen dogs in twenty-fourth position. He was a front-runner, often arriving at checkpoints an hour or two behind the other two or three of us. He pulled into Galena about dark and staked his dogs next to mine at Eddie's Place. Next morning, as I was preparing to head downriver, I heard the disquieting story. Race marshal Dick Tozier had instructed Johnny to return back toward Ruby, some twenty-two miles, and pick up and return with a dog he had left beside the trail on the way down to Galena. Coffin had lost one, that is, the dog actually died in harness. Unaware of our rule number ten—which states: all dogs dropped from a team, for whatever reason, must be accounted for by an official at a checkpoint—he simply discarded it beside the trail.

He went back. It was that or disqualification. He had to load his sled as it was on Saturday when he came in. Then he backtracked, picked up the deceased, returned, and checked in. He mushed forty-four miles and no gain toward Nome. In reality, a day of travel lost. I believe I was more disheartened than was Coffin, who seemed to accept his situation in the manner of a true stoic. Not a word of complaint was uttered. Nonetheless, I felt truly sorry for him. The irony of it all: As I was hooking up to head west, Johnny, right beside me, was doing the same to head back toward the east, away from the finish line. Johnny Coffin was an interesting, likeable man from the old school, as the saying goes, right down to the straw used as insulation in his mukluks. Age, about fifty. Very quiet. I believe English was a problem for him, which could explain some of his rule misunderstanding. Undeterred, Johnny persevered to finish in ninth place, two days behind Bobby Vent and myself. I cherish memories of our trail time together. Time only shall erase them.

A logical question to follow my recitation of the Johnny Coffin Affair is, did further dog mortality occur during the first Big One? I personally knew of no other. However, if full credibility is given to Pam Randles' observations in her account (see chapter 43) we will have to tally one more death, sadly, to our mortality list. That death was observed first-hand by Randles at Skwentna. It was more than likely the one reported in the press as belonging to Dick Mackey.

A further note on the topic seems appropriate here. In an April 2012 e-mail response to my queries on the subject of dog deaths during the first race, Dr. Terry Adkins, the one and only veterinarian covering that race, stated, "George Attla lost three…We made him rest at Galena. He put his dogs in Sidney Huntington's barn and fed them hamburger and rice for twenty-four hours, hence the mandatory twenty-four-hour rest rule." That brought our total to five known fatalities. A high number, perhaps, considering the relatively low number of animals entered in the inaugural race. However, bear in mind—there was little or no moral stigma connected with a dog death at that time.

Four decades of Iditarod racing has seen varying levels of dog mortality. Unquestionably, the goal of race officials and mushers alike has been zero dog deaths. Noteworthy is the fact that three extremely high-powered races—2010, 2011, and 2012—were completed without a dog death. This happy situation borders on the astounding, considering John Baker's 2011 record-shattering time of a bit less than eight days, twenty hours. That's over eleven days faster than Wilmarth's first race-winning time. Astounding, indeed.

If there is any downside to a deathless dog race, it is to be found among those of the PETA ilk. For Iditaroders, a death-free race is to be celebrated, a time to be jubilant. Not because we are particularly frightened by the anemic roar of PETA's paper tiger, rather because our beloved animals had been unscathed. For our antagonists, it signals a period of less finger pointing so necessary in expostulating their so-called ethics, so important to increased membership fees. OH! And liberal donations from those who have a need to feel ethical—moral, even.

Day 15: Galena, Koyukuk, Nulato, Saturday, March 17

On Saturday, March 17, we left for downriver shortly after 7:00 a.m. It was a clear sky, minus twenty degrees F, an estimated fifteen m.p.h.wind blowing downriver at our backs. George Attla remained at Galena in an effort to nurse his team back onto the trail. A successful effort, as it turned out, enabling him to eventually complete the race in fourth place, eighteen hours behind Vent and me. Poor Johnny Coffin was, as explained, mushing in the opposite direction at the behest of our race marshal. Now reduced to just three mushers in the front pack, Vent, myself, and Wilmarth had all cleared Galena in that order by 7:30 a.m. Trail conditions out of Galena were good. Trail was wind-blown, firm, and hard packed, which supported both dogs and sleds, allowing us to stay on top with very little punchy trail over the first half of the run. Of course, we were on the mighty Yukon, where we would remain until forsaking it at Kaltag. Our icy boulevard near Galena was, in width, perhaps one-half mile (a guess), whereas the total valley width was twice that. I recall no distinguishable bluffs or other noteworthy land features en route to Koyukuk other than three fairly large islands crossed near the mouth of the Koyukuk River.

Between three and four hours out of Galena and within an hour of Koyukuk, I stopped, snacked the dogs with frozen halibut, and treated myself to a thermos of coffee and trail cake. All team members were performing well during that run, with the exception of Eska, whose feisty little two-year-old sister continued to amaze me up front in single lead. Dick Wilmarth soon whizzed past without stopping. His sizable team was moving very well, I thought. A few minutes after pulling the hook, setting off again in the direction of Koyukuk, the wind began to pick up. Now, in addition to a beneficial tailwind driving down the Yukon, I started to feel the effects of a blustery breeze from the Koyukuk Valley to my right, the north. No new snow fell, but due to these contrary winds, I traveled through what seemed to be a building blizzard. During that stretch, going was noticeably more difficult due to soft drifted trail and the nature of the snow itself. Constantly blown around, snow crystals lose their rough edges, becoming like little round, smooth, frozen beads with just about zero compaction. "Sugar snow" it is called, for good reason. In that type of snow, each dog foot sinks, almost unhindered, to the bottom of its accumulation, as do sled runners. One gets the impression that he is being dragged through—well—sugar. Mushers with iron-shod sleds complained as loudly as I with plastic. A dumb, stoic resignation to the sugar snow pervaded those mushers who finally reached Nome. Coastal winds, it seemed, never gave a harassed coastal snowflake a moment's peace.

Koyukuk Village sits atop a high bluff on the north bank of the Yukon, some eight to nine miles west of where the Koyukuk River joins the latter. It is about twenty-five twisting miles west of Galena. Puzzled as to the whereabouts of Vent and Wilmarth, I parked my team on what I took to be a barge landing. I set my snow hook, and anchored the front of my team in place with a line tied to a skookum driftwood tree. The boy dogs were definitely beginning to show me at least one of Eska's problems. She was in heat. A few villagers lined the edge as I all but clawed my way hand over knee up a narrow, very steep footpath, cut diagonally into the bluff. Huffing and puffing my way up, the first building to greet me was the trading post, which also housed the U.S. Post Office. It was located dead ahead, maybe twenty-five yards beyond the upper landing. I made for it.

My whole Koyukuk experience was a bit odd. For starters, I did not discover until I began research for this book that Koyukuk was not an officially designated race checkpoint. Race literature given to mushers made no mention of Koyukuk. None. Talk about Johnny Coffin being unaware of our rules. The downriver trail lead me to that place, therefore it must be a check point—right? Frankly, I have no recollection of even such an elementary thought taking place. I never, until a year or so ago, suspected Koyukuk was not a first-race checkpoint. But, sure enough, checking back, there are no in and out times recorded for Koyukuk, no checker assigned, no reference in prerace literature promulgated by our race committee. Is it to be wondered then, why my arrival at that supposed checkpoint should be greeted as an uninvited moocher had shown up at dinnertime?

A Native welcoming committee of a dozen or more folks seemed solemn, reserved. No excited greetings made real by wide, sincere smiles. There were no children tumbling down to the barge landing in an effort to get near a dog team. And, as if an unseen barrier existed, none followed me up the steps leading to the trading post's Arctic entry. All had gone their separate ways by the time I was ready to go mine. An on-the-spot assessment was that Koyukuk wasn't very "doggy," as Joe Sr. would have put it.

Vernetti Trading Post/General Store/United States Post Office was housed in a large, two-story, aged log building with an ample entry. Another frame-type building, as I remember, was to the rear of the log structure, a warehouse, I presumed. Both, in my estimation, maintained a most precarious existence, teetering, as they did, on the very brink of destruction. Sooner or later, I thought, by earthquake or flood, they would belong to the Yukon. Details of the cluttered interior are admittedly foggy, but I was impressed, indeed thrilled, that I had paid a visit to an authentic, old-fashioned trading post. Store and post office claimed the front, while it appeared the darkened rear half or so housed the venerable proprietress, Ella Vernetti.

She, with husband Dominic, who had recently passed away, established that post way back in 1923, which was the heyday of the area's mining activity. They undertook a profitable "floating store" operation, as Ella called it, in addition to their trading post. This entailed running a well-supplied barge, both up the Koyukuk River and along the Yukon, trading with miners and trappers—gold and beaver furs—for needed items. At one time, those wilderness entrepreneurs maintained large fuel tanks, which supplied the local region with liquid fuel and a liquor license, which brought patrons from even more distant parts for liquid refreshment. When left to run things on her own, Ella had given up her liquor license because, "It wasn't worth the trouble that came with it," she explained. After Dominic's death, she was appointed postmaster, a common occurrence in Bush Alaska.

That lady absolutely fascinated me. Here was a Caucasian woman, with white hair, and still unbent under her nearly eighty years, widowed, continuing to live essentially as she had for the past fifty years. She was doing business as usual among the Yukon Athabascans. At first, she was not unfriendly but, I suppose, aloof. My initial impression was that here was a person who had seen fifty years of Yukon ice and water pass by her doorstep. She had seen it all, and survived it all, and, as a consequence, had no fear of the future. A true Alaskan pioneer woman. Had she been born earlier, I imagined she probably would have explained in her nonchalant manner how she packed a clothes scrub board over the Chilkoot Pass in the Stampede of '98. How with that icon of womanly drudgery, she established Dawson City's first profitable laundry service. Gradually, she began to warm to me. I believe because I somehow convinced her that I had a genuine historian's interest in her extraordinary life and a true curiosity about her village.

Had the two mushers ahead of me stopped in?

"Yes, they had coffee and left for downriver about fifteen minutes before you came. Oh, would you care for a cup?"

The more we conversed, the less important fleeting race moments became. I was enthralled. Ninety-eight people lived there. Most everyone spoke both Koyukon and English. There was no public water or power system. Most folks burned woodstoves for heat and cooking. Only two,"for fun" dog teams remained in the village at the time of my visit. But back when Ella and Dominic arrived, and until mining declined, there were many, many dog teams up the Koyukuk and along the Yukon.

"That is how we traveled in winter. Oh, would you care for chicken soup? I have a pot on the stove."

Over a bowl (or was it two?) of homemade soup and a half loaf of freshly baked bread, I continued my inquisition. I asked about trapping and learned that prices were exceptionally good that year, but as far as she knew, only two men were out on the trapline. She attributed its decline among local natives to the recent availability of public assistance. Ella volunteered commentary on their mail service. Back in the "dog team days," Koyukuk received mail an incredible four times per week, two times from each direction of the Yukon. "It was a lot better than today, because an airplane comes only once a week." As coincidence would have it, Vernetti and I shared mutual friends, Clarence and Louise Larson of Seward. Larson had been the Seward postmaster from our arrival there (1963) until his untimely death prior to the first Iditarod.

After carefully treading my way to my waiting, almost snow buried, team below, I took a few minutes to jot down my impressions under a scribbled heading, "Koyukuk Checkpoint." Checkpoint? I was completely oblivious to the fact that I had not seen a clipboard, had no inquiries as to my name, my bib number, number of dogs I was driving, and if I planned to drop any there. No one braved the steep path down to check to see if all mandatory gear was aboard my sled. Come to think about it, my sled was never checked by race officials, not even in Nome. Final Koyukuk "checkpoint" note: I thanked Mrs. Vernetti profusely for her wonderful hospitality. She said she was pleased I stopped by and that it was thrilling to see dog teams on the river again. Anyone hearing her could not possibly have doubted her sincerity.

Next stop—Nulato. With notes on Koyukuk completed, I retrieved my tie-down line from up front and did a quick inspection for towline and harness chews. Nothing amiss. By that time, all dogs had gained their feet, giving themselves a good shaking in an effort to be rid of the wind-driven accumulation of snow that clung to each. All of the dogs were eager, except Eska, who came to attention only after I pulled the hook in preparation for our departure. That was not like her at all. My concern for her was growing. Bobby Vent and Dick Wilmarth were ahead by maybe an hour when I set off downriver toward Nulato. At that point, with both Attla and Coffin, Warren Coffin held up at Galena, who would be pushing up from behind? Later, reviewing news articles covering this period of the race, I was more than a bit annoyed to learn that George Attla received way more "press," sidelined with a broken-down team than Bobby did—at fifty-nine, the oldest contestant in the race who led the pack into and out of Galena, and who, like Attla, had a crippled leg with which to contend. Vent's initial team of eleven had been reduced to just six by the time he left Rainy Pass. He dropped one more at White Mountain. "A Crippled Elder Drives Five-Dog Team to Second Place in One-Thousand-Mile Race." Now there's a story worth following.

37

Checkpoint Award Goes To…

If, as today, there had been a checkpoint award in 1973, Nulato would have won it hands down. Teachers and students did an amazing job in welcoming mushers and their teams. Teachers L-R: Bob Simpson, Dennis McKennen.

About six miles downstream from Koyukuk, toward the honest-to-goodness checkpoint of Nulato, the Yukon leaves its westerly course, bending sharply south-southwest. There, both the normal downriver wind and that draining out of the Koyukuk River valley to the north, combined to give us quite a push along our new direction. The twenty-mile distance was traversed in about two and one-half hours over hard, windblown trail. There were numerous wooded points and lofty mud cliffs along the northwest bank. There were several seasonal fish camps in various states of disarray. Their chief winter duty seemed to be that of depositories for the ubiquitous fish wheel. Know-how needed to build this ingenious automatic fishing machine came north with early gold rushers. Local, natural materials sufficed for construction and maintenance. Like shanties, boats and fish drying frames, the many fish wheels were mostly hidden under huge drifts of snow, driven by unrelenting winds.

Fish wheel design is clever by merit of its utter simplicity. It is essentially a water wheel with two large baskets affixed to a floating framework. Anchored in a river, the current turns the wheel, whose baskets scoop up the upstream migrating fish—salmon—depositing them in a tray leading to a holding box or basket. The several species of salmon can be caught using the same wheel. These fish are used for human food and, in some cases, sold on the commercial market. Back in the dog team heyday, huge numbers of chum (dog salmon) were sun and air dried, formed into bales, and stored away against winter as dog food. Indeed, demand was such that oft times, it supported limited commercial fishing enterprises along main arteries of dog team travel.

As one would expect, our first Iditarod Race set into motion many practices destined to become race traditions. Precedents were established. Not all was just blundering through. One such practice was checkpoint reception for mushers. None had done a better job of welcoming mushers off the trail than the community of Nulato. Where some did basically nothing, the village of Nulato did everything within its power to express genuine happiness and excitement over each musher's arrival.

The lion's share of checkpoint planning and preparation was performed by Nulato High School teachers and their students. A month or so after the race, I received in the mail a copy of the high school paper: "Fifteen cents per copy, Iditarod mushers free." In addition to providing a good picture of the checkpoint itself, the publication included short, usually complimentary, biographies of mushers who passed through their checkpoint with the following apology: "Some we missed because we didn't see them or never got the chance to find out anything about them. We're sorry…next year we'll do better."

From Files: Nulato High School publication (Postmarked May 1, 1973. No publication date.)

THE IDITAROD ISSUE
WILMARTH, VENT, SEAVEY, ATTLA AND NAYOKPUK TAKE TOP FIVE PLACES
IN
FIRST 1000 MILE IDITAROD RACE TO NOME

Dick Wilmarth, Bobby Vent, Dan Seavey, George Attla and Herbert Nayokpuk passed through Nulato recently. They, along with 17 other mushers, were on their way to Nome and the top money in the First 1000 Mile Iditarod Race from Anchorage to Nome.

Nulato High School students and the entire village anxiously awaited each musher's arrival. The students planned and set up what they hoped would be the biggest, best, and friendliest checkpoint from start to finish.

Over one hundred fifty blue oil drums were rolled into place to make a seventy-five yard chute for the mushers. Students cut willows and put orange flagging on them for trail markers. Others printed up humorous signs to put on the trail, in hopes that they would cheer up the tired mushers. The cross country ski club and the snowshoe club tramped down an area for a dog yard and provided spruce boughs for bedding. More students hauled water and heated it so the dogs could get a hot meal.

Excited students greeted each musher with hot tea, coffee, pop, and all the help he needed. While the mushers talked to the people, other students helped unharness the dogs and chain them up. With that done, the harnesses were taken to the school shop and dried out for the next day.

The musher was then led off to a warm Nulato house and given a meal and a bed. The excited hosts sometimes kept mushers up 'til the wee hours talking about dogs. Teachers who put up mushers were really guilty on this one.

The next day many mushers had the same help going out of town. Students all bid farewell and good luck to each musher on the last 300 miles or so left to go on the trip.

All of Nulato wanted to put a smile on the face of each musher. And all of Nulato saw them do just that. The first sign, 4 miles upriver from Nulato said, "HI NICE TO SEE YOU." Next year we hope to see them back again. It was great helping them make history and fun being just a small part of it all. We saw a lot, learned a lot, and had a good time seeing the Old Time Alaskan Spirit come out of hiding for a bunch of people we had never seen before. More than that, it was great helping someone simply smile after over 700 miles of mushing dogs hour after hour, day after day. We are proud to have met such a nice bunch of guys.

As stated, Nulato students were free with their compliments. Here is the bio published for me:

Dan Seavey

It really surprised us that first day when we found out that a teacher was in the Iditarod Race to Nome. Dan Seavey was that teacher. He said he teaches history in the Seward High School. He told us that he was taking personal leave for two months so he could train-up and get ready for this race.

Dan went down to Nulato Hall during the March 17th Potlatch. After everyone finished eating, Dan told everyone how the trip had been so far. He said all the mushers had had a tough time in lots of places before McGrath and all the way to Poorman and Ruby. Then he really made the people of Nulato happy. Dan said that Nulato was the best stop in the race. He said, "Nulato tops them all." That sure made everybody feel good, especially the school kids who had helped make the signs and helped the mushers.

Dan told us that he likes to take his dogs and go camping with his wife and family in the winter. He said this was the first time he ever raced them. They did pretty good too…he came in third when they got to Nome. Mr. Simpson is taking care of one of Dan's dogs that he left here. Mr. Simpson said it's not so sleepy as it was when it got here.

It is difficult to relate my true inner feelings as I neared one of Alaska's most storied villages. Truth is I had been riding high ever since beginning my descent at Ruby of the mighty Yukon, a river interlaced with so much Alaskan history. In my mind's eye, there came an endless procession of side wheelers, decks overflowing with cargo, and firewood for hungry boilers, impatient passengers heading upriver to Klondike gold fields. Also pictured were caravans of a dozen or more heavily loaded, sturdily built freight sleds being towed downriver by mammoth teams of mammoth dogs. Destination? The new strike at Nome. And here I was, not only reliving history, but, in a sense, making it as a participant in the first-ever one-thousand-mile sled dog race. Not an event to effect a change in the course of all future humankind perhaps, but history in the making nonetheless. There shall never, ever, be another first Iditarod Trail Sled Dog Race. Vent and Wilmarth ahead, as well as those many mushers and teams behind me on the trail, we were all pioneers. New pioneers, making new history.

Somewhere around the midpoint, between Koyukuk and Nulato, I decided to load and carry Eska. She was about in full season and just plain tuckered out. Truth be told, for what little she contributed and for her own well-being, I probably should have left her at the Galena checkpoint. Somehow, at that point, I suspected Nulato would be the end of her first Iditarod experience.

Arrival at Nulato was eagerly anticipated by me, history addict that I am. Nothing was heard of the place until a Russian Creole, Malakof, in service of the Russian American Company, built in 1838, a small fort of sorts, on the west bank of the Yukon, where it is joined by the unpretentious Nulato River. In short order, local natives burned the structure. The Nulato post was rebuilt by Vasili Dershavin in 1841. He remained in charge of the post, supervising trading ventures as far up the Yukon as the mouth of the Tanana, until he was killed in an Indian uprising in 1851, called the Nulato Massacre. Under its new owners, the United States, it was left to its own fate until, in 1887, when a Catholic mission was established. Prosperous steamship days were followed by a devastating measles epidemic in 1900. That and so much more rich history. And here I was, visiting the place by dog team, of all things. Soul stirring, for sure.

It started out as a clear, if snow-blowing, day at Koyukuk. By the time I reached Nulato, it was snowing—real snow from real clouds. There was, too, the ever-present downriver wind at my back, giving me a little boost, but reducing visibility. Darkness was settling in. About four miles out, I indeed began to encounter homemade signs stuck on bushes. Informative signs like—NULATO FOUR MILES, TIME TO CAMP WITH US, HOT COFFEE AHEAD, CHECKPOINT TWO MILES, and many others I failed to note. About two miles out, I was met by teacher and official checker, Leo Shanahan, astride a snowmachine. He extended a big Nulato welcome as hearty as it was sincere. "What's your pleasure? I have hot coffee, cold pop, and more sandwiches than I know what to do with." I don't remember something "hitting the spot" as much as that can of 7-Up Shanahan gave me. To Leo's obvious astonishment, two gulps and it was gone.

Come to find out, signs and welcoming, gift-bearing snowmachiners were just part of a grand communal scheme hatched up for the first Iditaroders. Movers and shakers of the operation were knowledgeable school staff and eager high school students. School was dismissed at least a day prior to our anticipated arrival. We arrived on Saturday, March 17. Working as a village team, they created homemade signs, fashioned an approach chute from blue oil drums, and I can still visualize that chute to this day. It guided teams into a holding area where tie-out chains waited beside a huge stack of freshly cut spruce boughs. The students were obviously accustomed to handling dogs; they capably unharnessed and bedded down my team. Others fetched supply bags, which surprisingly had found their proper place to be at a proper time. And, miracle of miracles—hot water! A whole bubbling barrel of the stuff, kept that way by attentive student firemen. No melting snow for dog water that night. Those foresighted folks had even provided for dogs to be dropped from the race. A separate area with extra-thick bedding and longer chain leads had been set up on a close by, out-of-the-wind location. As far as can be determined, only two dogs came to be lodged in that posh convalescence home—one of Herbie Nayokpuk's and my Eska.

Eska riding the last few miles into Nulato where she became the only member of my team of 12 to be dropped. It would be over 2 months before I would see her again.

At the place I encountered Shanahan outside town, I hooked Eska back into the string, but to no avail. In probably less than a quarter mile, she was back on her neckline again. I stopped and once more pushed, flexed, squeezed, and looked for every possible cause of her distress. Hydration good, gum color good, appetite good. Still she remained lethargic, uninspired, and she was definitely in the first stage of a heat cycle. Back on the sled she went, the decision was made for her to become a sojourner at Nulato.

It was toward the dark side of day when amid a goodly fanfare, I came to a halt within that elaborate holding area. I stood in a sort of shocked amazement as my team, in less time than it took to write about it, was unharnessed and resting comfortably atop spruce bough beds. Those kid handlers were simply marvelous. By the time I had completed my routine inspection and care of all the feet, both my "people bag" and "dog bag" had been delivered to my sled. We were fortunate to find our supply bags had been flown to the Nulato checkpoint and that an abundance of white fish had been made available by the villagers. My dogs ate well that night. They devoured halibut, beef fat, warm kibble soup, and whitefish for dessert. I didn't fare too badly, either, with an all-new allotment of Shirley's wonderful trail cake and several meals each of moose stew and chicken soup—freshness was assured as they obviously had remained frozen brick hard since leaving home.

Shortly after dark, nearly the whole population assembled at the community hall for a potlatch/dance to honor the first-ever Iditarod racers to have passed through their village. Well, to honor yours truly. Wilmarth was first to arrive, followed closely by Vent, both maybe an hour ahead of me. I never saw either all evening. Reports were that they had gone to bed, a situation that left me the sole musher representative in attendance. Undeniably, I would have liked to mimic their behavior. To do so, however, would have displayed terribly bad manners, a complete lack of gratitude, and grave injustice to so many folks who worked so hard to make us welcome. I went, and to this day, I am delighted that I did. We congregated in a most extraordinary building. This council house/community center was a huge, dome-shaped log structure. It had fascinating architecture in itself, without center support beams, just open, unobstructed floor space. How much, I do not recall, but upon entry, I was immediately impressed with its spaciousness. The fifty or more people present in no way made a crowd for that imposing structure.

After my third meal since reaching that checkpoint, I was asked to relate my experiences from the trail thus far. Fatigue, lack of sleep, an overly full stomach, and a superheated room were not, as one might imagine, conducive to coherent thought and un-slurred speech. In my presentation, I may have gotten to McGrath before Rainy Pass. A keen interest was shown in our floundering about, south of Ruby. All seemed very interested in the whole business, asking, perhaps, most questions about the functioning of my team. Of course, the event gave me opportunity to express my gratitude for what turned out to be an exemplary checkpoint. Formal "speech" over, I sat around—fighting sleep all the while—and talked with village leaders until about 11:30 p.m.

Bob Simpson and wife, both public school teachers at Nulato, served as my outstanding host and hostess. Their "bed and breakfast" was most beneficial and truly appreciated, albeit at a price in lost sleep. This interested and interesting couple managed to keep me awake long after midnight. I learned Nulato had a long tradition of dog mushing. That it was, at that time, considered a dog town. In fact, several teachers, including Simpson, kept hobby teams. Nulato musher, Fred Sommer, raced in the recent Alaska Purchase Centennial Race, precursor to the

Iditarod itself. We talked dog types for long-distance racing, strategies necessary for race victories in general. We surveyed my prospects for winning the first. I probably tossed and turned for all of five seconds after bidding a good night to the Simpsons. A very brief four hours later, my little alarm with its gigantic voice was insisting I hit the deck. It was 5:00 a.m., time to start my sixteenth day on the trail.

I got up, dressed, and headed over to the dog lot. Everyone was happy to see me—a good sign. Most dogs were up on their feet, wriggling with excitement—even Eska. I checked each over thoroughly, and applied neats foot oil and pine tar to every foot heading downriver that day. I fed and watered. Back to Bob's for a hearty breakfast of moose steak and eggs. By that time, it was getting fairly light, and with it, a promise of a beautiful day on the trail—clear, calm, not much below zero. Two to three inches of new snow had fallen overnight. Perfect!

Race or no race, I decided to cheat a bit on my trail time and go on a photo tour of the village. With youthful teacher Doug McKina as an enthusiastic guide, I set off a little before 7:00 a.m. Nulato was a picturesque, historic village. Most houses were constructed of logs. A plume of wood smoke was emitted from most chimneys, reaching straight up to the sky. Not even a downriver breeze that morning. The village seemed to sit securely on an elevated site. However, the highest ground, quite a lofty bluff, was reserved for the cemetery. That was the first feature observed coming from upriver and last leaving for downriver. Truly an unforgettable view. I now wish I had gone up to that hallowed ground and taken shots looking down on the town. But it was some distance and dog lot racket told me my competitors were beginning to hook up for the run down to Kaltag. I did manage a photo of the venerable Catholic Church. It was the original church, dating back to just after the founding of a mission in 1887. Doug, my informant, told me that the town was very devout and very Catholic.

Day 16: Sunday, March 18, Nulato to Kaltag

Huslia's Bobby Vent was off and running within ten minutes of my return from soaking up more of Nulato via exposed film. He was followed soon after by Wilmarth. Another twenty minutes and I was heading downriver in a somewhat restrained pursuit. Kaltag would be our last Yukon River checkpoint, some thirty-six to thirty-eight miles distant. Before nightfall, the second race pack comprised of Johnny Coffin, Herbert Nayokpuk, and Dick Mackey would take over our vacated space at Nulato. John Komak, a Teller Eskimo driver, joined them some time after dark. I had seen most of those teams in operation and reasoned that the best place for them to be was behind me—if I could manage it.

Our modern Iditarod Race is, at the same time, a model for volunteerism and a marvel when it comes to logistical support. A dog with a life-threatening condition, dropped, say, at the Cripple checkpoint, can, within four hours, be treated at an ultramodern facility in Anchorage. Closer to home, son Mitch became a beneficiary of the trail committee's amazing modern support system. Mitch, the 2004 champion, was on his eighteenth run in 2011 when an accident at the Ophir checkpoint rendered him unable to continue. Although, thankfully, not life threatening, an emergency operation was required on his hand. One of the checkers had a surgeon father on the East Coast whom he contacted by satellite phone—2:30 a.m. our time—and asked him to recommend a surgeon in Anchorage. Now, Ophir doesn't exactly have a lighted, paved airstrip, so things were put on hold pending arrival of daylight. Then came a bush plane ride to McGrath, an a.m. commercial flight to Anchorage, and surgery beginning at 5:00 p.m. Now that's service in anyone's book. Times have changed, as the saga of my Eska illustrates.

When I left Eska in Nulato—"dropped" her, in race jargon—I had no idea that two months would pass before I would lay eyes on her again. My thought, if I ever had one, was she probably would beat me to Nome to be flown to Anchorage with the rest of the team. Or, perhaps she would be flown out of Galena in a few days and be held in waiting by the committee somewhere in Anchorage. Imagine my surprise when my Nulato host contacted me by letter (that's U.S. mail), dated April 23, 1973, wondering what in the world he was supposed to do with Eska. Bob Simpson's letter is most instructive in light of modern fast track dog and people care practices by the Iditarod Trail Committee (see Appendix XIV, Simpson Letter).

Downriver from Nulato, there were numerous wooded islands, either crossed or avoided by the trail to Kaltag. It seemed the trail was put down on the most direct line feasible and was overall very easy to travel. It had a few inches of new snow, no wind to speak of; temperatures—mild.

I noted along the way, and more so nearing Kaltag, several holes cut in the river ice, where villagers appeared to have been fishing by means of gill nets set under the ice. Hope would have been for a catch of whitefish, an important winter subsistence item along the Yukon. Other noteworthy features came into evidence upon approach to Kaltag itself. Our path to town led us beside the dumping ground. Literally, every discarded item commonly found in landfills (dumps) of that day was in evidence—from household appliances to…well, paper diapers hadn't been invented yet, but you get the idea. While that pile of refuse in front of town dominated our approach, directly off to the right, a bit upriver, stood an eclectic collection of edifices serving as outhouses. All this debris was waiting for the inevitable "Big Flush" of spring. Kaltag Village itself was spread along a fairly high segment of the Yukon's west bank. That settlement of some two hundred souls was the eastern gatekeeper for the ancient Kaltag Portage. I drove my team up to where Vent and Wilmarth were parked in a large, open, loose snow area, close to the center of town, and set my hook. It was precisely 3:00 p.m. Vent had pulled in at 2:40 p.m. and Wilmarth right behind at 2:43 p.m. Our times were established officially by an honest-to-goodness official checker assigned to Kaltag by the committee.

For whatever reason, we seemed not to arouse much excitement with our arrivals. Certainly no holiday atmosphere, as was the case at Nulato. Nor did it seem like much of a dog town. There were plenty of loose dogs running about, but not a dog team lot that I could detect. I would fall prey to one or more of those ubiquitous, at-large critters during my stay.

Lawrence, (apologies, no last name) a pleasant, though not talkative, native fellow, pitched in to help care for my team. I hadn't pushed my team at all on the way down. I had stopped a couple of times to give fish snacks. It was obvious that Vent and Wilmarth intended to stay parked until morning. That, I considered good. In training, I had made several more or less nonstop runs of eighty to ninety miles, and the next run—the Kaltag Portage—from Kaltag over Old Woman Summit to Unalakleet was reported to be ninety-two miles. Good weather prevailed. A good trail was reported to have been made better by passage of the snowmachine race (from Nenana to Nome) over the portage a few days earlier. I figured that next run would be a good one to see if I had a dog team worthy of the name.

One reason expressed by some, including Dick Tozier, our race marshal, for the apparent cold shoulder at Kaltag was our checker. It seemed the committee rented space to house the checker and then assigned—of all things—a hippie to man the post. Remember, this was 1973, and to many folks, hippies fitted rather conveniently into a subhuman classification. Our hippie was, in fact, a very nice young man whose name was Doug, who happened to have long hair, as far as I was concerned. Doug, the checker, cooked both dinner and the next day's breakfast for us three mushers. He did a tolerable job of it, too. We dined royally at his rented cabin on macaroni and cheese, and oatmeal for breakfast.

Sometime, shortly after reaching Kaltag, I discovered that I had left my personal food bag back at Nulato. It was not a good situation, as there were no race supplies at Kaltag and I was contemplating a run of near one hundred miles the next day. I particularly wanted my two loaf supply of trail cake, as I knew from experience south of Ruby that it could sustain a person for days on end. What to do? I ended up asking the lady keeper of the one radio-telephone in town (and the one store) to call Nulato, requesting that news reporter, Orville Lake, bring my food bag when he flew down to Kaltag. Orville got the message. Next morning, I got the bag, minus the two loaves of trail cake.

Thanks to Seward friends, Kaare and Rae Elde, I was able to contact Shirley by phone. First, permission was given by the Kaltag store proprietress for use of her radio-phone. Next, I called the Eldes in Seward, who drove out to our place, contacted Shirley, who drove to town, and, using Elde's phone, called me at Kaltag. As noted elsewhere, the Seaveys hadn't entered the Telephone Age yet. Looking back on it, that call had to be one of our most humorous, caused by long delays, interruptions, and atmospheric interference. Still, it was wonderful to hear her voice after more than two weeks. Things were fine at home.

Kids were excited about the arrival of a new litter of pups. Someone in Anchorage was working on chartering a large airplane to Nome to see racers come in. I was to look for a letter that she and the kids had sent to Koyuk. Part of our conversation went something like this:

"How much longer to Nome?"

"Boy, that is a tough one to answer, since I don't even know how far it is from Kaltag here."

"What is the chance of getting lost again?"

"Not real good as we will be running over well-established trail—marked, even—they tell me. At the rate we are traveling, my guess is at least another week to Nome."

A lucky guess, as that was how long it did take.

One final transaction. The lady who minded the store and phone also had whitefish for sale. I purchased three at the going rate of one dollar each.

Soon after our dinner engagement with checker Doug, Dick Wilmarth and I topped off our evening out with a "coffee" arranged for us. Bobby Vent, as at Nulato, had retired to stay with a host family. It was a nice affair. Low key, and a wonderful opportunity to visit, especially with elder members of the community, who had, it seemed, a historic interest in dog mushing. It was pleasing to me to sit for perhaps one and a half hours, soaking up mushing lore of a bygone time. Locals seemingly deferred to a sage, whom I later learned to be Chief Franklin. Kaltag's younger generation, at that gathering, was most conspicuous due to its absence. After one last check on the dogs, I walked to the school where the trail-breaking snowmachiners, Wilmarth, and I were lodged for the night.

38

Canine Crooks

Approaching Kaltag, last stop on the Yukon. It was here that stray village dogs had an overnight banquet on the contents of my sled.

Day 17: Monday, March 19, Kaltag to Unalakleet

Five a.m. was clamorously announced by my little red travel clock with a firehouse-size alarm. Not bad, six hours of pretty good sleep, even allowing for a thin pad and a hard classroom floor. So as to avoid use of Orville Lake's flight service again, I collected all my gear, double-checked, and headed for checker Doug's cabin. I ate a hurried breakfast of oatmeal sweetened with brown sugar, buttered toast, and nice, thick, fat strips of bacon. I expressed my sincere thanks to that slightly built young man with a captivating smile and helpful manner. And long hair. Many a time I have wondered if Doug lasted in Kaltag long enough to check the last team through. It did dawn on me as I headed toward the dog park that Doug didn't seem to have a musher list for times in and out. For certain, he did not check my sled for required gear.

A disheartening, maddening scene greeted me upon reaching my team. Oh, the dogs were fine. Up, shaking themselves. Some uttering little groan-growl hellos, as if to say, "It's about time. Where have you been so long?" No, it was my sled bag. It had all but been cleaned out, unmistakably by some, or all, of the town's numerous strays. Dog food fish, gone. Beef fat for the team, gone. A bag with an assortment of mostly sweet people goodies, gone. What was left? Those nocturnal marauders, canine crooks that they were, alas connoisseurs with most discriminating palates, had not touched the commercial kibble dog food. To their credit, in a fleeting act of charity, they left, in their ruinous wake, exactly seven slices of dog-mauled bread for yours truly.

While kicking myself for not securing food items at the school overnight, I mulled over my situation. Bobby and Dick were hooking up. Nearly one hundred miles of uninhabited trail lay ahead to Unalakleet, with not more than twenty-five pounds of Purina to power eleven dogs the distance. My personal food was also in a sorry state. Not a soul stirred in the entire small village. At 7:00 in the morning, how could I go around hammering on doors, asking if they had fish for sale? By this stage of the game, there was an unspoken understanding that the race was about to begin. I had to see what could be made of my predicament.

Hustling back to Doug's cabin, I bummed a bucket of warm water, which I mixed with kibble and fed half of my total dog food on the spot. A hurried hook up and, without a villager's obvious notice, I set out in hot pursuit over the Kaltag Portage. It was probably around 9:30 a.m.

Ancient and storied, the portage trail was struck just behind Kaltag Village. It began to climb almost immediately through fair-sized spruce, which, after a few miles, played out into an area of stunted, wind-bedraggled growth. It was there, as a participant in the second (1974) race, I would find myself on all fours, looking for even a runner mark to indicate just where the completely blown-over trail lay. Actually, the climb up from the Yukon to the Upper Unalakleet Valley is just a gradual one, spread over forty miles or more. Somewhere near Old Woman Mountain, about midway between Kaltag and Unalakleet (around mile forty-five), timber starts doing some serious disappearing; the landscape becomes more open tundra. Descending toward Norton Sound, trees finally vanish except for stunted growth confined to river bottoms.

All things considered, that ninety-two-mile Kaltag Portage was the best trail segment of that entire first race. For starters, there would have been local (albeit minor, in that day) inter-village "snow-go" travel during winter. Add to that the twenty-man army team who drove double-track machines over it a week prior. Then came the second annual Nenana to Nome snowmachine race, which included nine teams, each of which consisted of four separate machines. They traversed the portage just days ahead of us. Finally, going out just in front of Bobby and Dick were our (the committee's) three remaining machines, driven by the indomitable Bill Copeland, Joe Smith, and Bob Stone. It was a good trail. The temperatures were perhaps a bit below zero when we got started, rising to the mid-twenties over the course of the journey. What better place for one steeped in Alaska's history to soak up its grand scope than the Kaltag Portage? History? How about prehistory? An elder at Nulato related that the portage was an ancient trade route between cultures. "In olden times," he said, "my people (Athabascan Indians) traded with Norton Sound Eskimos we call Inuits (meat eaters)." Old Woman Mountain area, it seemed, was considered neutral trade ground by those traditional enemies. It was there they met to carry on exchange of goods. In modern times came the Russians, during the 1830s and 40s, pushing their fur-gathering tentacles into Norton Sound, over the portage, and up the Yukon as far as Tanana. The U.S. military built a telegraph line over it, connecting Nome with the outside world in 1905. By then, the Nome gold rush was in full swing, and in its wake came winter commerce, and of even greater importance, the mail, via that ancient route. Walter Goodwin's 1908 preliminary survey out of Seward for a shorter mail trail to Nome was necessary only to Kaltag. From there to Nome, by way of the Kaltag Portage, a long-established, well-worn trail awaited the traveler.

Prior to Vent and Wilmarth's departure from Kaltag, we discussed the feasibility—wisdom—of breaking our run to Unalakleet in half, halting overnight at Old Woman. We had been told that two cabins were to be found there. One was an old "trapper cabin," mostly fallen in, which I suspect was a turn-of-the-century telegraph cabin. There was also, a relatively new "Fish and Game cabin," most likely belonging to the area's Federal Fish and Wildlife Service.

With little Kiana in single lead, backed up by Sonny and Bandit, two strong, steady male swing dogs, we took on the portage trail with gusto. That is, after the first hour or so of repeated bowel movements (dog), loosening up of stiff, sore muscles, and, bit by bit, falling into that brisk, easy, mile-eating trot I love so much to observe. Not a great distance up the trail toward Old Woman, I overtook Bobby, who remarked that he was having trouble "getting them cranked up." He lamented that he was unable to acquire beaver meat for his six-dog team since Galena. Beaver, in fact, became a much sought-after dog food for future races. The going rate became twenty dollars per carcass, which Bobby unwittingly set when he purchased a carcass from that trapper at Salmon River that first race.

Old Woman is a low, rounded, small, mountain-sized mound. It is prominent since it is standoffish from its more gregarious neighbors. The trail runs in its shadow. Here was the traditional boundary between two ancient worlds. Here, even the land began to change from a mostly forested Athabascan domain to that treeless, windswept tundra world of the Eskimo. I located the mostly gone telegraph cabin, but found not a trace of the supposed inhabitable structure. Most likely, it sat back on an unbroken loop off the main trail. Wilmarth's tracks continued on without apparent hesitation. My team was running well, I got to thinking, "What the heck, why not push on to Unalakleet?" Besides, from my map study, I knew the trail followed the Unalakleet River Valley downhill to the coast. Downhill meant easy going—I hoped.

Nearing Old Woman Mountain, a prominent feature of the Kaltag Portage on way to Bering Sea Coast.

From Kaltag, the portage trail runs toward the southwest to Unalakleet. Some distance beyond Old Woman Mountain—perhaps an hour's run—open tundra begins to dominate the scene. Remaining spruce, though twisted, and stunted, refused to give up the good fight. It was in that area I encountered a band of some twenty caribou. I say caribou, but they could have been descendants of Sheldon Jackson's imported Siberian reindeer for all I could tell. They had suddenly appeared on my right, from behind a barren knoll, taking off at a run, for all intents and purposes heading for Unalakleet ahead of us. I let the team give chase, which ended a quarter mile later, when the band decided it had provided enough entertainment for that weird-acting wolf pack, and disappeared into a thin spruce thicket to my left. Canine and human adrenalin levels soon tapered off to normal, but the incident had me thinking back to an earlier caribou episode, which ended way differently than this had.

It was early spring of 1968, and my youngest brother was visiting us from "the old country"—Minnesota. Dale Seavey, who was about eighteen years of age at the time, was already a well-developed hunting and gun nut. He worked all summer at Seward Fisheries processing plant to support his habit while in Alaska. During the fall season, we had done a successful dog team moose hunt on the Kenai Peninsula. Come the following March, this small in stature, but big in persistence, guy had me convinced we needed to go caribou hunting. Arrangements were made for Dale and me to truck two small teams from Seward to Tom and Kathy Johnson's place off Knik-Goose Bay Road (later

Joe Redington, Sr. Memorial Trial), near Wasilla, and overnight there. Next day, around noon, we were to connect with Dick Gilliand and his team at the Lake Louise Road Junction, Mile 160 of the Glen Highway. Gilliand, whose kennel supplied one of my early bloodlines, would come from Chistochina, likewise with a small team.

Since, in those days, the road to Lake Louise remained unplowed all winter, each big game hunter would drive a team with supplies and overnight with Dick's friends, Bill and Betty Poe, about twelve miles in on the sixteen-mile-long road. The next day, we planned to hunt along a certain seismograph trail, running in an easterly direction, south of the lake. Gilliand was to serve as our guide. Our mush into the Poe homestead was uneventful. We arrived over good trail with plenty of daylight to do dog chores. A pleasant evening was passed, allowing Dale and me to become better acquainted with our truly gracious, accommodating host and hostess. Next morning, with but a faint promise of daylight to the east, our little caravan moved out toward the hunting grounds.

Dick, with nine dogs in harness, led the way. Dale, a rank novice dog driver, was next, driving five of my most manageable dogs. I brought up the rear with seven of my older, steadier mutts. We took the trail (road) north toward Lake Louise, which was four or five miles distant. By the time we turned east on a well-defined "seismo trail," a gray, overcast day was in the making. It was warm, maybe zero degrees F, the kind of morning that gave notice that plans were brewing for delivery of snow by day's end. There had been recent snowmachine traffic over our route of travel, resulting in easy going for the teams. Dawn's early light revealed scores of caribou tracks going every direction, but seemingly no place in particular. The countryside ranged from small, snow-covered lakes, ponds, and meadows to heavy patches of quite dense spruce and hardwoods.

All three teams were "traveling light," as the saying goes, in anticipation of the necessity for hauling game on the return. Other than the "stay-put" survival items always on touring sleds, each carried only some lunch and a thermos of coffee. In addition, Dick and Dale each packed a rifle. Dale, for sure, wanted desperately an opportunity to use his. Following a short, mid-morning coffee stop, he would get his chance.

Sled dogs love new trails. The drive to explore unknown ground, to cover huge distances with pack mates, is genetic. In the wild, it is necessary for food gathering and survival. All canine senses come into play in this vital game of life. But, by far and away, the most important is the dog's astounding sense of smell, a million or more times that of a human, we are told.

A canine's innate desire to travel, to sniff out new ground, and this inborn compulsion to run with its kind, provides a key answer to the often-asked question: "What makes Iditarod racing dogs run a hundred or more miles per day?" In truth, nothing or no one really makes them run. They are, in fact, by their very nature, compelled to run. They were born that way. Selective breeding for those wondrous, wild instincts—in the case of the Seavey kennels, some twenty sled dog generations to date—simply brings to the top the very best of what has been there for centuries unnumbered.

Not more than a half hour after hitting the trail, following our "mug up," as we approached a low, barren ridge on our right (south), things began to happen. Almost as if on signal, all dog noses shot up, while being pointed in the direction of the ridge. Following Dick's lead, we stopped our teams. "I believe we have caribou behind that hog's back," Gilliand hollered back. The dogs were surprisingly quiet, no barking, just sniffing away in the suspected direction. As preplanned, I would stay and watch the teams while Dick and Dale did the hunting. Also, no more than three caribou were to be taken—one for each sled. Each musher, not trusting his snow hook to hold his team, maneuvered to a tree and tied off. The huntsmen quickly, but with stealth, rounded the far side of the ridge and disappeared from sight.

We waited. The dogs remained standing, but content to stay in place while they gave full attention in the direction of the unfolding hunt. Five minutes? Ten minutes? Fifteen, perhaps. Then the boys cut loose with a volley of riflery, which would have shamed the Chinese army. My first thought was, "My God, they probably went on a killing binge. What happened to the no-more-than-three we agreed on?" The thought was fleeting, for out from behind the far end of the ridge and onto the trail, bolted a band of wide-eyed, snorting caribou—ten or so animals. One glance at the now gone crazy, twenty-one barking, screaming, lunging canine demons and the caribou turned tail. With long, bouncing strides, they snorted their way down the trail ahead of us. Then came a snapping sound of wood breaking, and in close pursuit were Dick's nine dogs. They had demonstrated the results of good teamwork, and broke a four-inch spruce to which they were fastened as if it were a mere toothpick. The top portion of the tree remained holding on to Dick's snub line, for about a block, where it seemingly tired and released its grip. Meanwhile, the team had closed on the fleeing caribou to such an extent that they decided to add a bit of excitement to the race by taking an abrupt left and plunging down a very steep gully. The dogs followed.

I stood bewildered at the unfolding scene—more as if seeing it on a movie screen than in real life. I did come to my senses, but not until both the pursued and pursuers had left the scene. Bellowing like a madman, to distract remaining teams from lunging and possibly snapping other trees, I made the rounds and unhooked traces, which pretty much disabled each dog as a pulling force. Anyway, there wasn't anything to get excited over, unless it was a faraway sound of many dogs carrying on at a fevered pitch.

Dale had a successful hunt. Notwithstanding the extravagant expenditure of bullets, he bagged two animals, one, if not a trophy, a nice bull of admirable dimensions. Dick, true to his word, likewise downed a bull of admirable dimensions. Gilliand and I left Dale to do the skinning and butchering while we drove my team—Genghis in lead—to the ravine's lip. With much trepidation, we peered downward into its bottom. No caribou in sight. But the dogs—what a frightful sight they were. Never before, or since have I witnessed such carnage resulting from dogs fighting. Darkness was beginning to overtake our day by the time we had sorted out our sickening dog mess, loaded fruits of the slaughter, and struck out toward the Poe homestead. Total starless, moonless darkness had settled over our last hour on the trail. A fine, light snow began to fall.

From Dog Diary: (Saturday, March 29, 1969)

> ...back to Poe's between 8:00 and 9:00 p.m. Hung meat. Going was slow. Dick's team in bad shape from a big fight. He had to haul two in his sled, plus a caribou. Spent until midnight sewing up dogs' wounds by flashlight. Doubtful if two hauled back will make it—lost lots of blood. They are two of his (Gilliand's) best team dogs. Bad situation. Light snow. Mild. No wind.

Back to the First Great Race, a mile or so down the trail toward Unalakleet, the team settled back to its normal trot after the caribou chase. I halted beside a clump of dead, stunted spruce. Time for tea, made by melting snow over a small wood fire. All eleven sets of eyes were upon me with longing, expectant gazes. Each dog was accustomed to the routine: get the fire going, start melting snow for tea water, and throw snacks—fish and/or fat to eager eaters. Only this stop was different. Their canine cousins back in Kaltag had usurped, by foul means, this day's rations. Midway through tea preparations, Bobby Vent pulled in and parked his team of six large, rangy, very strong-appearing dogs. Could he join me? Absolutely. And we enjoyed yet another mug up together. Bobby said he had stopped and snacked his dogs on sheefish a ways back, which seemed to have perked them up considerably. I related my story of woe, how the Kaltag strays had partied all night on my tab. At that point, Vent remembered my "generosity," as he called it, back at Bear Creek Mine, when I shared surplus fat with him. He insisted I take his last bit of fish and feed it on the spot. Now, was that true generosity or not? After a half-hour stop, Bobby hit the trail once again toward Norton Sound. Having decided to give my gang a full-hour break, I lingered long enough to allow Bobby's half-pound fish snack for each dog to hit bottom.

Bobby Vent was one of many "Huslia Hustlers" originating in that Athabascan village located north of Galena. Of the twenty-one other first Iditarod finishers, I came to know and deeply respect that person the most. He had "hung up the harnesses," as the saying goes, and retired from mushing back in the 1950s. But, as with me, the lure of the open trail, the joy of traveling by dog team, proved to be irresistible sirens. He signed up for the first one and we hooked up quite by accident, becoming trail partners from Rainy Pass to Nome. Twice my age, experienced in wilderness travel and survival, I came to think of him more as a mentor than a competitor. He had gray, almost white hair. He was handsome—distinguished, really—by any standard. Short, but well-proportioned stature, with a fine, light copper-hued complexion of his race, Bobby was quiet, thoughtful, confident, given to an easy smile. Like his Eskimo counterparts, Vent had mastered the art of efficient dog team travel and trail craft. To my knowledge, no situation ever developed on our long march to Nome that he didn't meet head-on with a resolve and "it's all in a day on the trail" attitude. Not once did he complain of his physical infirmity that rendered it extremely painful just to stand on the runners. One can only wonder what agony he endured, driving his team and performing camp chores—all without complaint.

Notes are sketchy on my run from the site of the Vent-Seavey "mug up" on into Unalakleet. Someone noted our departure times from Unalakleet, but no known records exist for our arrivals. The trail continued firm and generally downhill. The weather was fine. Red Devil's Dick Wilmarth hit town first, followed by Vent and me twenty minutes later. It was dark, close to midnight, which would have placed the portage run in the neighborhood of thirteen or fourteen hours. As at Nulato, we were met as if we were returning, conquering heroes. A snowmachine escort guided us the last four miles to town. Village fire trucks with lights flashing marked our arrival.

What a contrast when compared to receptions given by most villages over in the Yukon Basin. It seemed the whole village turned out. Happy, smiling, laughing, excited, giddy to see us—at midnight. A wonderfully contagious, friendly atmosphere prevailed. It was as if in just ninety-two miles, we had been transformed to another country. Not, mind you, that Athabascan villagers were unfriendly. Plainly put, I related more closely with the open exuberance displayed by our Eskimo hosts. With abundant assistance, my team was escorted to the north edge of town and staked out. Of course, no spruce boughs were to be had for bedding, but an adequate supply of burlap sacks sufficed once the dogs figured out what in the world they were for.

Pioneer Iditaroders received royal treatment at the Unalakleet checkpoint from which I prepare to leave beginning my 18th day on the trail.

Twenty miles before Unalakleet, I had encountered an Eskimo fellow driving a snowmachine—Ray Foote by name. He kindly asked if there was anything he could arrange for me upon his arrival in town. Thinking over his offer, I said "Yes, are there fish to be had?"

"You're in luck," he remarked. "I have three pretty good-sized sheefish I can get for you." And off he blasted toward home.

Sure enough, when I got there, about ready to feed, here came Ray Foote with his three large, beautiful fish. At three dollars each, I was truly grateful to Ray for making them available to me. And, as icing on the Unalakleet cake, both my dog food and people food bags had been delivered to that first Norton Sound checkpoint. With water close by, dog chores went quickly. One-thirty a.m. and the last dog foot cared for, it was time to look to myself.

Al Lewis and his wife, both teachers in the Unalakleet system, hosted me. They had a six-month-old child at the time. Al was so helpful and accommodating. He helped get the dogs settled, helped me with my gear, and escorted me to his home. What a good host he was.

"Are you hungry?" he asked and, without waiting for my answer, began to fry up a big caribou steak and put the coffee pot on.

From somewhere, I got the nerve to inquire as to the status of his ice cream supply. Miracle of miracles. Not only had he a copious store of that commodity, he also, being an avid eater of the creamy white stuff, seemed to welcome my suggestion for the partaking of some. So there we were, 2:30 a.m., eating pumpkin pie with ice cream, washing it down with black coffee. The latter caused me, when I finally hit the sack, to toss and turn for—five seconds? After three hours, at precisely 5:30 a.m., that darned little travel alarm was again after me to get up.

39

Mail Must Go Through

Trouble along the way. I shredded a plastic shoe shortly after leaving Unalakleet, which made for an hour's delay and tougher sledding on to Nome. But, "The mail must go through."

Day 18: Tuesday, March 20, Unalakleet to Shaktoolik

Al Lewis's thermometer recorded a pleasant five degrees F at 6:30 a.m. The sky over Norton Sound was clear, with Besboro Island standing out prominently to the north toward Shaktoolik. More significant, the smoke from visible chimneys, lazily columned straight up. Good! No wind to speak of. Looked like a great day to continue my fabulous journey. By the time Al and his wife had gotten up, I was dressed, packed, and eager tend my dogs. With but little persuasion, however, I allowed myself to be convinced that breakfast would be in my best interest.

Vent and Wilmarth were in various stages of departure when I arrived at the dog lot. Greetings exchanged, a bit of shop talk, and I went to work packing my sled, watering dogs, tending feet, harnessing, and hooking up the team with Kiana in lead. No problem getting anyone out of bed. If not exactly tearing gear apart in eagerness to go, they didn't overtly resist the idea, either. Surprise! As I was hooking in my wheel dogs, Crazy and Casper, the Unalakleet postmaster showed up with a letter from Shirley and the kids, and an encouragement card created and sent by Seward artist, Dot Bardarson. What great morale boosters they proved to be. As events were to unfold, I would need all of that kind of boost I could get in the days ahead. No doubt about it, receiving that mail hand delivered on Norton Sound's barren shore added special meaning to special delivery. Al Lewis came along and was recruited to snap a few pictures, using my camera and his own. Most schoolchildren and many curious villagers were likewise there to see the teams off. Paul Ivanoff and E.M. Haugen were Unalakleet official checkers. Their record puts Wilmarth's departure at 7:55 a.m., Vent's at 8:00 a.m., and mine at 8:45 a.m.

The trail to Shaktoolik led across the face of town, hugging land along the east side of Norton Sound. It featured some substantial hills, necessitating an inordinate amount of side hilling and many deep draws containing calf-deep sugar snow. The ever-present Besboro Island loomed to the left (west), lying as it did some ten miles off shore, midway between Unalakleet and Shaktoolik. A minor disaster or perhaps a major irritant occurred well within sight of Unalakleet—certainly within the first five miles out.

My gang had no more than hit its stride when an icy, sloped stretch of trail sent me, sled, and wheel dogs skidding sidewise, striking a sharp, protruding rock The result left my left runner plastic flopping in the breeze. An hour's delay ensued while I unpacked sufficiently to locate my repair kit, remove the now worthless plastic, counter sunk (using a pocket knife) four protruding bolt heads into runner wood and bolt everything back in place. Oh!—and repack my sled for the trail. Lacking foresight to carry extra plastic, it was now "to Nome or Bust," riding one runner of wood and the other of plastic. Anticipating tougher sledding as a consequence of this setback, I abandoned an estimated fifty pounds of probable surplus dog food—fish mostly. This was done much to the delight of a half dozen very vocal ravens, who stood by at a respectful distance, waiting for us to get the heck out of there so that the feast might begin.

The run to Shaktoolik turned out to be the most difficult to that point .Temperatures kept climbing, reaching above the thawing point by midday. The Flat, coastal running of my fantasy, materialized into very rugged hill climbing. I had pictured plastic runners gliding, with little friction, over coastal sugar snow, they, in fact, felt and acted more like unpainted two-by-six-inch planks being dragged through desert sands. Throw in a fair amount of serious side hilling and the result was the most exhausting run to that point in the race. We all paid our dues getting to Shaktoolik that day—Bobby, Dick, and myself.

We came out of the hills several miles before reaching the village of Shaktoolik, running on low-lying land that necked down to a mere spit along which the village was located. Our approaching trail ran right through the first evidence of civilization—the cemetery. Next, we arrived at the village itself, constricted by the spit's narrowness to only one dwelling width, but stretching for perhaps a distance of one mile. My most exhausting day thus far came to an end beside Shaktoolik's National Guard armory, our roadhouse for the checkpoint. It's been said, "Nothing is so bad that couldn't be worse." As disagreeable as my first jaunt between Unalakleet and Shaktoolik was, it did get worse—a lot worse—for son Mitch and others in 1982, as revealed in Chapter 32.

Midway into my inaugural run to Shaktoolik, I made a stop to snack dogs, allow them to cool down a bit, and regain my own breath. It was then I remembered my mail crammed in a parka pocket. First, an original humorous, artsy card from friend and now famous Seward artist, Dot Bardarson. I sat on my sled in warm sunshine and laughed aloud at sled dog antics according to Dot. Shirley's letter with notes from Mitch and our kid's friend, Dale Hoogland, came to me by a route that remains a mystery. Mailed at Seward—eight-cent stamp, those days—with a March 17 postmark. It was addressed to me in care of "Iditarod Trail Race Checkpoint, Koyuk, Alaska." That address was crossed out with a note, "Return to" and an arrow pointing to our Seward return address. Still, it was handed to me at Unalakleet the morning of March 20, two checkpoints prior to Koyuk. In my book, that truly does give special meaning to special delivery. Dale gave me a vivid account of a rather bloody dogfight the kids had while running puppies, yearlings, that is. From Mitch, I learned Hyda had five pups, good looking, black and gray masks. This then thirteen-year-old future race champ observed, "According to your tape I get the idea that Attla isn't all that great. Radio, TV, and the paper make it sound like he owns the trail." Shirley started out: "Sure appreciated your tape, although you sounded like maybe we should perform last rites." She continued by saying that news coverage was much more complete now. "You can't imagine how excited we are about you're being up in front of the pack. Actually, the whole town is talking of nothing else." Both boys made mention of a special race charter plane and plans to "See you in Nome." That bit of info was the best news of all.

With checkpoint chores wrapped up, I had time at day's end to reread those letters from home. In my reading while on the trail, I completely missed the abundant humor inherent in eleven-year-old Dale Hoogland's narrative of an at-home communal dog mush done while I was headed to Nome. Actors in that drama (comedy?) were Dale (family friend, writer), Gary Elde (family friend), Darian Seavey (son), all age eleven, and Mitch Seavey (son, handler for my 1973 and 1974 Iditarods), age thirteen.

From Files: March 17, 1973. Letter received at Unalakleet.

> …we were hooking the pups up yesterday. Wow! We had a hard time. First Boo [Darian], Gary, and me were holding the pups. Then we missed our ride. So we ran up to the road and caught him [Mitch]. Then Sinuk [Sinook] ran off the road, chasing after moose. Then we went up the road past the bridge. Ther[e] Gary took off his shoe to itch his foot. Also, the dogs ran over him. Then the yellow one in the back of the kindergarten section chewed his harness.
>
> All of a sudden, Garf and Adam [Oden] got into a big fight. So we tied Adam to the tie down line. Then we got home and took them to their dog houses. May God Bless You. From Dale.

Later, as freshmen at Seward High School, Darian and Dale often drove a team to school and back home when the school day ended. One cold and very windy morning, the boys took off for school per routine, only to lose their team, which ran off following a nasty spill into a deep, hard, wind-carved gully. The incident happened while crossing Resurrection River flats. One could reasonably expect the team to either continue on to school or retrace their tracks home. Wrong! The five-dog team decided on a tour upriver. The school morning was pretty well shot by the time the truant kids and canines reported to our attendance director with an excuse written by Shirley, which read simply, "Lost dog team on way to school." Believe it or not, the boys were given an excused tardy. When a fellow can't "itch his foot" without being run over by a dog team, or going to school necessitated a six-mile, on-foot detour to retrieve a troop of errant canines, can any wonder remain why one only (Mitch) of that gang of boys in the end became a dog musher?

Here is a bit of trivia for us modern Iditarod fans who make the annual air trek to Nome for the race finish. The March 16, 1973 *Anchorage Daily Times* carried an announcement by Joe, Sr. that the Iditarod Trail committee would sponsor a group charter flight to Nome with a 9:00 a.m. departure on Monday, March 19. At least forty seats were available on a first-come and first-serve basis. Arrangements were with Wein Consolidated Airways, who, if more fans wished to travel, would provide a larger airplane. And the fare? Eighty-four dollars (that's $84.00). One way, right? No! Round trip. Sewardites snapped up a goodly portion of those forty seats. Those arriving by charter on Monday found a good deal of forbearance necessary, as they did not see their first musher until nearly noon Thursday. Still, during Nome's long period of waiting, excitement was maintained at high levels, as it remained until the last musher was off the trail. That musher was John Schultz of Delta Junction, who finally crossed the finish line to lay claim to the Iditarod's first red lantern, over thirty-two days after pulling his hook in Anchorage.

Back in Shaktoolik, I parked my weary team on the armory's lee side around 5:30 p.m. After a most fatiguing, frustrating day, I was third in, Bobby had clocked in at 5:05 p.m., and Wilmarth at 3:04 p.m., posting a nice lead for sure. I remember thinking another day like that and I would need to consider taking one off. Of course, Bobby and Dick had to deal with the same trail conditions as I had. The unknown for me was just how much extra drag my shoeless, wooden runner caused. In truth, it didn't seem to be a whole lot. I reasoned, if I stayed off the rocks so as to prevent gouging the wood of the shoeless runner, the sled would make it to Nome. There wasn't a lot to be done about it anyway. I gave it little thought from there on to Nome.

I have no record or recollection—nor does the race committee—of a specific checker at Shaktoolik. What I most remember are the kids. Lots of them—everywhere. Curious kids, in and out of the armory at all hours. Cute, happy kids. Their elders, in true Eskimo fashion, were friendly, helpful, and generous. Over protest by their owner, I purchased, for five dollars, two feedings of what was called "last year trout." It was Dolly Varden, caught the previous fall and kept frozen all winter. I inquired of the elderly dog musher if those fish made good dog food. He gave them a short but effective testimonial, with a chuckle, by declaring, "Me eat 'um." The meaning being, if they are good enough for him, then most certainly, my dogs shouldn't have a problem with them. And they didn't. He added that a little fermentation would have made them even better, easier for dogs to digest.

Trail condition north to Koyuk came up in conversation and my informant assured me it was well marked with tripods on land and bushes, periodically placed across the long, long expanse of Norton Sound. I inquired about the flooding on Norton Sound sea ice that I had "heard about." Actually, I was, due to a rather vain sense of pride, hesitant to reveal to that local sage that I had read of the flooding phenomenon in Frank Dufresne's book, *My Way Was North*. He wrote that it happens quite often. Since Norton Sound is very shallow, often no more than fifteen to twenty feet, its ice freezes to the bottom. Storms building out to sea and blowing on shore can push a five- to six-foot head of water over anchored ice. Not a good condition for the traveler to be caught up in, as Dufresne had once experienced. With but a slight breeze evident as we spoke, I found comfort in his concluding remark: "Today, no wind, not worry." These were reassuring words for a Cheechako in that country.

Close attention was given my gang that evening. A couple of young boys were talked into fetching a bucket of water for me. This entailed going some distance to the river, where a communal hole in the ice had been insulated against freezing. Everything about my team was encouraging. All eleven ate ravenously, both fish and fat. By way of very soupy kibble, they became well hydrated. There were no trees for spruce bough beds in that barren, windswept place. Snow was scarce and blown brick hard. Consequently, the best I could do was to dig a bowl-shaped depression for each dog as a bed. No wind, evening temperature around fifteen degrees F. It would have to do. Finally, I took great pains to care for all dog feet. Generally, they were good. My pine tar and neats foot oil ointment, by all evidence, was doing its job. I daubed Bag Balm, my old reliable, on the few nicks that I found.

Finished with my dog chores, I performed an on-foot reconnaissance of the outward-bound trail to Koyuk. It was then I chanced to meet Joe Smith and Bill Copeland, two committee trailbreakers, whom I had not seen since way back at Ruby. Bad news—both of their machines had become inoperable and they were waiting for an airlift over to Nome. Recall that Carl Fitzler had dropped out due to mechanical problems. Don Rosevear was, at the time, in Nome, still trying to figure a way to retrieve his dead machine, abandoned south of Poorman. With Smith and Copeland out, only one of the five remained: Bob Stone of Anchorage. Bob has a story of his own. He was not a motor head by experience and had not driven a snowmachine until just before our race. Talked into joining the committee's civilian trailbreakers, Stone purchased a used 1969 Scorpion machine, getting to ride but little before setting out ahead of dog teams. I had a connection with Bob's Scorpion. As a high school student, I worked weekends for a stretch of time, making shipping crates for Scorpion machines. The factory was located at my high school town of Crosby, Minnesota. About every time I talked to Bob, he was fixing to quit. At Poorman, he was hiring a plane and going home. At Ruby, for sure, a private plane and he was gone. By Shaktoolik, that sole survivor had apparently made up his mind to finish the job. He and his old Scorpion did just that.

We three lead mushers, by 9:30 p.m., had teamed up in an attempt to convince the score or more village kids that it was time to vacate the armory due to our dire need for sleep. Bobby was already out. Dick and I had all but persuaded the youthful hoard to abandon the premises when the doors burst open, allowing admittance of yet another draft of kids. Young girls, mostly. "Aunt Mabel wants you guys to come and eat right now." Wilmarth shook Bobby into a semi state of consciousness, explaining the necessity for becoming mobile. Not desiring to be labeled disobedient to Aunt Mabel, and quite sure we heard the word "eat" spoken, we willingly fell in behind a cute little supposed niece. We were escorted just a few doors up the spit—

toward land. The niece threw open the door, softly announcing our arrival. "They're here, Auntie." Then she left us to go join her friends. Search as I did, I could find no description of Aunt Mabel among my notes. I do remember thinking, however, that she must have been "Auntie" to the whole village, due to her gentle, giving nature. She served, I recall, a huge platter of golden-brown trout and, never to be forgotten, hot, homemade bread. If Aunt Mabel expected eager, appreciative eaters at dinner that night, we, the first Iditaroders ever at her table, did all in our power not to disappoint. Stuffed to the brim with all manner of good things to eat, I made a quick check of the dogs, and lights out at the armory.

When one is closely connected to a newsworthy event such as the first Iditarod, it is soon realized just how prone to error news reporting can be. Not that half-truths or outright no truths are necessarily intentional. Usually, misinformation comes about as a result of faulty information and/or faulty reporting of the same. The unfortunate result here is that folks often accept and believe what is conveyed via the press. Given time, and repeated often enough by enough people in enough places, original error becomes historic fact. Iditarod number one received a full quota of press prattle, which, with passage of forty or so years, has converted to history. In my case, perusal of news articles of the day had me arriving in Nome with twelve dogs (my original number), as well as seven, when the real number was eleven, a minor error for sure, but demonstrative, nonetheless. Or, the news report to the effect that our first champion departed Shaktoolik on Tuesday evening, March 20, for Koyuk—shortly after Bobby and I pulled into that checkpoint. Out went Wilmarth, according to press accounts, only to be swallowed up and stopped in his tracks by a fierce ground blizzard, forcing a retreat back to Shaktoolik. That bit of fiction was, in turn, used by editor, Dorothy Page, in compiling the first of her wonderful Iditarod Race Annuals. Tomorrow, ten years, fifty years from now, a researcher of the first race will latch onto that bit of misinformation and again print it as fact, that the first Iditarod champion, way back in 1973, wimped out in the face of a storm hardly noticed by modern racers, and turned tail and limped back to comfort and safety. Cognizant of how such distortions of reality occur, and the frequency of such occurrences, can one be condemned too soundly for doubting history itself?

40

...All the Whiskey You Can Drink...

Between Koyuk and Elim a severe storm developed which stopped Vent and me in our tracks at Moses Point and dashed hopes for a first place finish for both. Note spruce trail markers.

Day 19: Wednesday, March 21, Shaktoolik to Koyuk to Moses Point

For several days previous, my compact, red, gold-trimmed travel clock received a silent cursing for its 5:30 a.m. promptness in siccing its obnoxious alarm after me. That morning at Shaktoolik was somehow different. Seven hours of undisturbed sleep helped ease the transition from mostly dead to semi alive. A dull realization of the date—March 21—spring had arrived, adding a measure of excitement. Then, too, the goal was nearing—perhaps two long days would put me in Nome. Day nineteen dawned clear with a temperature of ten to fifteen degrees F. The wind was moderate from the north. It would be a beautiful day to be on the trail.

Breakfast before leaving Shaktoolik consisted of a can of army C-rations, beans and wieners, which were placed on the stove the night before. They were compliments of General Gettys's army snowmachine team, which donated its surplus to Shaktoolik villagers. On top of this went a generous half-loaf serving of Shirley's trail cake with all the goodies—honey, eggs, nuts, candied fruit, mince meat, to mention a few.

To say I did my morning dog chores without trepidation wouldn't be true. Stories of Norton Sound's fickle weather had me on edge. Special attention was once again given each foot of each of my loyal and, by now, truly loved and appreciated trail companions. All had eagerly sprung up to greet me, tails signaling delight. All ate and drank ravenously—a good indicator of an ardent desire to once again hit the trail. Here is as good a place as any to note that I did a fair amount of switching dogs around in the team—from side to side to alleviate strain on a dog's outside shoulder, caused by the slight angle of pull for each dog inherent in our tandem-hitch arrangement. Anybody willing to have a go at leading either single or doubled up with Kiana or Genghis, had opportunity to do so. Positions within the team also varied from run to run. Today a leader, tomorrow a wheeler. Except under extreme, dire circumstances, I removed harnesses after each run.

The uneasiness felt that morning while readying my team resulted from the unknown, in particular, the thirty-mile crossing of Norton Sound ice. Villagers assured me the ice wouldn't move until spring. Even in a severe storm, I reasoned, there was not a big chance of getting dangerously lost. Recalling my conversation with the well-aged village musher concerning storm-driven flooding, I took special note of northerly wind, thankful it wasn't being generated out east toward the Chukchi Sea.

Doubling Sonny with Kiana at lead, I pulled the hook on Shaktoolik, according to my notes, at 6:45 a.m. I was right behind Bobby Vent, and a short time ahead of Wilmarth. The trail led perhaps ten miles across the low, flat, and barren Cape Denbigh, marked with typical tripods. Before hitting sea ice, Wilmarth passed me, cruising nicely, I thought.

Once on the ice, markers became small (three to four feet) willows and stunted spruce, wrested from river and stream bottoms of that area. Placed at roughly fifty yard intervals, those most welcomed safety beacons were stuck into hard, drifted snow and seemed to stay put remarkably well. Brief halts were made on the way over to Koyuk. One for dog snacks and another to photograph my team among building-size chunks of pressure-ridge ice, a phenomenon completely foreign to me, save vicariously by way of books. Trail conditions were hard, windblown snow—good going. We did have a building headwind, constant, at maybe twenty-five miles per hour by our arrival at Koyuk. That wind had strength enough to turn the last twenty miles into some real work. Mile upon mile of pedaling.

En route between Shaktoolik and Koyuk, Sonny in lead. Pressure ice was a new experience for me. The clear, windless condition was to change drastically in just a few hours.

About ten miles out of Shaktoolik, I overtook Bobby. Shortly after, our trailbreakers, who had borrowed a machine from a Shaktoolik villager, passed all three teams on the way to recover one of their broken "Iron Dogs." Wilmarth pulled into Koyuk officially at 1:08 p.m. I was next, clocking in at 2:25 p.m., followed by Vent one hour and fifty minutes later. We gained an hour according to the official clock between Shaktoolik and Koyuk. In those days, Shaktoolik was in the Alaska Standard Time Zone while Koyuk kept Bering Sea Time. Though not knowing for sure, my guess is Bering Sea Time was used to clock us in which explained what appeared to be good travel times made over that trail segment while facing strong wind. Alaska no longer spans multi time zones. Nonetheless, Iditarod Race officials, in most recent years, have had to deal with the nationwide "spring ahead" into daylight saving time, which occurs after racers are underway to Nome. Computer viewers, due to a built-in program feature, have access to true, on-the-trail times. However, for the official clipboard record, one hour—caused by the hour leap ahead—has to be deducted from total elapsed new clock time for each arrival under the Burled Arch. For forty years, pioneer Iditaroder, Nome and race promoter, Leo Rasmussen, has checked in hundreds of official race finishers and has overseen the process in general to insure such details are not overlooked

At Koyuk, the checkpoint was in an identical National Guard armory as that in Shaktoolik. And, again, I was unable to recognize any one person designated to be an official representing our race committee. Our dog food bags had managed to find Koyuk, so while I enjoyed coffee and a stew of undetermined ingredients, provided for us at the checkpoint, my team chowed down fat, rich halibut heads.

Dick Wilmarth had preceded me to Koyuk by an hour and twenty minutes. It was apparent that he was preparing for another push that day. I had as good a run that day as a lousy one the day previous—into Shaktoolik. My dog team was not overly eager, but resigned—slowing down, it seemed, but steady. Kiana, who, at such a young age, had, I now realize, unfair demands placed on her at lead. She was unmistakably showing signs of being tired of it, more than physically fatigued. I had my eye on her partner on the way over. Sonny, a sixty-pound, yellowish-white male, had migrated from wheel to lead since the race start. He appeared to like it up there. With several daylight hours remaining, Wilmarth getting nervous, and a dog team with gas still in its tank, I decided to make the hop over to Elim. I would tag Wilmarth for another checkpoint and then make a dash for Nome. Bobby had probably the worst run of his race to that point. Constant need to peddle against strong wind caused him to suffer terribly with an arthritic knee. It was painful just to observe him hobble about, tending to his unwavering team of six. He grimaced with each step, but nary a word of complaint did I ever hear from that fine Athabascan gentleman.

Wilmarth hit the trail toward Elim about one and one-half hours after I arrived—ten minutes before Vent arrived. Cutting my planned rest from four to three and one-half hours gave him an hour and three quarters' jump on Bobby and me. We both cleared the Koyuk checkpoint at 5:05 p.m. Yes, I would trail along behind Dick to Elim, give my guys a good rest, and then pull the stoppers for Nome. Ah, such are the "plans of mice and men." The general direction when traveling from Koyuk to Elim is southwest. This provided a welcome relief from back-breaking pedaling, as we could expect a push from strong wind, now at our backs. Sledding, even with one plastic-less- runner seemed good. We had a hard trail with occasional sugar snowdrifts. On that run, Kiana was doubled at lead with Bandit, a steady male, deep-red coat, black muzzle, probably—like Sonny—a sixty-pounder.

Wilmarth was long gone, leaving in spots plenty of evidence of his having been there. In addition to sight evidence—dog tracks, runner marks—even more significant was a hot scent trail. With two good leader noses at work, there is little danger of straying too far. Our route alternated between low coastal ground and shortcut sea ice segments, connecting points and promontories. Neither Bobby nor I had learned the actual distance between Koyuk and Elim before starting out. Later, we settled on forty-six miles, derived from computations employing the most scientific instruments obtainable—a map and a length of string. Markers, as on earlier trail, were a combination of permanent wooden tripods and expendable willows.

Those familiar with prairie country know that storms, dust, and grasshoppers can come and go with amazing rapidity. With nothing but vast openness, devoid of impediments, winds have unobstructed playgrounds. We hadn't been on the trail an hour when, within fifteen minutes, a blizzard, ground storm, whiteout, you name it, descended upon us with unbridled fury, the likes of which would have made a good, old-fashioned Dakota blizzard jealous. In short order, I went from being able to see Bobby's team coming along about a mile and a half behind, to being unable to distinguish the next trail marker some fifty yards' distance. We must have been close to Bald Head (Point), on the Koyuk side, at the time.

The off-shore north wind built to a gale force. My poor dogs. They would hit a wind-polished spot, loose traction, and literally get rolled into a knot, requiring a frustrating untangling, under something less than good picnic conditions. Other times, away would go the sled, skidding sideways, with me firmly attached, until it struck an immoveable drift or a crusted snow patch, and over I went, taking the entire team with me, ending, one time, a half block off the trail. What a storm. What an experience. Blinding and, at times, breath-sucking. Dangerous, scary, but exciting and exhilarating at the same time. One remembrance I have kept—all these years—is thankfulness for the relatively mild temperature at the time. And another is an absolute, set-it-in-concrete admiration for my dogs. In the course of many untangles, I rearranged my front end. Genghis, my old faithful, went in front with Kiana. Bandit was placed back in swing. We went. In spite of roll-overs, roll-ups, wraparounds, and tangles, we went. And even when a couple of males—Kuchik and Casper—repeatedly attempted to dive behind snowdrifts, out of the punishing tempest, we went. How gratifying it was to witness my years of training pay off. Uncounted hours back on Kenai Lake and Resurrection River flats, driving this never-say-die team head-on into fiendish, violent snowstorms.

During one of my disentanglement exercises, Bobby "caught me up," as it is said along the Yukon. From all appearances, he was doing much better in the tangle department than I was. This, we agreed later, was due to metal runner shoes on his sled being less prone, he thought, to sidewise skidding. Also, with fewer dogs in harness and his smaller stature, he had fewer "sheets offered to the wind."

Upon leaving sea ice and ascending a promontory called Bald Head, a couple of surprises were in store. First, I was amazed—expecting none—at the size of trees through which the trail passed. Certainly cabin-size, some being twelve inches at the base. This timber offered welcomed protection from the scathing wind below. A second amazement was that in less than an hour's climb, we broke out of the storm completely, into a beautiful, starlit, calm winter's night, much to my wonderment and relief. Even with my Cheechakoish understanding of northwest coastal weather, I knew below us, on the ice, that ground storm was still churning away. And so it was. Too brief was the respite before descending Bald Head's west side, plunging again into an awaiting stark surrealism.

As we neared sea ice to begin the twenty-five-mile run over to Moses Point, I passed Bobby, who was having leader problems. Darkness was now complete. A two C-cell handheld flashlight was my sole illumination. Snow swirled, driven by a fully fledged ground storm whiteout. Protection of eyes became an urgent concern. I pocketed my pathetic little light, giving up as futile attempts to hone in on trail markers. In essence, as well as in fact, I was running blind, totally dependent on my leaders' ability to ferret out the trail. For twenty-five miles, and for what, in time, seemed an eternity, my drive into that vast emptiness ground on. Spooky as it was, there was nothing to do but forge ahead. Like flying an airplane, once one lifts off, he is committed.

Dangerous as that run may have seemed as it was playing out, it had some mitigating elements as well. Frequent, quick flashlight checks revealed that both leaders, Genghis and Kiana, had noses to the ground. They were on dog scent. Wilmarth was somewhere ahead. Occasionally, I caught a glimpse of a willow bush marker, seemingly marching by on my left side, a reassuring occurrence for sure. Also, if not balmy, the temperature that night remained mild to an extent that, with off and on pedaling, I was able to keep warm. To the rear, a flicker, though seldom, from Bobby's light, gave comfort in knowing he had tagged on and was on the move.

Somewhere near Moses Point, the wind's most fierce force was unleashed. As before, we went sailing, ending in the inevitable tangles, labor, and slowing of progress. There must have been three or four miles of that treachery and frustration before striking land. Still, the wind raged. Still, visibility remained practically nonexistent. Still, with unfailing confidence, Genghis and Kiana led on. I remembered wondering how that night would end.

Well, one may say it ended—abruptly. From my perspective, standing on the runners, and driving my team more by feel than by sight, it ended with a simultaneous emergence of a faint light ahead and a quick halt. An assessment of the situation, with aid from my—about one-candle power flashlight—revealed that my team had made an executive decision to call it a day. Collectively, it had dived under and around a cache, which, due to wind action and snow accumulation, had provided a large, out-of-the-wind depression. Beyond, on the lee side of a building, was Dick Wilmarth's team. Two snowmachines were parked near the entrance of what turned out to be a summer fish camp dwelling, situated on Moses

Point, some twelve to fifteen miles from our Elim checkpoint. A wave of relief ran through my entire being at the realization we had gained refuge. A feeling not unlike coming to anchor in a calm, quiet bay after being thrashed for hours on end by a violent, angry sea.

From Files: (Notes on latter part of race)

> I did have my flashlight, but it was of little use for locating trail markers. Mostly, I trusted the leaders to sniff out the trail. I finally came to a fish camp. It was before Elim, on the east side of Moses Point…By this time, the wind had really built in velocity. It got to the point that if I stopped the dogs, some would dig down immediately to be out of the wind as much as possible. Of course, I would have a tough time getting them going. Some, while passing an ice clump or anything that served as a wind break, would attempt to dive behind it. Dog coats in my pack did come to mind. But how to get to them, much less put them on under such adverse conditions?
>
> Fortunately, this cabin came along. Actually, my dogs turned right in there and were under a cache before I really knew what was going on…I left them there and followed the light streaming from cracks in the building and a small, glass door pane. Wilmarth's team was to the left, sheltered side of the cabin…Had to step around two snowmachines parked out front.

Huddled around a lighted, but not yet hot, wood stove, were Dick and two middle-aged Eskimo fellows. All fully dressed for outside, all obviously elated over having found refuge from the storm, as indeed I was. That fish-site cabin had been built for summer use only. The unabated wind played weird music through numerous cracks in its four walls. But it was heavenly. Just getting in, out of the wind, was akin to stepping off an airplane in Miami in mid-winter.

I thought it strange that no real acknowledgement of my arrival was made. No greeting. No small talk. No comparing of trail notes, as was done on previous runs. One got the impression he had ignorantly interrupted a juicy family fight. Wilmarth seemed restless, eager to again face the black, hellish night, but reluctant to do so.

Stating my reason, I moved the one mantle Coleman lantern, which wasn't doing well from its perch on a small table, to a wire hanging near the door, hoping it would help Bobby locate us. Not ten minutes later, Bobby's team made the same "under the cache" dive mine had. It was a tired, painfully limping "Huslia Hustler" who burst in, trailed by a cloud of swirling snow. "Whuh! What a night," was his understatement as he collapsed into a rather ratty, overstuffed chair, facing the stove. Flakes of snow that clung to his wolf-skin ruff, in an instant, turned to beads of water. At that point, Wilmarth's quandary became clear.

From Files: (Dorothy Page's first Iditarod Trail Annual, page 28.)

> Robert Vanderpool, Jr., twenty-two year old pilot, who *flew cover for Wilmarth from McGrath to Nome*, also said he planned to enter the Iditarod race. (Emphasis mine.)

Vanderpool did, in fact, "fly cover" for Wilmarth. On two separate occasions south of Poorman, I witnessed plane and dog team parked together in open ski-landable spaces beside the trail. Certainly, to have someone fly cover could be construed as violation of Rule 14, which prohibits motorized assistance.

Dick's Moses Point vexation was a people problem, really. Simply put, how to get two reluctant, and probably wise Eskimos, to drive their snow-machines ahead of his team so that he could make further progress that terrible night. And, by so doing, finally get the jump on Bobby and me. His people were limited to the two machine drivers only. Bob Stone, the remaining official trailbreaker, was not there. Vent and I watched, un-consulted, ignored, as if ticket holders to a mostly silent drama. Finally, Wilmarth threw his cards on the table, uttering, "You boys stay ahead of me and I will buy you all the whiskey you can drink when we get to Nome." As God is my witness, those were his, almost, if not exact words. They had effect. Within fifteen minutes, the sound of the last machine blended into the music of wind playing through the cabin.

From Files: (Notes on Latter Part of Race.)

> As Wilmarth was preparing to be led up the trail by the (two) machines, the storm still raged. I asked Bobby if he wanted to

> follow, stating I would go if he did. He said, in his matter-of-fact way, that his leg was "on fire," that he had been beat up enough for one day, for me to go ahead. "I will catch you up tomorrow." … easy decision on my part (to go or not). Bobby and I had been trail partners from way and gone back there…and with him hurting… besides, both my team and I had gotten walloped pretty well that run, too…decided to stay until daylight.
>
> We (Vent and I) talked about Wilmarth's use of airplane and unauthorized snowmachine assistance toward Nome. We both remembered rules outlawing outside and mechanized assistance, and pondered if we should make an issue of it…In the end—by our arrival in Nome—we had decided to overlook the whole affair. By so doing, Bobby and I unwittingly began another Iditarod tradition, albeit a subliminal one: "Let sleeping dogs lie, for the good of the race."

Rule19 stated: Outside assistance will be allowed only if the team is unmanageable. Rule 14 forbade motorized assistance altogether. However, the reader must realize that the first race was an experiment, a pilot race, if you will. Things didn't always go as planned, or even as hoped. Bad plans or absence of plans at all, were mostly results of lack of knowledge and/or experience among planners, volunteers, and racers. I was as happy as the next musher when, after stomping out the words "DOG FOOD" in the snow, south of Poorman, an airplane showed up with dog food. I didn't ask if the pilot was a certified, bona fide Iditarod volunteer. Volunteer snowmachiners were to travel ahead of race leaders to assure a useable tread. Yet, I never laid eyes on one of those fellows between Ruby on the Yukon and Nome on the Bering Sea, save going the wrong way near Shaktoolik. That includes the controversial Moses Point night. Still, there remain the questions: Was it legal, under our rules, to hire trailbreakers when none of our own was present? Was such an action a violation of the spirit of our race? Apply these same queries to the matter of one receiving private "air cover" from McGrath to Nome.

There was, for the first race, a list of only twenty-one vaguely stated rules. Questions were bound to come up on conduct and interpretation as indeed they have throughout four decades of Iditarod racing.

The result is a much more imposing body of rules of small-book thickness. Modern Iditarod race rules are reviewed annually—"for the good of the race," it is hoped.

Day 20: Thursday, March 22,
Moses Point to Elim to Golovin to White Mountain

Dick Wilmarth pulled into Elim that stormy night of Wednesday, March 21, at 11:00 p.m. After a lengthy rest of nearly nine hours, he struck out for Golovin and White Mountain at 7:55 a.m. the following morning.

Meanwhile, Bobby Vent and I were holed up at Moses Point over Wednesday night, March 21. We fed our dogs and moved them around so as to gain as much protection possible from the howling wind. My team of eleven remained under the cache, and Bobby's were bedded down on the lee side of the fish shack. After partaking in about a half loaf of Shirley's trail cake, I hit the sack. Luxury at its finest. There was a bearskin sleeping pad that I placed atop a mattress on a cot. Next, I put down my sleeping bag, and finally, my tent as a loose cover over the works. It was about midnight. Our fire had burned out long ago. Bobby, sitting in the dilapidated, overstuffed chair, snored the snore of an exhausted man at peace with the world. A constant and gusting wind continued to whistle through our place of refuge.

I awoke fifteen minutes before my 5:00 a.m. alarm sounded. Its persistence brought Bobby to his feet. The cabin was cold and very drafty, and as there was not enough wood to melt snow for dog water, we skipped the formality of kindling a fire. A few chunks of solid trail cake served as my breakfast. I retrieved the dogs from their snowy beds and fed fare, which must have become monotonous by that stage of the race—chopped, frozen halibut heads. While packing up my sled, it seemed the wind was diminishing, and it did so as we progressed down the trail toward Elim. The temperature was mild, perhaps in the upper teens. With young Kiana once again in single lead and the team quickly falling into a slow but steady pace, we cleared Moses Point by 7:00 a.m. Bobby Vent was close behind. For the most part, the going over to Elim was good. The trail was adequately and permanently marked overland with traditional tripods. Snowdrifts, though four to five feet deep in places, were wind driven, brick hard, which made relatively easy sledding over them. I encountered only moderate hills. In places, however, the sledding was such that the drag on the team resembled that expected while driving through loose, fine sand. Whether due to absence of plastic on one runner or compact, wind-smoothened snow, I couldn't decide. It might have been some of each.

Moses Point fish camp morning after the big blow. I had parked the team here the night before for what little protection offered by the structure from a full-fledged ground storm.

This photo of Elim villagers and me is one of my most prized. Bobby and I were treated to a mid-morning breakfast and sent on our way with fried caribou steaks for "trail food."

Unlike the present-day overland approach to Elim from Moses Point, we traveled the beach both in 1973 and 1974, pulling off the sea ice directly in front of the village. My arrival was recorded as 10:40 a.m. on Thursday and Bobby's was 11:50 a.m. It seemed the whole village had declared a holiday, with most villagers in full regalia, turning out to greet me. Many cameras were put to use as I snubbed the team to a mostly snowed-in boat that had been pulled high up on the beach. I was greeted by happy folks, smiling, handshaking, welcoming folks. No place en route had I felt more welcome than at Elim. Their camera craze overtook me as well, resulting in one of my most cherished photos—me posing amid a score or so of Elim villagers, taken on that First Great Race.

Leaving Moses Point, my intention was to breeze through Elim as quickly as possible—"Hello, good-bye"—like. But following our photo session, an invitation to breakfast at a nearby residence was extended. After checking and ascertaining that Wilmarth was some three hours ahead at that point, I gratefully accepted—a tactical error, as it would prove. I had just sat down to a steaming bowl of mush and a mug of hot, strong coffee, when a shout from outside went up. "Dog team!" Soon Bobby joined me. We learned that all the apparent fanfare was not for Bobby and me, necessarily. Fact was, the village was waiting with eager anticipation for the weather to clear when several planeloads of church parishioners could arrive to begin a weekend, statewide denominational convention.

Bobby left Elim ahead of me by about ten minutes at around noon. We were both given a heartfelt send-off and two nicely fried caribou steaks, compliments of the lady of the house, for "trail food." Little wonder I have reserved a warm, soft spot for Elim over all the passing years.

For another ten miles, our trail hugged the shoreline on its way to Golovin and White Mountain. Except for an occasional stretch of "sugar snow," the going was good. It was a level trail with moderate wind on our right side. The level nature changed drastically upon reaching Cape Darby. Crossing the cape entailed some of the most serious hill climbing encountered anywhere on the trail. There were some ten miles of it before dropping down to sea level again, onto Golovin Bay, and then, another five miles north into Golovin Village. Uncle Sam's long arm was evident when I met and visited with a man in Elim who was working for Social Security. He was being conveyed over his route in a sled pulled by a snowmachine. While traversing the mountains of Cape Darby, en route to Golovin, he passed me and stopped to chat a bit. Then this civil servant was off to White Mountain to enlist more seniors in his program.

Golovin struck me as an unpretentious little village, unaffected by the passage of time. Folks turned out in the same excited manner as at Elim, but fewer in number, bearing fewer cameras. Golovin, named for an early Russian naval captain, is situated on a former native village site. I was told that after John Dexter established his trading post on the village site in 1890, Golovin rose to prominence as a service center for Norton Sound mining operations, in particular those of the Council District. It would remain so until Nome came into existence and displaced it in importance. Still, in 1973, all the features of a healthy village were in evidence—people, airstrip, school, post office, and trading post.

Vent and I arrived together shortly before 5:30 p.m. Bobby was limping badly, due to his painful, arthritic knee. His dogs, like mine, were moving at a slowed, but strong, pace. To my surprise, the first to greet me was Mrs. Francis Wright, a former Golovin resident, who then lived in Seward. We had become acquainted with her through church activities. It was Francis who provided us with a dog bootie pattern and helped Shirley get started on the sewing. She was in Golovin to visit her brother. We had a nice visit while I rested my dogs and, at the same time, enjoyed a cup of coffee at one of the village homes. Our host was an old-timer born in the village and whose first name was Floyd. His last name has escaped me.

Before pulling the hook on Golovin, I paid a visit to the trading post and, fortunately, was able to purchase a much-needed pair of sunglasses. I had misplaced, or otherwise lost, two pairs up to that point and was experiencing the early stages of snow blindness—burning eyes. There at the post, I met a man by the name of Erickson, from my "Old Country"—Minnesota. His hometown was Cloquet, which he had left to come to Golovin to teach in public school.

It was getting dusky at 5:30 p.m. when Bobby and I struck the trail for White Mountain. Weather-wise, it was warm with light snow falling, wind in our face, but of moderate velocity, perhaps ten to fifteen miles per hour. Between Golovin and White Mountain is about eighteen miles of mostly flat trail, most of which is over Golovin Bay, with a few overland miles and up Fish Creek. Bobby and I ran together, mostly in the dark, with teams, as they neared twelve hours on their feet, displaying little enthusiasm for their jobs. Where we came off Golovin Bay, a fellow on a snowmachine met us and escorted us overland to the Fish Creek, which we followed upstream three to four miles, arriving at White Mountain at 10:00 p.m. Thursday evening.

White Mountain was the community that went into such an uproar over the race committee's announcement that we were going to bypass it. In truth, White Mountain is about twenty miles out of the way, compared with the straight west route out of Golovin. The committee gave in to the collective pleas of White Mountain and, at the last minute, agreed to route the race through there. The problem was little had been done to establish it as a checkpoint. Consequently, no dog food reached that location for the front teams.

As at Poorman and Kaltag, I again found myself in a dog food deficiency – like a zero amount. Beating local bushes the best I could do was a sack of frozen herring, for which I poured into the local economy, ten dollars. I gave half to Bobby Vent, as he, too, was in a dog food crunch. Except for a few, saved for a morning snack, I fed it all amid serious misgivings, as the lot appeared rather shopworn. Herring is extremely fat, rich fish. I knew my dogs were not accustomed to such rich fare. At home, most had refused to eat the stuff at all, the few times I had given it a try. But at White Mountain, it was a situation of herring or nothing. To my surprise, they all chose herring. Next day, on the final run to Nome, my misgivings proved valid. Three dogs were very ill, plagued by vomiting and diarrhea over the first-half day. The remaining eight showed no obvious adverse effects.

White Mountain was a checkpoint in every sense of the word, except a dog food depot. Amiable Howard Lincoln was the village checker, as he would remain for more than three decades to come. People cut boughs for dog beds, and a fellow named Johnny invited Bobby and me to stay at his place, which we gladly did. I polished off three helpings of caribou stew and drank what must have been two quarts of coffee and water. After setting my alarm for 5:00 a.m., I collapsed into a deep, much-needed sleep somewhere close to 11:30 p.m.

41

The Indomitable—Bobby Vent

Bobby Vent, my most cherished trail mate, leaves White Mountain. Nothing on the long, punishing trail deterred him from reaching Nome. (Photo: Terry Adkins)

Day 21: Friday, March 23, White Mountain to Nome

As was my habit, it seemed, I woke at 4:45 a.m., once again beating my alarm by fifteen minutes. Bobby and I had breakfast with our host. The race's only veterinarian, Terry Adkins, was at White Mountain, and while we readied our teams for the trail, he examined each dog. Where mine were concerned, two or three were showing signs of dehydration. A couple also had web splits (between toes), which I had been doctoring, and from which they were recovering, or at least holding their own. Another, Shiak, had a badly torn pad on a rear foot. This I treated and placed a bootie on it, the second one used the entire journey. Bobby had one dog in terrible condition and, upon the vet's advice, dropped him at White Mountain. Sore footed, dehydrated, it also suffered ill effects of its new herring diet. Vent was now at legal rock bottom (five) for dog numbers. Fortunately, they proved to be five super-tough animals, and like their master, indomitable to the end.

From Files: Information edited from Adkins/Seavey telephone interview, January 20, 2011.

Terry Adkins was a sharp, young airman stationed at Elmendorf Air Force Base when he first fell under the Joe Redington spell. A trained and licensed veterinarian notwithstanding, his assigned job was that of meat inspector for the base. As such, Adkins made many flights to the Aleutians to inspect fish plants selling seafood to the air force under government contract. Another job was to oversee operation of base dog kennels and stables.

A motley collection of pound and giveaway dogs comprised Terry's earliest team. Since its members were housed on base, they became the "Air Force Team." They were run in local fun races, providentially including those sponsored by the Aurora Dog Mushers Club. Enter Joe, Sr., who, after his convincing manner, made Adkins feel he was the keystone of the entire planned race. He was needed to keep the Humane Society of Alaska at bay. Without his help, all would be lost. The good doctor consented to Joe's insistent plea that he become the official "race vet." Big problem. Adkin's commanding officer said, "NO!" Not to worry. Joe Sr. went to army General Gettys, who had already consented to supply an army team of advance trailbreakers for the race. General Gettys went to the air force commander and came back with the use of Adkins assured.

Flying in small airplanes is the name of the game for a vet covering the vast Iditarod Trail. And when one is the only vet over the thousand-plus-mile course, there is no option. Joe, Sr. was Terry's first pilot. He dropped Terry at Skwentna, intending to return to Knik to pick up a forgotten item. On takeoff, he flipped his plane. No harm done, the pilot, even the plane, escaped with minor injuries. Art Petersen, who was to become the granddaddy of all Iditarod air force pilots, took over and stuck with Terry for the duration.

Adkins stated there wasn't much medically among the dogs that were memorable. However, certain extraneous occurrences are unforgettable. He was flying with Petersen when they air mailed, via the plane's window, a new set of dentures to Raymie Redington near Galena. Again, it was Petersen and Adkins who dropped bags of dog food south of Poorman in answer to my stomped-in-the-snow appeal, "DOG FOOD." Their timely arrival spared George Attla and me the chore of a planned and imminent moose hunt. A severe windstorm, with accompanying blinding snow, prevented Petersen from rounding Cape Nome and flying on into Nome. Solution? He taxied his aircraft the twenty-two miles, staying glued to the Iditarod Trail for guidance.

In Nome, it seems Terry was attracted, like so many visitors, to the famous (infamous?) Board of Trade watering hole. He was amazed to find the place packed to capacity, not an available stool in the entire joint. The fellow accompanying him suggested, instead of leaving, they exercise a bit of patience, waiting for drunks to topple from high, well-used bar stools, packed cheek to jowl along what seemed a half-block long, heavy wood bar. Sure enough. Within five minutes, Adkins relates, four stools became vacant. Two by natural topplings and two when their occupants, by mutual agreement, repaired to the outside in an effort to settle a loud, nasty, verbal disagreement in a more physical, man-to-man fashion. While there, our vet engaged in his own game of fisticuffs. Seemed native driver, John Komak, eighth place finisher from Teller, disapproved of Adkin's insistence that he drop a certain dog back along the trail. As situations of that ilk are wont to do, this turned combative. Adkins claims he suffers from an arthritic right hand to this day.

Herbie Nayokpuk's dog, Patti, was dropped due to a hernia, at Adkin's suggestion, and sent to Anchorage for an operation. A year or so later, Adkins visited Nayokpuk at his Shishmaref home. Herbie offered to carve ivory tusks as a gift for saving his dog. This Terry refused, reminding the race favorite that it was his duty as a vet to do so. Without another word to Adkins, Herbie instructed his son to fetch Patti. Handing the leash to an astonished visitor, Herbie said, "She is your dog now." Not wishing to offend his host a second time, he accepted. Terry has perpetuated Patti's line (white dogs) for over forty years.

By the second (1974) Iditarod, Adkins had palmed off his voluntary veterinarian chores onto three army vets and took the first steps toward an amazing twenty-two Iditarod Race career.

Dr. Terry Adkins, first and only veterinarian, checks my team at White Mountain. An 18 hour almost non-stop run to Nome was to come.

One of two booties (muttluks) used the entire race goes on at White Mountain. (Photo: Terry Adkins)

Dick Wilmarth had arrived at White Mountain five to six hours ahead of Vent and me, at 4:30 p.m. Thursday. We saw neither hide nor hair of him in the checkpoint. No record exists of his departure time, though the checker thought it to be "before midnight." If so, Vent and

I reasoned, he would be about eight hours down the trail toward Nome by the time we left White Mountain. Realistically not catchable, unless his team crashed and burned or some other disaster befell him. Still, there was no harm in driving hard—just in case. Further, we had heard that George Attla and Herbie Nayokpuk were closing in on us from the rear. An added incentive not to tarry. As it evolved, Isaac Okleasik, Dick Mackey, and John Komak were also nipping at our heels.

Dorothy Page published the first of a long series of her delightful race annuals under the heading: *The Iditarod Trail Annual – Anchorage to Nome Race, 1973*, by Dorothy Page. (No copyright evident.) One section of that annual is Dorothy's compilation of race reports, written by Gordon Fowler of the *Anchorage Daily Times* (no longer published) and those by Ralph Lee, writing for the *Anchorage Daily News*. Below are a few excerpts:

> Most of the mushers left Anchorage with the longer freight sleds and had their sleeping bags, dog food and other paraphernalia piled high on the sleds as they embarked on the long journey to Nome.
>
> ...Barry McAlpine of Goat Creek, number 19, didn't have his team ready to start when his regular turn came up. Officials ruled he could start after the rest of the regular field left. On the second try, McAlpine's team got 100 yards down the trail and became involved in a tangle and started fighting among themselves. McAlpine called it quits at that point.
>
> Alec Tatum of Anchorage, number 28, scratched at Knik when he was disqualified for arriving at Knik two dogs short on the string he started with.
>
> Portions of the Matanuska and Knik Rivers had opened and instead of crossing on frozen rivers themselves, mushers had to reroute themselves over the concrete bridges and problems were many.
>
> Joe Redington Sr. reported he's dropped off a pair of boots to Howard Farley at One Stone Lake to pass on to Dr. Hal Bartko who'd worn out his boots and needed new ones.
>
> The double team of Ford Reeves and Mike Schreiber, number 30, had made it to Skwentna...It was reported that Reeves had walked

the entire 55 miles from Susitna to Skwentna as the team was laboring under 400 pounds of freight.

Vent and Wilmarth had even camped near each other one might and had added incentive to break camp earlier than usual the following morning when a pack of wolves moved in close enough to sniff their camp.

...Casey Celusnick of Fairbanks – who'd been running with John Schultz of Delta Junction as a double team – sprained his leg at March Creek in Ptarmigan Valley and had to be flown by Air Force helicopter to an Anchorage hospital. Schultz elected to remain in the race and continue on alone.

John Luster of Chickaloon, number 25, scratched on Monday morning, March 12, at McGrath...he was running yearling dogs and figured they'd had enough...another factor..."I run out of cinnamon rolls." Luster had left Anchorage with 20 pounds of cinnamon rolls which his mother had baked for the trip as his sole source of food.

Reporters noted that in talking to the mushers as they arrived in McGrath in anything but nice weather, that the majority of them were cheerful, laughing it up about the situations they'd encountered and might still find ahead.

Fans who'd been following the race by radio had been told matter-of-factly that mushers were tackling glare ice, gusty winds, cold chill factors, overflow which was two or three feet deep in places, and many tough hills. In addition to mushing, the men were busy repairing sleds, caring for sick or lame dogs...but they certainly weren't complaining.

...Raymie Redington, number 21, had arrived in Galena on Saturday night and announced he was scratching..."I'm gonna take them home and rest them up"...Raymie Redington had experienced one of the most unique problems of any musher in the race...he had broken his dentures just outside of Knik and had been reduced to eating dog food as it was the only thing he could "chew." Help came when his father, Joe Redington, Sr., had air dropped a most welcome package – containing new dentures.

Five mushers had left Ruby close together. They battled for the lead down the frozen Yukon River. The running was easier down the river and the mushers made as much as 100 miles a day in places

> running 16 – 18 hours. By the time the leaders reached Unalakleet, on the Bering Sea coast, the teams of Wilmarth, Seavey and Vent were scrapping for the lead.
>
> It appeared a total of 22 teams – barring any more drop-outs – would complete the grueling test.
>
> Few people in Nome were planning to get much sleep the night of March 22, 1973. Instead, the whole town planned to keep a 24 hour vigil on the incoming Iditarod sled dog trail…"No matter what time of the morning – even 3 a.m. Mayor Robert H. Renshaw told reporters, "You can bet the whole town is going to turn out."… The night passed and morning came – but still no mushers.

Vent and I pulled out of the White Mountain checkpoint close to 7:00 a.m., bound for Solomon, fifty miles distant, we were told. Perhaps three inches of new, overnight snow covered the outbound trail. Snow continued to fall most of the day, but without much accumulation. The temperature was twenty degrees F by my thermometer. With Bobby bringing up the rear, our route took us up the Fish River, about two and one-half miles above White Mountain Village, where it left the river and wound its way westward through the White Mountains to Solomon. On the river, there were tree boughs marking the trail and, with only a strong breeze blowing, were easily discerned. This pleasant situation changed drastically shortly after leaving the river and heading overland. In a matter of minutes, I went from being able to see the old trail, even with new snow on it, to perceiving only a vast, white nothingness. About the time I stopped the team, both my eyes had developed a mild, burning sensation, to which a little fine sand seemed to have been added. Being a cloudy, snowy day, I had completely overlooked putting sunglasses on. I would pay for that blunder, suffering the effects of snow blindness for the remaining daylight hours—even after donning my "shades."

Vent came along while I was in the process of trying to discover the trail's whereabouts by zigzagging the team over a general course of travel in the hope that Kiana would pick up Wilmarth's trail scent and line us out. Bobby agreed to go ahead and, sure enough, in a quarter mile, he ran across one stake, then another, and another. My eyes noticeably improved as the day wore on. Still, it was comforting to follow someone with an abundance of trail smarts and good eyesight to boot. Hills and more hills with the trail marked by use of permanent tripods characterized the route through the White Mountains. At Topkok, we left the mountains via an abrupt drop onto a rather windy lagoon, then on land along their sea coast to Solomon. It took our weary teams eight and one-half energy-sapping hours to cover that stretch. My official check-in time at Solomon was 3:41 p.m., and Vent's was 3:39 p.m. Wilmarth had cleared Solomon, bound for Nome shortly after 6:00 a.m. that morning. That gave him an eight- to nine-hour jump on his pursuers, with less than thirty-five flat miles of travel remaining to the finish line. Bobby and I acknowledged that if any more racing was to be done, it would be between us for second and third positions.

In truth, I didn't know what to expect at Solomon. I figured it was probably another Eskimo village. Actually, I learned there had indeed been a native village on its site along the Solomon River until the Nome area gold rush of the early 1900s brought about its demise. In its place sprang up a rather typical pacer mine boom town, which, too, went into a tailspin after dredges worked the river bottom prior to World War II. A few intriguing reminders of its past glory remained for us mushers of '73 to wonder over. A few weathered buildings, some rusty railroad equipment, a long, deserted railroad bed, and telephone line marching off toward Nome were the most visible features of a distant and better time. Two Iditarod Race checkers, out from Nome, were lodged in the old general store. When I inquired if, in fact, Solomon was a ghost town, I was informed that three Eskimo brothers, whose last name was Green, were the sole inhabitants at that time.

Even the checkers could not agree on the distance between Solomon and Nome, with guesses ranging from twenty-five to thirty-five miles. We chatted with these good-natured volunteers as Bobby and I polished off a large, steaming-hot bowl of chili and a mug of coffee, giving our teams an hour break in the process. There was no dog food at Solomon. I debated the wisdom of feeding the last few herring in view of the intestinal distress it was causing. Throwing caution to the wind, I distributed the very last morsels to the dogs that had seemed to have survived the fishy feeding at White Mountain. My three poor, ill pooches didn't seem to mind being shortchanged. Officially, Vent and I departed Solomon at 4:50 p.m., Friday, March 23, during our twenty-first day of travel. While hooking up, Bobby asked me if I wanted to leave first, stating, "If you want to get ahead of me, now's the time to do it." My response was, "Well, it's only twenty-five or so miles to Nome. I figure because of our starting positions in Anchorage, I'd have to gain about half an hour on you. I don't think I can squeeze that much out of this team. Tell you what, you take off, and if I catch you in the next hour, I'll go ahead." Finding that arrangement agreeable, Bobby pulled the hook on what had to be the toughest five dogs in the race, for the last leg of the first race. I waited, certainly not more than fifteen minutes, and took off in pursuit. During the wait, I switched dogs around in the team. I ended up with Sonny in single lead and he would take us on into Nome. An hour's travel brought Vent into focus, but not within passing range. The run to Nome, by the way, turned out to be closer to thirty-two miles, than twenty-five, as we had guessed.

From Solomon, we ("we" meaning Bobby and me plus our dogs) stayed on the coastal spit and followed the old rail and telephone line for some twelve miles, along which a few ancient-appearing mileposts remained. There was a break in the spit where, in bygone days, a ferry operated to Port Safety (Safety) , about four miles distant. There we elected to drop onto the sea ice, where we mostly stayed until reaching Nome. As we neared Cape Nome, the snow seemed to turn to sand again, dragging us down to a maddening crawl over the next three-mile stretch. By the time we hit good snow again, darkness had overtaken us.

Modern Iditaroders are routed over Cape Nome, located fifteen miles east of Nome. There are two reasons why they do not round the cape as earlier racers had done. First, it often happens, as it did before the first race, autumn storms push mountainous amounts of jumbled ice up against the cape, rendering travel around it difficult, if not impossible. Second, in modern times, the cape is slowly disappearing as huge portions of it are being barged off to perform rip-rap duty at locations all over Northwest Alaska. Gale-force winds of winter scour the quarried section nearest the sea, completely bare of snow. Not the best trail for dog team travel. So the long haul over Cape Nome has become standard in recent years.

42

OK, Guys, One Last Time

Near Solomon I prepared to move Sonny (left swing) to lead position, relieving Kiana for our final run to Nome. (Photo: George Sabo)

It was a strange visual sensation. I peered ahead through lightly blowing snow into the black of night. I could make out only an outline of Bobby's incredible team. Strange indeed. His dog team appeared to be climbing an almost straight-up hill, and in another instant—poof, it vanished. After a few more yards travel, it started to sink in. Our trail had begun to traverse house-sized chunks of sea ice deposited against the shore by an earlier Norton Sound storm. Checkers back at Solomon had alerted us to that formidable trail impediment, and estimated rough going for "about a mile." Vent didn't stop, but somehow plowed through the mess unaided by even a flashlight. I stopped to retrieve my parka, which was attempting an escape from under the rope used to secure my sled tarp. That was when I first became aware of it.

"There! Ahead and a bit to my right. Could it be? Yes, it had to be, for there, on the landward side of the frozen Bering Sea, loomed Cape Nome." Even the almost total darkness of that Arctic night could not hide such a massive headland. "Whoa!" My tired team, of eleven huskies, that had been in harness since early morning—sixteen hours by then—gladly obliged. That distant glow in the night sky had to be Nome. Nome, Alaska, end of a punishing twelve-hundred-mile sled dog trail, now just twelve miles distant. I had been traveling by dog team for over twenty days in the first-ever Iditarod Trail Sled Dog Race. What a beautiful sight!

Oh, the thoughts that whirled through my fatigued, confused mind. Thought flashes, I suppose. Like watching a slideshow being flashed on a wall: A fierce blizzard, caribou, vandalized sled, native villages, lost and near starvation, a trailside turkey dinner, buffalo chase, knee-deep water, minus forty degrees F campouts, Anchorage race start, my family, our Seward homestead, Good Friday Earthquake, move to Alaska, and how it all had its beginnings in a little country school, so far away in time and distance.

The spell was brief. Reality took over. I had twelve miles to go. The finish line was just two hours away and I was a front-runner in the First Great Race. No time to tarry. Those lights beckoned. "Ok, guys, one last time. Let's go!"

My family and I were not home from Nome more than two weeks when who showed up with his tape recorder but the Gentle Bully—Doug Capra. Capra thought it most imperative that I relive the last dozen miles or so of the race while events surrounding them hadn't escaped me. Since our narrative thus far has delivered us within sight of Nome, it seems a good spot to insert pertinent parts of that interview, conducted forty years ago.

From Files: Last Twelve Miles (From a transcribed and edited audio tape dated April 11, 1973).
Interview conducted by Doug Capra with author.

C: Dan, you mentioned to me that as you traveled those last few miles into Nome, you did a good bit of reflection on the race itself and what it had come to mean to you. You mentioned that this contemplation began with an actual stop you made about twelve miles from town. Is this right?

S: Yes. That's my estimate. I stopped for a few minutes just after rounding Cape Nome at about 10:00 p.m., when the lights of Nome first came into sight. The reason I remember stopping was that we had passed through a real rough section of trail, where house-sized pieces of ice had been stacked against the lower bluff of the cape by an earlier storm. With all the slamming and banging going on, I was about to lose my parka, tucked under a cord used to secure my sled pack. I braked the team to a halt in order to regain control of my wayward garment, and there it was—Nome! All the lights of New York City could not have shined a brighter welcome than did those of Nome that evening.

C: Now, think back and describe as much detail as you can about those lights.

S: There is an airport in Nome, and the very first light I zeroed in on was the airport beacon, making its rounds in the sky over Nome. Also, several communications towers located on the cape side outskirts of town had flashing red lights atop them. Individual lights in town were too distant to be distinct. Even headlights of moving cars were not distinguishable. The overall impression was that of a large spot of illumination up ahead. Really, like a big city, since it had been a while since seeing so many lights.

C: Your parka was lying on top of your pack; does that mean the weather wasn't cold the night you finished?

S: When we arrived in town, there was a slight east wind—five to ten miles per hour, I judged. Someone noted the temperature to be minus two degrees F. Even though I hadn't diminished my physical activity a great deal as I neared Nome—pedaling, running up small hills—I could feel the air cooling. There was light snow or maybe frost in the air.

C: Describe the last twelve miles of trail, its condition, location, terrain.

S: It was a pitch-dark night, except for the residual illumination from town lights and occasional use of my trusty C-cell. I do not believe Bobby—ahead of me somewhere—had a useable flashlight. I do not remember seeing it. One could not tell where the trail was unless you looked directly down by your feet, where Bobby's runner marks could be seen. We were informed in Solomon that after rounding the cape, we would be on sea ice nearly to Nome. Four miles out, at Fort Davis, we would leave the ice and be on a road to town. I don't know if I was getting rummy or what, but even though the trail was smooth, it seemed I was climbing a slight grade most of the way in. Traveling on the ice below the shore berm probably accounts for that strange, unreal sensation. Near the cape, there was a long stretch of pushed-up jumbled ice to go through.

C: How far ahead could you see the ground?

S: That's not the way it is. All I could see were outlines of dogs, forms of dogs, not the trail under or ahead of them. The few times I did overtake Bobby, I could see his form, probably fifty feet ahead at the most.

C: Was it clear, stars out?

S: At Solomon it was definitely clear; however, as we neared Nome, there developed what is called ice fog, I believe, or maybe light snow. What I assume happens here is that during the day, a certain amount of evaporation occurs. The air being relatively cold and heavy, this moisture isn't lifted very high in the atmosphere. Then, as the sun goes down, the air cools further, moisture turns to crystals, resulting in what feels like light snow against you face. Of course, visibility is greatly reduced when this occurs.

C: Now for some physical details, how you felt as you were covering those final twelve miles.

S: Well, I was still pedaling for sure. That's one foot on a sled runner while the other pushes off the ground in rhythmic fashion in an effort to assist the team. After the fashion of a child propelling his scooter down a pathway. Long before Nome, this action had become a reflex, automatic, involuntary. I pedaled throughout the entire trip. At times to aid the dogs or to keep warm. At others, out of sheer boredom. I remember thinking that I should take a break from my incessant pedaling; it is pretty good going. The dogs can handle the job without my help. So I would stand with both feet on the runners. But wouldn't you know it? Without a conscious thought, pretty soon, there I would be, pedaling away. All that is to say, my legs were in super good shape.

C: They didn't feel tired, even during those last few miles?

S: No. And keep in mind we were ending an eighteen eighteen-hour mush. Twelve miles from the goal, it would have been a good fifteen hours of actual work—standing, pedaling, running, up hills.

C: And overall, you were warm?

S: Yes, generally speaking. Certainly by this point in the venture, I had learned to use my parka wisely. The simple rule here, when you are out in cold weather, especially for days on end, is—no sweat. Hard work up ahead? Off comes the parka. Reduced activity? Back on it goes. Thus avoiding, as much as possible, chilling dampness. My blue wool watch cap proved inadequate in preventing frost-nipped earlobes. How I longed for a cap such as Bobby wore, magnificently made of martin skin, a masterpiece.

C: Were you preconceiving what it would be like coming in to Nome?

S: It may not make sense, but I remember thinking that it really couldn't be over. Wanting it over, but somehow, hoping it wouldn't end. Ridiculous, I suppose, not to want off the treadmill. Fatigue-induced thoughts, no doubt. After coming all that way, only to be overcome by a great reluctance to bring things to an end. But that doesn't answer your question about anticipating what it would be like upon arrival. In truth, I envisaged a very short dash up the main street, wherever that may be—a dash of a block or so. There would, in my imagination, be a few people to greet me—a handful, so to speak. A modest level of excitement. I was quite spent and wasn't looking forward to entering the town as a conquering general.

C: Was there a crowd to greet you?

S: Yes. A much larger crowd than I pictured. Keep in mind, Bobby and I appeared on the scene shortly after midnight, Bering Time.

I hadn't expected many spectators out that time of day, nor to be so excited. It had been twelve hours since the winner had appeared on Front Street, Nome. I thought there wouldn't be much hubbub occasioned by our middle-of-the-night debut, but there was. Race officials, a large, boisterous, cheering throng on hand to welcome Bobby and me to journey's end. Mayor Robert Renshaw even ordered the town fire alarm sounded in way of announcing to the community that we were there.

C: In what pace were you going those last twelve miles? What were your feelings about the dogs?

S: I would guess about six miles per hour. Perhaps a little less, but still a fairly fast trot, which is twice as fast as a man can walk, even at a hurried pace. Throughout this first race, I gained nothing but admiration, not just a deep love for dogs, but an absolute admiration for them. I knew the distance traveled had to be something over one thousand miles. On this particular day, by the time we got to Nome, we'd been on the road eighteen, going on nineteen, hours. Still, I look out there and see those dark forms in silent motion, look down at the runners and see the trail melting behind me, and ask myself, "Why? Why do they do this?" What is it about a dog, or collectively, a dog team, that keeps it going day, after day, after day? This was the twenty-first day that they had been stuffed into harness and told to go. And they go without question. Here they were, pushing nearly twenty-four hours that last day, and they kept going. Many a time, I marveled at what truly remarkable animals they are.

C: You said you were thinking more about dogs those last twelve miles than anything else.

S: Yes, as I mentioned, the thought of what propelled those animals down the trail, day upon day, and that together, we were accomplishing something never attained before. That being one dog team and each individual comprising that team, running over one thousand miles in race mode. What a testimony to an indomitable spirit residing within the very souls of these marvelous creatures. Miraculous creations, in truth. A number of folks along the route honestly never expected racers and teams to show up. For instance, the caretaker at Rainy Pass Lodge said he was not prepared because he thought teams weren't up to the task. Perhaps, the race committee had a similar idea, explaining our four-hour wait at Rainy Pass for dog food. One suspects that same dim view prevailed up along the trail as well as with the general public.

Fifty-nine year old musher, Bobby Vent, up front over that final stretch, provoked no little dog thought. They altered from, "I should pass the guy and gain on him" to "Forget racing. I just want to get to the end." In Anchorage, we had a common race start. That is, regardless of one's starting position, all are considered to have left at the same time, 10:00 a.m. One's overall race time is calculated from 10:00 a.m. to arrival in Nome. Since we left at two-minute intervals, number thirty, let's say, would have to gain an hour-plus on number one in order to arrive at the finish line with less total elapsed time than that first team out of the chute in Anchorage. Truth was, I could not remember Bobby's number, all along believing he had a lower start number than my number fourteen. All I needed to do was to stick to him and I would beat him by a few minutes less elapsed time. All bunk, as it turned out. Bobby was number twenty-seven, which meant he had twenty-six minutes to spare on me. I would have to beat him into Nome by, say, a half hour for second place.

In lead was Sonny. Young, athletic, he had worked his way forward in the team from wheel in Anchorage to lead leaving Solomon. He shared the dubious title of lead dog on an alternating basis with petite, and nearly exhausted, Kiana over the last roughly two hundred miles. Sonny had no command leader training, but seemed adept in staying glued to the trail scent laid down by Vent's and Wilmarth's teams. Good enough for me at that stage of the game. We rode that scent into Nome.

C: So Sonny turned out to be one of the best?

S: He did. Without the training, I had no idea how he would function in town, if I would be able to get him to the finish line. But I was very proud of him—aggressive, forward-oriented to the end. It is no fault of the dog that he wasn't trained. I now see I need to have more trained leaders in a team. At any rate, I was popping vest buttons over that dog in particular and the whole darn team in general. Without doubt, most of those final miles were spent pondering the team's performance. I was pretty pleased, pretty proud of the whole bunch to be perfectly frank.

C: It seems common for one finishing a task, such as you did, to have strange or unusual thoughts pop up. Did you?

S: Yes. This may be taken as strange. There were the lights of Nome drawing closer and closer. In that town, among all those lights, there has to be some, there has to be lots of ice cream. I pictured myself eating a large bowl of ice cream with an oversized spoon. Then, as already pointed out, I had that strange mechanical feeling of being on a pedaling treadmill, wishing for it all to end, but at the same time, being torn by a desire to go on and on. Now that's strange. Right?

C: Your last day on the trail was your twenty-first. Did you have a concept of time?

S: I did not know for sure what day it was. I thought we must be pushing twenty. It seemed a long time since leaving Anchorage. By the twenty-first day, time didn't have much meaning in terms of days of the week, day, night, time of day.

C: Even those last twelve miles seemed long?

S: For sure. Of course, it was dark and I couldn't look back on the cape and say, "Well, it looks like I'm halfway there. That means I have traveled an hour and have about that to go." No watch for me, not since 1958. My time was measured more by going to bed and getting up to the redundant tune played on my little alarm clock.

C: Did you know your family and others from Seward were waiting for you in Nome?

S: From the letter I received at Unalakleet, I was aware that a plan was being hatched to fly to Nome. While out on the trail, frankly, I didn't have time to become too lonesome, being as I was either busy or sleeping. Nearing Nome, I became progressively more eager, more impatient to be there, suspecting my gang would be on hand to greet me at trail's end.

43

Please, Lord, Don't Make Me Pee

Pam Randles at Bear Creek Mine. An incredible lady with an incredible first race story she delightfully shares with us in this work.

My last post-race contact with Pam Randles—the newspaper lady of my tape transcription—was a letter I received from her dated May 5, 1973. On pink stationary in a very neat, definitely feminine, hand, she offered photos she managed to take of my team during our sojourn among the snowdrifts of the Innoko country. And offering, me as well, a taped copy of the "Dan Seavey Song," sung by the Seward contingent at the Nome finishers' banquet. Like other first-race material, that letter, with all its generosity, was marched off for a long nap in my card- board repository of Iditarod Race history.

Sometime in 2009, after an extended self-pep-talk, resulting in a decision to get going on this book, I was able to contact Pam, then living in Southeast Alaska. She had distressing news. Much of her first race materials had been ruined by floodwaters some years back. However, with a return of her old, pink letter generosity, she offered what pictures she had. Would she also be willing to give a written account of her unusual experiences between McGrath and Ruby?

That latter request resulted in an amazing fifteen-page e-mailed mini-history of the first race. Delightfully informative, it comes from a unique perspective—that of the wife of a participating Iditarod musher, Slim Randles, and a deputized Iditarod Race official. But her most unique first-race experiences resulted from being, like all of the mushers, a pioneer. No other woman got as close to the first race as she did. A woman news reporter bumming rides in airplanes and on snowmachines, reduced during our wanderings to cooking a common stew in a dog food bucket for all the Fourteen Mile Creek "strandees." No other woman known to me wanted an Iditarod story so fervently as to consent to bunking in a tent filled with strangers, filled with strange, odiferous men, that is. Pam states of the first Iditarod: "It was the first great adventure of my life." So it was for me as well. But Randles' little adventures that added up to her grand adventure were of a far different nature than mine. Life-threatening hypothermia and fear of an airplane crash were just two such mini-adventures. In Nome, race officials high-tailed it back to Anchorage following the first of several banquets to be held. Race keys were turned over to a still willing Randles. She volunteered to the bitter end. An end marked by John Schultz's arrival under the finish banner after more than thirty-two days on the trail. For Pam, there was no banquet, no purse, no acclaim, no prize. No prize, that is, in the conventional sense. Pam concludes her captivating story by claiming, in fact, she did receive an Iditarod prize. This prize was as unconventional as its recipient, as you will see at the end of her narrative.

My intention was to sprinkle a few Randles paragraphs throughout a portion of this book—enough for flavor. Several rereads, however, drove me to the conclusion that to do so would have cheated both reader and book. So here is Pam's story with minimal editing on my part. Enjoy!

My First Iditarod
By Pamela Randles
Haines, Alaska, 2010

Let's see. Where can I start? It was the first great adventure of my life. I had done other things in my life that could count as adventures, but this one was the first real venture into a complete unknown all by myself.

I was twenty-nine years old and married to a man and a team of sled dogs. When I had married Slim, I had married the team as well. It took a little while, but I became hooked, as dog mushers do. We lived with our dogs in a little log cabin we had crudely built with our own hands, 12.5 miles north of Talkeetna, a little village of 110 souls at that time. We used our dogs to haul firewood, groceries, laundry, and mail in and out of town. I use the word "town" advisedly. Talkeetna was pretty small and rustic at that time.

We hung around with dog mushers in the area, many of whom went on to run that first Iditarod: Ron Aldrich, Tom Mercer, Terry Miller, Dick Mackey, Raymie Redington, and Rod Perry. Living in the Upper Susitna Valley was living in Dog Mushing Central. We were all Bushrats—living in cabins and homes with few amenities but a big dog yard. While dogs were a hole to sink money into, they were also more fun than a barrel of monkeys. There is nothing quite like hooking up a team of dogs who are raring to go. They bark and dance and just can't wait. When you finally pull the hook and they take off at full speed (probably 25 miles an hour), there is a swish of sled runners and the wind in your face. Perhaps six furry behinds running ahead like a house afire. It is wonderful. You charge out into the boreal forest where there are no human sounds; no roads, no TVs, no nothing but you and your dogs and your wits.

On one of our thrice annual town trips, we were shopping at Army-Navy Surplus, and we ran into Dick Mackey. He told us that Joe

Redington was finally going to do it. He was going to have that race he had been talking about for years: a race from Anchorage to Nome by dog team. It seemed an imposibility. There was no trail from Anchorage to Nome. How could you carry enough food? But at the same time, it was a wonderfully exciting prospect. Slim immediately decided he had to run it. Had to. The word that the race was finally going to happen traveled like wildfire through dog mushing circles.

Little by little, the pieces fell into place. There would be a team of snowmachiners to break trail. There would be checkpoints where you could send supplies and dog food. It would start after "Rondy," the first week in March, in downtown Anchorage, and go around Knik Arm to Knik, and then into the wilderness.

Slim and I got busy. There were miles of training to be done; the race was a thousand miles they said, so at least that many miles should be on the dogs before Slim left. There was money to make, as well as dog harnesses and a parka for Slim. There were food and supplies to amass and send out to the checkpoints. What was the best food for the dogs? Had to be high fat. What kind of stove would you use to cook on the trail? How much food was needed? How many dogs would we take? Which ones would be best? Would they use the same race rules as for other races? This kind of race hadn't been done before, and we didn't know what it would be like. Joe Redington Sr. said there would be a $50,000 purse, $50,000! Whoever heard of such a large purse? Most races were run for 50% of the entry fees, if anything.

I felt like I sewed 10,000 dog harnesses. In truth it was only a couple of harnesses per dog, but each harness had eight places where the nylon webbing had to be sewn together. We were living in a tiny cabin in Girdwood, where I had gone to make money while Slim trained the dogs.

As the time for the race got closer and closer, I began to realize that my entire "family" (Slim and the dogs) would be taking off, and I would be left alone with maybe a radio report a day if I was lucky. It made me sad and I told Slim so. He said, "Why don't you cover the race for the *Daily News*?" He wrote for the *Anchorage Daily News*. I told him I wasn't a journalist. He told me I could certainly write, and I should call Stan Abbott to propose that I send him stories in exchange for expenses. I didn't quite have the courage to do that. I had never written a newspaper story in my life.

One evening when we were out for dinner, Slim excused himself for a few minutes. When he returned, he told me there was a phone call for me. It was Stan. Oh, crap. Now what? Stan said he would love to have someone cover the story. He thought the *Daily News* would have an exclusive. No one else was covering it that he knew of…yet. I should just call in daily to the Sports Editor, Ralph Lee, and keep receipts. I hung up the phone in a state of shock. I couldn't figure out if I was more scared or excited. I had absolutely no idea what I was doing.

The Start

The normal procedure for a dog race is to have mushers draw for starting position a couple of days before the race. On race day (usually a Saturday), mushers left at two-minute intervals in the order that they drew. The drawing was attended by old friends in the mushing community, as well as mushers from the more remote part of the state—Huslia, Noorvik, Shismaref, Anvik, Tok, Nome, Delta, Aniak. In this race, it was possible to run two-person teams, and there were three of them. There were big teams and little teams. There were first class teams with color-coordinated harnesses and REI jackets. There were village teams with mukluks and parkas. There were rural teams with Bunny boots and U.S. Army sleeping bags. There were professional racing teams, like World Champion George Attla. There were local race teams like the Redingtons. There were working teams and recreational teams. And there were a few complete unknowns like Dick Wilmarth of Red Devil. (Who the hell is Wilmarth, and where the hell is Red Devil?)

Come race day, the mushers came with their dog trucks or, in our case, a car. With the help of their handlers, they tied out their dogs and got their gear ready. There was a cacophony of dog talk and hundreds of well-wishers. I was handling for Slim. It was mayhem, as only a dog race can be. I was nervous, as were our dogs. I stood by the leaders, A-Bob and Fade. "It's okay guys. Good dogs. Easy now."

One by one the teams took off from Tudor Track, the Alaska Sled Dog Racing Association's track in Anchorage…5…4…3…2…1…

GO! When it was our turn (Slim was musher twenty of thirty-four teams), I ran with A-Bob and Fade to the starting line. The dogs were jumping and lunging and pulling on the lines. They couldn't wait to go. 5…4…3…2…1…GO! Off they went. I looked after them. Take care of yourselves, guys. Don't get hurt. Sigh. Time to jump in the car and drive to the Knik River Bridge to help escort the teams across, then on to Knik to see them off. Then I had to start figuring out how I was going to follow the race and cover it for the *Daily News*. By then I had agreed to call in to two radio stations in Anchorage as well, KYAK and KHAR. The local reporters were covering the start but had no plans to cover anything else just yet. They were unsure it would be completed. And if it did, they would get a report from Nome.

The Knik River Bridge was a two-lane bridge over the wide Knik River. Cars would be competing with dog teams to cross. Several handlers were there on either end of the bridge to direct traffic and teams. There had been some passes already by the time the mushers got to the bridge. They were no longer in starting order. Some had passed several teams. I made notes for my first news stories. Next stop, Knik.

Knik was a small settlement, and the teams departed down a trail across Knik Lake headed for Susitna Station, the checkpoint on the Susitna River.

Next morning, I hopped on a plane for Su Station. I was with an Air Force veterinarian, Terry Adkins. (He got the bug and became a musher. He ran the race many times.) We landed on the river at the Su Station checkpoint, a cabin on the Susitna River. The small cabin was up on top of a steep bank of the Susitna River. As the teams came through, Terry checked them and I made notes. There were some sore feet. Terry gave the mushers something green to put on the dogs' feet. For the rest of the race, there were green splotches in the snow. There were tired dogs. Mushers readjusted their loads and took off for Skwentna. Each checkpoint had a ham radio operator, so I could ask them to help me file my stories. They would contact an Anchorage ham operator, who would then call on a landline to the paper and radio stations. After the first batch of mushers went through Su Station, Terry and I flew on to Skwentna.

Skwentna

The Skwentna checkpoint was at Joe Delia's house on the banks of the Skwentna River across from the airstrip. Dogs and mushers were arriving by the dozen. There were teams all over the snow-covered landscape. Teams were parked and mushers were cooking food for the dogs and checking gear. The snowmachine trail-breaking team had passed through, staying a day ahead of the mushers. There were airplanes around as well. Planes were flying race support as well as just coming to see what was happening. They carried the Race Marshall, Dick Tozier, and his friend, Race Commentator, Orville Lake. They carried judges and veterinarians and radio operators. They were bringing in the supplies the mushers had sent along for the checkpoints—food and gear. All mushers were required to carry minimum gear—axe, snowshoes, two days' food for the dogs…but the rest of the dog food and replacement gear was shipped on to each of the eighteen or so checkpoints.

I filed my stories with the help of the ham operator. He would radio someone in Anchorage who would call the *Daily News* on a landline. In like manner, I would call the radio stations and file stories. The reporters on the other end would write up the stories and put them in the paper or air them on the radio. It was complicated, but it worked.

Everyone knew I was covering the race for the News. There is a dog mushing community, and everyone knows everyone, or everyone knows *of* everyone else. Slim, as a journalist, was well known among the mushers. He had made a couple of highly publicized runs with our dogs. One was a publicity event to encourage people to get dogs from the pound. He took a bunch of "Pound Bummers" on a trip south from the North Slope. He ran into heavy weather near the Sagavanirktok River and had to abort.

One musher had arrived in Skwentna with a sick dog, and the dog had died. There was great concern over that. Joe Sr. told me not to tell the News or the radio station. It would look bad. Some others agreed with him. This was always an issue with dog mushing, because there are people who think it is a cruel sport. Those people should try it, or at least watch a race. The dogs love to run. One of the best ways (if not THE best way) to correct a dog for bad behavior, like chewing or picking fights, is to leave that dog home. They really want to go, so leaving them behind is a strong punishment. When you wave a harness in front of the dogs, they get really excited and can't wait to go. In fact, the toughest time running the dogs is the first few miles—they go like bats out of Hell. You really have to hang on tight!

The critics will point out that there are mushers who are harsh to their dogs. As with any sport, there are those who do bad things. But, as with any other sport, those few do not represent the many who love their animals and treat them well. Fact is, you can't run a thousand-mile race if you don't treat your dogs well. It is an endurance contest more than it is a race. You have to feed them and care for them extremely well, or they won't get you there. Most Iditarod dogs are cared for better than most house pets. They are fed carefully formulated diets and exercise regularly. They have all their shots and all their veterinary needs are met.

There were nearly 400 dogs in that race. Odds are that if you took any 400 dogs over the period of a month, at least one would get sick or die.

So, what to do about the dead dog. This was 1973, the year Richard Nixon resigned in a storm of controversy. A big part of that controversy was his efforts to cover-up his misdeeds and the misdeeds of his cohorts. Cover-up was a nasty word. I felt that it is better to report the loss of the dog along with the autopsy results so the public would know the truth, and they would know that there were no cover-ups. The autopsy on this particular dog showed that it had died of intestinal intussusception, a problem that can happen to any dog, any time and is not a function of mistreatment on a race. That is how I reported it, and there was no fuss.

I kept a lookout as mushers came into Skwentna. I was watching for the front-runners, for my friends, and of course, for my husband. He came in towards the back of the pack. I was glad to see him and our dogs. The dogs were part of the family. I was as worried about them as him. Joe Delia gave Slim and me a place to sleep at his house. That was the last time we were together for the next six weeks.

In the morning, I watched as the mushers took off one by one. They were headed up into the Alaska Range to Finger Lake and Ptarmigan Pass. I felt I should stay with the front-runners so I could report on who was ahead, so I started looking for a ride to the next checkpoint. I was completely on my own for rides. I was essentially hitchhiking from checkpoint to checkpoint. There were no roads between these small communities. There were no jet airplanes, just small planes—Super Cubs, Cessna 185s, and the like. The first plane that landed at the airstrip turned out to be a new pilot who was soloing and couldn't take me anywhere. The next one was going the wrong direction. The race planes had all taken off at first light and were long gone. I spent hours standing on the snowy airstrip.

But then I got the news via the ham operator that my husband had been injured and had been flown to Anchorage. The sleds for this race were heavily loaded for cross-country travel, and they weighed quite a bit. It seems that somewhere near Finger Lake, our sled had run over his foot and damaged it. He had been sent to Providence Hospital. I don't even remember how I caught a flight in, but I did. I was really worried and rushed to the hospital. Slim was in the emergency room. The first thing he said to me was, "What are you doing here? You have a race to cover." He assured me that he was all right. He hadn't broken anything, but had gotten contusions on his foot. He couldn't continue the race, but he certainly made it clear to me that I had to.

All the planes following the race were now way out of range for me to hitch a ride, so I called my editor and asked if he would pay for a plane ticket to McGrath, the nearest large airport to where the race was heading. As I recall, it cost $85, which seemed like a princely sum to me, but the News paid the tab.

McGrath

The McGrath airstrip runs along the Kuskokwim River and next to "downtown" McGrath, a town of about 600 souls. After I picked up my duffle bag, I asked where headquarters was and was pointed to McGuire's Tavern, a typical bush Alaska bar—lots of Bunny boots and flannel shirts and fur hats…and beer and laughter. I spoke with the checkpoint folks and managed to find housing with the town nurse. I dropped my bag there and called in my story. I asked Ralph if he wanted me to stay with the front-runners, or to hang around McGrath for a day or so and interview some of the other participants, get some color and background. He said to stay for a bit, then catch up in Ruby.

The trail out of McGrath led north through Takotna to Bear Creek, then Ruby on the Yukon River. There would be a long stretch of no communication. Bear Creek, the next checkpoint, was Tex Gates' cabin at his old gold mine in the middle of nowhere. After that was the Athabascan village of Ruby. Joe Sr. estimated the distance from McGrath to Ruby to be 88 miles. The idea was that mushers could go to Bear Creek on the first day out of McGrath, then on to Ruby the second day. No problem.

I got something to eat at the Roadhouse and returned to the nurse's house. She wasn't there, so I couldn't get in. McGrath was celebrating the arrival of the mushers in grand style. So everyone in town was whooping it up. The nurse had gone to one of the two bars, McGuire's or the Roadhouse, like everyone else. So I went looking for her and looking for some of the fun. This was pretty exciting stuff! First time it had ever been done. And it was happening, really happening. The mushers had made it through the Alaska Range, the part I figured would be the toughest country. They had also made it through the white man settlements. The next stretch, from McGrath to Kaltag, was Athabascan country. From Unalakleet on, it was Eskimo country. I felt quite competent in white man country, but way out of my league among Alaska Natives. I knew a lot about taking care of myself in the wilds of Alaska, but I didn't think I knew anything next to Alaska Natives. I was thrilled at the opportunity to test myself and my outdoor skills.

McGuire's and the Roadhouse were hopping! Music was playing and people were dancing, drinking, and talking. They were starting to place their bets on who would win the race. Who had the best dogs? Who was the most experienced? George Attla of Huslia, eight-time winner of the Fur Rendezvous, was one of the favored, as was musher Isaac Okleasik. But there were so many mushers who came out of the Bush, people who probably knew better how to run this kind of race than the sprint mushers. Ken Chase's father had delivered mail by dog team. Bobby Vent of Huslia was an experienced musher from a village known for its mushers. Johnny Coffin looked good. My friends, Ron Aldrich, Tom Mercer, and Terry Miller, had all run good races near my hometown of Talkeetna.

In many ways, it was anybody's race. Since it was the first of its kind, no one really knew who had the skills that would be needed. There was a lot of talk about how this was really a camping trip, not a race. It was an endurance race, not a sprint race. Some of these guys who had village teams and trapline teams probably knew a great deal about running out in the tule bushes, but how were they at competitive racing? The townies may have the corner on racing strategies, but did they know how to run a long race with heavy sleds and camping out?

So far, they had shown themselves to have fast teams, but it was long race. You had to pace yourself. At the same time, you didn't want to lose sight of the lead teams and not be able to catch up. All the mushers were watching each other to see who would do what. For example, at Rohn River, Ron Aldrich had breezed through and camped a mile out of the checkpoint. His strategy was to psych out Dick Mackey and others and cause them to take off before fully resting their teams.

They had to be careful of hazards as well. Nobody knew the whole trail. Nobody knew where all the tricky spots were. Where were the steep switchbacks? Where was the overflow? Not to mention moose. The trail at Happy River had been treacherous. In Ptarmigan Pass, Terry Miller's team had been following the river when they found an open hole in the ice. The overflow water had been swirling down into the hole like water down a drain. Some of his dogs had fallen in. He had grabbed his axe and sunk it into the ice to hold the team from being washed in. He held on until someone came to help him and his team out. That was a close call. Too close.

The Eskimo teams were used to more open spaces, and the forest made them nervous. They didn't know if they could trust the Athabascan Indian mushers. Historically, there had been conflicts. So they camped out on lakes and in open spaces. The Indian mushers didn't understand why the Eskimo mushers camped out in the open instead of in the shelter of the trees. But later, they were the ones in uncharted territory, on the coast.

But in McGrath, it was time to celebrate. They had made it through the mountains. Nine mushers had scratched, leaving 23 teams in the race. McGrath was a town with stores and restaurants and bars. They had been on the trail five days and were ready for a little "civilization." They were able to stay in people's homes, instead of camping out. They had been running hard and felt they could take a rest here…for a little while…carefully watching all the other mushers.

I decided I could relax and enjoy myself. I didn't have to go anywhere tomorrow, so I could drink and dance and enjoy the festive atmosphere. I started at McGuire's and moved on to the Roadhouse. Great fun! At about two in the morning, I met up with the snowmachine trail-breaking team. There were five of them from Knik and Wasilla, and they were going the entire way to Nome. I told them I was reporting for the *Daily News*, KYAK, and KHAR. They asked me if I wanted to ride with them to Ruby. I thought about that for two and a half seconds. My Lois Lane instincts screamed at me to go and get a firsthand look at the race on the trail. They said they had to leave ahead of the first musher, so as not to give that musher the advantage of a freshly broken trail and chasing. Dogs will chase a snowmachine, so if the first musher is too close to the machine, that team has an unfair advantage. George Attla had told the snowmachiners that he was going to leave about 6 a.m., so they had to leave no later than 4 a.m. Yikes!

88 Miles, My Foot!

We took off from the airstrip, five snowmachines. I was riding double with Joe Smith on his little machine. I didn't really want to ride double because I thought I would get cold, but I wasn't going to argue with these guys. After all, they were taking on an extra person, and I was not going to be a complainer. Especially, I was not going to be a complaining woman. It is a burden to have any extra person along. One more responsibility; one more mouth to feed; one more potential problem.

I didn't have much experience with snowmachines, just dogs. So I sat there behind Joe. We got to Takotna and stopped at the military cafeteria for coffee and orange juice. Then off we went. There had been a trail to Takotna. There was quite a bit of traffic on the 23 miles between there and McGrath, but once we left Takotna, the trail all but disappeared. The snow was deep. If I stepped off the trail, I sank up to my waist. The only trail was the one we were making. The snow was soft and sprayed up along my legs as the machine floundered along. Joe's machine was smaller than the others, so he struggled a bit more. Pretty soon, I began to notice the snow was soaking my snow pants. I was getting wet. Not good. But don't complain. Just get up and move when we stop so you warm up. And we were stopping often as the machines floundered around in the snow and got stuck. There is nothing anyone can do anyway. It's not like there is a hotel anywhere nearby, or even a cabin.

When we stopped to heft a machine out of the snow, the men wouldn't let me help. It is that gender thing again. "No, no. That's fine. We can do it. You just relax." I was worried about getting chilled or worse, but I refused to complain (which was not only stupid, but dangerous). I just sat there. As we went on, my fingers and toes got cold and then they hurt. My face was cold and hurt. I shivered. Then I stopped shivering. I felt sleepy. Towards afternoon, we stopped once again to dig out the machines. Joe noticed that I was holding my arms to my chest and rocking back and forth. He had worked on the Slope and had training in recognizing the signs of hypothermia. This was it. He told me to get up and walk. It was hard to do. I stumbled and it hurt to walk. It hurt enough to make me cry. They decided to find a place to camp and get me warmed up.

We found a cabin out there in the middle of nowhere. Seems to me the name on it was Aho. You could see daylight through some of the logs where the chinking had been lost. It had a barrel stove. It was an old one with places where it had rusted through. They got me inside and built a fire. They got the fire roaring. You could see it through the sides of the stove. I stepped behind a blanket by the side of the stove to change out of my wet clothes, into dry ones. They put buckets of snow on the fire and threw tins of food in to thaw. They had been given cases of military K rations. I had some dried fruit and some other snacks.

I was starting to warm up. Coming out of hypothermia like that hurts. As you get circulation back into your limbs, they cry out in pain. I began to shake powerfully. They handed me a cup of coffee, but I was shaking so badly, I could hardly get it to my lips. It was a struggle to get the wonderful, hot liquid down, but I did. I slopped some of it on my clothes as well, because I was shaking so violently. In my foggy brain, I thought, "Don't do that! You must not get wet in wintertime. It is dangerous." No kidding! I had learned that this day. Then they offered me a can of peaches that had been heating in the hot water on the stove. I have never tasted anything so wonderful in my entire life! Those peaches were nectar from the gods. I swear they saved me. The shaking diminished, and I began to relax. The pain abated. I was tired but felt fairly comfortable for the first time in many hours.

We all rolled out our sleeping bags in a row on the theory that if we all slept close together, we could keep each other warm. I was somewhere in the middle. If felt so good to get inside the sleeping bag and be warm. Sometime in the middle of the night, I awoke to find an arm around me. I said something like, "Get your arm off of me!" He did. That was that.

Next morning I chose to ride on the back of the sled that was being towed by Don Rosevear on his big, double-track Ski Doo. I knew how to ride a sled. I was comfortable there. I was moving and staying warm. No snow wetting my snow pants. Much better. We started for Bear Creek in the morning. There were pieces of trail to follow. We were now a day behind schedule. According to Joe Sr.'s estimations, we should have gotten to Bear Creek last night and Ruby today. But we hadn't gotten to Bear Creek yet. Hopefully, we would find Bear Creek today and our supplies would be there. We hadn't seen any mushers since leaving McGrath. Partway through the day, Joe's snowmachine blew a clutch. We had to leave it. We were down to four machines for six people, plus a sled full of gear.

We arrived in Bear Creek before dark. Tex Gates greeted us and showed us to a cabin that the race participants could stay in. It had a couple of cots and a woodstove. It was pretty comfortable. But none of the supplies for the mushers had arrived. We were okay, but they might be in trouble. A fire was built and food prepared. We settled in. As the evening progressed, mushers began to trickle in. People were drying out boots and gloves, checking out dogs and gear. People rolled out sleeping bags on the cots and the floor. There began to be wall to wall people. It got late and we went to sleep. Lights out. Sometime in the middle of the night, Dick Wilmarth arrived. His boots were wet, so he took out the liners and set them on the oven door of the woodstove. Then he fell asleep. When felt boot liners start to burn, they really stink. Imagine half inch thick wool felt from boots. He awoke and let off a stream of obscenities to run the air blue.

Some one said, "Hey! Keep it down. There is a woman in here."

Wilmarth didn't believe him, saying something like, "Right. Sure there is."

I said, "Yes, there is a woman here." Chuckles followed and the language cleaned up. There can be benefits to being a woman, as well as drawbacks.

In the morning, there was discussion about what to do. Since there were no supplies, notably no dog food, it was decided that we needed to plan some relief. Wilmarth went to Tex Gates' cabin and got on the radio. He was hoping to be heard by his friends, the Vanderpools in Red Devil or Georgetown. They had an air service and could potentially bring people food and dog food. He couldn't raise anyone, so he just radioed in the blind, hoping that they would hear, or someone else would hear who could relay the message. He explained that there were five teams and the snowmachiners at Bear Creek with no supplies.

We took off, headed for Ruby again. The new snowmachine team led. There was supposed to be a marked trail, but there was no trail. We were just heading north. Someone had said to look for the twin mountains on the northern horizon. As far as I could see, there was an endless row of mountain peaks. I couldn't see any twin peaks. We were struggling to find a way through deep snow. It was tough going. At one point, Rosevear rode over a log under the snow, and the sled caught on it. My husband told me what a New York Spin was to a rodeo cowboy. But now I found out for myself. I literally went head over heels, over the handlebar of the sled, and landed sitting on the tongue between the sled and the snowmachine. Rosevear's machine had a double track with a single ski in front. It was a vulnerable part of the sled. He had repeated problems with that ski.

Somewhere midday, I began to think, "Please Lord, don't make me pee." The snow was so deep, it would be difficult for a person of the female persuasion to find a place to relieve herself without making a public spectacle of herself or sitting in the snow, which sounded unpleasant. And then it occurred to me that I had a bigger problem. It was coming up on that time of the month, and I was not prepared. Please, God, make me late. At least until after Ruby, where I can get supplies.

We slogged through the snow all that day, not really knowing where we were going. Hoping we were headed the right direction. That night, we pitched a tent on the crest of a small hill. I had never slept in a tent in winter. Stalactites formed in the tent from our breath.

When we woke in the morning, George Attla had caught up with us. Several other mushers also caught up. Dan Seavey, Bobby Vent, Johnny Coffin, and Dick Wilmarth had joined us. They all got together and made a plan. We were near the North Fork of the Innoko River. We, the snow-machine team, would try to locate the trail. Vent and Coffin would work on an airstrip in case the Vanderpool plane came, and the others would go look for a moose for food. We were now three days out on what was supposed to be a two-day trip. We were at the North Fork of the Innoko River, which was quite a distance from Ruby. There had been no food at Bear Creek. We had ten people and 55 dogs and no food. Not good.

The going was extremely difficult. There was no trail, it was cold, and there were deep drifts. We made little progress. We would go a few dozen feet forward, and then some machine would get stuck. I was on the biggest machine with the sled, so we were at the rear. Repeatedly, we had to stop and help each other get unstuck.

George Attla caught up with us. He put on his snowshoes and got out in front to break trail. He was very skilled on those snowshoes. He had simple bindings that were just a loop. He could slip the shoes on and off just by twisting his foot. George had had TB as a child, and he had one stiff leg, but he could move on those snowshoes. He was impressive. His dogs just trotted along behind, followed by the snowmachines. Attla broke trail for everyone for most of that day. It was slow going. We were getting nowhere fast. Vent, Coffin, Wilmarth, and Seavey had joined us. We were slowly snaking through the hills, crossing lakes and streams, heading north. We were all keeping one eye on the sky, just in case…

I had Army mukluks. They had a canvas top and cowhide soles. They were warm enough, but not as well made as the Native skin boots. They were wearing out, coming apart. My feet were warm enough, but the soles were coming away from the uppers. Bobby Vent took pity on me and gave me a pair of his calfskin boots. They were wonderful. I still have them, 36 years later. I wore holes in the moose hide soles years ago, but kept them as a souvenir. They fit perfectly and kept my feet warm.

Toward afternoon, we heard a plane. It was Vanderpool! He air-dropped us his emergency food and a sack of dog food from his plane. We set up camp. George Attla built a long fire in the snow. Someone gave me a bucket; one of those old five-gallon coffee cans with a wire bail. It had been used for dog food, so it was a bit greasy. They also gave me all the freeze-dried packets from the Vanderpools airdrop. I mixed them all together—Chili Mac + green beans + scrambled eggs. Not exactly what you would choose, but beggars can't be choosers, can they? The men got firewood and cut spruce boughs for beds for us. They made two big piles of boughs for sleeping. The order would be the elders in the middle and youngsters on the sides. Made sense to me. They cobbled together whatever they could find to cook up some dog food.

My fingers got so numb I grabbed the bail of the bucket to check the food and didn't feel the heat. My flesh burned and I smelled it. I finally flinched, but had a nasty burn on my finger. It was cold. It was bitterly cold. Seavey asked if we wanted him to check his thermometer for the temperature. We all said no. Attla had a tea bag. I had a Sierra Club cup. We made some tea and passed it around, each person taking a sip. Attla said he had a little piece of sheefish left from his dog food that we could share. We sat around the fire, trying to stay warm and cheerful, trying to conserve what resources we had, trying to keep our spirits up. We did pretty well. After sharing our meal, caring for the dogs, gathering firewood, and making sleeping platforms of spruce boughs, we all crawled in our sleeping bags. I wore everything I owned. I even wore the boots Bobby Vent had given me. It was bitterly cold, but I was able to sleep.

In the morning, there was still some fire. It had sunk into the snow, but it was still going, and it gave warmth. We were all getting up and gathering around the fire to warm up before taking off. Seavey announced that it was 36 below. Too much information. I really didn't want to know that. I was happily ignorant of how cold it was. Of course, it WAS that cold, and knowing it didn't change anything. We packed up and took off.

Again, it was slow going. Vanderpool flew back to us and waggled his wings, indicating the direction we should be going. We knew there was a road, the Long-Poorman Road, that connected Ruby to some mines in Poorman 75 miles to the south. We were hoping to find that road. Somewhere in the middle of the day, Rosevear's snowmachine finally gave up. He had to leave it right where it was. We were down to three machines for six people and a big sled. I felt like a real liability. I was coming along to report the story. I was out there out of the kindness of the snowmachiners. But I was stuck now. I couldn't just bail out at this point. We wound on between open country and forested areas. We could see the mountains on the northern horizon intermittently. Those mountains were at the Yukon River, and that is where Ruby was. Somewhere up there.

We began to realize we were coming to a settlement. There were signs of a road, some buildings. No people, but something. We had been out for five days and four nights. No way was this 88 miles! Even with the slow going, dogs aren't that slow. We discussed it and, based on what the snowmachine team knew about their machines and the mushers about their travel time, estimated the distance to be about 256 miles. I think that is pretty close to the reality. The official race distance is now given as 241. Interestingly, the mileages from checkpoint to checkpoint vary from year to year, depending on conditions. Before there was an established trail, they varied even more. Trailbreakers have to deal with local river and lake conditions, as well as snowfall for that year. In the early years, when possible, the trail followed local village trails or trapline trails. Over time, a race trail has developed, but is still subject to local weather and geography.

Ruby

As we pulled into Poorman, we saw Vanderpool's Piper Club parked. He was going to Ruby and I asked if I could go with him. I felt like a burden to the racers and the snowmachiners. I could stop being that now. I climbed into the plane. Bobby Vanderpool was the pilot, and I sat next to him with the instrument panel in front of me. I noticed that only one gas tank had gas in it. The other was empty. Well, hopefully. there was enough fuel to get to Ruby. We took off, following the Long-Poorman Road north. We hadn't been in the air long when the plane lurched and fell. Oh, my God, we're out of fuel! I must have turned white as a sheet. Vanderpool smiled as he switched tanks and explained that one of his fuel gauges didn't work.

He flew to Ruby and landed on the Yukon River in front of the village. I had absolutely no idea what I was going to do in Ruby or where I was going to go. But I didn't care. I think I was pretty far gone in some ways.

As I walked up the riverbank, I noticed a girl, about 10 years of age, at the top. She beckoned me to follow her. I did. She went to a house, and I was welcomed in and offered a seat. The woman of the house offered me a glass of water from a half-gallon pitcher. I drank glass after glass. I had no idea I was so thirsty! They showed me to the room I was to use. They acted like I was expected, so I assumed they took me for someone else. I asked. They said, "You are the reporter who has been traveling with the mushers." Mukluk Telegram. News travels fast and far in rural Alaska. They asked me about their Uncle Bobby. I told them he was doing well. He knew what he was doing. He was fine. I was at the home of Florence and Harold Esmailka. They were kind to me and took me in. I am eternally grateful.

I asked if there was any way I could call the *Daily News* and the radio stations and file a story. They hadn't heard from anyone in five days. First, I talked with Ralph Lee at the *Daily News*. The last he had heard, I would call him from McGrath five days ago. But I never called. I related the tale of the five days of travel, the lack of trail and food, the 36 below. It was quite a tale. Then I called KYAK. Whoever was on the air asked me to wait a minute, and I heard him say on the air, "We have Pam Randles calling from Ruby to report on the Iditarod Sled Dog Race. She doesn't know she will be live on the air." Oh, my god, he's going to put me on the air live! I can't do this! I have never been a radio person. I have not had any training! But not much I could do about it now! He interviewed me on the air, and it went just fine. But my husband happened to be listening on the car radio. He hadn't known where I was for the last five days. He later said he had nearly driven off the road when he heard the story.

The next day, I hitched a ride to Galena on a small plane.

Galena to Kaltag

The village of Galena is situated between the airstrip and the Yukon River. When I got off the plane, I asked where the checkpoint was. They told me it was at Hobo's, a local watering hole. I went there, and they directed me to Sidney Huntington's house. Race Marshall Dick Tozier and Orville Lake were there. I was offered a seat by Angela Huntington, who then asked if I wanted a cup of coffee. I said yes, and she pointed to the coffee pot.

The Huntingtons were gracious hosts, especially considering they were being inundated by all sorts of people. One was Mel Carter, an Anchorage television journalist. Well, I wasn't the only reporter anymore! Angela sent Mel and me to get water. That involved putting a large trash can (used for water, not trash) in the back of a pickup truck and going to fill it. Mel drove and got stuck in a ditch temporarily. Getting that much water back into the house was a bit of a challenge. That can was heavy!

Mel asked me if I could identify all the mushers. Yep, sure can. He had arranged for a plane to fly him for the rest of the race, and offered me a seat if I would do the aerial identification. Deal. So I rode in that plane until we got to Nome.

The going on the river was much faster for the mushers. Compared to what we had all just left, it was a superhighway. So now the camping trip was over, and it was a race! George Attla arrived first into Galena, but his dogs were tired, and there were rumors he might scratch. That put Wilmarth, Coffin, Vent, and Seavey in the lead. Attla decided to lay over in Galena for a day, but continue on after that.

The race went from Galena to Nulato, Koyukuk and Kaltag. At this point, it cut through a pass to Unalakleet on the coast. Raymie Redington had scratched in Galena, so that left 22 teams, and 22 teams would finish.

Unalakleet to Nome

I was traveling in luxury at this point. I actually knew where my next ride was coming from. We stopped at Unalakleet, Shaktoolik, Golovin, Elim, and White Mountain. The race was on. The stretch between Shaktoolik and Golovin looked scary to me. It was across sea ice with sticks and branches stuck in the ice to mark the trail. But the wind howled at times, and the visibility was poor to nonexistent. I was glad I was in the air, and my heart went out to the mushers.

We (Mel, the pilot, and I) arrived in Nome ahead of the mushers and I was offered a place to stay with some folks affiliated with the radio station KICY. It's odd what sticks in your mind sometimes. I remember they were very nice people, and I remember that they served chocolate chip muffins for breakfast. I must have been a pretty odd sight. I had been wearing the same clothes for the whole race. I only had two changes, so I had to wear one when I washed the other. And there weren't many Laundromats on the trail! My clothes were actually beginning to wear out.

Nome

A little ways out of Nome, the Nome Race Committee had set up a siren to go off when a musher was sighted. That was the signal to run down to Front Street. And the first time it went off, it seemed like the whole town and all its visitors crowded near the finish line. There were two radio stations in Nome at the time, KICY and KNOM. They had their people ready to go, and I was with them to talk about the race, identify mushers, and interview them as they came across the finish line. What an exciting time that was!

The first musher was spotted down at the end of Front Street. It was Dick Wilmarth. His team was trotting well. He looked relaxed. It felt like time slowed down. We were all excited and wanted his lead dog to cross the finish line. There is a law in Nome; lead dogs are supposed to wear bells in town. So on his way up Front Street, Wilmarth saw a lady run out and hang bells on his leader.

It seemed to take a long time for his team to get to the finish line, and when he did, the crowd exploded. He was surrounded by excited fans, and microphones were stuck in his face. But I remember the first thing he did was talk to his lead dogs. Then he allowed himself to be interviewed. He had taken 20 days, 49 minutes to get to Nome, a distance estimated to be 1,064 miles that year.

About ten hours later, Bobby Vent arrived, followed by Dan Seavey. George Attla took fourth place. Fifth place went to Herbert Nayokpuk, sixth to Isaac Okleasik, seventh to Dick Mackey, and eighth to John Komak.

After the eighth musher came in, the race officials and Nome committee decided to have an awards banquet. Knowing there were still 14 mushers out on trail, Nome mayor, Robert Renshaw, promised a second banquet for them.

After the first banquet, the race officials decided to head back to Anchorage. It upset me that they wanted to leave before the race was over. I voiced my opinion to them, and their advice was to tell me to do it. They would even give me their hotel room. Well! Okay then! So I ended up being the quasi Race Marshall/Judge/Timer for the rest of the race. We brought them all in and welcomed all of them to Nome.

Over the next ten days, the remaining 14 mushers arrived, one by one. The place where everyone congregated was the coffee shop in the Nome Nugget Hotel. The conversations were unusual but not unexpected. Dog foot care. Feeding. Race strategy. Gear. The run from McGrath to Ruby. Ptarmigan Pass and Happy River.

"Man, look at that! Nice, deep chest. Good, strong leg muscles!" They weren't talking about a passing woman, but a passing dog.

The last musher to arrive was John Schultz of Delta. His dogs crossed the finish line. He stepped off his sled and said, "I came to Nome to have a beer, and that's what I'm gonna do." And he walked into the nearest bar.

There was a second banquet to honor fourteen mushers. It had been a remarkable achievement. Twenty-two dog teams had crossed the State of Alaska on remote and difficult trails, to arrive in Nome three weeks later. No one knew how this first race would turn out, but it turned out well and began a legend.

I climbed onto the last plane to fly teams out—55 dogs, 8 sleds, 8 mushers, me, and one terrified stewardess flew back to Anchorage. It was over, but it had just begun.

I even got a prize. The last time I had seen my husband was at Joe Delia's house in Skwentna. When our daughter was born, Joe said we should name her Skwentna. Are you kidding?

44

The Goal Was At Hand

Shirley and Tracie being interviewed for local radio while awaiting Bobby's and my appearance in Nome which occurred a few minutes past midnight.

Eight miles of the final run from Cape Nome was down below beach level on the frozen Bering Sea. Running time was something over two hours. Nome proper stayed hidden from us behind high banks lining the beach until, at long last, our trail turned and mounted the beach at Fort Davis. From that point, the Nome-Council Highway, closed for the winter, served as the last segment of trail to Nome. Soon after crossing the bridge at Fort Davis, we had passed the darkened village of displaced King Islanders and a derelict gold dredge.

Today, that dredge is a trail feature well known to all Iditaroders. It officially marks the beginning of no-man's land, the zone in which a racer need not yield the trail to teams attempting to pass from that point to the finish line in Nome. Nome! Praise be to God! The goal was at hand, brightly looming ahead. Bobby's team picked up the pace, as did mine, in eager anticipation of something new, something more alluring than the tedious boredom of the past seventeen-hour march.

Sonny never missed a beat. As we neared the outskirts, a growing number of vehicles and bystanders were in evidence. A few snowmobiles began to pace us. Folks shouted out, "Welcome to Nome, Bobby! Welcome to Nome, Dan Seavey!" Sonny led on, unfazed. Then the last three blocks of our incredible journey. What a heartwarming, never-to-be-duplicated surprise. People everywhere, fire siren blared its deafening welcome. Bobby stopped ahead, under an orange banner, bedecked with fluttering pennants of assorted colors. The crowd pressed the teams from all sides. Still, Sonny and teammates pushed on until further forward progress became impossible, blocked by a jubilant phalanx of spectators. We had conquered the trail. We—eleven of my twelve dogs—and me. It wasn't a quick or easy conquest. We had been at it for twenty days, fourteen hours, thirty-five minutes, and throw in sixteen seconds. Bobby Vent crossed the finish line about twenty-five yards ahead of me in second place, but some twenty six minutes less total elapsed time than mine.

There was a familiarity about the banner that stretched overhead from the old post office to the building opposite. And well there should have been. It was, in fact, the very one that saw us off in Anchorage with words "Starting Line" inscribed. Now, in Nome, the backside was hung facing incoming teams with lettering boldly proclaiming, "Welcome to Nome." Joe, Sr., later remarked the reason for the banner's reuse in Nome was that the committee was so broke that purchase of two separate banners was out of the question.

Crowd-size estimates vary, as they seem to enjoy doing, regardless of the occasion. From Sewardite, Dot Bardarson's twenty-five hundred, to the announcer's thirty-five hundred, or "almost as large as when Dick Wilmarth arrived." Both of our teams immediately became engulfed by a human wave. My team was halted, probably twenty-five yards from the finish line. Once stopped, there was no further headway possible. Officially, I never did cross that line. Familiar faces. Radio men, KYAK's Orville Lake and John Carpenter, Race Marshal Dick Tozier, obviously tired, sleep deprived. A hand shake and an excited, "Welcome to our city!" from a dapper, straight from the Gay Nineties—waxed mustache and all—Mayor Robert Renshaw.

A handshake and an excited, "Welcome to our city" from a dapper...Mayor Robert Renshaw. He greeted all mushers day or night.

"And there was Shirley, prettier than I had remembered..."

The crowd was still operating at a clamorous pitch when I turned from greeting the mayor. There was Shirley, prettier than I had remembered. While embracing, there materialized before us an ebullient, banner-waving,Seward contingent. Before I was able to grasp the meaning of all the commotion, I was totally overpowered by Seward family and friends. What pure joy to know all around me were those who truly cared about the event, cared about me! In a moment, hardships of the long, taxing trail melted into insignificance, were elbowed aside by my children, Mitch, Tracie, and Darian. Sent fleeting by teacher friend, Joanne Hoogland, and offspring, Dale and Carol. There, too, was friend and official Seward representative, artist Dot Bardarson, who, with our Seward friends, Bob and Shirley Hill, screwed the cap down tight on all remaining trail discomforts. A wonderful, never-to-be-forgotten homecoming. Hugs, handshakes, back slapping, laughter, and, yes, tears of joy.

"… there materialized before us, an ebullient banner waving contingent…of family and friends."

"What pure joy to know all around me were those who truly cared about the event, cared about me! In a moment, hardships of the long taxing trail melted into insignificance."

My chief handler, Mitch, with help from friend, Dale Hoogland, sister Tracie, and kid brother, Darian, took charge of the team. It was driven to a lot set up on the edge of town, next to the old airstrip. The teams were provided with the first straw seen on the race and gang chains thoughtfully laid out with wind protection in mind. I remember thinking, no dog lot arrangement was too good, no amount of food and straw too much for my eleven: Sonny, Kuchik, Bandit, Koyuk, Shiak, Snippy, Kiana, Genghis, Flame, Crazy, and Casper, they and little Eska, back at Nulato, all my personal trail champions.

The entire Seward delegation was housed at the Nome Lutheran Church. It was to that welcome retreat I was led by all except my youthful and willing dog attendants. Even at 1:00 a.m., there followed the inevitable question-answer session. An eighteen-hour mush notwithstanding, my trail fantasy was fulfilled with a heaping bowl of ice cream, voraciously devoured. Photos were taken, aided by flashbulbs. What a stark transformation three weeks of trail wear produced. Shirley and I, the beauty and the beast. Sitting beside Shirley, with flashbulbs exploding, was the last I remember. I was tired, very tired.

"What a stark transformation three weeks trail wear can produce. Shirley and me, the beauty and the beast."

Some of the "Seward Gang" in Nome for the First Great Race.
L-R: (Adults) Joanne Hoogland, Dot Bardarson, Shirley, Shirley and Bob Hill, (children) Dale and Carol Hoogland, Darian.

Sometime after daylight, I awoke, at first completely disoriented, reaching for my nonexistent alarm clock. It took some doing to reason through my foggy mind just where I was and to come to grips with the realization that my race was over. Somehow, I had showered, changed clothes, and gotten to bed without a speck of recall. All was now quiet, everyone off somewhere, allowing me to sleep off three weeks of accumulated fatigue. I recall lying there, luxuriating; to be truthful, thinking of all that had transpired the past few weeks. Then, as if re-seeing a familiar movie, my mind began to drift over the trail's length, revisiting recent scenes: In Anchorage, the frenzied start, after our frantic neighborhood search for Genghis. A heart-sinking discovery of having left my parka thoughtlessly behind. Tank ruts for a trail along Fort Richardson. Snowless hummocked trail from Eklutna to Knik, a harbinger of worse to come. Beauty of the Rainy Pass country, balanced against a frustrating wait for arrival of dog food. Genghis to our rescue from waist-deep water above Ptarmigan Pass. Parts of two days spent in unadulterated agony and frustration on the Kuskokwim's South Fork, battling its overflow, knifing wind, snags, glare ice, gravel bars, buffalo herd, and a missed turn near Egypt Mountain. Turkey dinner with the Forsgrens at their Ophir cabin. Unsurpassed hospitality showed us by Tex Gates at Bear Creek. Our "wandering in the wilderness" south of Poorman, when competition was replaced with cooperation as we went into survival mode.

That wonderful reception staged for us by teachers and students at Nulato on the mighty Yukon. Kaltag, where local dogs enjoyed an overnight banquet on my sled contents. Unalakleet, where I ended up shy plastic for one runner. Traveling Norton Sound with Bobby Vent, tough competitor, true gentleman, an embodiment of the indomitable Iditarod spirit. Our unforgettable night pinned down at Moses Point. Wilmarth's escape. Our last eighteen-hour haul from White Mountain into Nome. Everything topped off by an end-of-the-trail welcome of the grandest proportions.

Yes, it all happened and a lot more. But I was there in bed in Nome. It was over. Or was it? After such an experience, could it really ever be over? Wasn't it the adventure of my lifetime? Had it not been branded deeply in my heart, there to remain as long as it beats? By some mystical means, that adventure had, to a degree, changed places with my being. Left behind are my acquaintanceships with fellow mushers, villagers, volunteers, my cold campfires, impressions on others, and no doubt a whole lot more, all exchanged for many of the same things,mixed together with beauty of the land, the joy, and satisfaction of driving and working with an incredible dog team, and rising to every level of challenge necessary to prevail. Such were my thoughts when my three pride-provoking kids burst in on me, jolting me back to the real world of—now.

By mid-morning, Saturday, March 24, the Seward gang assembled down at the North Star Restaurant for breakfast. It was pleasant to be able to converse without slurred speech, to complete even a lengthy sentence without taking a nap midway into it. It was wonderful to spend time with friends and family (non-canine beings) again, talking, and laughing. Not surprising, our conversation gravitated to "the race." Speculation, mostly. Who will arrive—in what order? What teams are capable of setting a record between Solomon and Nome? It was Bud Smyth who would do so. When would Attla, the next expected musher, arrive? That question inspired one of my favorite first-race photos.

L-R:Wilmarth, Vent, me. A posed shot: Looking for Attla coming down the trail into Nome in fourth place.

"Shirley and I walked to the Nome Post Office with my dog team mail. I poked the souvenir letters into a letter chute. Mail over the race trail had to be a first."

Shortly before noon, both Vent and Wilmarth put in an appearance at the North Star Restaurant, which was fast becoming unofficial race headquarters. One of them, I believe Bobby, asked, "Where is George?" An idea popped into my head. I said, "How about we three go out and pose as if looking for Attla coming down the trail?" That's what we did. Several cameras clicked away, resulting in several different angles of the same pose. Later that day, a *Nome Nugget* photographer positioned the three of us in front of Nome's gold rush era gold scales. He handed us a gold-filled poke, and snapped another great first-race shot. While at the North Star that afternoon, someone handed me a fistful of congratulatory telegrams. Ninety-four good people of Seward sent their best wishes by that means.

Leaving the North Star, most of our group walked over to the dog lot. I wanted to check on the dogs and fetch the packet of souvenir letters reposing somewhere in the bottom of my disheveled sled pack. Tired, most of the dogs were content to stay curled up on their straw beds as I went down the line, checking each over. The kids had fed them earlier, reporting all had eaten with gusto. My notes from our Nome sojourn simply state, "Shirley and I walked from the dog lot over to the Nome post office with my dog team mail. Mitch and Bob Hill accompanied us." I unwrapped the bundle, and poked the letters into a letter chute. Shirley took pictures. Mail over the race trail—it had to be a first.

Everything unique to the first race was a first. Meaning, for example, a sled dog race—nothing first, nor unique, here—but one of one thousand miles or more, using the same dogs, is decidedly a first and, without question, unique. There are many Iditarod Race traditions, whose origins are traced to the 1973 inaugural event. Easily coming to mind is the first weekend in March start, Anchorage start site (ceremonial, nowadays) trail mail (mine in 1973 was adopted by ITC in 1974), keeping record of the fastest time between Solomon (Port Safety or Safety, nowadays) and Nome, the town siren and police escort at Nome, use of veterinarians during the race, publishing dog deaths, employment of the "Iditarod Air Force," multiple finisher banquets, red lantern award (adopted from earlier races), and reliance on volunteers.

Julie Farley, Howard's wife, was one busy lady before, during, and after the first Iditarod. Howard was one of those who could not, or at least did not, say no to Joe. As a result, he ended up consenting to handle all things Iditarod in Nome. It took a while for the magnitude of his commitment to sink in. Housing arrangements had to be made for mushers, visitors, dignitaries, like Governor Egan, and others. He had to arrange a place for dogs to be kept and provide for shipping dogs home after the race. City officials dealt with traffic control, police involvement, finisher banquets, and how best to utilize the media and how to answer the hundreds of questions that would come from new Nome volunteers about tasks totally new to most, as they were to Howard himself. When things were reaching their overwhelming worst, the unthinkable happened. Howard became severely bitten by and incurably infested with the mushing bug. He sought relief through intensive dog team training in the Nome area, to no avail. Finally, out of desperation, with consent, indeed encouragement from his noble wife, Howard agreed drastic measures were necessary. Yes, he would travel to far-off Anchorage and enter his team in the first Iditarod Race, leaving fate to run her course. And wife, Julie, was left to run her large household and Nome's Iditarod affairs as well. No mistake about it. Julie Farley became extremely busy, performing yeoman service for the Iditarod.

But she was not too busy to throw a very nice party at her home that (Saturday) evening. Undaunted that Howard was out on the trail, she handled the whole affair with grace and self-confident charm. Shirley, son Mitch, and I welcomed George Attla and his six-dog team in, a bit before dark, and made our way over to Farley's house. There was standing room only, with a good mix of Nome folks and a predominance of Iditarod-related visitors. Good food, lively conversation, with opportunities to meet some wonderfully warmhearted Nome folks. Not least of whom was hostess, Julie Farley.

The next and final affair that day was something new and totally captivating for Shirley, me, and the kids. Word was out that the world-renowned King Island Dancers were performing down the street at the armory. Exhausted though I was, nothing would do but to troop on over and join a large, appreciative audience. Our arrival was accompanied by a general murmur throughout and wide smiles of recognition. Six magnificently attired male Eskimo dancers and drummers had already begun. They wore beautiful skin parkas, traditional sealskin pants, and ornately decorated skin mukluks. There were two drummers, one seated on the floor, one moving energetically with the dancers. We were enthralled. A story completed, told in voice, body movement, and vigorous drumbeats, all came to a sudden and dramatic halt. Then, without a word of explanation, the elder of the troop beckoned me front and center, and, again, not uttering a sound, handed me a pair of fur-trimmed dance gloves. Big, toothy smiles ensued, followed by drums and chants, lighthearted laughter from a polite, if not totally appreciative, audience. I danced, Eskimo style. Well, sort of, until the drums were silenced and my gloves taken away. I tendered my talent to the headman, expressing my wish to join that famous entertainment company on a permanent basis. I never heard back from him.

I perform with the famous King Island Eskimo Dancers while in Nome. Their leader didn't seem overly interested in my offer to join them on a permanent basis.

Nome's Sunday morning (March 25) dawned clear with a blustery east wind. Temperatures remained mild, around zero degrees F. Before evening, that east wind would give a welcomed push to four more teams, enabling drivers to complete their races in time to attend the banquet being set up for them over at the North Star.

For the Seavey family, early Sunday morning was family time, after feeding dogs, that is. I was, by then, at least partly back in the world—functioning, though in slow motion. We began to talk of home and to think through what was necessary to get us there. We arranged to fly dogs down to Anchorage, and to get us there on the same flight. We mapped out necessary shopping that had to be done in Anchorage before heading south to Seward. The kids filled me in on school, on the dogs left at home, in particular, the new puppies. Mitch informed me that he had removed dew claws from them. Then, off to church.

By Sunday night's banquet, eight teams had reached Nome. George Attla was fourth, followed a couple of hours later by Herbert Nayokpuk, who reached Nome in fifth place, which was worth three thousand dollars to him. Recall that he had also garnered one thousand dollars for being the fastest team between Anchorage and Knik. From his very first Iditarod Race until his last in 1988, "Herbie" would remain the race's favorite competitor. Seven hours behind Herbie, Isaac Okleasik, of Teller, the 1967 Alaska Purchase Centennial Race Champ, mushed down Front Street in sixth position. Mid-Sunday afternoon saw teams driven by Dick Mackey and John Komak enter Nome in seventh and eighth places, respectively. Seventh place paid two thousand dollars, and eighth place paid one thousand eight hundred. Competitors in the First Great Race were paid down to twentieth place. By way of contrast, entrants in a modern Iditarod are paid to thirtieth place, while all finishers receive a minimum of one thousand forty-nine dollars. Funds to finance the payout to all finishers come from what is called the Iditarider Program. Race fans bid (Internet auction) on their favorite musher's sled for a ride over the "ceremonial start" course in Anchorage. The forty-nine attached to the one thousand dollars is symbolic—Alaska is the forty-ninth state—as is the claim that our race course is 1,049 miles. More Joe, Sr. salesmanship here (see Appendix XV, Final Standings—1973).

Everyone who wasn't sleeping off the effects (or the after-effects) of the trail, showed up at the North Star Restaurant for lunch, and to pass the time until the evening banquet. City of Seward's official representative, Dot Bardarson, was there. Not allowing the artist in her a vacation, this creative friend was busy sketching key actors in that first trail drama. I remember one sketch of race judge, Joel Kotke. In it, Joel was blissfully asleep under a table. She also did excellent pencil drawings of Dick Tozier and George Attla. Years later, Dot told me she had done upward to a dozen and turned them over to "the committee." Over the years, I have made several fruitless inquiries as to the whereabouts of these historically important items. George Attla, sprint-racer extraordinaire, related at the banquet that while Dot was sketching him, there occurred a mad rush of mushers present to a window overlooking Front Street. Thinking such excitement must have been occasioned by "a pretty girl walking by," George excused himself and joined the supposed oglers. George recorded his disappointment when, to his dismay, he beheld—"an old, black Lab strolling by."

Had I taken better notes, I could identify the site of the first "Finishers' Banquet" with unquestioned authority. Such, unfortunately, is not the case. Dorothy Page's race annual has it simply at the Nugget Inn. An audio tape of teams arriving in Nome recorded a radio announcer stating that the banquet would be held at the North Star Hotel's Nugget 3 Room. Howard and Julie Farley, collaborated by Leo Rasmussen, placed it in the North Star Hotel's "Sea View Room," next to the N.C. Building. Nome residency for all three informants predates the first Iditarod. All three, in one form or another, were participants in the first race. They went on to reveal that the North Star was later taken over by the Nugget Hotel of today. In modern times, mushers of the trail meet to critique their race and decide on various awards and recognitions to be made public, come banquet night. Recent past meetings, for that purpose, have taken place in the bar/restaurant of the Nugget Hotel, facing the ocean. Every time I enter, there develops a strange sense of familiarity of having been there before, a long time ago.

Top finishers of the First Great Race. L-R: Dick Wilmarth (1st), George Attla (4th), Dan Seavey 3rd), and Bobby Vent (2nd). (Photo: Terry Adkins)

The Seward contingent put in its banquet appearance well ahead of the appointed hour. I was met in the lobby by none other than Joe, Sr., looking well rested, if not worry free. Calling me aside, he stated in a very confidential manner that the committee needed a loan, that we were still a little short on the purse. "We were thinking since you at least have a job waiting for you, that you might loan us some of your prize money to pay the last few mushers." I asked how much was needed. Joe answered, "Around half your six thousand dollars." I thought it over quickly, realizing that I, after all, did have something to do with getting mushers committed to the race, and thus bore responsibility for their payoff. We agreed he could shortchange the six thousand dollars to half, as needed.

Our banquet room was way overstuffed at three hundred persons, while many had to be turned away, simply because it was impossible to wedge more in. Race Marshal Dick Tozier was still out on the trail. Joe, Sr. was present, as was "Muktuk" Marston and Orville Lake, who served as the master of ceremonies. Of course, the eight "off the trail" mushers who ranged from refreshed to bedraggled in appearance, occupied honored guest tables up front.

We were a pretty tight-lipped bunch of mushers, compared with today's free-wheeling motor mouths and an occasional eloquent orator. As a result, it didn't require a great amount of time to award trophies and distribute prize money checks. Each musher also received a copy of Colonel Marston's book: *Men of the Tundra*, an accounting of his work in organizing the Northwest Coast Eskimos into the Alaska Territorial Guard for defense during World War II. This treasured keepsake was inscribed and signed by both Marston and General Gettys.

First finishers banquet in Nome. Joe, Sr. prepares to hand off the first place trophy to Dick Wilmarth of Red Devil, Orville Lake emcees.

Second place trophy went to Bobby Vent. Mrs. Vent gets the check from Orville Lake.

I received my third place trophy, an inscribed copy of Col. Muktuk Marston's book, *Men of the Tundra*, and half my pay. The other half I loaned to the race committee.

Alaska Governor Bill Egan sent congratulations, as did Senators Ted Stevens and Mike Gravel. Army snowmachiners and all civilian volunteers came in for well-earned praise. Vital parts played by volunteer pilots were duly recognized. Colonel Muktuk Marston was formally inducted into the Musher's Hall of Fame and presented with a stunning portrait of his likeness in oil, painted by artist Evaline Rowsey. As our champion, Dick Wilmarth, in addition to a trophy, and cash, was given a painting by Bessie Moses, a gift from her husband. Wilmarth had his name inscribed on a perpetual trophy that was to remain in Nome, awaiting new champions to come along.

For me, the most memorable event of the evening came at the end when things were all but wound down. Joe, Sr. came to the microphone and, with a smile that clearly displayed happiness and satisfaction, asked all assembled, "Is there anyone present here tonight who would like to see this race next year?" There was a couple of seconds of silence as the question soaked in to the crowd's collective mind. Then, as if on cue, a resounding, "Yes!"

"We'll have one then, and I promise you it will be bigger than ever and (out comes the promoter) we anticipate that perhaps one hundred teams will be entered a year from now."

Like the other first banquet mushers, I received, in turn, my check, trophy, and the colonel's book. But the real treat, the real prize—and surprise—was the song: "Dan Seavey Was a Musher" sung as a prelude to me going up to claim my formal laurels. Artsy Dot Bardarson (and daughter Dori) wrote it and Dot accompanied the singers with her guitar. The singers? Mitch, Tracie, and Darian Seavey, and Dale Hoogland. To watch and listen to such youthful exuberance and sincerity truly was the frosting on the entire race cake. The crowd loved it as well. Give it a try, if you dare. It was sung to the tune: "Stewball was a Race Horse" (see Appendix XVI, "Dan Seavey was a Musher").

Big surprise at first finisher's banquet, Nome, 1973, was the performance of the "Dan Seavey Was a Musher" song. Seward artist, Dot Bardarson accompanies. L-R: Mitch Seavey, Dale Hoogland, Darian and Tracie Seavey.

Student-made banners adorn my Seward High School classroom upon my return to duty following participation in the First Great Race.

Following the banquet, we bid adieu to the Sewardites, Bob and Shirley Hill, Dot Bardarson, and Joanne Hoogland and her two great kids, Carol and Dale, as they scurried about preparatory to heading to the airport to catch the evening flight to Anchorage. I shall remember always what a grand, welcome sight they were. Waving the Dan Seavey banner, folks from home in Nome, because they were excited about what I was doing. At the finish line because I was coming in. Now, if that isn't true friendship, I don't know what is. Scheduled for the first flight out Monday morning, we did what packing we could before retiring from an interesting, eventful day. Our last in Nome.

Monday morning dawned bright and breezy. My faithful little alarm persisted until I was up. I dressed hurriedly and rousted Mitch. The plan was for Mitch and me, with volunteer assistance, to get the dogs placed in sky kennels and transport them, sled, and other mushing gear to the airport for loading. Shirley, Tracie, and Darian would complete packing and, again, with help from volunteers, make their way to the airport in time for the 9:00 a.m. flight. There was no airport security in those days, just show up in time to catch your flight.

It was 6:00 a.m. when Mitch and I struck out to load dogs. Mitch, our oldest son, on whom so much responsibility had fallen at such an early age, simply by merit of being the firstborn. He was at the same time intelligent, competitive, with a perfectionist bent. Nothing was ever done halfway by Mitch. At age twelve and thirteen, he was my one and only trainer-handler for my 1973 and 1974 race efforts. The most cherished memories I have carried forward into my old age center around the days and nights we spent driving dog teams over remote trails together by day, camping beside them by night. At no time had I felt closer to the Creator or His Creation. He must have taken a bit more time when He put together the sled dog and exercised a bit more benevolence when He gave over to my stewardship, such a magnificent animal, in company with a son.

Our dogs were stowed forward in an Alaska Airlines 737 jet. It was a fairly packed flight, but we were in the air on time. The kids, Shirley, and I were excited to be heading home. It had been a long haul for me, and a long wait and lots of uncertainty for them. Already, several times before leaving Nome, I had answered the question: "Well, what was it like?" Meaning the race experience. Already, my answer had become pat: "It was the greatest adventure of my lifetime." If I verbalized all I was thinking, I would have to add, "Regardless of what other adventure or misadventures come my way." The adventure of a lifetime. I drove a dog team into history, through history. For me, it was not the great camping trip as George Attla called it, but a thousand or more miles of new country. Beautiful country. A thousand miles of new cultures, new villages, and new people, who were wonderfully warm, open, and giving. A thousand miles of barren ground, deep snow, knee-deep overflow, rocks, gravel, glare ice, fierce winds, mind-numbing cold and fatigue, each a test of one's true resolve. It was a thousand miles of comradeship, trail-side campfires, sharing in hard times, and in good competition balanced with cooperation, each man attempting the untried. A thousand miles of space and time spent with one of God's most marvelous creations, the sled dog. Mile upon mile, days stacked up twenty high. They were always up, positive, uncomplaining, tough, adaptable, and indomitable. Each evolving in my eyes from a dumb draft animal to a valued trail partner, admired in truth, loved beyond words.

We were facing east as our plane lifted from the runway and began to gain altitude. My mind had already drifted toward home, wondering what would await this wayfaring teacher back at Seward High. I remember thinking I was taking the easy way home, two hours by air compared to twenty and one-half days by dog team. Glancing out a portside window, I recognized the incoming Iditarod Trail, stretching out toward Fort Davis and beyond in the direction of Cape Nome. I attempted to point out the trail to Shirley, seated beside me as the plane turned more south out over Norton Sound. It was then that I uttered undoubtedly the understatement of my entire life. Looking at Shirley, the light of my life, who, at fifteen years into our marriage, had already shared so much with me, I said, perhaps more to myself than to her, "Well, the First Great Race is over. My first and my last."

How was I to know that my Iditarod had just begun?

Epilogue

How naïve it was of me to think, as our airplane lifted off from Nome following the first Iditarod Race, that my involvement with things Iditarod was over – for good. Fact is, there was no escaping them. From 1970 to present, 43 years, they have been my constant companions. Same with sled dogs, though dating back an additional seven years.

I have made reference to my participation in the second Iditarod in 1974 and the 25th Anniversary Race of 1997. In the latter, I had the honor of sharing trail with Joe Sr. between Kaltag and Nome. Sadly, it was to be Joe's last. Then, in 2001, I was privileged to travel to Nome in company of son Mitch and grandson Danny to become the first three generation trio to complete an Iditarod. Finally, in 2012, I once again hit the trail highly motivated. For that year was the fortieth running of the race. Forty years since we twenty-three race pioneers drove our teams down Front Street, Nome. Also, the Iditarod National Historic Trail Alliance had sponsored me to promote trail awareness along the route – part of its historic trail centennial celebration. An added incentive was both Mitch, and this time grandson Dallas, were competing, making for a repeat of a three generation race.

Where we of the First Great Race can justifiably lay claim to being Iditarod Race establishers, successive generations of racers have bragging rights for elevating our race to an extremely competitive international sporting event. Unquestionably, younger generation Seaveys have done their bit for that cause. Mitch, my 13 year old handler in 1973 has, to date, over twenty races to his credit, including a 2004 championship which was repeated in 2013 when, at age fifty-three, he became the oldest competitor to win an Iditarod. All four of his sons are Iditaroders. Danny, Tyrell, and Dallas came up through Junior Iditarod ranks to become veteran senior racers. Dallas in 2012, at age twenty-five, became the youngest champion in Iditarod's forty year history. As an aside, Dallas won the one thousand mile Yukon Quest in 2011, his rookie run. On the same note, Mitch took home $100,000.00 for his victory in the centennial run of the All Alaska Sweepstakes held at Nome in 2008. Mitch and Janine's teenage son, Conway, has one Junior Iditarod championship captured with eligibility for one more.

In truth, most of my Iditarod activity over the years has centered on the historic trail, not racing. As a member of the Aurora Dog Mushers, I advocated in the early 1970's for a national status for the Iditarod Trail, and served for thirty years on an advisory board for the same, once established. In 1982, I joined with fellow Sewardites to form the Seward Iditarod Trail Blazers. Our thirty year goal has been to re-establish the Iditarod Trail on the Kenai Peninsula. Some ten years ago, there was organized the Iditarod Historic Trail Alliance, a private, non-profit dedicated to preservation of the historic trail and associated properties. In the past, I served as its president and currently occupy a position on the board of directors. Likewise, I did a nine year stint on the Iditarod Trail Committee (race) board. In March of 2013 I was greatly honored to be inducted into the prestigious Iditarod Hall of Fame, sponsored by the *Anchorage Daily News*. All of which has been both interesting and rewarding.

A couple winters back, there occurred an incident equally rewarding when Shirley and I witnessed – wonder of wonders – our 5 year old great-granddaughter, Allikz Seavey's solo run with her one-dog team and a Christmas present sled. The display of sheer joy by child and her lead dog, Hootch, was truly heart-warming. A fourth generation Seavey musher in the making? Perhaps not. But the Iditarod National Historic Trail is there for her – just in case. That marvelous creature, the Alaskan Husky has earned a secure place in Alaskan culture and will be there for her – just in case. I believe I spoke for the many who have devoted a large measure of their life's allotment to the trail and sled dogs when earlier I wrote: "I can think of no greater legacy for us to hand over to future generations of Alaskans."

Dan Seavey
Seward, Alaska
May, 2013

Appendix

1. Retired in honor of Leonhard Seppala
2. Richard Frank, Minto
3. Keith Poppert, Wasilla
4. Danny Ewan, Gulkana
5. Earl Norris, Anchorage
6. Pete Shepherd, Fairbanks
7. Johnny Rine, Anchorage
8. Harold Greenway, Fairbanks
9. Phil Hodgkin, Willow
10. John Wallace, Wasilla
11. Gil Hagen, Anchorage
12. John Nielsen, Iliamna
13. Bergman Sam, Hughes
14. Gareth Wright, Fairbanks
15. Carl Mosher, Anchorage
16. Hudson Sam, Hughes
17. Gloria Jones, Anchorage
18. Ray Redington, Anchorage
19. Joe Redington, Sr. Anchorage
20. Dick Mackey, Anchorage
21. Vern Chernesky, Big Lake
22. Jerry Riley, Nenana
23. Warner Vent, Huslia
24. Fred Sommer, Nulato
25. Elia Anelon, Iliamna
26. Steve Losonsky, Fairbanks
27. Orin Bowles, Eagle River
28. Isaac Okleasik, Teller
29. Bill Taylor, Fairbanks
30. Barney Anderson, Palmer
31. Herbert Nayokpuk, Shishmaref
32. Thomas Napageak, Point Barrow
33. Dick Wolff, Anchorage
34. Orville Lake, Anchorage
35. Dick Kopsack, Big Lake
36. Stan Barney, Anchorage
37. Shirley Gavin, Peters Creek
38. Ed Evens, Anchorage
39. Lee Twing, Big Lake
40. Ed Carney, Wasilla
41. Larry Westlake, Kiana
42. Warren Coffin, Noorvik
43. Bob Arwezon, Anchorage
44. Bill Sturdevant, Anchorage
45. Don Bowles, Eagle River
46. George Attla, Huslia
47. Chester Topkok, Teller
48. Al Hibbard, Big Lake
49. Jimmy Malemute, Galena
50. Marvin Snow, Anchorage
51. Charles Belford, Deerfield, Mass.
52. Lester Sam, Allakaket
53. Ray Carter, Wasilla
54. Joe Redington, Jr., Anchorage
55. Andy Simon, Allakaket
56. Roland Lombard, Weyland, Mass.
57. Charles Stevens, Palmer
58. Mike Stephan, Anchorage
59. Ray Folger, Tanana

IDITAROD TRAIL COMMITTEE

KNIK ALASKA

BOX 6108 ANNEX
ANCHORAGE ALASKA

March 23, 1970

Fellow Dog Mushers:

Sled dog racing in the past few years has become increasingly popular throughout the United States and Canada. We have been following with great interest the growing list of dog mushing clubs and races in Team and Trail.

This enthusiasm over mushing is most encouraging to us as we make plans for the longest and richest race in dog mushing history. We'd like to tell you about it.

First of all, the purse will be $50,000, which doubles the $25,000 we raised for the 1967 Leonard Seppala Memorial Iditarod Trail Race.

We plan to run from Knik, the start of the 1967 race, all the way to Iditarod and back to Knik, a total of about 800 miles, following the historic Iditarod Trail. The Iditarod was once the main winter route between south-central Alaska and the interior. The race trail traverses some 400 miles of Alaskan wilderness and passes through the village of McGrath.

We intend to construct cabins approximately 50 miles apart the entire length of the trail for storing food and supplies that will be needed by dogs and mushers. News media personnel will be welcome to make use of these cabins.

Mushers will travel as far and as fast as they choose, making camp along the trail wherever they wish. We are still toying with the idea of a required layover at the halfway point in Iditarod.

Our plans also include a provision for aircraft surveillance along the entire trail. In the event of an emergency the musher and team will be air-lifted back to a population center.

Because of the immense task in planning and organizing this race, we are setting a 1973 date for the first of what we hope will be an annual 800 mile Leonard Seppala Memorial Iditarod Trail International Championship Race.

In 1971 and 1972 we intend to have races in the 100 to 300 mile class on the lower end of the Iditarod. This would provide an opportunity for mushers to work up to the big one.

A 1973 date will give your club members plenty of time to raise and train dogs for the championship of all championship races. We hope you will seriously consider sponsoring a musher from your club for the race.

We are enclosing reprints of two booklets on the famous Nome races held between 1908 and 1916. While these were "only" 400 miles in length, an examination of the breakdown on times and distances covered in one day should provide some idea of what can be expected in the 800 mile race.

If you are interested in receiving progress reports on the organization and planning of the 800 mile Iditarod race, we will be happy to put you on a mailing list.

Also, if you have any questions or suggestions we would like to hear from you.

As a fund raising project for trail work and promotion expenses, we are selling copies of the two enclosed booklets for $1.50 each. Would you show these to club members? We can fill orders for any number of booklets your club may want to purchase.

Sincerely,

Thomas L. Johnson

Enclosure

rjw

Alaska State Legislature

REPRESENTATIVE
IRWIN L. "IRV" METCALF
SEWARD, ALASKA
9TH DISTRICT

COMMITTEES:
JUDICIARY
LOCAL GOVERNMENT
LABOR AND MANAGEMENT

House of Representatives

Juneau, Alaska 99801
April 20, 1970

Copy

IDITAROD TRAIL COMMITTEE
P.O. Box C108
Anchorage, Alaska

Attention: Mr. Thomas L. Johnson

Gentlemen:

It has recently been called to my attention by Mr. Dan Seavey of Seward that the IDITAROD TRAIL COMMITTEE is planning a "Dog Sled" Derby race from Knik to Iditarod and return, a round-trip distance of 800 miles, duplicating, for the most part, the pioneering days of Alaska, when mail and supplies were moved by dog team and professional mushers from the coast of Southcentral Alaska to Iditarod from Seward, Alaska, via Girdwood, Crow Creek Pass, Eagle River Valley, Knik, thence cross country to Iditarod, as evidenced by some of the old photographs of that activity, and I would like to take this opportunity to endorse your proposed cross country "Dog Sled" Derby Race and to personally commend you for your efforts in trying to get this new activity started.

Inasmuch as the Alaskan winters are long and general employment is somewhat short, which is a typical characteristic over all of Alaska more or less, it is felt that your proposed "Dog Sled" Derby will stimulate a much-neded economic activity, as well as providing opportunity for outdoor wintertime recreation, which is much needed here in Alaska, when many people are prone to engage in indoor recreational activities.

In answer to your invitation for suggestions, I would like to take this opportunity to make two suggestions as follows:

1. I would like to see the "Dog Sled" Derby start at the Port of Seward, instead of Knik, as the Port of Seward was the real and original beginning point, in early days, for the mushers and dog teams handling passengers and freight between the Southcentral coast and Iditarod, as I am told by some of the old and former dog mushers, such as Martin Lanning. They used to travel from Seward to Iditarod via Girdwood, Crow Creek Pass, Eagle River Valley, and Knik. Such an itinerary route would provide a genuine duplicate replica of the early day "Dog Team Sled" travel.

2. I would like to suggest that the Committee compile a booklet, establishing as much historical background information on early day dog team travel, the outstanding dog teams of early days, as well as some of the outstanding experiences of some of the early day mushers. Also, I would like to see reprints of pictures of early day dog team mushers published therein. Such a publication would undoubtedly create and stimulate interest in your proposed program of cross country "Dog Sled" Derby. Some of the early day dog team mushers endured severe hardships and, in my opinion, were outstanding men of their era, similar to the "cowboys" of the early days of our Southwest.

Trusting that the foregoing may be of value and assistance to you in your proposed "Dog Sled" Derby and with very best and kind wishes for the success of your new venture, I remain

Sincerely,

Irwin L. "Irv" Metcalf
c/o Legislative Affairs Agency
Juneau, Alaska 99801

ILM:pl

cc Mr. Dan Seavey

United States Senate

COMMITTEE ON COMMERCE

WASHINGTON, D.C. 20510

March 9, 1972

Mr. Daniel B. Seavey
Intructor
Seward High School
Box 923
Seward, Alaska 99664

Dear Daniel:

Thank you for your February 8 letter expressing your strong interest and support for designating the Iditarod Trail and the town of Iditarod as historic landmarks.

Please be assured that I support the measures being taken to preserve and restore historic relics within our state.

I appreciate your conveyance of concern for our State's historic past. Please feel free to call on me if I can every be of further assistance.

With best wishes,

Cordially,

TED STEVENS
United States Senator

IDITAROD TRAIL

International Championship Sled Dog Race
Anchorage to Nome March 2, 1973

1000 MILES-$50,000.00

The longest & richest sled dog race in history, over the old Iditarod trail-

Iditarod Trail Committee
Box 6108
Anchorage, Alaska 99502

Fellow Musher,

The big race is on, and we want to invite you to enter the longest and richest dog sled race in history.

Just a little news on our progress at this end. Joe Redington and many helpers are, at this moment, working on putting in and marking the trail. Most of the trail was put in last winter, but of course, it needs to be gone over again. Much of the race trail is used throughout the winter so will require no further preperation.

We are presently working on procuring aircraft, so mushers, dogs, and equipment can be flown back to Anchorage when the race is over.

Most of the other information, you will find in the accompanying brochure. Race rules and a racing contract will be sent on receipt of the interest form.

The excitement of the Anchorage to Nome Race is beginning to grip all Alaskans and dogmushers with its magnitude.

Be a part of it, send your entry blank now and become part of history.

Happy Mushing,

Gleo A. Huyck

Iditarod Trail

Anchorage-Nome International Dog Sled Race

HISTORY

In the early years of our state, the Iditarod Trail was considered by many as the primary route into the Alaska interior until the mid 20's. The trail began at Knik, located across the Knik Arm from Anchorage, and stretched across the rugged Alaskan terrain until it reached the gold rush city of Nome on the Bering Sea. Many portions of the Iditarod Trail are still in use by trappers and Natives who find that even in this day of modern transportation systems and snowmobile travel, a dog team is sometimes still the best and most reliable way to travel.

REQUIRED EQUIPMENT

An equipment check-out will be conducted prior to the start of the race to insure that every contestant will have an adequate survival package. Mushers will be notified well in advance what gear they should have in order to enter the race.

Basically, the equipment will include: sleeping bag, one day's ration for man and dogs, matches, axe or saw, tether chain or individual tie-outs, sun glasses or goggles, snowshoes.

RULES

The International Dog Sled and Racing Association race rules will apply to the race. Since the uniqueness of the race will require some modifications, a complete list will be sent to all interested parties on request.

PURSE

The largest purse in the history of dog-sled racing — $50,000 — is being offered to the top twenty finishers. The top prize for first place is $12,000, with the second place winner receiving $8,000 and the third place winner getting $6,000.

The remaining purse wil be awarded in the folowing manner:

4th	$4,000	10th	$1,400	16th	$ 750
5th	$3,000	11th	$1,000	17th	$ 700
6th	$2,500	12th	$ 950	18th	$ 650
7th	$2,000	13th	$ 900	19th	$ 600
8th	$1,800	14th	$ 850	20th	$ 500
9th	$1,600	15th	$ 800		

REGISTRATION — $100 PER ENTRY

Hundreds of inquiries have already been received from across the nation regarding this historic race . . . and hundreds more are expected in the weeks ahead. The race committee is especially enthusiastic regarding the active participation by Native mushers from remote Alaskan communities. The competition should prove to be spirited and rewarding.

We invite all interested mushers — from the professional to the recreational week-ender — to join us in the race. If you are interested in more information, simply fill out the form below and return it immediately. You will receive specific details and a registration form by return mail.

DETACH HERE

Sounds great!! I'm very interested. Send me more information and an entry form right away.

(PLEASE PRINT)

NAME ______________________________

ADDRESS ______________________________

CITY/TOWN/VILLAGE ______________________________

ZIP ______________________________

Deadline for registration is February 28, 1973.

PLACE
STAMP
HERE

IDITAROD TRAIL RACE COMMITTEE
BOX 6108, ANNEX
ANCHORAGE, ALASKA 99502

RACE ROUTE

The race will begin in Anchorage on March 3 and the contestants will continue, at their own pace, until they reach Nome. Each participant will be required to check in at periodic check points, namely — Knik, Susitna, Skwentna, Rainy Pass, Rohn Roadhouse, Big River Roadhouse, McGrath, Placerville, Ruby, Galena, Nulato, Kaltag, Old Woman, Unalakleet, Shaktoolik, Koyuk, Elim, White Mountain, Solomon, and finally Nome. A look at the state map will give interested participants some indication of the length and challenge of the 1,000 mile route.

APPENDIX VI: Race Sign-Up Information and Entry Form

THE IDITAROD TRAIL INTERNATIONAL CHAMPIONSHIP RACE

Anchorage to Nome

1,000 Miles

$50,000.00 Purse

March 3, 1973

Introduction

The longest, the richest, and the most grueling sled dog race in history will begin in Anchorage, Alaska, on March 3, 1973, and end anywhere from 10 days to 3 weeks later in Nome, about 1,000 miles from the starting point.

Man and dog will experience the hardship, as well as the companionship, of the trail as they make their way from the Pacific coast of southcentral Alaska to the shores of the Bering Sea in northwest Alaska, over countless miles of rugged and relatively untouched wilderness.

Essentially, the race will be patterned after the Great Nome Sweepstakes Race which took place in the early part of this century. Each musher will proceed at his own pace, covering as many miles in a day as he is able, making camp along the trail at night or mushing on to the next checkpoint where he may find an extra space in a cabin or ten to spread out his furs or sleeping bag.

The Iditarod Trail Race committee is sponsoring this unique event in order to promote the rapidly growing sport of dog mushing, and to secure the restoration of historic trails in Alaska.

For a good share of the distance, mushers will be following the historic old Iditarod Trail, which is presently being considered for inclusion in the Nation Historic Trail System.

History of the Iditarod Trail

Shortly after the turn of the century, a winter route was established from the coast in southcentral Alaska into the rich gold fields of interior and northwester Alaska. Dog teams, horses, and back packers traveled from the seaport of Seward north to Knik, located across the Knik Arm from present day Anchorage. Knik was the staging area for those hardy souls seeking adventure and fortune to the north and west. The route leading out of Knik went to the bustling gold rush towns of Iditarod and Flot and from there on to Nome. In 1910 the Alaska Road Commission marked and improved the trail from Knik to Iditarod for use as a primary winter access to the interior. This trail became known as the Iditarod Trail.

Heavy use of the Iditarod continued up until the Alaska Railroad was completed to Fairbanks. Since then it has been traveled less frequently by homesteaders and others making their way west from Cook Inlet.

Today, at the lower end of the trail near Knik, dog mushers are still using the Iditarod. Sled dog races are held on nearly every weekend of the snow season.

In 1967, fifty-nine mushers entered the $25,000 Iditarod Trail Centennial Race held at Knik. Probably this many or more dog teams will be running in the 1973 race.

Route

Beginning in Anchorage, contestants will mush out around Knik Arm to Knik, where they proceed west and north, covering a major portion of the Iditarod Trail until they reach McGrath. Along this stretch, dog mushers will pass many historic old roadhouses that thrived in the early gold rush days. Susitna Station, Mountain Climbers Roadhouse, and Happy River are a few. Some outposts on the Iditarod Trail, such as Skwentna, Rainy Pass Lodge, and Farewell are presently inhabited.

From McGrath, a village of 300 souls, the race trail heads north to the Yukon River gold rush town of Ruby. At that point mushers travel down the frozen Yukon passing the Indian villages of Galena, Nulato, and finally Kaltag, where they will leave the Yukon and journey through the Unalakleet River Valley to the Eskimo village of Unalakleet on the Bering Sea coast.

Out of Unalakleet, drivers and teams generally follow the coastline, passing through a number of small villages such as Shaktoolik, Koyuk, Elim, and Solomon. From Solomon, the last of 20 checkpoints along the race trail, mushers will make the final push to the finish line in Nome.

Trail Conditions

Over some stretches, such as those between villages, the race trail will coincide with other well used trails. Where the race trail is not commonly used, mushers may encounter some soft trail conditions.

As a minimum standard, a well marked broken trail will be established over the entire route.

Weather Conditions

During the month of March, days are getting longer and warmer in Alaska. Mushers could find ideal mushing conditions for the duration of the trip.

However, this is Alaska, and weather conditions may vary considerably. Extremes which may be encountered along the way would include sever cold at night, high winds, heavy snows, and intense glare from the sun on the snow.

Check Points

Check-points will be established at old roadhouse sites along the trail or in villages. In some cases tents will be set up where there are no existing structures. Intervals between check-points will average approximately 50 miles.

Functions at all or most of the checkpoints would include:

1. Radio contact to keep track of the progress and welfare of the mushers.
2. Vantage points for news media.

3. Storage for dog food.
4. Shelter for mushers, on a first-come-first-serve basis.
5. Collecting point for dogs being dropped from teams.

Dropped Dogs

Dogs may be dropped from teams at designated check-points. Planes will transport these dogs back to Knik, the first check-point about 65 miles from Anchorage by highway, or on to Nome, whichever the musher prefers. It will be the musher's responsibility to pick up his dogs within a limited time after the race is over.

Dog Food

Final arrangements are being made to have a reputable brand of commercial dog food, such as Kosco or Purina, placed at designated check-points in sufficient quantity to insure that every musher will have an adequate supply of dog food waiting for him along trail. The check-points where dog food will be available are approximately 100 miles apart.

Musher's Food

Mushers are to assume responsibility for providing their own food whether they carry everything with them from Anchorage or plan to purchase supplies in one of the towns or villages along the way. The first check-point where food is available is McGrath. From that point on there are several villages with small stores where food may be procured.

There will be a limited supply of emergency rations at each of the check-point.

Equipment

Each participant will have his own preferences as to the type of sled, gear, and other paraphernalia he will take with him on the trail. However, an equipment check-out will be conducted prior to the start of the race to ensure that every contestant has an adequate survival package.

Mushers will be required to show race officials that they have in their possession the following items:

Arctic type sleeping gear — One day's ration for man and dogs
Matches — Axe or saw
Tie out chains for dogs (trees may not always be readily available)
Sun glasses or goggles — Snowshoes

It is highly recommended that mushers take along an extra set of warm clothing.

Return from Nome

Arrangements are being made for air transportation from Nome to Anchorage after the race in large cargo planes for mushers and dogs.

THE IDITAROD INTERNATIONAL CHAMPIONSHIP RACE

Anchorage to Nome

1,000 Miles

$50,000 Purse

March 3, 1973

Anchorage to Knik (Merrill Field): 51 Miles

Knik to Susitna: 27 Miles

Susitna to Skwentna: 40 Miles

Skwentna to Rainy Pass Lodge: 55 Miles

Rainy Pass Lodge to Rohn Road House: 59 Miles

Rohn Road House to Farewell: 26 Miles

Farewell to Big River Road House: 48 Miles

Big River Road House to McGrath: 20 Miles

McGrath to Placerville: 80 Miles

Placerville to Ruby: 54 Miles

Ruby to Galena: 49 Miles

Galena to Nulato: 34 Miles

Nulato to Kaltag: 36 Miles

Kaltag to Old Woman: 38 Miles

Old Woman to Unalakleet: 33 Miles

Unalakleet to Shaktoolik: 32 Miles

Shaktoolik to Koyuk: 52 Miles

Koyuk to Flim to White Mountain: 39 Miles

White Mountain to Solomon: 34 Miles

Solomon to Nome: 30 Miles

Total: 853 Miles

THE IDITAROD TRAIL INTERNATIOAL CHAMPIONSHIP RACE

Anchorage to Nome

1,000 Miles

$50,000 Purse

March 3, 1973

Rules

The following rules are subject to slight modification. Any changes or additions will be made known to mushers at a drivers meeting prior to the race or by mail.

1. The race will be held as scheduled regardless of weather conditions.

2. Drivers must start the race with no less than five (5) dogs.

3. Each driver has the choice of his own sled, subject to the condition that some kind of sled or toboggan must be drawn. At the option of the driver, sleds may be changed during the race.

4. No dogs may be added to a team for any portion of the race.

5. Two or more teams may not, in any way, be secured together.

6. No driver shall allow any of his dogs to be hauled by any other team or vehicle.

7. Cruel and inhumane treatment of dogs is prohibited.

8. Any driver quitting the race must notify the nearest check-point.

9. Two mushers may drive one team, provided that both mushers cover the entire distance either on the sled or on foot. Both mushers of a two-man team must pay the $100.00 entry fee.

10. Dogs may be dropped from teams at designated check-points; all dropped dogs must be accounted for by the official at the check-point.

11. Outside assistance will be allowed only if the team is unmanageable.

12. Musher and team must check in at all check points.

13. Mushers setting up camp must clear the trail of their dogs and gear.

1. In case of a lost team, the team will not be disqualified if the driver regains control of the team, provided that the team completes the entire length of the race trail. In no case shall a driver accept assistance from a motorized vehicle.

2. All drivers must be 18 years of age or older.

3. Any driver quitting the race must use good judgment and not create an obstacle for any other team still in the race.

4. Official finishing time will be determined when the musher (or mushers in the case of a two man team) and all of his dogs (except those dropped at designated check-points) cross the finish line.

5. Every person entering the race will observe the general rules of good sportsmanship.

6. No driver shall tamper with another driver's dog or gear with the intent of handicapping that driver.

7. Any drivers, dogs, or teams coming to the starting line unfit or incapable of completing the race, in the opinion of the judges, will be disqualified.

8. Any violation of any of these rules may result in the disqualification of the team and driver, subject to the judgment of the race marshal.

IDITAROD TRAIL INTERNATIONAL RULE COMMITTEE

ENTRY FORM

WHEREAS the Iditarod Trail International Race committee is planning to stage, administer, and promote a dogs sled race from a point near Anchorage, Alaska to a point near Nome, Alaska, in March, 1973; and

WHEREAS the individual undersigned dog sled racer desires to participate in such a race; and

WHEREAS the individual undersigned dog sled racer is confident of his ability to finish said race and has no desire to hold anyone other than him or herself responsible for a failure to so finish said race or for any other damages caused directly or indirectly by said participation; and

WHEREAS there is the possibility of great financial reward through endorsement fees and similar instances of race-related remuneration in which the individual undersigned would benefit from the services of an agent skilled in such matters,

IT IS THEREFORE AGREED THAT:

I the undersigned individual dog sled musher for and in consideration of the right to participate fully in the aforesaid Iditarod Trail International Championship Race agree as follows:

1. To pay the sum of one hundred dollars ($100.00) as a non-refundable entry fee on or before February 17, 1972, and if payment is not made between February 18 and February 28 the entry fee shall be $150.00, and

2. To hold harmless the Iditarod Trail and International Race Committee and its successors, assigns, and members for any property damage or personal injury arising from or caused by or relating to my participation in the Iditarod Trail International Championship Race, and

3. To grant to the Iditarod Trail International Race Committee the exclusive right to represent me, my successors, assigns and heirs, in any and all negotiations relating to or arising from my participation in the Iditarod International Championship Race and furthermore to share equally with the Iditarod Race Committee any benefits, monetary or otherwise, that inure to me as a result of or arising from my participation in the Iditarod Trail International Championship Race; provided however, that the sharing of monies or other remuneration shall be limited to such received through advertising fees, commercial product endorsements, television or radio fees, and the like. The foregoing is not intended to interfere in any way with the individual dog musher sponsor relationships; i.e., providing of dog food, transportation costs, equipment, entry fees, etc.

DATED this ________ day of ______________________________, 19____.

Entrant ____

Witness: __________________________________

Approved for Entry: _______________________________________

Iditarod Race Committee Date

IDITAROD TRAIL

International Championship Sled Dog Race
Anchorage to Nome March 2, 1973

1000 MILES-$50,000.00

The longest & richest sled dog race in history, over the old Iditarod trail-

January 4, 1973

Iditarod Trail Committee
Box 6106
Anchorage, Alaska 99502

Dear Friend:

We welcome you to the growing number of Alaskans who are helping to make the Anchorage to Nome Iditarod Trail International Championship Sled Dog Race a successful and enriching Alaskan heritage adventure.

It is through the planned running of this Alaskan gold rush trail that present day dog mushers will experience the same trials and joys as those who first came to Alaska.

Just as many of these gold rush participants came to our state looking for that Bonanza that was rumored from Seattle to Florida, we offer a rich strike to the modern Alaskan...a race lottery! Aside from the enjoyment that the Alaskan public will experience by participation in the lottery, we believe that an outlet in your business will provide many an hour of enjoyment for your patrons in trying to figure the best time, especially as the race draws near and excitement mounts.

The operation of this pool can be compared to the Nenana Ice Classic. A customer will purchase a ticket and guess the number of days, hours, minutes, and seconds that it will take for the winner to cross the finish line in Nome. The ticketholder or ticketholders of the winning time, or the closest to the winning time, will receive a purse of roughly 50% of total ticket sales. The Ice Classic, by means of comparison, generally pays out around $100,000 per year. We hope to be able to do as well. Especially since the race pool is tied to such a dramatic event as a thousand mile sled dog race.

In Alaska it is legal to gamble if the group doing so is registered as a non-profit organization with the state and is registered as such for five years. The organization is then eligible to apply for a gambling tax permit. The Iditarod Trail Committee meets that criteria. However, along with the state's permission, the federal government requires each seller to have a federal gambling stamp. This means that each individual in your establishment who actually SELLS a lottery ticket must have a federal tax stamp. Information on how this is done will be provided. However, nothing prevents employees from promoting sales as long as the sale itself is performed by a federal tax stampholder.

Brochures, Race Rules, Mileage Sheets (between checkpoints), and other data, as well as posters, will be provided to you for promotional purposes, and as conversational background for your customers. The main part of the ticket the customer will keep, recording the time that he indicated on the stub. The stub should be put into a clear marked container such as a one or two gallon glass jar. TICKET SALES MUST BE CONCLUDED AT THE CLOSE OF BUSINESS ON MARCH 2, 1973.

Collections will be made within a few days after the race begins, and an accounting of tickets and/or money will be made at that time.

After winners are determined, a book will be sent to you with the names and addresses of the winners, the winning times, and where the ticketholders purchased their tickets.

If you have any further questions, please ask your local representative or write to the Iditarod Trail Committee, P.O. Box 6108 Annex, Anchorage, Alaska 99502.

Thank you for your assistance in making this the truly greatest race in the history of dog mushing.

Sincerely,

Joe Reddington, Sr., Chairman
Iditarod Trail Committee

Iditarod Trail, Alaska
Land Deed

Warranty Deed

THIS DEED Made the 20th day of May 1987, between the Iditarod Trail Committee, Inc., Party of the First Part, and, Daniel B. Seavey Party of the Second Part;

WITNESSETH: That the Party of the First Part, in consideration of TEN DOLLARS ($10.00) lawful money of the United States paid by the Party of the Second Part, does hereby Grant and Release unto the Party of the Second Part a portion of the IDITAROD TRAIL as follows:

An unspecified, undivided 1/998,600th interest in that portion of Government Lot 5, U.S. Survey Number 1726, Palmer Recording District, Third Judicial District, State of Alaska lying north of the Right-of-way for the Knik-Goose Bay Road as it exists this date.

It is hereby expressly agreed by and between both Parties that the Party of the First Part or it's assigns has a permanent easement to enter and occupy the above described lands of the Party of the Second Part for the general purposes of holding sporting races, including "The Last Great Race", other events, and maintenance and repair as the Party of the First Part deems appropriate;

TO HAVE AND TO HOLD the above granted interest in land unto the Party of the Second Part, his heirs and assigns FOREVER;

IN WITNESS WHEREOF the party of the First Part has set his hand and seal the day and year first above written.

IDITAROD TRAIL COMMITTEE, INC.

Lavon Barve
Iditarod President

Joe Redington Sr.
Father of the Iditarod

State of Alaska)
Third Judical District)
On this day 20th. day of May 1987, before me, the undersigned, A Notary Public in and for the State of Alaska duly commissioned and sworn personally appeared Joseph E. Redington, Sr. and Lavon A. Barve of the IDITAROD TRAIL COMMITTEE INC. to me know to be the authorized members of the Committee that executed the foregoing instrument and acknowledged said sealing was their free and voluntary act.

WITNESS: My hand and seal hereto affixed the day and year first written above.

Violet E. Redington
Notary Public in and for Alaska My Commission Expires 8-11-90

1068

Title certified by
McKinley Title & Trust, Inc.

Personal

Snowshoes
Flashlight w/ batteries
Cassette Player/batteries/ tapes/mic.
Camera
Extra clothes
Sock, wool, 2 pr
Insoles, wool 2 pr
Underwear, wool, 1 set
Liners, boot, wool, 1 pr
Pants, down filled, 1 pr
Souvenir letters
Toilet paper, 1 roll
Maps
Compass
Wind meter, pocket
Thermometer, pocket
Bible – pocket size
Clock, small, travel size
Spoon
Cup
Sunglasses
Paper/pencil
Aspirin
Chapstick
Needle, thread
Pocket knife
Film, 4 rolls, 36 exp
Toothbrush/paste
Sleeping bag
Sleeping pad
Gas stove w/ gas
Gas, 2 quarts
Sterno
Matches, water proof
Candles, plumber, 6

Food

5 day's rations
Trail cake
Tea/coffee
Chicken soup
Moose stew
Sandwiches

Sled

Tarp
Nylon cord, 40 ft.
Pliers, 1 pr.
Rough lock chains
Gun, 22 cal. Rev. /shells
Wrench
Screw driver
Rawhide, 2 strips
Wire, light, 4 ft.
Bolts, 1⁄4", 6

Camp

Axe
Tent

Dog

Tethering chain
Booties, 1 dozen w/ tape
Coats w/ pins
Buckets, 2
Whip
Foot oil
Harnesses
Towline, 1 section
Collar,1
Lamp black
Can/paint brush
Food sent to check points
Fish, 4 pounds per dog, per day
Kibble, 4 pounds per dog, per day
Beef fat, 1 pound per dog, per day

Total Gear Weight on Sled – 121 pounds.

APPENDIX X: Shirley Seavey's Trail Cake Recipe

1 (9 ounce) package mince meat (dry variety)

½ cup water

1 cup mixed candied fruit

1 ½ cups pecans or walnuts, coarsely chopped

1 cup dates

1 cup raisins

1 cup evaporated milk

$^{1}/_{3}$ cup honey

1 egg

1 cup flour

½ teaspoon soda

Break mince meat into small pieces in a pan. Add water, place over heat; stir until lumps are thoroughly broken. Boil briskly for one minute, stirring constantly. Cool. Add next seven ingredients; blend well. Stir in flour and soda just until blended. Pour into 9x4x3 inch baking pan that is greased, wax paper lined, and greased again. Bake at 350° for one hour or until cake tests done with a toothpick. This makes one large loaf; Shirley doubles recipe for three loaves.

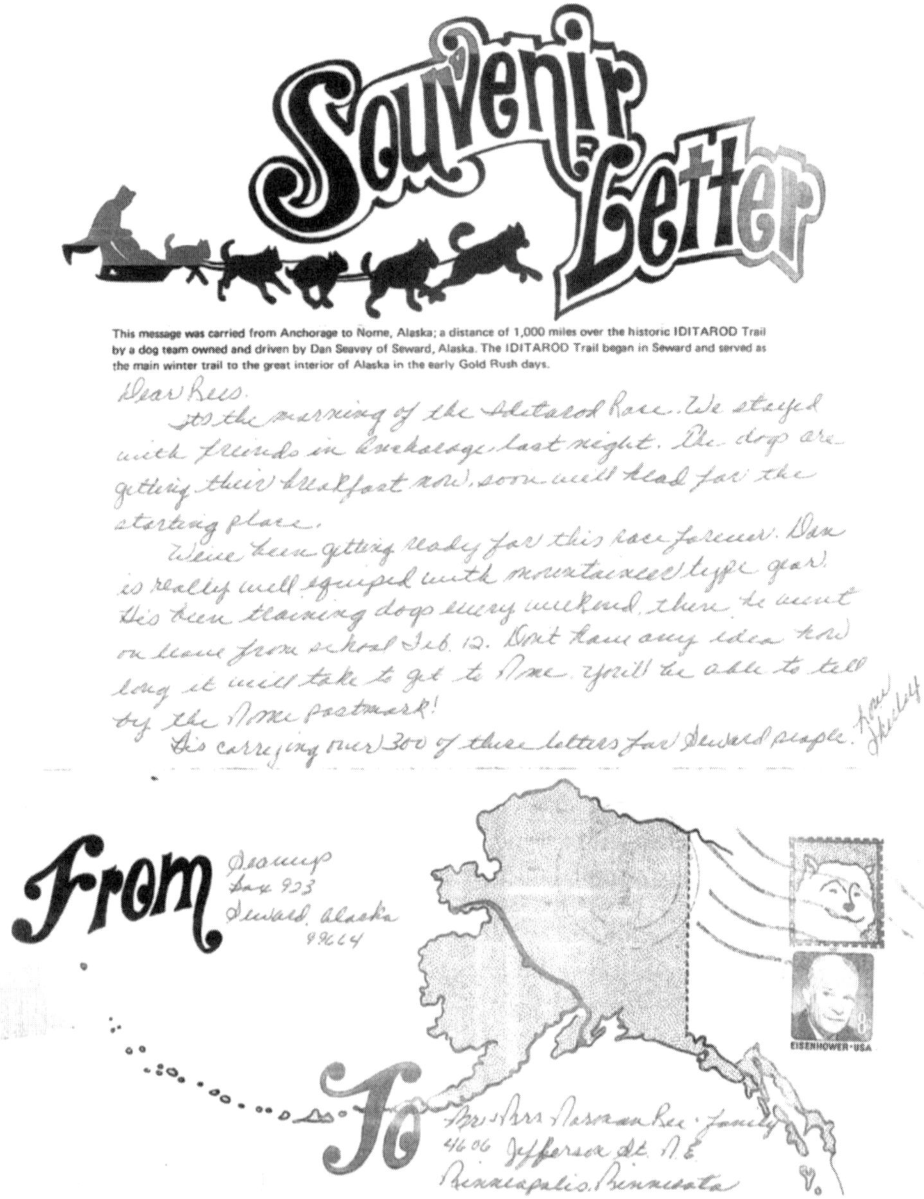

Souvenir Letter

This message was carried from Anchorage to Nome, Alaska; a distance of 1,000 miles over the historic IDITAROD Trail by a dog team owned and driven by Dan Seavey of Seward, Alaska. The IDITAROD Trail began in Seward and served as the main winter trail to the great interior of Alaska in the early Gold Rush days.

Dear Rees.

It's the morning of the Iditarod Race. We stayed with friends in Anchorage last night. The dogs are getting their breakfast now, soon we'll head for the starting place.

We've been getting ready for this race forever. Dan is really well equiped with mountaineer type gear. He's been training dogs every weekend, then he went on leave from school Feb. 12. Don't have any idea how long it will take to get to Nome. You'll be able to tell by the Nome postmark!

He's carrying over 300 of these letters for Seward people.

Love Shirley

From Seaveys
Box 923
Seward, Alaska
99664

To Mr. & Mrs. Norman Rees & family
4606 Jefferson St. N.E.
Minneapolis, Minnesota

EISENHOWER · USA 8

APPENDIX XII: Starting Order – 1973 Iditarod Race

Bib Number	Name	Home	Number of Dogs
1	Bud Smyth	Houston	20
2	Hal Bartko	Palmer	13
3	John Schultheis	Knik	12
4	Ron Oviak	Point Hope	13
5	John Komak	Teller	13
6	Ron Aldrich	Montana Creek	13
7	George Attla	Fairbanks	14
8	Ken Chase	Anvik	10
9	Robert & Owen Ivan	Akiak	13
10	Darrel Reynolds	Anchorage	13
11	Isaac Okleasik	Teller	12
12	Herbert Foster	Kotzebue	10
13	Bill Arpino	Tok	13
14	Dan Seavey	Seward	12
15	Dick Mackey	Wasilla	16
16	Rod Perry	Anchorage	11
17	Herbert Nayokpuk	Shishmaref	13
18	John Schultz/ Casey Celusnick	Fairbanks	10
19	Barry McAlpine	Goat Creek	7
20	Slim Randles	Talkeetna	7
21	Raymie Redington	Knik	9
22	Terry Miller	Palmer	10
23	Bruce Mitchell	Ester Dome	9
24	John Coffin	Noorvik	13
25	John Luster	Chickaloon	11
26	Conrad Killigruk	Point Hope	11
27	Bobby Vent	Huslia	11
28	Alec Tatum	Anchorage	9
29	Dave Olson	Knik	10
30	Ford Reeves/ Mike Schreiber	McKinley Park	14
31	Howard Farley	Nome	15
32	Tom Mercer	Talkeetna	10
33	Dick Wilmarth	Red Devil	12
34	Victor Katongan	Unalakleet	7

Dear Dan,
May 10, 1973

Congratulations on the great showing you made in the Big Race. I think it [Seavey team] was the best of the lot because of the condition your dogs came there in. Hope we see you next time.

I'll try to answer your questions the best I can.

1. Skwentna is composed of five families and consists of a Post Office and a small [FAA] installation. The original settlers was Max and Belle Shellabarger, who trapped, guided, and ran the Post Office here since the 1920's. In 1945 the [FAA] was built here but was called the [CAA] Office and a number of transients which varies according to fur prices.

2. I'm 43 years old and began trapping in partnership with Max Shellabarger at Skwentna in 1949 when I was 19 years old. Prior to that, I had worked a while in Ketchikan and in Anchorage for Ward Gay of Sea Airmotive. I acquired my first dog team in 1949 and used from 6 to 8 dogs for freighting and trapping. Used dogs until a couple years ago when salmon fishing for subsistence purposes was stopped and it became too costly to feed a team. Max and I kept about 20 dogs and had a fishwheel which we used to catch about 4,500 salmon which were dried for dog feed. Max was killed in an aircraft accident in 1957. His wife still lives at Skwentna where she has resided for 50 years.

3. The people present at my house when you came in were as follows:

1. Myself
2. My wife, Carlene
3. My daughter, Christine (7 yrs.)
4. My son, Pat (4 yrs.)
5. Fred Blumer, Anchorage, race official
6. Dave Sanford, Eklutna Road, official
7. Terry Adkins, Elmendorf, veterinarian
8. Pam Randles, reporter and wife of Slim Randles, one of the mushers

The fiberglass igloo belongs to Ralph Eldridge of Anchorage and is used as a moose hunting camp.

4. Skwentna to Finger Lake – 45 miles

Finger Lake to Rainy Pass Lodge – 32 miles

Rainy Pass Lodge to Rohn River – 79 miles

5. The owners of Rainy Pass Lodge are Bud and Mike Branham and the caretaker of Rainy Pass Lodge is Allen Budinski of Colorado.

The owner of Hayes River Lodge (Finger Lake) is Dennis Branham and the caretaker of Finger Lake is Gene Leonard

6. The only comment I can recall about you was how good your team appeared. There were so many comments by people about each musher and his team it's hard to remember any particular one. I believe every musher before you had dropped a dog, Attla dropped 2, and that was the most particular thing I can remember about your check-in.

7. Enclosed are some pictures. Hope you can make something out of all this hodge-podge. The clipping from *Time* will give you a little info about us and the country. The color slides are mine and the others are shots taken by Joe Rychetnik now of California.

My wife and I got rid of our last 3 sled dogs a couple years ago but now have a good female for breeding and 3 pups from my wife's sister's team. My wife's sister is a musher and keeps a team of 16 dogs so I hope to build up another team in a few years so I can get in the big race. Don't have much hope of getting a team like I used to have since we don't have a trapper in the valley with dogs anymore. Doesn't give a fellow much chance to pick and weed stock. Sort of have to take pot-luck now. As you can see from the photo, we use toboggans and the Canadian tandem hitch for trapping in deep snow and brushy country. On more open freighting trail where I used more than six dogs, the tandem harness wasn't no good, and I used a harness similar to what you mushers in the race used. Didn't bother the dogs much when I switched harness. Also used a runnered freight sled on hard trail.

We're losing one family and two kids here, so it would take four kids to have a school now.

Dan, I don't know how you feel about traps and trapping, but there is a bill, S.B. 1637, put before the Senate on April 18, that would outlaw traps and snares and almost kill the fur trade. I don't need to tell you what that would do to the bush residents of Alaska. I for one don't want to go on welfare or leave my home. The only thing that can keep this bill from being passed is a strong letter campaign opposing S.B. 1637. I hope you feel as I do about this and will help spread the word. The preamble to this bill in the Congressional Record is filled with half-truths, misrepresentations, etc. and is based on the presumption that what is good for Florida is good for Alaska.

Trapping was exceptionally good this year, and prices were the best in 30 years. I ended up with 90 marten, 50 beavers, 25 mink, and a nice bunch of wolverine, fox and otter plus a large batch of squirrel, weasel and rats.

If you can think of anything else I may be able to help with shoot me a line.

Yours,
Joe Delia

P.S. Never had anything stop me on the trail with dogs, but these snowmachines seem like it's one thing after another goes wrong. That was the main reason we kept a few dogs after we got a snowmachine, to haul in the haywire snowmachine engines.

The best distance I ever made in one day was 57 miles with a big load of beaver and six dogs. Suppose I could have gone further, but there was no reason to. The dogs weren't particular tired. I was feeding nothing but beaver at the time.

Nulato, Alaska 99765

April 23, 1973

Dear Dan,

I was pleased to hear that you finished third in the race. I also appreciate you taking time to talk to the village about the race at town hall.

The dog you left here is doing fine. The vet came through here about 3 weeks ago. He looked at her and said that she looked alright.

Last week Ken Chase, one of mushers, came to Nulato for the carnival. He told Dennis that the trail committee has picked up all the dogs that were dropped from the race. This can't be true because Herbert N ?? [Nayokpuk's] dog is still here and so is yours, and from what I gather, quite a number of dogs are still in Galena.

I will be leaving Nulato to go to Seattle around May 24. I have a native who will be talking care of my dogs for me this summer. However, he doesn't understand English too well, and I am afraid that a mix-up will occur if they come to get the dog after May 24.

There is also the possibility that the dog won't even be in the village, but at the native's fishcamp, some 18 miles outside of Nulato. Would you please advise me what to do with her?

Sincerely yours,

Bob Simpson

APPENDIX XV: Final Standings - 1973

Team	Total Elapsed Time Solomon to Nome	Days	Hours	Minutes	Seconds
1. Dick Wilmarth Red Devil	5:37	20	0	49	41
2. Bobby Vent Huslia	7:11	20	14	8	46
3. Dan Seavey Seward	7:10	20	14	35	16
4. George Attla Fairbanks	6:47	21	8	47	53
5. Herbert Nayokpuk Shishmaref (1st to Knik)	6:33	21	11	0	19
6. Isaac Okleasik Teller	8:15	21	18	21	25
7. Dick Mackey Wasilla	7:51	22	4	3	49
8. John Komak Teller	7:56	22	4	36	34
9. John Coffin Noorvik	10:36	23	6	43	29
10. Ron Aldrich Montana Creek	7:23	24	9	58	26
11. Bill Arpino Tok	9:47	24	12	12	0
12. Bud Smyth Houston (Winner)	4:42:25	26	11	25	35
13. Ken Chase Anvik	4:56	26	11	45	35
14. Ron Oviaak Point Hope	8:41	26	15	54	1
15. Victor Katongan Unalakleet	10:00	28	23	41	4
16. Robert and Owen Ivan Akiak	7:45	29	11	24	25
17. Rod Perry Anchorage	5:13	30	1	39	21
18. Tom Mercer Talkeetna	6:43	31	3	35	45
19. Terry Miller Palmer	7:06	31	4	20	7
20. Howard Farley Nome	6:20	31	11	59	11
21. Bruce Mitchell Ester Dome	6:09	31	12	5	6
22. John Schultz Delta Junction	7:25	32	5	9	1

Did Not Complete Race: Dr. Hal Bartko (Palmer) •John Schultheis (Knik) •Darrel Reynolds (Knik) •Casey Celusnick (Fairbanks) •Slim Randles (Talkeetna) •Raymie Redington (Knik) •John Luster (Chickaloon) •Conrad Killigruk (Point Hope) •Alec Tatum (Anchorage) •Dave Olsen (Knik) •Ford Reeves (McKinley Park) •Mike Schreiber (McKinley Park)

12 Total

APPENDIX XVI: "Dan Seavey was a Musher"

by Dot and Dori Bardarson
(To the tune of: "Stewball was a Race Horse")

Dan Seavey was a musher
And his dogs couldn't fail
For three weeks he drove them
On the Iditarod trail

Dan Seavey was a postman
As he carried the mail
From Anchorage to Nome
On the Iditarod Trail

In McGrath he was snowbound
He ran into a gale
And he took a vacation
On the Iditarod Trail

And way up yonder
You could hear his wild call
Was rugged Dan Seavey
Ahead of them all

The prize was awaitin'
And when he reached Nome
All the people from Seward
Would welcome him home

With dogs in the basket
Other teams fell behind
But Dan's pace was steady
And the dogs didn't mind

I bet on George Attla
I thought he would pay
If I'd bet on Dan Seavey
I'd be a rich man today

There's a moral to this story
If you don't want to fail
Keep all of your doggies
On the Iditarod Trail

Then Bobby Vent faster
With Dan on his tail
His friend and companion
On the Iditarod Trail

We might mention Wilmarth
A name we recall
Though not from Seward
The fastest of all

Index

A

B

C

E

F

G

H

I

J

K

R

S

T

U

V

W

Y